The Nature of Theatre

Under the Advisory Editorship of J. Jeffery Auer

The Nature of Theatre

VERA MOWRY ROBERTS

Hunter College of The City University of New York

HARPER & ROW, PUBLISHERS

New York, Evanston, San Francisco, London

Calligraphy by Jeanyee Wong

THE NATURE OF THEATRE
Copyright © 1971 by Vera Mowry Roberts

Library of Congress Catalog Card Number: 72-137814

This one is for Ellen

Contents

Preface ix

Introduction: Theatres and Theatre 1

I
The Experience of Theatre

1
Seeing a Play 11

2
The Nature of Art and the Art of Theatre 31

II
Ways of Seeing

3
The Play Itself 47

4
The Development of Dramatic Forms and Modes 74

5
Conventions 117

III
The Predominant Genres

6
Tragedy 131

7
Comedy 175

8

Mixed Genres: Melodrama and Tragicomedy 213

9

New Forms 243

IV
The Artists of the Theatre

10

Actor and Director 283

11

Designer and Architect 331

12

Playwright and Critic 372

V
The Allied Arts: Movies and Television

13

Cinema 395

14

Television 448

Postscript: Vocations and Avocations 479

Selected List of Books for Additional Reading 487

Index 493

Preface

This is a book about theatre. Its stance is firmly center-stage. It is intended as an introduction, a look around at the marvelous complexity that is theatre. And because movies and television are these days so often spoken of as theatre, a part of what follows is concerned with them.

Preparing this volume has been a real learning experience for me. I have been involved with theatre for something close to a quarter of a century now, and might be thought to be something of an expert. My involvement has included acting, directing, producing, writing, researching and teaching—on several levels and in varying situations, both professional and educational. Perhaps therein lies the difficulty. How could anyone sum this all up? How could it be clarified? How could one make *experiential* the beautiful arc of action that is theatre? How could I convey the exquisite intensity of this object of my ruling passion? I had a lot of things to sort out.

This book is the result of a long and agonized search for clarity and effectiveness. No one who reads it, in part or in whole, can be any more aware than I of seeming deficiencies and neglects of this or that playwright, this or that production. I apologize beforehand; piece out my imperfections with your thoughts.

What this book *does* represent is not only my own experience of theatre, but what I have been able to assimilate from the experience of others through reading, talk, and study—not only hours and days of it, but months and years. I am indebted beyond the possibility of payment to the host of wonderful people who have shared with me their own intense involvement with theatre over many years, on stages, in rehearsal halls, in books and in other publications. All these theatre people—actors, directors, technicians, designers, critics, playwrights, alive and dead—whose insights and points of view they have shared with me, are all a part of this work as they are a part of me. I thank them.

The student of theatre (and anyone committed to theatre is for all his life a *student* of it) never stops learning. Another quarter of a century from now I might very well write a quite different book. "We never step into the same stream twice," because the water is always changing. But the *stream* is there, not only as a Platonic *Idea*, but also as a moving, actual entity. It is my sincere hope that this book (as I have tried to make it) will body forth both the *Idea* of theatre (in the full implication of the Platonic concept) and the moving and ever changing *Reality* of theatre.

The illustrations have been chosen to show a variety of theatrical experiences. They can be used to study and compare various types of performances and materials. In some cases, the captions will refer the reader to specific comparisons of this sort. Many of the illustrations are from my own collection of theatre pictures; for others I am indebted to the persons and/or institutions listed with the illustrations themselves. I also wish to thank Leslie Carola, Gayle Jaeger, and William Monroe of Harper & Row, and J. Christopher Roberts for their invaluable assistance in the arduous problem of illustrations.

Vera Mowry Roberts

January 1971

The Nature of Theatre

Introduction: Theatres and Theatre

We are all actors. From the first moment that we are conscious of ourselves as individuated human beings each of us assumes a variety of roles, shifting easily from one to another. We are the obedient child, the obstreperous child, the mimic, the Little Leaguer, the Girl Scout, the student, the careerist, the lover, the parent, the grandparent. We are even aware that tiny babies "cry for attention." We enjoy the *action* implicit in these many and varying roles, and we learn their limits by playing them. "Let me try that." "Let's see if I can do it." We are all actors, consciously or subconsciously. "Each man in his time plays many parts." In the process, the fortunate discover themselves and, as we say, "assume their life role." The less fortunate never find their "true role," or have great difficulty in doing so.

We are all directors. The whole rhetorical superstructure of request, persuasion, and command is the outcome of this directorial impulse. "Come here." "Get away." "Watch your step." "What do you think you're doing?" "Why don't you try it this way?" We are constantly trying to shape others to our image of them, to make them *act* as we wish. We are all directors in our effort to shape our environments to the structure of our dreams, our images of the way they should be.

We are all critics, constantly passing judgments upon what we see and hear. "Great!" "What a wash-out!" "How beautiful!" "Now, that just won't do!" From isolated instances of approval or disapproval, from the assessment of the fitness of things to their purpose, whether it be the length of a girl's skirt or the way someone handles a fork, to progressively more complicated situations of the way a class is conducted, or a party given, or a game played, or an election held, we declare: right, not so good, passable, terrible. We include in this judgment appearance and action, how well a particular thing serves its purpose, and we make the judgment according to standards we have acquired in each matter either through our own experience or by accepting certain "rules" formulated by others.

We are all members of various audiences. The very role of critic puts us squarely in this group as well. But we are very often uncritical members of audiences, too. We say that we "watch the passing show," from a park bench, or a subway strap, or a street corner. We are "sidewalk superintendents" at a construction site, or spectators at a boat regatta, a baseball game, or a hockey match. We gather in crowds to listen to a street-corner or park-square orator; we sit at a table on the Via Veneto or the Champs Elysées to "see what we can see." What are we watching; what are we listening to? People in action, people *as actors*. And we enjoy the observed activity all the more when we have someone along to share it with us.

What Francis Fergusson calls "the histrionic sensibility" is at work here, "a primitive virtue of the human mind." In the last short appendix to his book, *The Idea of a Theatre*, he talks about "the histrionic sensibility: the mimetic perception of action." He seems to limit it to that sensibility which "perceives and discriminates actions," as the ear "perceives and discriminates sounds." But I would submit, as illustrated above, that it has much larger and more profound implications. We are all—our whole lives—performers/spectators/directors/critics in an action that stretches from birth to death. "All the world's a stage." It is because this histrionic sensibility is implicit in the nature of being human, is preconceptual and instinctive that there is hardly a man alive who does not enjoy "a good show" and deplores a poor one. Such value judgments are based upon the nature of the event being judged and the knowledge and experience of the judge in just such events. No one is called upon to be the umpire in a game about which he knows nothing; if he is, he will not last long at the job.

The histrionic sensibility is the basis of theatre, just hearing is the basis of music and taste the basis of the culinary arts. In a later chapter we will deal in some detail with the implications and refinements of art as a particular manifestation of human activity and with theatre as one of those arts. Let us simply say here that theatre, in some form or other, has been a constant human activity since the beginning of human activity, that it is derived from the very nature of life itself, and that, therefore, it will continue to be a vital human activity. The theatre "holds the mirror up to Nature" and shows us ourselves—the complicated, contradictory, joyful and sorrowing things that we are, the pattern of tensions between hopes and fears that constitutes human life, the inward and outward conflicts that accompany and comprise human existence.

Because theatre is the very stuff of life itself it has been particularly susceptible to misunderstandings and misconceptions. It has been loved and hated, praised and reviled, adored and scorned, and even (worst fate of all) treated with indifference. In the modern world: i.e., in the twentieth century, much of its historic function has been assumed by movies and television.

It is almost impossible to conceive that any young American entering college these days has never seen a movie or watched television. It is easier to assume that many of these have never seen a stage play, and a much larger number have never seen a first-class professional production. The reasons for these assumptions are easy to come by. Availability of TV is limited only by sufficient affluence to own a set, or acquaintance with someone who does. Even the bars and coffee houses these days are often equipped with outsize sets, and the TV departments of merchandisers invariably have many sets going at once, so that any ambulatory person can watch, at almost any moment he so desires, what is being broadcast on this ubiquitous medium. As for the movies—even the smallest of small towns has at least one movie house, or a "drive-in," and the portability of the canned film makes dissemination easy.

It is not so with theatre, which requires a specially prepared environment, a sizeable body of cooperating people, and a span of time for the preparation and presentation of the performance. Expenses in relation to income are almost invariably more precarious in theatre than in either of the other forms. True it may be that any given television program, any given movie may be initially more costly to prepare than any given theatre performance (although the astronomical sums—as high as $900,000— spent on some recent Broadway musicals might seem to belie this point). But the advertising revenue, which is the chief sustenance of television, makes huge sums constantly available to that medium. Initial cost in movie production is always reckoned against possible and probable distribution of the canned film. Several prints are often distributed simultaneously so that, at any given moment, an aggregate audience of potentially hundreds of thousands can be viewing the same production, all having paid admission prices.

Theatre performance, on the other hand, is created anew (although on an agreed upon plan through a series of rehearsals) each time a different audience comes to share it. Continuing expenses for performing space, actors' salaries, and such make the amortization of the initial costs for sets, costumes, and lighting a much slower process than the similar amortization of moviemaking costs. If the show travels, the process is cumbersome and expensive, and it is still tied to one-at-a-time performances with limited audience-capacity and hence limited income from ticket sales. Even noncommercial theatre of high quality is ruinously expensive. Joseph Papp, the entrepreneur of the now famous and institutionalized New York Shakespeare Festival, announced in the spring of a recent year that he needed something over a million dollars for his next season of free summer Shakespeare in Central Park and his productions at the renovated Astor Place Theatre during the winter months (where the top ticket price is $5.50). Except in the case of the rare "hit" shown on Broadway, or the long-term financing of isolated community theatres, theatre production does not pay for itself. (The 2000-odd college and university theatres in the United States are obviously subsidized by the various academic administrations involved, even when ticket sales reach capacity.)

What then, makes theatre worth all this money, and time, and trouble? What is there about theatre which causes the governments of every European country—and of many in other parts of the world—to channel public funds to the support of theatre? Even the disgracefully laggard United States Congress has, in recent years, permitted such an expenditure of some public funds. Why are increasingly larger grants being made by reputable foundations and businesses to theatre activities? Why are theatre departments being established in more and more schools and colleges? There must be something about this form of human activity which makes it worth all this attention. And there is, of course.

Theatre activity of whatever kind—from the remotest degree of audience participation to the deep commitment of the director and/or producer—is potentially the most humanizing, the most life-enhancing, the most spirit-freeing of all possible activities. It requires commitment and involvement at every level; it demands concentration and attention; it stretches the mind and the heart. It is no accident that the glorious periods of history, to which we look back with awe and nostalgia—Periclean Athens and Elizabethan England—were both marked by the widest possible participation in theatre by all levels of the populace. It is not happenstance that many of the great minds of previous ages were involved in theatre: Goethe, Wagner, Voltaire, Lessing, Molière, Shakespeare, Shaw, Lope de Vega, Cervantes—to name only the most obvious. It is no cause for wonder that one of the proletarian triumphs of the French Revolution was the opening of dozens of theatres in Paris; that the government of West Germany, after the holocaust of World War II, allotted precious funds from its straitened treasury to open again immediately its hundred state theatres; and that most of the theatres of Russia were open and playing even in the darkest days of Revolution and economic stringency thereafter.

For theatre is as necessary to the nurture of humanity as bread and meat. Whole segments of the American population, though well nourished in other respects in this affluent society, are suffering from malnutrition of the soul, lacking theatre. What then, can be said of the whole populations deprived even of bread and meat? What functions does theatre perform for the starving populations of India, for the struggling proletariat of China, for the emerging nations of Africa that they should be concerned to spend time and energy and money on theatrical endeavors? But we are back where we started. There is something in the human composition that demands theatre, that over and above the necessities of keeping body and soul together asks for the ritual of theatre to feed that which is human in him. And as he is deprived of this he is so much less human. The movies and television will satisfy a little of this urge, but, once exposed to theatre—good theatre—no person will accept these mechanical contrivances as a total substitute for the excitement, the engagement, the transaction of live and living theatre itself.

It is beyond calculation how many performing groups people

how many stages in how many communities of the world if we include all kinds and persuasions of people, part-time amateur as well as full-time and professional. The HUMAN values of even the least skillful of these multitudinous performances cannot be argued. Their participants no doubt enjoy and derive benefit from the sense of commitment, the involvement, the identification with mutual goals, the cooperation, the communication, the feeling of community which are all a part of the activity. And it must be recorded that often the fascination with amateur theatricals is mere love of "showing off." *Any* theatre activity, I sometimes think, is better than NO theatre activity. On the other hand, it is by no stretch of the imagination that a great many of these performances can be called ART (in the terms which we will hereinafter define) or can make any pretensions to ARTISTRY. And that in itself is a serious deprivation. For what too many people are getting is a pale and watered-down imitation of the real thing. And if too long fed on these inadequacies mankind will be woefully undernourished. It is mandatory not only that ever widening groups of people be given their first involvement in the art of theatre, but that all those who have been subsisting on inadequacies be brought as quickly as possible to the real thing itself. Such an improvement in taste can only transpire as more and more people develop understanding and judgment about the nature of theatre, the use of its basic materials and methods, how its whole is created and what one can and must expect of it. Art and humanity demand no less.

It is perfectly true, of course, that for an unsophisticated enjoyment of any of the arts, knowledge about the materials, techniques, and accomplishments of a given art is quite unnecessary, as one could, for instance, simply enjoy the movement of a tennis ball through the air without any knowledge of the rules of the game. But just as in tennis the spectator's enjoyment is keener when he knows the rules of the game and can appreciate the skills of the players, so in art works in general and theatre in particular the knowledgeable person's perceptions give his enjoyment a keener edge. If theatre has, over wide reaches of time and space, proved itself at once one of the most humanizing of man's social activities, as well as one of his most intricate art forms, then it behooves us to inquire rather closely into this phenomenon in order to enlarge our understanding as well as our appreciation.

Just as Jefferson insisted that democracy needs an educated electorate, theatre needs an educated audience. But just as a representative democracy is an exceedingly complicated organism, so too is theatre. In fact, being a much more ancient organization than the democracy Jefferson was talking about, theatre is just that much more complicated. It has been overlaid by centuries of practice and malpractice, by infinite incrustations. So we shall try to simplify the process of understanding by beginning with the naive assumption of the thing seen, then inquire into what it is that has been seen, and how it got that way. Theatre is a *thing made* by man for his use and his enjoyment and shares this quality with many other art forms. It is obvious, of course, that no one statement—no one book—can say all that needs to be said. But the only way to accomplish any task is, as William Saroyan advises, to make a beginning. This book is our mutual beginning. It will take the rest of our lives to make an ending. And that ending will be only our personal ending, and not that of the theatre.

I
The Experience of Theatre

1
Seeing a Play

The eclectic theatregoer these days is offered a variety of experiences. If, like Pepys of Restoration fame, he were to keep a journal detailing his activities, the theatre entries over a short span of time might read something like this:

TUESDAY. What better way to spend a summer evening than to watch Shakespeare under the stars at the Delacorte Theatre in Central Park? The weather is warm and a little muggy, but the weatherman says it won't rain, so off we go. Finally the long line of people is seated; the "minstrels" who were entertaining the arriving crowd have finished their songs, and *Henry IV, Part 2* is about to begin. The sun is setting behind us, and the long shadows are creeping over the lake that we can see beyond the stage. There are about 2500 of us on wooden, outdoor-type seats mounted on rising stands in wedge-shaped sections of an approximate semicircle. The stage is a big open platform slanting upward toward the back, with solid, boxlike "houses" to either side. There is a construction up and center which looks very ingenious, with a stairway leading to a platform, and an arrangement of what look like swinging doors below. There is a lot of open space. Suddenly batteries of lights from great towers to either side of the audience beam on and Rumour, in a variegated costume chiefly of floating strips bursts on to the stage, and delivers his prologue while he sinuously moves up, over, and around that central construction. As he leaves, Lord Bardolph enters from the side, bangs on the post: "Who keeps the gate here?" and in a moment Northumberland enters from under the raised platform, and we get the conflicting reports of the great battle in which Hotspur was killed. It is an ominous beginning. But no sooner do Northumberland and his retainers "go in" to write their letters and make their plans

Figure 1–1
New York Shakespeare
Festival's Delacorte Theatre

*A scene in the tavern
from* Henry IV, Part 2.
See also 5–7. *Directed
by Gerald Freedman
(George E. Joseph)*

than Falstaff enters—that outsize parody of a human being in
immense boots and plumed hat, with a small boy as his page,
looking even smaller beside that immense bulk. We will watch for
every entrance of this pair, now; they have won our hearts. Falstaff proceeds with that marvelous avalanche of words in a voice
as big as his belly (what needs he of the microphones without
which we could not hear the others?). So the play proceeds:
back to the Archbishop's palace for further intrigue; to Mistress
Quickly's tavern and Falstaff again, with Prince Hal, weary from
the wars, making sport of Falstaff disguised as a waiter. (Clever
how they have arranged to carry on the table, stools, and food
as a part of the opening action of the scene.) So we see them all:
the dying King, Shallow, and Silence, and that hilarious conscrip-
tion, the parleys in "the forest," the death of the King, Prince
Hal's toying with the crown, Falstaff's anticipation of patronage,
and that sad reversal, "I know thee not, old man" in the midst of
the splendid procession which attends the new King's coronation.
There has been only one intermission, and it is almost four hours
now since the play began. It has moved swiftly from scene to
scene with necessary properties being carried on quite naturally

12

THE EXPERIENCE

OF THEATRE

Figure 1–2

Théâtre de la Cité
*Roger Planchon's
production of* Tartuffe
*at the Lincoln Center
Festival 1968. See also
3–5 and 7–14.*
(René Basset)

by the actors. The costumes are richly Elizabethan and colorful.
Though the warm air makes us sticky, we do not notice the hard
seats until the lights finally dim for the last time, and we are glad
to get to our feet for the tumultuous curtain call. The plain flood-
lights that illuminate the audience area seem garish after the
colored lighting of the stage, and we pick our way down many
steps and out through the park to our bus, in something of a daze.

SATURDAY. Tonight we go to the Vivian Beaumont Theatre at
Lincoln Center for *Tartuffe*. It is Roger Planchon's Compagnie
du Théâtre de la Cité de Villeurbanne, here on a visit. Curious
how this beautifully appointed indoor theatre reminds one of the
Delacorte. The seats are again in rising wedges over a semicircle,
and the stage (for this production) is also raked. But the seats
are beautifully upholstered and comfortable, and the setting on
the curtainless stage is incredibly ingenious. It is a system of pipes
carrying upstage in diminishing perspective a series of variously
shaped and decorated painted pieces which disappear and return
to make the playing space larger or smaller, while maintaining the
illusion of a seventeenth-century interior. That frantic opening
scene is played in the smallest of the possible spaces, down front,

and the compression gained thereby immediately involves us in the serio-comic situation. So alive and real are these characters that we do not find ourselves (as we usually do at a performance of *Tartuffe*) impatiently waiting for the long-delayed entrance of the title character. Orgon, for all his preoccupation with the as yet invisible Tartuffe, is not a doddering fool, but a brisk man who knows his own mind and intends to see that his family does as he wishes. When Tartuffe finally appears, we know why Madame Pernelle and Orgon are so taken with him: he is not a slathering old hypocrite, but a handsome young man, smooth as silk. This is going to be interesting. At once Orgon's insistence that Marianne marry Tartuffe in understandable; Valère will have a hard time of it. And the seduction scene with Elmire has a suspense and a dual sexuality that is startling and alive. We are almost sorry that this Tartuffe is duly punished. It is a thunderously perfect show, set in a social context that is both seventeenth century and curiously modern, and the enraptured audience responds with thunderous applause. It is an eminently satisfying evening in the theatre.

SUNDAY. It's the Pocket Theatre tonight for Claude van Itallie's

America Hurrah! with The Open Theatre performing. The theatre is an off-Broadway house, long and dark and narrow, but the seats are more comfortable and the sight lines better than in most of such houses. It looks a bit cramped; there must be every one of those 299 seats which is the maximum for off Broadway, and every one of them is filled. It's a rather affluent-looking uptown crowd; the production has made a name for itself. Will it really be as good as its reputation? We notice that the performance is subtitled "Three Views of the U.S.A.," and that the stage, curtain-less, is a box lined with aluminum foil, one side missing so we can see inside. The first "view" is something called "Interview"—a company of eight people who seem to multiply, divide, and sub-tract in number, size, and volume before our eyes. There is no continuity, no story. Interviewers become applicants and vice versa. No characterization is constant; it is impossible to "iden-tify" with any one character. Yet the impact is unmistakable: just so are people hounded in these remarkably false situations; we have been inflating the importance of the "interview" out of all proportion. The second "view" performs the same courtesies for the idea of television rating. With the same eight actors we are in the viewing room of a television rating company: the same aluminum foil box with the addition of a few stylized properties. But the triumph of the evening is the third "view," called "Motel." The stage, with its same aluminum foil walls, is now the interior of a motel room, decorated with garish curtains and an outsize bed. The exaggeration of size is pertinent when two huge and grotesquely dressed "dolls" enter—one male and one female. They are actors who have been "fleshed out" with papier-mâché additions; the motel-keeper is a huge female figure only remotely human, with no live actor visible at all under the papier-mâché form. While this comically terrifying figure moves about the room extolling its virtues in a lengthy monologue, the man and woman systematically and obscenely demolish the room and its contents. It is a grim but hilarious view of the irreverence and violence of American life, with all its disregard for things human, embodied in an *action* which takes the side of humanity in destroying *things.* The action is so effective, the meaning so implicit in the *action* that we are lifted out of our seats to cheer. So this is what the new theatre is all about!

WEDNESDAY. Tonight we are going to see the APA-Phoenix pro-

Figure 1–4

APA-Phoenix Company
Pantagleize. *Ellis Raab
as Pantagleize in the
Hall of Justice.*
(*Van Williams*)

duction of Ghelderode's *Pantagleize* at the Lyceum Theatre. It is
a musty old Broadway house with the paint peeling from the
plaster figures and moldings that decorate the proscenium and
boxes. The seats are comfortable enough, but there is not sufficient legroom between the rows; people must have been smaller in
the days when this was built, almost seventy years ago, long before the play which we are to see was written. We have been
interested for a long time in this Pantagleize, this innocent, this
"last poet," as Ghelderode calls him, who is "bound to Parsifal
by purity, and to Don Quixote by courage and holy madness,"
and we want to see what this fine company will do with him.
They do not disappoint us. From the moment we meet the tall,
thin, white-clad figure of Pantagleize as he wakens to that "lovely
day," through all the mishaps he encounters with revolutionaries
and revolution, to his arrest, trial, and execution ("particularly
in our time, the Innocents must be slaughtered: that has been the
law since the time of Jesus"), we are enthralled with the stage
action, which so aptly makes concrete and vital this abstract play
about the way a person may be caught up in a revolution without meaning to be, and which sees revolution as a condition of

Figure 1–5

Act IV Experimental Theatre, Provincetown
Father Uxbridge Wants To Marry. *Interested spectators participate in the action of the play at close quarters with the actors.*

man's life. It is an open stage, albeit a definitely proscenium one, and the action flows effortlessly. Scenes are transformed before our eyes to the revolutionists' cafe, the street, Rachel Silbershatz's house, the bank, the hall of justice, the prison: all with a modesty of detail and simply indications of place that sometimes used the whole stage, sometimes only a spotlighted part of it. The movement of dozens of banners behind a wall "acts out" the revolution, and the spotless and graceful figure of Pantagleize moves in Chaplinesque fashion through it all. Surely this is the definitive production of *Pantagleize*. Who else could touch it?

FRIDAY. We are in the tiny Act IV Café Theatre to see Frank Gagliano's *Father Uxbridge Wants To Marry*. We had seen its initial performance at the American Place Theatre and thought it rather heavy-handed and "over-produced." What will it be like here, we wonder, where about sixty or seventy people crowd around little tables under a low ceiling, and there seems to be no "acting space" at all? When all who want them are supplied with coffee and sweets, the lights quickly dim, high sweet music surrounds us, through it we hear the tick of a metronome, and there, somewhat off-center in the rectangular-shaped room is a spot of light on a small, low platform which contains a man, asleep, standing at what looks like a lever, with a small seat in the opposite corner. As we become aware of him, the voice of Mrs. Bethnal-Green assaults him, "Well, Mr. Morden . . ." as she steps into the "elevator" and he awakens. Elevator sounds and the music of angels over the sound system punctuate this scene. It ends with Morden's cry for help as the elevator sticks and Mrs. Bethnal-Green faints. The cry is answered by a voice from somewhere in the dark; Morden goes toward the voice through a succession of downspots which light before him and go out behind him; the elevator has disappeared, and we are in the softly lit rectory of Father Uxbridge against a wall of the cafe upon which are hung two stained glass windows (both a part of the permanent decor of the house). Mysterious music and a green spotlight introduce the dream figure of Father Ungar in a location somewhat removed from the rectory area when his name is mentioned; it fades quickly. Again the Mother's Voice, this time on tape, leads Morden to another small area of the cafe, where the desiccated figure of the mother is a store dummy in a wheelchair. So the performance moves through and around the seated audience, in half a dozen different locations in various paths from one to the other, lights and music making a continuous and undulating path from beginning to end. Now Morden's nightmare is real and immediate to us; now it makes sense for one actress to be playing all the women's roles, for Morden sees only the one woman in his dream, no matter who she is supposed to be. We are involved inexorably in this action which swirls around us, even though the performers are completely self-contained, making no eye contact with us, nor ever touching us. It is a new and exciting theatre experience, and infinitely more moving than the dispersed and grandly staged original production.

THURSDAY. Tonight we will see Arthur Miller's latest at the Morosco Theatre. It is *The Price* with Kate Reid, Pat Hingle, Arthur Kennedy, and Harold Gary. The Morosco is a standard Broadway house, old but well furbished, with a gracious faded red and gold air about it. It seats about 1000 people in the sloped orchestra and the single balcony, or mezzanine as it is called these days. The audience gathered for this performance seems affluent, not particularly intellectual (if one can surmise such a thing from appearance), and in a good frame of mind. When the curtain

Figure 1–6

The Price. *Kate Reid and Pat Hingle confront each other in the cluttered apartment. (Inge Morath, Magnum Photos)*

goes up, there is spontaneous applause for a minutely detailed realistic setting of the attic floor of a Manhattan brownstone house, jammed to the rafters with very obviously real and solid furniture. More than half the stage space is consumed with the stored household effects; a few pieces down front will give seating possibilities to the four members of the cast at various times. There are no sound effects, no music, no intermission. It is about two hours of talk; elapsed time is the same as stage time. The effect is eminently *real*. So are the people: two brothers, one of whom left this house years ago to become eminent and successful and returns momentarily, the other who took a job as a policeman to support his father in this house and who is here with his wife to sell off the accumulated belongings. The fourth person is the secondhand funiture dealer who has come to see if he wants to buy. That is all; it is enough. Obviously, many people in that audience—men and women—identified very closely indeed with the characters on the stage. You could hear indrawn breaths, sighs, small bursts of laughter, sobs; you could see the nods of recognition, the eager bending forward of approval, the slumps of dismay. This was a sophisticated Broadway audience, and yet they were entirely caught up in the action on the stage. The applause at the end was deafening.

MONDAY. Our week of theatre-going, spread over many weeks, ends tonight with a revival of Shaw's *Arms and the Man* at the Sheridan Square Playhouse, one of the better off-Broadway theatres. The playing area is the open end of a squarish rectangle with the banked seats arranged in three sections: one facing the open area and two flanking it along the sides and extending a little further into the open area. The intervening aisles are used by the actors as well as by the audiences; the actors also have some means of getting on and off in the playing area itself. The designer has filled the open space with an ingenious arrangement of platforms and set pieces which will start as Raina's bedchamber, be transformed into the garden of Major Petkoff's house, and then become the library for the last act. It does not do this instantaneously; at the intermissions between the acts stagehands come on and move the pieces, but very expeditiously. Many of the members of the audience stay in their seats to watch these changes. The lighting fixtures are in view, but out of sightlines; the light plot is varied and effective. And, of course, Shaw's delightful spoof of the romatic disposition is perennially amusing. It is almost actor-proof; but this cast is particularly competent and get from the action every nuance and every ounce of fun. Though the audience is a little cramped for space, and the seats are not the most comfortable, they are obviously enjoying themselves immensely. Perhaps the proximity of the players and the action involves the audience more intimately. At any rate, the talk afterwards as the audience goes out is all delighted and cheerful.

Now, in these manifestly varied evenings, what are the constants? Why can we label all of these "theatre"? And why might literally hundreds of experiences—similar and not so similar—be called by the same title? Some of the common features are obvious:

1. In each case a specific group of people gathered together at a specific time in a specific place to watch and listen as another smaller group of people pretended to be persons they were not, acting out a story invented by yet another person.

2. In each case the space occupied by the acting group was more brightly lighted than that for the watcher-listeners and was

Figure 1–7

The audience, in close proximity to the stage, enjoys the production of Arms and the Man *at the Sheridan Square Playhouse. Designed by Lloyd Burlingame.*

equipped with various articles of furniture, painted frames of cloth, disguised boxes, steps, and various other articles, and

3. All the performers wore clothes which were different from their usual habits, which disguised their own personalities, and which seemed to belong to the characters they were impersonating.

These features (with the possible exception of special lighting) have been common to theatre since its beginning—a group of specially costumed performers acting out a story for a live audience. But when we have said that, we have only begun to explore the phenomenon of THEATRE. Why, for more than two thousand years of man's history, have such occasions continued to occur? Why, in spite of political upheavals, war, and a multitude of natural disasters, have self-selected groups of people continued to isolate themselves for varying periods of time to participate in a patently invented happening, and generally paid a not insignificant portion of their income to be allowed to do so?

Let us return to our journal for a moment, and extract some other observations.

1. One of the performances was first seen by audiences in the last decade of the sixteenth century; one in 1664, one in 1894; the others in very recent years. Yet all seemed to speak to that contemporary audience of which the diarist was a part. Here is the first mystery.

2. So far as could be observed, all of these audiences—from the 1009 filling the plush-covered seats of the Morosco to the 67 sitting on hard chairs at cramped little tables in the Act IV Café Theatre—were at one with the performances. Eager, attentive, relaxed, involved, they laughed with the performers, cried with them; at many and frequent intervals could be felt that intense and breathing silence which means rapt attention. And at the end of each performance came that release of the collectively held breath, followed by the storm of applause signaling the conclusion of a mutually shared and mutually enjoyed experience. And here is the second mystery.

Compare, for a moment, the events described above with the more ubiquitous and more easily available form of entertainment —the cinema, or with television. Few indeed must be the people who have not at some time or other slipped into the dark of a movie house, stumbling over feet and knees, to find an empty seat while the picture continued to move on the screen at the front of the house. Entering in the dark, the spectator also probably leaves in the dark, when the pictures on the screen before him come round once more to the sequence at which he entered. During the cycle for which he paid his admission price he has scarcely been aware of those in the seats surrounding his, except as they intruded upon him with popcorn eating, conversation, or love-making. He has been isolated from the world about him, from his fellow men, as he was transported to a never-never land of brilliantly colored fakery in which even the beautifully dressed people seem like objects which the camera uses as it does furniture or landscape. (I am speaking here of the typical Hollywood product so familiar to American audiences.) He has been overwhelmed by the size of the images projected before him; he has had his senses drugged by their kaleidoscopic effect and the all-pervasive soundtrack on which there is not a moment of silence, and he leaves the movie house in a state of semisomnambulism which requires a real wrench to place him once more among the world of men. Though this view of movies may here seem partial and somewhat cavalier, it is at any rate deliberate. In several significant ways, it is perfectly true that the film experience, no less than that of theatre, depends upon participation in an action through means of perception; such perception and participation are often life-enhancing. But in these early stages of our consideration of the nature of theatre, it seems useful to make a distinction between the immediacy of live theatre and the once- or twice-removed stance of film in relation to its audience. We will explore film more impartially and more thoroughly in Part V.

In watching television (in his own home or elsewhere), the viewer has an experience similar to movies, yet different. Now the figures on the screen before him are mini-figures; only in close-ups do faces assume life-size, and then the isolated face is attached to nothing and has no relationship to other people or to things. At frequently recurring intervals the watcher's attention is violently displaced to the virtues of an antiperspirant, soft drink, or airline before another segment of the show he is watching comes dutifully into view once more. He carries on a conversation with his fellow watchers, not only during these interruptions, but frequently through the main event itself. His attention is peripheral, fragmented, and unstable. The television is simply an accompaniment to the concerns of everyday, as convenient as a pressure cooker or an electric stove and not much more significant.

Going to the theatre, however, is a special event to our mythical man. He arranges for tickets in advance, and pays for a particular location in the house. He arrives somewhat in advance of the stated starting time and mingles in the lobby and the aisles with other like-minded people; he speculates about who these people are, where they come from, why they have gathered to see this production; perhaps he chats with friends or acquaintances who, by chance, are attending the same performance. He looks at the program handed to him by the usher who shows him to his seat, and he orients himself to the time and place and personages of the performance which is about to begin. The houselights dim, there is an expectant hush, and the performance begins. He gives himself over to the enactment, tacitly agreeing that the actual human beings he sees therein are, for the duration of the performance, what they say they are, and that they are moving and speaking in a locale which is amended by his imagination to *be* whatever the play requires. He is conscious of the breathing audience around him; he enters into the group spirit; his laughter is quicker and louder as it is supported by that of others; his tears or indrawn breath or silences are a communion not only with the actors but with other members of the audience. He joins in the applause at the end of the performance, and as the actors take their bows in their own persons, though still in costume, he is aware of a shared experience which has given his life an added dimension of humanity.

What he has done, of course, is to have shared in a ritual as old as man himself. Consciously or subconsciously, he has become one with the long march of the ages through which theatre has reflected the concerns of man: his fears, his desires, his aspirations. He has figuratively joined hands not only with the immediate participants in this particular ritual occasion, but through them with all of mankind everywhere and at all times. He has made a statement about his human-ness and reaffirmed his faith in humanity. For above all, theatre is and always has been a PEOPLE-activity, created with, by, and for people in direct communication, face-to-face. When it has lost sight of this fact, when it has allowed this confrontation to be sullied or distorted by the interposition of nonhuman agencies of machinery in whatever form, it has become nonvital, or other than itself. The rediscovery of the human principle once more has made it rise again like a phoenix from the ashes to new vitality. Always the most important elements in theatre have been the actor and the audience. Playscripts, costumes, settings, lighting, music, song, and dance, even theatre architecture itself, have at various times and in varying proportions been present solely to support the actor and his audience. And again, whenever any of these elements has, in the long reaches of theatre history, become more important than the actor-audience relationship, at that moment theatre died, only to rise again. "It is the waves of love I feel from audiences that make me an actor," a young friend of mine said to me recently. He was talking about the human communication which is the essential factor—perhaps the *only* essential factor—in the art of theatre.

Theatre is experiential. Like life itself, it appeals simultaneously to a number of the senses, and its impact is emotional. The large numbers of people who voluntarily place themselves in theatre seats night after night in all the theatres, large and small, through-out the world, are looking for an EXPERIENCE, preferably life-enhancing. They seek not only (and certainly not primarily) to enlarge the borders of their knowledge, but also to MAKE THEM-SELVES FEEL—to LIVE with the performance a life not otherwise available to them. These impulses are largely unrecognized and certainly seldom expressed. Yet they are fundamental, and the recognition of them tells us much about the nature of theatre and explains perhaps all of its miraculous persistence from the earliest times to the latest, among all manner of people and in all sorts of places. For theatre is one of the most persistent of art forms and one of the earliest.

As an art, theatre shares with music, dance, painting, sculpture, and literature the quality of ordering materials so that they are expressive. Unlike the observed world of surfaces, where order is often undetectable, the world of art always reveals the hand and mind of the artist—selecting, arranging, and giving meaning. An example from what Marshall McLuhan calls the Gutenberg tech-nology will clarify this statement. Words by themselves are refer-ential; they have no existence apart from the THINGS to which they refer; the further they ascend Hayakawa's "abstraction ladder" the less communicative they become. Taken singly, or grouped in random order, they convey little or no meaning; the pages of a dictionary are useful for reference, but not for com-munication. It is only when the system of grammatical order is applied to words—only when a process of selection and arrange-ment takes place—that they become intelligible. But even then they are intelligible only in a symbolic way—as convenient codi-fications of the things, persons, and ideas which they represent, or to which they refer. No one would pretend that WORDS are substitutes for THINGS, for PERSONS, for IDEAS. They are the CON-VENTIONS by which these items are EXPRESSED, are communicated, are ordered, or arranged. They are the code, or the shorthand of the world past, the world present, and the world to come. But they are no more than a code, a shorthand. "Words, words, words, words," said Hamlet, and with reason.

For words leave out the SEEN image, the FELT image, the image heard and smelled and tasted. Only by implication and the ex-perience of the word-consumer can these qualities accrue to the progression of black marks on white paper which have been invented by man to be the record of his existence. But he knows that existence is more than this code, this shorthand, and, consciously or unconsciously, he keeps making the translations from the code. He not only translates the written word, but the spoken word as well—"What you do speaks so loud that I cannot hear what you say," "I hear what you say, but what do you *mean* by what you say?"

The nonverbal worlds of music, of dance, of painting, and of sculpture are more direct in their communication, in that they are closer to the THING itself, and not a shorthand, a code, or a reference. Yet each in its way is an abstraction, an ordering of elements selected by an artist to convey his particular meaning. The musician uses pitch, tone, and timbre in varying arrangements; the dancer uses line, movement, and space; the painter uses line, color, and space relationships; the sculptor uses line and mass and space itself. The musician makes his appeal almost solely to the sense of hearing; the painter and the dancer, almost solely to the sense of sight; and the sculptor, to sight and touch. And though these appeals are direct and unencoded, the experience of these arts is amplified and made meaningful to the "consumer" by his total life experience and his awareness of their patterns and conventions.

What, then, of theatre, which is a composite art, and in many ways the most ephemeral of all of those which I have mentioned? It partakes of some qualities of all of these—music, dance, painting, and sculpture. Like the Juggler of Our Lady, it keeps several balls in the air at one time, making a beautiful pattern so long as each ball is in its proper relationship to every other one, and so long as the balls are in action and interacting. But let the juggler disturb the pattern, or his skill fail, and down the balls come in a heap, and chaos results.

It is this very quality of simultaneous multiple appeals that makes theatre (as opposed to literature, where the shorthand of words puts the burden on the reader to supply both multiplicity and simultaneity of appeals) so potent an art, and—alas, too frequently—chaotic. For the demands on the theatre artist for balance and proportion, for rhythm and harmony, for interest and variety, are very great indeed. Yet when superbly achieved, theatre speaks to its audiences as life itself does—with a multiplicity of appeals and a directness, yet with an order and a meaning that transcend life, as all abstractions and arrangements (which are the essence of art of all kinds) do. Theatre is, indeed, an imitation of life intended to convey some perceptions about life.

I have always been somewhat suspicious of artists who declare that they create their works of art FOR THEMSELVES, in order to express themselves, with no thought of an audience. Even Emily Dickinson, who wrote so many of her poems in private to exorcise her particular daemon, sent many of them to Thomas Wentworth Higginson for his criticism, and many more accompanied small gifts to other individuals. The musician's work does not exist until it is performed, and performance in itself mandates an audience of one or many. Music itself predated the system of notation which makes a record for performance possible. The dance world is still struggling with systems of notation whereby movement patterns, originally created for audiences, can be recorded and re-created. Painters and sculptors have for centuries worked on private and public commissions to produce their works for audiences of individuals, states, organizations, and nations. Even for those freely created and intuitively inspired works which have had no prior incentive, the artist seeks exhibition space and ultimate sale. One of the prior conditions for the architect to begin his work is a clear vision of the "audience" for whom it is intended. The poet's eye "in fine frenzy rolling" seeks primarily the outward expression of his inward feeling, but few indeed are the undiscovered and unpublished "great" ones. Any writer—poet, novelist, essayist, journalist—has always in his vision his potential audience, the person or persons to whom his work is directed, and who will eventually read it.

Perhaps more than any of these, the theatre is and always has been acutely aware of, indeed completely dependent upon, its audience. For THERE IS NO THEATRE without an audience. Theatre does not and cannot exist unless and until there is an audience. It is the mutually enjoyed experience of performers and audience which constitutes theatre; it is the LIVING TOGETHER of an ordered existence, the interchange of spoken or unspoken thoughts, ideas, emotions, actions—in other words, transactions—which make theatre.

It goes without saying, then, that the fullest and most meaningful experience of theatre (as indeed of the other arts as well) will

be enjoyed by those who most deeply and fully know its nature, its possibilities, and its pitfalls. Robert Frost once said that to understand Poem A you must read Poem B, to understand Poem B you must read Poem C, to understand Poem C you must read Poem D, and on *ad infinitum*, as if poetry were like eating olives, where all you have to do to develop a taste is to keep on eating them. Of course, there is a grain of truth in this procedure. Undifferentiated, unexamined, and unclassified experience would, if mortality did not intervene, eventually teach us everything. But what a waste of time! And more importantly, what a waste of the precious store of human energy and a dissipation of the possibility of enlarged and knowledgeable enjoyment! For poetry, like any art form—like theatre—has its principles of ordering which, mastered early on, make subsequent encounters with the poetic phenomenon more satisfying and life-enhancing.

So it is with theatre. Although it sometimes seems that the more one knows, the more one finds there is to know, the training of one's sensitivities to the components of theatre will make all subsequent experiences of theatre more meaningful and life-enhancing. Theatre is not the mere words of the play itself, it is not a visual image, it is not a pattern of sound or of movement—it is all of these, and more than the sum of all its parts. Nothing exists by itself, but in its relationships to everything else—the author's words, the actor's person, the costumes, the setting, the lighting, the sound, the music—all must work together so that the meaning intended by the original creative artist, usually the dramatist, is conveyed to his audiences, not the linear meaning only of the grammatical composition, but the total meaning of text and sub-text and supratext, if you will. And in theatre, all of this must happen with live human beings gathered together in one place, at one time, so that the communication can be instantaneous and sensitive to the electricity of that one time and place.

Needless to say, no one is more aware than this author of the inadequacy of words to express what is beyond the power of words to express. But just as Carl Sandburg once defined poetry as "the binding in fetters of permanence a transient dream," so it is incumbent upon us to attempt the discussion of the totality of theatre (which is far more than words alone) in the "fetters of permanence" which ARE written words, the "transient dream" of theatre. Piece out our imperfections with your thoughts, and per-haps we shall at last succeed in doing what James Weldon John-son has his Negro preacher do: "explain the unexplainable, ponder the imponderable."

You will gather, and rightly so, that the diffuse definition of theatre at which we have thus far arrived seems to exclude the movies and television, those "Johnnies-come-lately" on the scene. The exclusion is deliberate and intended. But from the benignity of our comprehension of theatre (at which we will hopefully ar-rive), we will also consider these "second-cousin" (I almost said "sister") arts. For both movies and television borrow largely from the theatre and (largely because of a lack of comprehension of their true nature) seem too often a bastard, although all-pervasive, form of theatre. The similarities and differences we will explore. But, for the moment, let us hold to the thought that theatre happens wherever a live actor confronts and communi-cates with a live audience, and the transaction that takes place between them is the essence of theatre, although to that essential confrontation has been added, over the long stretches of its exist-ence, a multiplicity of structures and conventions which have be-come a part of the total construct implicit and explicit in the term theatre.

We proceed on the premise that understanding enhances appreciation. Theatre audiences do not go to the theatre, by and large, forearmed with neat classifications of types and styles of drama nor the wide reaches of theatre history in their minds. They go for an experience—all the rest is post facto. Theatre criticism is a literary art; the theatre itself is a social art. Theatre is and always has been a microcosm of the world in which it exists. Its constant is humanity, and from this fact derives its universality. It is people-oriented. And the people-problem with respect to theatre is how to experience more, to enjoy more, through understanding more clearly and deeply just what the theatre is in its constant becoming. Let us explore these concepts in some detail.

2
The Nature of Art and the Art of Theatre

At this juncture it might be profitable for us to explore for a moment or two the nature of art and its relevancy to the human condition. It is not our intention here to produce a definitive tome in aesthetics; the reader is referred in the appended biliographies to useful extant works in this field. But the progression or development of our investigation does require that we begin at the same beginnings.

There are probably as many definitions of art as there are people to concoct them. In its earliest sense, the word was applied to anything which required skill and ability acquired through practice and directed to a definite end. Thus, in the aesthetic sense there were the Fine Arts, in the ethical sense the Arts of Conduct, and in the useful sense the Liberal Arts. Vestiges of the latter two applications are with us still in such phrases as "the art of living," "the art of cooking," "the art of war," etc. But for a long time now the word art has been more exclusively applied to the static arts of painting, sculpture, and architecture, as well as the dynamic arts of music, dance, and literature (poetry and drama). Many writers on aesthetics, from Plato to Schiller and Herder and Susanne K. Langer, have attempted to explore and explain the essential nature of art as distinct from other manifestations of human activity. Many of these recognize the nonutilitarian, immaterialistic character of art; some regard it as a form of play; some as an empathic phenomenon; some as "nature seen through a temperament"; some as the equivalent of intuition; some as "objectified pleasure"; and some as dependent upon the artist's emotional impulse. But all (with the evidence of history and archaeology to support them) have insisted upon its necessity to man's existence, to its life-enhancing qualities.

Primitive man found an impelling weapon in art to allay his superstitious fear of the unknown forces of nature. Through his art products he tried to placate the mysterious or hostile powers; he created symbols of stability and rest in the turmoil of the universe; he created a whole, a unity, over which he had domination and power. This need to see a selected whole is still a basic and compelling impetus to the creation of art. In unselective nature our vision is naturally limited, and natural processes are still largely out of our control. We are part of a process of becoming, with first causes inscrutable and ends unforeseeable. The peculiar quality of a work of art, as differentiated from natural or accidental beauty, is the order, the composition impressed upon his materials by the skill or technique of the artist as he shapes them to express the emotions or feeling awakened in him by the world around him.

Art, as we understand it today, does still include the old meaning of skill acquired through practice and directed to a definite end. It also includes the idea of a product not directed primarily to utilitarian ends, inspired by the emotional response of the artist to the impact of the world, of nature and of man, upon his sensitivities. As D. W. Prall puts it in his early work, *Aesthetic Judgment* (p. 292):

This world [of art] is different from the world of life only in being clearly bounded, separated from the universal context of nature by a distinct beginning and end beyond which it does not reach at all, and in being composed of select and perspicuous material also clearly outlined in explicit temporal and spatial relations, which, instead of being embedded in a confusing and overwhelming matrix of other relations and events, as the realities of nature and of life are obscured in the moving universe of all reality, stand out clear and emphatic and consistent and whole and independent, a bounded and ordered unity, an anagram of life and nature, humanly composed whole, exactly what we call a work of art, and a work of fine art, since its sole aim is its own achieved definite and unique expressiveness, not practical communication or any other ulterior sort of usefulness or purpose.

Susanne K. Langer, in her detailed and coherent book *Feeling and Form* (pp. 36 ff.), puts it thus: art is

an autonomous, creative function of a typically human mind. . . . Art is the creation of forms symbolic of human feeling. . . . Every real work of art has a tendency to appear thus dissociated from its mundane environment. The most immediate impression it creates is one of "otherness"

Figure 2–1

National Theatre
of the Deaf
*Sculpture and music
These sculptural forms
are musical instruments
used as part of the décor
on stage.*

from reality—the impression of an illusion enfolding the thing, action, statement, or flow of sound that constitutes the work. . . . the true power of an image lies in the fact that it is an abstraction, a symbol, the bearer of an idea.

She goes on to say that the process of art creates a "virtual" or *seeming,* or *made* object having no actuality in the familiar world; it is an *illusion,* acts as a symbol, becomes "expressive of human feeling." Aristotle, that ultimate source of all aesthetic theory, called the various arts "modes of imitation" (*Poetics,* Chap. 1) with a meaning very much like that more fully quoted from Prall and Langer.

Such definitions of art allow us to see its realization in the temporal arts of music, poetry (in its widest application), and dance, and in the spatial arts of painting, sculpture, and architecture. In each, the artist uses the qualities inherent in the nature of his medium to express through his technique of ordering an individual response or manifestation of feeling. A brief exposition will illustrate the point.

Music is the purest of the arts; it appeals only to the sense of hearing and has the fewest number of variables, all derived from nature. Its predominant characteristics are pitch and rhythm. In music, natural high and low sounds and the gradations between them are marked off and systematized into a scale with set vari-

Figure 2–2

Painting
Leon Bakst's painted
setting for Lâcheté.

ations between the changes in pitch. So, too, the recurrence of
stresses or emphases which constitute rhythm are, in music, selected, controlled, and composed into rhythmic patterns. To these
are added tone (a musical sound of a single pitch is composed of
a fundamental tone and its harmonics or overtones), timbre (the
qualitative difference of pitch and tone delivered for the same
musical sound by different instruments), and intensity (comparative loudness). By dealing with these intrinsic qualities of sound
in a selective, systematized fashion, the musician *composes* a
work which *expresses* his emotional state, his *feeling*. All music,
from the simplest tune to the most complicated symphonic score
for a hundred-piece orchestra, uses these qualities inherent in the
nature of the medium, their complication and the effectiveness of
their ordering being dependent only upon the skill or technique of
the artist and the strength of his emotional drive, or inspiration.
We call music a *temporal* art because its qualities function over a
period of elapsed time, and time periods of varying length are
manipulated to produce one of its characteristic effects. Music,
says Miss Langer, "makes time audible, and its form and continuity sensible . . . it is *virtual* time." (p. 110) Yet even this
purest of the arts, unadulterated by any sense impression save
that of sound, becomes infinitely complex in the manipulation of
its inherent qualities, as anyone who has listened to a Beethoven
symphony, for instance, can attest.

Figure 2–3

Sculpture
Lee Simonson's unit
setting for Hamlet. *The*
total effect of the setting
is a sculptural one.
See also 6–6.

As music is a temporal art, so painting, sculpture, and architecture are spatial arts, operating in and manipulating *space* as music operates in *time*. The inherent qualities in these arts are hue, line, area, and mass, and it is these which are systematized and composed to create the final art object. Painting operates in two dimensions and so has at its disposal hue, line, and area. Even the much vaunted and exceedingly useful principle of perspective, discovered by Renaissance painters, is a two-dimensional tool used to give the optical illusion of a third dimension. Or one might say that representational painters *perceive* in three dimensions, then work these three into an illusion-giving two dimensions. Paintings have length and breadth; they are flat surfaces. Length and breadth are qualities of lines, which are in turn extensions of points marked off in systematized units of space. Points extended into lines traveling in different directions intersect and so create areas, or flat forms, or designs. Sketching, lithography, and etching stop at this point. Painting uses color, or hue, for the lines and areas, either creating line and area by the direct application of color or by applying color to a previously prepared drawing. Hue is that element of color which corresponds to pitch in sound—the basic quality which can be marked off in gradations, although in nature itself there is no such definite demarcation. While pitch gradations, however, travel in a straight line from low to high, the gradations of hue travel in a circle, from yellow to orange, red, purple, violet, blue, blue-green, yellow-green and back to yellow. Then, each hue, or gradation of clear color, can be intermixed with white or black to create lighter or darker shades, depending on the proportions of constituents in the mixture. The painter, working consciously within these orders, produces a structural whole which is expressive of his own passionate and vivid feeling. Hence we conclude that representation alone is not art, for it is a mere copying of nature. Interpretation is art, for it entails, through the use of acquired skill and technique, the qualities inherent in the nature of the medium structured to express in space the feeling, or vision, of the artist.

The sculptor and the architect work in three dimensions as compared to the painter's two—length, breadth, and thickness or mass. To the sculptor, hue is less important than to the architect, but he no less consciously uses line, area, and mass to create a construct in space. Modern abstract sculptors even use enclosed space itself, as when we see an abstracted human figure with a hole through its middle, or a structure of shapes enclosing variously shaped open spaces. The architect, of course, has always been concerned to manipulate empty space in his constructs.

In recent years some painters have been experimenting with the problem of adding an actual third dimension to the length and breadth which have hitherto been used; thus we have collages. Further extensions of this idea, coupled with the experiments of some musicians in "chance" or "noise" music have led to an experimental form of theatre, as we detail more fully in Part III, Chapter 9. Experiments also by painters and sculptors to extend the boundaries of their arts have recently led to the creation of "environments," about which we will also have something to say later in our discussion about new forms in theatre. In the minds of many people, these experiments have yet to prove themselves as viable art forms; they are still very much "avant-garde," or perhaps improvisations on the way to a form.

Despite the complications inherent in the conscious ordering of set gradations in hue, line, area, and mass, we may say that painting, sculpture, and architecture are spatial arts—appealing primarily if not solely to the sense of sight—whereas music is a temporal art appealing solely to the sense of hearing. These four, working in materials inherent in the sensory impressions of sight and sound, for which an order has been discovered and system-

Figure 2–4

*Architecture
Norman Bel Geddes'
design for Reinhardt's
The Miracle. The effect
is that of a Gothic
cathedral.*

atized, are clearly in the fine arts, as traditionally and presently viewed. We may note here in passing that constructs using sensory impressions of the other three senses—smell, taste, and touch —are not considered *arts* since the mind of man has not discovered nor systematized gradations or orders in them so that they can become the materials which can be put to use by the artistic technique. Touch, of course, does enter into the spatial arts as texture, but its use is incidental to the total work.

From these more easily seen examples of temporal and spatial art we move to the composite arts, such as dance, which uses both spatial and temporal elements. Patterned movement, inherent in the possibilities of the human body, makes shapes in space, moving from one configuration to another in accordance with selected rhythms which exist through time. The fact that dance is almost invariably accompanied by music makes no alteration in the fact that one of its inherent qualities is that of rhythm, "the setting up [of] new tensions by the resolution of former ones." (Langer, p. 127) Here, too, it must be noted that the avant-garde of dance rejects musical accompaniment and insists on the autonomy of the patterned movement which is the essence of dance as an art. This patterned movement, or *gesture,* is the basic abstraction which the dancer makes and organizes, and through which he symbolizes the play of powers, the relation of forces in a polarity of tensions, with rhythmically changing patterns.

Rhythm is the basic quality of poetry also, the only branch of literature which has consistently and from the beginning been considered an art. No doubt this classification is traditionally founded on the fact that poetry was originally not written down, but descended by oral tradition and hence made its primary ap-

Figure 2–5

Dance
A moment in the New
York production of
Your Own Thing.
(Bert Andrews)

peal by its sound. But there is much more to an art form that uses words than simply the sound thereof. For the very nature of words is referential rather than actual; here literature departs from the other arts which use actual aesthetic surfaces as materials. Literature is the most remote of the arts from perceived surfaces; hence it is that we often find certain groups of studies labelled "Literature and the Fine Arts." The communication that particular groupings of words have for a given audience will depend to a large extent upon the experience and background of that audience, how much reference it can bring to the words presented. Words, as we have mentioned before, are simply the agreed upon symbols for actuality which given social groups accept as descriptive of that actuality. But they are indeed the materials of literature, and the artist in literature acquires the techniques and skills of selection and arrangement according to an agreed upon structure—grammar—to body forth his statement. All artists in words use not only their denotative values but their connotative values as well, and in poetry particularly the use of imagery is paramount. In all of this the sound values are not neglected; who was it said that the word "carminative" seemed to him the most beautiful sound in the language until he learned what the word meant? Thus the literary artist, no less than those in the temporal and spatial arts, uses the inherent qualities of his medium (words) to express in ordered and struc-

THE EXPERIENCE
OF THEATRE

tured form the intent of his genius, depending upon his audience to bring to the conventions which are words the implications and memories of sense impressions which are a vital part of his referential medium. The writer of poetry, fiction, and drama, as distinct from the historian or the reporter, uses discourse (the arrangement of words in understandable form) to create an illusion, an appearance of experience, "the semblance of events lived and felt . . . so that they constitute a purely and completely experienced reality, a piece of *virtual life*." (Langer, p. 212) Literature creates its own world from the first word. The dramatist, of course, differs from the novelist chiefly in that his words are what Francis Fergusson calls the "last actualizations" of the perceived action which is basic to his conception. They are the outgrowths of action, whereas the novelist's words are the very medium through which the reader enters whatever action there is.

Theatre, like ballet, is a composite art but, unlike ballet, uses not just two or three of its sister arts, but all of them. The musical qualities of pitch, tone, intensity, and timbre are present universally in the voices of the actors even in nonmusical plays where instruments and/or songs are not used. One is reminded irresistibly in this respect of Sarah Bernhardt's advice to the novice who asked what three things were most important to develop as an actress. Said the great one: "Voice, voice, and again voice." The spoken word as sound alone is of intimate concern to the actor; the French have perhaps realized this more keenly than any others —voice culture has always been of primary concern in French theatre. (One almost suspects that it has always been of least concern in American theatre.) Even the least perceptive of persons must have had the experience of being affected by the tone and intensity of utterance more than by the words themselves, as when in compassion, understanding, and love someone might have said to him, "You are a perfect fool!" Even the most elementary reader of poetry is struck with the added dimension of its vocal delivery:

The lone and level sands stretch far away

is beautiful to look at on the page and conducts an image to the reader's eye, but the *speaking* of the words makes them more and other through the music of the tones and overtones, the rhythm, the alliteration. The words of a play are set down to be spoken,

Figure 2–6

Polarity of tensions in a theatre scene. Iphigenia in Aulis.
(Friedman-Abeles)

are the stuff of speaking, and the dramatist must ever deal with his vocabulary in its *audible* aspect.

Literature—the art that deals with words—is but one of the structural elements of the art of theatre, though one must keep in mind the differing priorities of words in novels and in drama. One would not deny to the playwright the importance of his words to the total concept of theatre; in many times and places it has been the impelling vision implicit in the words set down by a writer which has made great theatre. And since words have been and will continue to be (despite Marshall McLuhan) a primary means of communication for human beings, the words the dramatist writes will continue to be of prime importance in the theatre, because through them is conveyed the essence of drama, which is the emotions, goals, and actions of the characters as they have significance for the audience. But the words he chooses and the construct he erects with them must always be chosen and arranged with eye and ear trained to the exigencies—the possibilities and the pitfalls—of the total art of theatre. He must ever be aware of the fact that words are simply an easy way of preserving sense impressions, but are in no wise the thing itself; that plays which have become "literature" cease to be theatre; i.e., when the exclusively literary qualities of a play are divorced from

Figure 2–7
Hunter College, CUNY
*The power of words.
The oath scene from
Othello. See also 6–7.*

a consideration of the play's use in theatre, the play is diminished thereby. Reading a play is a very poor second to experiencing it in the theatre. What an impoverished idea of theatre is to be had from "play*reader's* handbooks"!

Not only are words just convenient referentials, they also are frequently submerged or changed in meaning by the action which accompanies them. "Actions speak louder than words." "What you do speaks so loud that I cannot hear what you say." Action—the movement of the human body in space which is the essential quality of dance—is a third composite of theatre art (the first being music or sound, the second literature or the selected arrangement of words). Dance in its own image may be—and often is, of course—a part of a theatrical production, just as music often is. But more important to the total art of theatre is the expressiveness of movement as integrated with the spoken word: an amalgam of literature, music, and dance which becomes other than any of these arts in their purer or more restricted state.

The basic abstraction of theatre is the *act*, which may be briefly defined as any sort of human response, physical or mental. It includes both word and gesture, thus transforming into *other* the basic abstractions of literature, dance, and music. Any *act* springs from the past and is directed toward the future; it transpires in

Figure 2–8

Minnesota Theatre
Company
*The basic abstraction of
theatre is the* act. *Mrs.
Antrobus defends her
values in a scene from*
The Skin of Our Teeth.
*Directed by Douglas
Campbell.*

the present. "It is only a present filled with its own future that is
dramatic," (Langer, p. 307), it is the "occurrence of virtual life"
(Ibid., p. 325), the *semblance* of futures appearing as embryonic
in the present. The *words* of theatre cannot be separated out because they are an intrinsic part of the *act* which is the basis of
the theatrical art.

The spatial arts, too, are a part of theatre art. Painting and
sculpture as such are a part of the visual elements of the theatre,
and architecture is so obviously inherent as to need no demonstration. But again aside from their use as recognizable entities,
the qualities inherent in the spatial arts—hue, line, area, and
mass—are in theatre used in a particularly theatrical way. None
but the most naive of spectators would assume that the soaring
arches, stained glass windows, and stone cathedral walls of Norman Bel Geddes's design for *The Miracle*, for instance, were an
actual architectural structure rather than the wood and lath and
colored gelatins of the actual set. Nor that the damask-seeming
walls of a Jo Mielziner drawing room were indeed damask. But
the spectator's acceptance of the theatrical reality is gained
through his feeling, to which the elements of the spatial arts speak
in the context of theatre. The inherent qualities of the spatial arts
are used in costuming and in lighting, as well as in scene design,

and in these new combinations become meaningful as a part of the whole.

Thus, in the line of our argument, we come to the conclusion that the art of the theatre can be called a composite art, using elements and structures native to other arts. But one more point must be made. As other arts become a part of the art of theatre they are *fused* and *transformed* into a single object of felt intention: that of theatre. Just as one does not separate the spatial from the temporal elements in experiencing the art of dance, so one does not separate out from theatre art an individual entity which under other circumstances might be one of the other arts. For each loses its separate identity in theatre, and the whole becomes greater than the sum of all its parts. As D. W. Prall has so poetically put it (Op. cit., p. 281):

For the theatre is relentless, more clearly than any other art, in its domination of all its constituent elements and constituent arts, which it presents only in its own theatrical perspective, from which, if they are separated, they fall to pieces as worthless rubbish, like stage-jewels or stage costumes from an old actor's chest.

If we were here to hazard a definition of *theatre*, we might phrase it thus: Theatre is that performing, or occurrent, art whose basis is the *act*, through which are perceived both the character and the range of human experience in the semblance of virtual life. It is, in other words, that art form which most vividly explores and represents what is meant by the state of being human.

It is this composite or combined art of theatre which transcends its components and becomes a particularized and meaningful aesthetic experience, whole and different from any other, that we shall be talking about in subsequent pages. Just as one can write about music, or painting, or architecture without being deluded for a moment that the words are in any sense *the thing itself*, so we can write about theatre. Because there are so many elements operating in the total construct of theatre, it is expedient that we deal with them individually in some depth. But we must never lose sight of the fact that each becomes not just the element known and used in the other arts, but a component in the theatrical art and hence other than its separate self. Though we would seem by this method to fragment the total art of theatre, we shall try never to lose sight of the whole, and before we close we shall hope to put it all back together again. Fortunately, theatre is no

Humpty Dumpty, but a dynamic organism in growth and change and perhaps the most meaningful and overwhelming of all the possible forms of art. It is, in itself, an ordering, a composition, through which the artist expresses his emotional reaction to his world in terms that speak to his audiences directly.

II
Ways of Seeing

3
The Play Itself

Having established that a play experienced in the theatre is a transaction between artists and audiences, we are ready to inquire more deeply into the nature of that transaction. In so doing, we shall call upon the accumulated wisdom of the ages while at the same time never losing sight of the fact that theatre is NOW, always NOW, always something transpiring in the present. This perspective and this immediacy is both its glory and its danger. For the theatre of past ages is irrevocably lost to us by its very nature—we cannot resurrect, except by indirection, either audiences or actors—that mystical communion which is at the center of theatre. The fragment of theatre which we have inherited from past times is the play itself, expressed in words alone, words which have either become the stuff of literature or the pursuit of esoteric scholarship. From this fragment a new theatrical experience can be reconstituted for a modern audience by talented and knowledgeable theatre artists, but it will never be the same as it first was. In fact, it should not be the same—antiquarianism in theatre is a sorry embalming of a live body. Since every theatrical production is done for a NOW audience it must be done anew; thus enters the basic problem of "revivals." How can a play written centuries ago be made to "live" for a modern audience? Artistic tastes and values—along with the fundamental worth of the revived play—dictate some answers. But one of these is NEVER a redirection of the playwright's original intention, his original expressiveness, his basic theatrical statement. We will deal with the problem of revivals in more detail in our later discussion of the director as an artist in the theatre. For the moment, let us say only that it is the primary obligation of the director to convey the intention of the playwright to his audience with as much artistic truth and fidelity as his capabilities allow.

Benedetto Croce insisted that the play, as any other singular work of art, is unique, subject to no rules. If this basically sound and partially true statement were universally applied, artistic standards would be impossible of achievement, and critical judgment nonexistent. It is true, of course, that the individual theatrical event *is* unique, but just as an individual painting or an individual musical composition also becomes a part of the total corpus of the arts of painting or music while maintaining its uniqueness, so too the individual theatrical event becomes a part of the totality of that art form. Just as an understanding of the principles and practices of painting or of music in their historical perspective conditions the response of their audiences to the immediate presentation and makes not only enjoyment keener but true value judgment more likely, so a knowledge of the principles of theatre art enrich its audiences and render just judgments more likely. One must bear in mind, of course, that criticism follows creation, that even the earliest and most famous of works in theatrical criticism, Aristotle's *Poetics*, was written about a hundred years later than the plays upon which its observations are founded. One must remember, further, that no work of art in any field ever was truly and brilliantly created simply by following rules of composition. But critical criteria, derived in the first instance from excellent creative work in a given field, can provide shortcuts to understanding, appreciation and judgment of a wide body of singularities in that field, provided always that the user thereof is constantly aware of the uniqueness of any given work of art. With this chastening thought in mind, let us explore the varying ways in which the art of theatre has been achieved, what the nature of those variations has been, where the excellencies lie, and what, if possible, has been the reason for failures and near-failures.

Let us begin with the play as the most durable entity of the theatrical phenomenon, as that which exists over a long period of time as a musical score does, as that which is handiest for extended study and analysis. But even here we must not—indeed cannot—analyze a playscript as if it stood as a sole artistic creation, complete and adequate. For even the principles that we shall discuss and apply are predicated not solely upon what playwrights have written down over the ages, but what has appeared in theatres as theatrical presentations.

Even the word "drama" itself, which modern thought tends to associate chiefly with the words the playwright has written down, is a transliteration of a Greek word δρᾶμα meaning "a thing done." That is to say that drama is realizable only in performance; we are dealing with blueprints only (in the architectural sense) when we deal with the playscript. Drama *transpires* before our eyes; we hear it with our physical ears; its time is always NOW.

A few representative definitions may prove useful:

Drama consists of emotions and opinions and occurrences presented in three dimensions with more or less approach to imitation by human agency.
—*Ivor Brown (Encyclopaedia Britannica)*

A play is a story devised to be presented by actors on a stage before an audience.
—*Clayton Hamilton, 1910*

A performance [is] to give expression to the significance of the movement, gesture, and speech of human bodies in a plotted whole of emotionally charged action, presented as spectacular pattern or as representation or as both, to eyes and ears and minds capable of grasping a defining artistic intention, thus uniquely revealed in all its determinateness of expressive specification.
—*D. W. Prall, 1929*

A play visibly represents pure existing.
—*Thornton Wilder, 1941*

A play is an image of human life created in the minds of an audience by the enactment of a pattern of events.
—*Clay and Krempel, 1967*

If we may be allowed to appropriate a phrase used in another context by Archibald MacLeish, we might say that not only a poem, but a drama "does not mean, but be."

Perhaps the most influential treatise ever written on the construct called a play is the *Poetics* of Aristotle in the fourth century, B.C. As the work has come down to us, it is fragmentary—notes from a series of lectures—and even in the oldest manuscripts there are differences from one to another. Many scholars have spent much time over several centuries in exegesis and explanation, and much weight has been attached to Aristotle's words. Roger Bacon is supposed to have observed, in the thirteenth century, that "Aristotle hath the same authority in philosophy that the Apostle Paul hath in divinity." This air of holy writ attached to the *Poetics* for centuries after that as well, and many critics and playwrights strained or explained away Aristotle's text to make their own plays or those of others seem to conform to it. What must be remembered, of course, is that Aristotle's statements are based on literary models which, although perfect in their kind, do not exhaust the possibilities of literature. A dogmatic insistence upon the infallibility of his specific statements can be only a frustration. Indeed, the long history of such insistence has led, in the present day, to a body of work which calls itself "non-Aristotelian criticism."

But if one is not a dogmatist, one can justly say that perhaps no subsequent critic has been so impartial and so insightful in penetrating the very nature of the theatrical art. Aristotle seeks primarily, if not solely, to find out what plays are *in themselves*, and how they produce their distinctive effects. It is a scientific inquiry; it is descriptive, not prescriptive. Contrary to the point of view of many other classic Greek writers (Plato and Aristophanes included), he is not concerned with the use of drama to educate or to inculcate morality; the theatre is not the school, it is itself. Thus, because of the perspicacity of their author, and not solely because they have for so long been held in high esteem, we find that the basic definitions and categories of the *Poetics* are even today applicable and seem contemporary. Many modern critics, of course, still use it as a basic pattern of exploration into dramatic techniques. What is to be remembered is that the whole of the treatise cannot be regarded (as so many generations following its appearance have regarded it) as an immutable "law," to be applied as a whole to all theatrical phenomena without question or proviso. The obscurities of portions of the work would seem effectively to prevent this, in any case. But when Aristotle talks about what a play *is*, in its essence and its expression, in its Being and its Becoming, the applicability of his observations are at once apparent.

Aristotle said that there were necessarily six elements in every tragedy: Fable, Character, Thought, Language, Melody, and *Mise en Scène* (according to Potts' translation of the original Greek words). The elements are "necessary" because of the nature of the medium: an *action* presented to an audience by actors. Subsequent theatre practice has demonstrated that the six elements are present not only in tragedy but in all types of dramatic presentation, only the stress varying from one type to another. In other words, these elements constitute the very basis of drama itself, the first three dealing with *structure*, the last three with with *style* or texture. Though we are now dealing with a single entity, that "uniqueness" which Croce says is a play, our aim is to see how these six elements are "necessary" parts of all possible unique creations in the art of theatre. Only by such demonstration of universal application is Aristotle's thesis validated. Let us consider them individually, therefore, changing the order somewhat and in some cases using synonyms for the designations.

It is curious and wonderful that Aristotle divined at once the nature and uniqueness of drama by putting first in his listing of elements Plot, or Fable, for in doing so he was following the method of the playwright, who conceives first an *action*, a thing done. Concerning the nature of Plot, the *Poetics* (as it has come down to us) is fairly specific and complete. The treatment of Character is also fairly clear, and fittingly comes second in Aristotle's listing, since the nature of theatre requires character as the agent of plot, the means whereby the virtual life of the play is enacted. Thought, he said, comes third, and here we are on more tenuous ground. Its treatment is sparse in the fragments we have and seemingly contradictory. Therefore, its interpretation has varied considerably. At the risk of seeming to put words in the mouth of Aristotle, I shall choose a particular stance with respect to Thought and put it first in the listing of elements—for reasons which I trust will become apparent.

First, then, *Thought* or *Theme*. Aristotle says of this element that it "controls all the effects that have to be produced." (Chap. 19) His previous reference to Thought (in Chap. 6), puts it, presumably in order of importance, after Fable and Character, and he seems there to be concerned with it as a manifestation of character, a method of expression. Even in Chapter 19 he refers to Thought as that which he has more fully treated in his *Rhetoric*, including proof and refutation, the manipulation of feelings such as pity, fear, anger, etc., the suggestion of importance or its opposite. But he immediately follows with: "Clearly also you require Thought on the same lines for the incidents, whenever you need to make them pathetic or terrible, or larger than life or probable; with this much difference, that you have to make the point clear without stating it, whereas in the language the effects are produced by a speaker in so many words." Clearly, Aristotle

Figure 3–1

Hunter College, CUNY
*The Thought, or Theme,
of Sophocles' Antigone
is complex and many-
layered, with wide
applicability. Its
universality is the main
reason for its continuing
popularity in the
theatre. Designed by
Charles Elson.*

is struggling with the rhetorical orientation of his time, is using words and modes of expression available to him in his milieu, but does apprehend that the rhetorical application of the term, Thought, is not adequate for the operation of the principle in theatre, that Thought indeed "controls all the effects that have to be produced." We therefore listed it first, rather than third.

In the light of our previous discussion we may consider this to be the drive of the artist to express a felt significance, a governing concept for the play. It is his conscious or unconscious reason for creating a work of art, his "Idea." It is what he has, fundamentally, to say. It is the artist's point of view; it is his way of looking at the world. It dictates his use of all the other elements, of all of his materials as he structures them into a whole. It is the impelling reason for the application of his technique. It is not simply a discursive statement which can be made in a single sentence. As a matter of fact, any dramatist who figuratively or literally writes himself a single sentence which is his theme and then scrounges around for characters and plot to illustrate that theme will undoubtedly write a very bad play. History is full of such examples. Diderot, that notorious pedagogue, wrote *The Father of the Family* in 1758 to show audiences how a father ought to behave to his family. Has it ever been restaged, I wonder?

It is Thought, then, that determines the large strategy of the play, which informs its action, which is its meaning. It is much larger and more encompassing than a thesis which is a logical or rational reduction of the play's action by a critic or analyst in order to comprehend the play; a thesis cannot exhaust all the play's Thought. Nor is the Thought simply subject matter, or what the play is, presumably, about. Sophocles' *Antigone* is not just "about" the conflict between the moral and the civil law, nor the education of Creon in the mercy that seasons justice, nor Antigone's staunchness in holding to what she knew to be right, without compromise. *Othello* is not just "about" the ravages of jealousy, nor the pervasiveness of evil, nor the rashness of precipitant action. *Tartuffe* is not just "about" the come-uppance of a hypocrite, nor the tyranny of religious form, nor the oppressiveness of paternalism. These plays have become "classics" because the Thought that pervades them, that gives them life, has more than one level of meaning, so that we can come back to them again and again with renewed insight and renewed interest. A great play does not give up its Thought easily and on the first asking, although as more and more meanings become apparent, so too does the sensitive audience realize the oneness of all of them, the unity that vitalizes the whole, the singleness of vision.

Every playwright who ever wrote is conditioned by his audience. Since plays are written to be performed, and there is no performance without an audience, he must take the audience into account. He must know its loves and hates, its desires and fears, its hopes and its frustrations. He must be sympathetic to its mores and understanding of its point of view. He does not, of course, limit his Thought to the narrowest potentialities of his possible audience, but neither does he scorn them. He loves humanity with a great and understanding love that accepts both aspiration and despair. He is not always benignant; he can be cruel and harsh, but never contemptuous and condescending. The great playwright sees life steady and sees it whole; he invites his audience to share his vision.

How much of life an individual playwright sees, of course, depends upon how wide his sphere of vision is. In what light he sees it depends upon his total life view, the tint of his figurative glasses. If they are rose-colored, he is a romanticist, if they are gray he is a naturalist or a realist, if they have magnifying lenses he is probably a satirist. If his field of vision is limited to the upwardly mobile middle classes he writes bourgeois drama; if to the wrongs of the submerged minorities, propaganda plays; if to sophisticated social circles, drawing-room comedy; if to the futility of existence, plays of the so-called absurd.

The size of his vision and the color of his glasses dictate the *tone* of his work, that is, the *feeling* which it evidences and the emotional response it elicits from its audiences. This tone establishes the mood of his work and directs his choice of materials and his method of handling them. It determines his *style*—not just the style of his writing (though it is that, too), but his life style, and above all the style of his work for the theatre. Arthur Miller, for instance, sees today's "little man" with infinite compassion, and writes *Death of a Salesman, The Price,* even *The Crucible.* Genet sees life through a crazyhouse mirror and writes *The Balcony, The Blacks,* and *The Screens.*

Now, we have chosen to give first consideration to Thought, which Aristotle placed third in his listing of the six necessary elements. We have done this because Thought "controls all the effects that have to be produced," and is therefore of overriding importance. But from his own point of view, Aristotle was right in putting Plot and Character ahead of Thought in his listing. For he was assuming the point of view of a practicing playwright, who first thinks in terms of an *action* and of *characters.* That is, he thinks first in these terms unless he is a didactic writer who uses plays to illustrate a proposition rather than letting his theme be implicit, or an end product. No audience attends theatre to view an illustration of a copy-book maxim; they go to see a set of characters performing an action. And the successful playwright's first inspiration is—nine times out of ten—a dramatic action, something happening in a certain set of circumstances to and with a certain set of characters.

So let us now consider *Plot,* or *Fable.* In naming this element of the drama, Aristotle says it is "the imitation of the action; the whole structure of the incidents . . . a whole and complete action of some amplitude." He uses the word "imitation," of course, in the sense that it applies to any work of art—nature-derived but systematized and man-created, as we have detailed in Part I. A play, he says, is a *structure* consisting of *incidents.* It is *whole* and *complete* and of *proper size.* Now what does all this mean?

The function of plot is to provide structure in order that the audience may see, appreciate, and share in a dramatic action which has a beginning, a middle, and an end, which is, as it were, a complete and free-standing unit of experience, a unique work of art, a "virtual life." By and large, over the wide span of the

Figure 3–2

Arena Stage,
Washington, D.C.
*The complications of
the plot are no small
part of the fun of
Wilde's* The Importance
of Being Earnest. *See
also 7–17.*

history of dramatic literature, plots tell a story. It is easy to see why, for rare is the human being who does not enjoy a good story. The joke, anecdote, short story, novel, ballad, narrative poem, epic—all are forms of stories which have held the attention of audiences over long periods of time. Even history is primarily enjoyed because it tells a story—which fact Herodotus would no doubt witness to were he called upon to do so. From primitive times to the present, from childhood to old age, people have loved and longed for stories. No wonder then that the people-oriented art of theatre has told so many stories, from that of *The House of Atreus* to *The Deputy*, from myth to documentary, from fact to fantasy. No wonder that all possible sources of stories have been used to lend plots to the dramatist—history, legend, current events, folklore, fantasy, novels, poems—wherever an action of possible human interest could be found it has been translated into theatre pieces. "What's happening?", "Where to?" "What next?" These are universal questions, and the good storyteller has always been a privileged member of society. Occasionally there have been plays which triumphed by subordinating the story line to other elements: spectacle, or mood, or witty dialogue, or character revelation. And the newer playwrights seem intent on eliminating

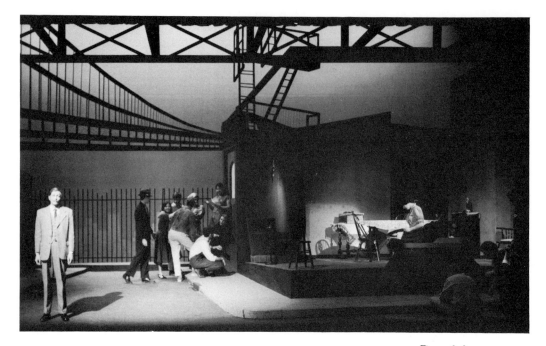

Figure 3–3

Illinois State University
*Playwrights sometimes
use a narrator-character
to supply exposition, as
the figure on the left is
doing in this scene from
Arthur Miller's* A View
from the Bridge. *See
also 13–19. Directed by
Jim Zvanut, setting
designed by Charles
Howard.*

story almost entirely: *The Bald Soprano, Waiting for Godot, The Caretaker.* But only consummate handling of the other elements make these viable theatre pieces, and often today one hears the plaintive query at the end of a theatre evening, "Now what was *that* all about?"

The telling of a story, whether long or short, falls naturally into four divisions: exposition, complication, climax, and dénouement. Again, these are convenient labels to aid in understanding the play's action. The second and fourth of them Aristotle likened to the tying and untying of a knot.

EXPOSITION is the sketching in of necessary background so that the audience can follow the story. "I met Joe Carmody today. You remember—he's Mike's friend; we met him at Cynthia's party a week ago Saturday." Or to quote the opening of a famous play, "This play is called 'Our Town'. . . . The name of the town is Grover's Corners, New Hampshire—just across the Massachusetts line. . . . The First Act shows a day in our town. The day is May 7, 1901. The time is just before dawn." It is Wilder's Stage Manager speaking, of course, in a frankly man-to-audience, this-is-a-play-you-are-seeing kind of manner, so that the audience receives quickly and directly the information that it needs to understand what happens next. And whenever more information is necessary in this play, the Stage Manager is there to give it, directly and unequivocally, and outside the action of the play itself. The character of Andy Tracy does the same thing in the first of the two plays that make up Brian Friel's *Lovers*, "The Winners." At the beginning of *Henry V*, the character of Prologue sets the scene, and *Henry IV, Part 2*, opens with Rumour doing the same.

Innumerable plays open with minor characters engaged in incidental activity while they bandy back and forth statements containing information the audience needs to know—the "feather-duster" scene of exposition. Thornton Wilder makes delightful fun of this convention in the opening monologue of Sabina, the maid, in *The Skin of Our Teeth*. Molière's *Tartuffe* opens with a family gathering during which the basic situation is outlined and the characters introduced. The short opening scene of the witches in *Macbeth* sets the mood and intimates a story, then the immediately following conversation among Duncan, Malcolm, the Sergeant, and Ross gives the necessary background information. The playwright is always faced with the necessity of making clear the circumstances which give rise to the dramatic action, and in most plays these are outlined as rapidly and clearly as possible as early on in the play as the writer can manage.

Sometimes the stage setting, particularly in realistic plays, serves the purpose of exposition, as the carefully detailed stage setting in Pinter's *The Caretaker* immediately tells the audience much about the tastes, interests, personalities, and background of the characters. In less carefully detailed settings, background characters sometimes perform similar functions, as the theatre crowd does in the opening scene of *Cyrano de Bergerac*. Or stock characters—servants, family friends, etc.—as mentioned above, provide the exposition.

Exposition needed during the subsequent scenes of a play are often provided by a conveniently arriving servant, friend, or *confidente*, while the convention of the soliloquy or the aside supplies direct information to the audience about the inner state of the character thus speaking. A similar device to the soliloquy or the aside, used primarily in more realistic plays, is the monologue,

Figure 3–4
Lincoln Center
Repertory Theatre
*The inciting incident,
or point of attack, in
King Lear is the
judgment scene in the
first act. See also 4–8.*
(Martha Swope)

motivated by a telephone call, or a letter, or some other "real" device. In any event, it is the playwright's business to supply the audience with whatever information they need in order to understand the dramatic action. The skillful ones integrate this necessary information into the main action of their plays, or frankly and often amusingly present it directly. With less skillful playwrights the exposition halts and stumbles and is awkwardly introduced in a way that seems not germane to the action, a mere excrescence.

COMPLICATION begins after the audience has been made aware, through the initial exposition, of all the circumstances that it needs for orientation to what follows. That moment in the play which sets off the precipitating momentum of the action is called *the point of attack;* it is the beginning of the "tying of the knot." Creon decrees that Polynices shall remain unburied; Macbeth meets the witches on the heath; Viola meets Orsino; Romeo sees Juliet at the ball; King Henry decides to make Becket the Archbishop of Canterbury; Honey and Nick arrive at the home of George and Martha; Agamemnon comes home from the Trojan War. The point of attack is the inciting force which triggers a line of action.

The complication (or development, as it is sometimes called), proceeds to add incidents, or detail minor crises, until the knot is fully tied. If the dramatic action of the play is a single complex situation, like that in *Oedipus, Phèdre,* or *The Misanthrope,* where the dramatist chooses for his starting point a place near the climax of the total story, the plot is said to be an *unfolding* plot. If, on the other hand, decisive factors are introduced cumulatively as the action develops them, the plot is said to be *accretive*, as in *Hamlet, Cyrano de Bergerac, Becket*. In either case, the discoveries unfolded or the factors accumulated are selected and arranged by the playwright to keep the forward thrust of the play moving. The compression of the theatrical form demands that these incidents be chosen rigorously and that, in addition to each being interesting in itself, it be relevant and necessary to the whole action. The playwright generally uses an incremental progression; i.e., an arrangement by which each successive scene of a play builds upon those which have preceded it and in turn adds a new increment. These increments are not necessarily in a *causal* relationship; they may be handled through another scheme entirely, as in Chekhov's plays, or in O'Neill's *Long Day's Journey into Night*. But suspense and/or increasing tension is built into the progression; through them the interest of the audience is maintained. Oedipus, as King of Thebes, is obliged to do something to lift the plague from Thebes. He undertakes the task. He discovers from Creon that this can only be done by discovering and punishing the murderer of the former king, Laius. Oedipus appeals to the prophet Tireseus to assist him in the search, and Tireseus refuses, predicting disaster for Oedipus (a particular instance of *foreshadowing*, which is very frequently used to good effect in the action of plays). Oedipus, dismissing him in anger, then appeals to his Queen, Jocasta (formerly married to Laius) for details concerning the murder. He has misgivings when he hears of the place where three roads meet but is reassured by Jocasta's statement that her child who was, by prophecy, to be the murderer of Laius has "perished." The news comes of the death of Polybus (whom Oedipus thought to be his father), but with it also the fact that Polybus was not his father, but he was a "found" child, delivered to the Messenger himself by a herdsman of the House of Laius. Jocasta knows the truth now, and urges that the inquiry cease; Oedipus "will not hear of not discovering the whole truth," and sends for the Herdsman. Thus simply and successively, revelations add to the tension of the action to its maximum point. Other plays achieve this complication through different choices: the adding of *new* factors, as Shakespeare does in *Othello*, or *Macbeth*, as O'Neill does in *Mourning Becomes*

Figure 3–5

Lincoln Center
Repertory Theatre
*The dénouement of
Molière's Tartuffe is
Orgon's discovery of
Tartuffe's treachery in
this famous scene. See
also 1–2 and 7–14.*

Electra. But either way, the audience must feel, as the complication develops, that the reasons for whatever occurs are acceptable, that they have *probability:*

CLIMAX is that point in the play at which the complication reaches its greatest tension. For this reason it is also most frequently the point of greatest emotional intensity. It is the point from which there is no turning back.

> *. . . I am in blood*
> *Stepped in so far that, should I wade no more,*
> *Returning were as tedious as go o'er.*

Oedipus' questionings finally lead to the answer of the Herdsman, and Oedipus exclaims, "All brought to pass—all true!" Polonius' "Lights, lights, lights!" at the end of the play-within-a-play marks the climax in Hamlet's action: he is now sure of his course; the rest is unravelling of the knot.

The climax is generally immediately preceded by the chief *obligatory scene* of the play, that action which is the final one of the development and the end of which marks the climax, the crisis, the turning point of the play's action. It is, as William Archer

Figure 3–6

American Shakespeare
Festival Theatre
*All difficulties are
resolved in the
dénouement of a
comedy, usually by a
celebration, as in this
scene from
Shakespeare's* The
Taming of the Shrew.
(Friedman-Abeles)

puts it, "one in which the audience (more or less clearly and consciously) foresees and desires, and the absence of which it may with reason resent." One of the most famous of all obligatory scenes is the handkerchief scene in *Othello*. In addition to the chief obligatory scene, there may be minor ones, and sometimes even good dramatists neglect one of these, as when Ibsen has that important fondling of Regina by Oswald take place offstage.

DÉNOUEMENT is the untying of the knot. It is what happens in the action after the climax; it is the solution to the problems which have been raised. Creon relents at the urging of the Leader of the Chorus, but it is too late; Antigone hangs herself, Haemon runs on his sword, and Eurydice in an excess of grief commits suicide. Lady Macbeth goes mad, Birnam Wood comes to Dunsinane, and Macduff slays Macbeth. The action comes to a close; equilibrium is once more established in the imagined world of the play. In comedy, the dénouement usually follows quickly after the climax; in serious plays the dénouement takes longer.

In a dramatic action handled skillfully by the playwright, the dénouement is said to be *inevitable*; i.e., the closing action grows organically out of the preceding events and characters; it is logical and hence satisfying to the audience, whether it end in disaster for the chief characters or in the accomplishment of their objectives. Millamant and Mirabell will be married, as will Viola and Orsino. Nora will leave the "doll's house"; Oedipus will go into exile; Margery Pinchwife will be a good wife; the Trojan War begins. Less skillful playwrights may bring their plays to a resolution by the introduction of a letter, or a telephone call, or the arrival of a long-absent character, or the intervention of a king, or a god—a *deus ex machina*—an agency that does not grow generically out of the logic of the action. Even Homer nods occasionally, but we forgive him, as we forgive Molière the ending of *Tartuffe*. Sometimes—as in Pirandello's *Right You Are*—the playwright deliberately leaves an "open ending," so that the audience goes away with a question as to the outcome. But such a practice is dangerous, for the audience almost always wants to feel that the action is completed, that equilibrium has been reestablished, that there is nothing more to say on the subject.

So much for the Plot, or Fable—exposition, complication, climax, dénouement—these are its parts, varying in proportion from play to play, but generally present and generally discernible in most of the plays of our revered tradition. Plays of the modern period often operate within a different pattern and we will consider them later.

The third of Aristotle's elements in a dramatic action is *Character*. Even a moment's reflection will reveal how impossible it is to separate character from plot, or either of them from language or dialogue, since the theatre medium is one in which the construct has its embodiment in the action of human beings. For that matter, as we have already established, none of the elements can stand alone; all are equally necessary to the completed work of art. Therefore, just as we have given separate consideration to Thought and to Fable, we can consider Character as an entity, remembering the while that all work together. Actually, of course, these separated elements are more in our minds as logical, as applied to the functioning of the play on our consciousness in order to explain the effects produced on us.

It is an old dictum of journalism that nothing interests people so much as people; hence the human interest stories, the society columns, the "man behind the news" kind of reporting. The fact is no less true in theatre. By and large, audiences want to see on stage people they can believe—for the duration of the play—are *real* within the construct that the play presents. The transaction that takes place in theatre is between the people on the stage and the people in the audience. Here is the very soul of theatre. Indeed, for a very long time in the history of theatre, dramatists were judged on their skill in creating "characters against the sky" —memorable figures. It is particularly true that the *reader* of plays (as the reader of novels) is first struck by and longest remembers the characters in plays: Hamlet, Grandpa Vanderhoff, Clytemnestra, Tartuffe, Lady Wishfort, Tony Lumpkin, Mr. Antrobus, etc., etc., etc. The person who *sees* these characters in action on a stage in a theatre, with all the other elements present and working, will have a better perspective on the relationship of Character to the whole. But even he will, nine times out of ten, carry away with him the memory of the characters over and above anything else that he experienced. The phenomenon is simply a part of what it means to be a human being. It is finally true, of course, that characters make the action, and action makes the characters—to a greater or lesser degree on one side or the other, depending on the Thought and the Fable.

It is a basic human characteristic to be interested in contests of all kinds: lotteries, games, athletic events, and tests of skill. Nothing gathers a crowd quite so quickly as an argument that might eventuate in a fight. Tests of skill, mental or physical, on a wide variety of levels, are the very breath of life to most people. Theatre capitalizes on this propensity. Or rather we should say that since theatre is the reflection of life as it is lived, such conflict is implicit in it. But the conflict in theatre (since it is an art form) is systematized and regularized and its outcome is determined by the selection of incidents and the delineation of characters in a controlled situation—hence its satisfactions. Aristotle defines Character as that because of which "we ascribe certain moral qualities to the persons." (Chap. 6) Characters in a play are defined by the goals which motivate them. Hence it follows that a playwright must stress certain traits in his stage characters because of his concept of the characters' appropriate goals. Thus character grows from plot.

At the very beginning of our theatrical history, terms were invented to designate the two chief opponents in the conflict

Figure 3–7

Hanover College
*John Proctor is the
protagonist in Arthur
Miller's modern tragedy,*
The Crucible. *Directed
and designed by Tom G.
Evans. See also 14–15.*

presented on the stage: protagonist and antagonist. As stated designations the words are not so much used today, but the functions are still present, and an understanding of the terms is necessary if one is to appreciate the dramatic presentation. The protagonist is the chief character in the dramatic action, the one about whom the Fable moves, the one who most deeply and consistently engages the sympathetic attention of the audience; he is the "home team," as it were. The antagonist is the visiting team, the opponent, whose action is to foil the attempt of the protagonist to reach his goal, to attain his desires. This opposition, this antithesis, forms the central action of the play. The protagonist is almost always easy to identify. Very often the title of the play is his name: *Hernani, The Caretaker, Coriolanus, Medea, Bérénice, Le Cid, The Good Woman of Setzuan, The Jew of Malta, The Country Wife, The Madwoman of Chaillot.* Even in plays whose titles describe an action rather than name a character, the protagonist is easy to identify: in *The Taming of the Shrew* Petruchio is the tamer; in *She Stoops to Conquer,* Kate Hardcastle is the "she." In plays more generally titled, an even cursory acquaintance with the action will identify the protagonist: Mak in *The Second Shepherd's Play,* Hieronimo in *The Spanish Tragedy,* Madame Ranyevska in *The Cherry Orchard,* Mr. Antrobus in *The Skin of Our Teeth.* The antagonist is the chief opponent: Comte de Guiche in *Cyrano,* Claudius in *Hamlet,* Creon in *Antigone,* The President in *The Madwoman of Chaillot,* Agamemnon in *The Prodigal*, Célimène in *The Misanthrope*, Mephistopheles in *Faust*. In the simple terms of melodrama, the protagonist is the hero, the antagonist is the villain, and the line of conflict is sharply drawn. But in more complicated and hence more lifelike drama, the antagonist need not be a double-dyed, mustache-twirling villain (as Creon certainly is not), but just the agency which stands in opposition to the goal of the protagonist. There are even plays where the central conflict takes place *within the mind* of the chief character, as in O'Neill's *The Emperor Jones*; he is his own antagonist. But the conflict has to be objectified in the theatre, so the audience sees The Little Nameless Fears, the Slave Ship, the Auction, etc., in the succession of scenes in O'Neill's play.

Audiences usually demand of chief characters—those central to the dramatic action— that they are believable; i.e., that what they are and what they do is a logical extension of human experience. Given the circumstances of the dramatic action, does the behavior of the characters in the play conform to the human impulses and reactions of the audience under comparable circumstances? Selection is the key. We do not expect to see Orgon washing his face, nor Kate Hardcastle making beds since neither of these actions (though germane to the human-ness of the characters) have anything to do with what is going on in the play. Goals define actions; actions for goals define character.

Characters are revealed to an audience in four ways: by what they say, by what they do, by what others say about them, by what others do because of them. We might add a fifth: the appearance of the character. Aristotle, in discussing Character, said that there were four things to "aim at": (1) that it "should be good of its kind"; (2) that it "should be appropriate"; (3) that it "should be lifelike"; (4) that it "should be consistent." (Chap. 15) By and large, these aims are still viable. We ask of a character that his behavior is that demanded by the dramatic action, that it is in line with what we know or can imagine of an actual human being in similar circumstances, that no detail seem wrong, or inappropriate, or inconsistent with what we know or can guess of human nature. Again, within the circumstances of the play, we unquestionably accept the extravagant character of Cyrano, even though we suspect that a man so brave and so intelligent would not usually be so motivated by the size of his nose. We even accept—nay, delight in—the almost dehumanized characters in

Beckett's *Waiting for Godot* because they belong in the given dramatic action. Disruption occurs only when we cannot make sense of Character within the circumstances of the play.

The chief characters we want to know well. From what they do and say, from the reactions of other characters to them, we derive a sense of "roundedness" or completeness which is satisfactory. Of minor characters we are not so demanding. We will accept those whose function is background, exposition, or service if they seem right for their position in the action so far as appearance, movement, voice, and dialogue are concerned. We do not ask to know them well, since they are subordinate to our prime interest. However, when, as with Shakespeare, we get a brilliant delineation of minor characters, often in very few words or actions, we are delighted, and the texture of the whole presentation is immeasurably enriched thereby.

Finally—and here is the secret of the connection between Fable and Character—we get to know people in real life by what they *do;* we realize that what they *are* is revealed by what they *do.* We apply the same criteria to characters in the theatre, realizing all the while that "the best in this kind are but shadows; and the worst are no worse, if imagination amend them."

The next of Aristotle's elements is *Language,* or *Diction.* To some extent, the preceding three elements (Thought, Fable, and Character) can be considered those used in the *structure* of a given play, while the second three (Language, Melody, and *Mise en Scène*) deal with *texture,* tone, or style. The distinction is not clear-cut, however, for language in its particular aspect of dialogue is the material which the playwright manipulates to form his construct. All the words used in a play must be spoken by the characters in the play; this direct and immediate use of dialogue is the very nature of the dramatic form. All exposition, characterization, and the conveying of emotional states must be done through the dialogue of the characters as it, in turn, is determined by the *action* of the play. Unlike the novelist or poet who can interpolate explanatory passages, the playwright must incorporate whatever explanations are necessary into the speaking parts in his play. He is, of course, aided in this task by the "speaking power" of the other elements; but words carry the burden. Much of the "appropriateness" and the "consistency" which a character has depend on the words he is given to speak. It is the business of the play-wright to have his little fishes talk like little fishes and his whales like whales—if we are to sort out the accusation of Boswell that Dr. Johnson "made all his little fishes talk like whales." Kings and commoners must use the language appropriate to their respective stations in life (unless, of course, the playwright deliberately distorts the expected for comic effect). The dialogue must "ring true" to the ear of the audience, so that they experience the "speaking image" which is the peculiar province of theatre. Yet even in a realistic play, the words heard on stage, if they are to be effective, must not be the usual discursive meanderings heard in ordinary life, but a selected arrangement that gives the *illusion* of life. Stage characters speak not the way people do, but the way they would if they could.

Aside from the use of Language in developing Character, it is also used structurally, as we have seen above, in presenting ex-position, in the aside, the soliloquy, and the monologue. Speech itself is a form of action. In the theatre a given line of dialogue must be immediately clear to the audience, since there is no time for turning back or for rumination. Sometimes a playwright will use repetition to remind an audience of points or ideas he wishes them to remember, but by and large the language of theatre must be immediately comprehensible.

In addition to all these matters, Language also contributes to the texture or tone of the play. It does this chiefly through the pro-clivity of language to symbolic or metaphoric expression. Figura-tive language has the psychological effect of transferring images directly from the spoken word into the consciousness of the hear-ers, with a consequent stimulation of the imagination and an enrichment of mental imagery which helps to establish a mood appropriate to the dramatic action. The recurrent imagery of night and darkness—moon, stars, moonlight, dreams, and water—which are threaded through the language of *A Midsummer Night's Dream* contribute to the magic quality of that play. The images of night and darkness in *King Lear*, on the other hand, are linked to those of storm and destruction, so that the atmos-phere which is conveyed is very different. The unfailing rightness of Shakespeare's imagery has been the subject of considerable investigation. (See C. F. Spurgeon, *Shakespeare's Imagery and What It Tells Us*, London: Cambridge University Press, 1936.)

Imagery, of course, is the very stuff of poetry. Perhaps its propensity to arouse the imaginative response of listeners is a clue to the reason why poetry is the initial form of literary expression and the one generally conceded to appeal most to the emotions.

But even dramatic prose uses imagery, as Shaw does so superbly in the "Don Juan in Hell" sequence of *Man and Superman*, as Beckett does in *Waiting for Godot*, as Tennessee Williams does in practically all of his plays. For it is the shortest way to operate upon the sensibilities of an audience, and draw them into the life of the play. In the best dramatic constructs the imagery arises inevitably from the world which the play asks to be compared with.

In the last few years we have had a spate of playwrights who insist that language has lost its ability to communicate in this age of mass communication chiefly because language has suffered a recession in meaning in the modern world, which seems to have discovered that we so often lie with language. We talk about these playwrights more in detail later. But even the absurdities in the dialogue of such a play as Ionesco's *The Bald Soprano* are carefully composed to achieve the effect the playwright wants to convey to his audience. No human being is immune to the beguilements of good talk, since talk is so definitively a human activity, and playwrights since the beginning of theatre have used it as one of their essential materials. Language is in itself a creative force, the symbol of the public world through which a man becomes himself. The denigration of language is, hence, an ultimately self-destroying and even life-destroying activity.

Next in Aristotle's catalogue is *Melody*, or *Music*, or, as some interpreters of the *Poetics* would have it, *Mood*. He was, of course, writing in a time when actual instrumental accompaniment to parts of all the great tragedies was ubiquitous; he had never known anything else. Poets were musicians and skilled in dance as well. He calls Melody "the chief of the enhancing beauties" of the drama. We have seen that the intrinsic qualities of music are pitch, rhythm, timbre, tone, and intensity, and that the skillful manipulation of these qualities expresses the inner feeling of the composer-artist. How effective music can be in stimulating controlled emotional response in theatre audiences is apparent to anyone who has experienced a "musical," and the uses to which music is put on the sound tracks of innumerable motion pictures is notorious.

But the human voice alone is a musical instrument, possessing all the intrinsic qualities mentioned above. These function in non-musical drama in ways similar to their function in pure music. The succession of sounds, their rate and tone, their intensity and pitch, convey to the audience the emotional state of the speaker. Macbeth's "tomorrow and tomorrow" speech, simply by the succession of long, deep vowel sounds—even without the attendant denotations of the words—conveys something of the despair and weariness of the speaker. Not only in this speech, but throughout skillful dramatic writing everywhere, the word choices, the grammatical structure, the pattern of the syllables, when combined with the sense being enunciated, contribute largely to the tempo of the production. The quick and playful banter of Wilde's *The Importance of Being Earnest* derives not only from the wit of the statements themselves, but also from the sound pattern. On the other hand, the thoughtful progression and the seriousness of the famous "To be, or not to be" soliloquy are implicit not only in the conceptual idea of the statement, but also in the careful composition of the sound pattern. Generally speaking, complicated ideas, complex sentence structure, involved phraseology, and abstruse meaning slow the tempo as they slow enunciation and comprehension. Commonplace ideas, idle chatter, short phrases, and simple sentence structure, on the other hand, are easily comprehended, quickly spoken, and impart a faster tempo to the movement of the play. And tempo is a quality of music, having its subtle but unmistakable effect on listeners.

The element of Melody, however, may be thought of as embracing not only pure music itself and the human voice but also the total sound pattern of the theatrical performance. The drumbeats O'Neill insists upon in the *The Emperor Jones*, the chopping sounds at the end of *The Cherry Orchard*, and the carefully orchestrated musical effects in *The Glass Menagerie* are integral parts of the transaction between play and audience. Modern playwrights have made great use of nonverbal Melody in their plays. Frank Gagliano's *Father Uxbridge Wants To Marry*, for instance, could not function without its elevator sounds and offstage vocal music.

Figure 3–8

American Shakespeare
Festival Theatre
*Costume and gesture
reinforce the romantic
and fantastic qualities
of* A Midsummer Night's
Dream, *with Cyril
Ritchard portraying
Oberon. See also 4–9.*

All sounds: music, voice, or otherwise, become a pattern in the
play which expresses audibly the intention of the playwright in
emotional underscoring and content.

The last of the six elements present in the theatrical entity is
the *Mise en Scène*, or *Spectacle*. Simply stated, this element includes all the visual aspects of the performance—scenery, properties, lighting, costumes, and the movements of the actors—the
total "stage picture," as it changes from moment to moment in
the play. In Aristotle's day it consisted chiefly of the costumed
actors and chorus members moving in patterned rhythm, underscoring and making visible the emotional pattern of the dramatic
action. From the beginning, even in primitive times, the costumed
actor moving through his part in harmony with his fellow performers was a vital part of the Spectacle, as he remains today.
Properties too were always present: chariots, thrones, vases,
swords, shields, and baskets—all of these were used in the classic
Greek plays; properties of some sort have always been a part of
the *mise en scène*. Lighting and scenery began their development
chiefly in the Renaissance, and scenery especially has gone
through many metamorphoses. Though there was a brief period

when scenery bid fair to overwhelm the actor, and did indeed demolish the playscript, there has been an equilibrium among the elements, by and large, in this century. Spectacle, like the other necessary elements, serves to give expression to the artistic conception of the playwright and serves the actor in his presentation. As we have mentioned above, the visual often serves as exposition in setting the scene and orienting the audience to the time and place of the supposed dramatic action. Costume serves the same purposes and can be used as well to heighten the dramatic conflict and reveal character. Modern electric lighting is a flexible instrument for the setting of mood or tone. All of these use the intrinsic qualities of color and line; lighting adds the quality of intensity and, often, area. Settings use color, line, area, and mass, as do the graphic arts and architecture. Spectacle will be treated more in detail later as we discuss the modes and forms of drama.

In a successful work of theatre art, these six necessary elements are in balance and proportion; they have unity and harmony both in themselves and in the aggregate; they have variety and contrast, balance and proportion, as well as a total rhythmical relationship. Finally, the construct called the play *as performed* should possess unity, amplitude, and probability—three qualities first detailed by Aristotle but still of important magnitude in the theatre.

Just as, says Aristotle, "in the other imitative arts the object of each imitation is a unit," so should it be in theatre. He applies the rule primarily to the Fable, but it may well apply to the whole. Because of the nature of the theatre he knew, he conceived that the unity of action which was the Fable would "tend to keep within a single day and night or thereabouts." And from these statements Renaissance critics evolved an immutable rule of the three unities of time (no more than twenty-four hours covered in the action), place (all action transpiring in an area no larger than a single city), and action (a single line of action with no subplots). But it is far more likely that, since he begins his *Poetics* with a brief consideration of other arts, he is thinking of Unity as an attribute of a work of art, complete within itself, having all the units that are needed to fulfill its end, but none that are not needed.

So, too, as he speaks of amplitude, he says: "a picture, or any other composite object, if it is to be beautiful, must not only have its parts properly arranged, but be of an appropriate size; for

Figure 3–9

Bavarian State Theatre
*Elaborate scenic
investiture creates an
interesting spectacle in
this Munich production
of* Ciboulette. *Directed by
Fritz André Kracht.*

beauty depends on size and structure." (Chap. 7) As a picture
that is too big overwhelms us because we cannot take in its unity
or its wholeness, so a play which is too big, one that has too
many incidents, will be dissipated in its effect because we cannot
keep it in our minds. Conversely, the amount of time covered by
the action should be commensurate with the "chain of probability" necessary to the conception. The play should be neither too
long nor too short but of its proper size. And finally, probability
is to be kept in mind; "it is not the poet's business to tell what
has happened, but the kind of things that would happen—what
is possible according to probability or necessity." (Chap. 9) The
truth that is stranger than fiction is not the proper material for
theatre, because plays are played for an audience which must
accept what they see and hear and feel as a reflection of their
delights, apprehensions, fears, and hopes. "All the world's a
stage" only in that it offers an infinite variety of possible materials
which the theatre artist can perceive, select, and arrange. The
stage, on the other hand, is and always has been a reflection of

the world in which it exists, a microcosm of life, sorted out, structured, and presented (as all works of art are) to a live audience which brings its mind and its emotions to enter into a transaction, a mutual sharing, with the artist and his interpreters. Theatre is a combined art, a composite art, composed of many elements yet in its totality transmuting those elements into a new whole, a unique and powerful art form in its own right.

4

The Development of Dramatic Forms and Modes

In the previous chapter we dealt in some detail with Aristotle's analysis of dramatic form, with its six necessary elements. We saw that these six elements have remained a basically valid means of understanding what a play is as it is performed in the theatre. We also mentioned briefly that his treatise had resounding influences down through the centuries, not only in critical theory but in theatre practice. We shall be dealing with these influences more fully and directly in Part III. In this chapter our aim is to trace the developmental and historical progression of form and mode, and how they have interacted with the changing intellectual climate of the Western world to produce an ever expanding number of *kinds* of plays, the names of which are repeatedly found in theatrical documents: cycle play, bourgeois tragedy, sentimental comedy, problem play, epic theatre, and many others.

In trying to comprehend the extent of these changes and developments, it will be useful to keep in mind three pairs of terms, one dealing with the *social reasons* for theatre, one with the *form* of theatre, and one with the *modes*. The first is the antithetical spheres called *religious* and *secular*; the second the opposite forms of *tragedy* and *comedy*; the third the contrasting modes of *classic* and *romantic*. These will overlap and interact. Sometimes both form and mode will be unmistakably clear; sometimes they will not. We had better begin with some pertinent definitions.

The *form* that we dealt with in the preceding chapter is the archetypal *dramatic form* itself: the Aristotelian "necessities" which are the elements most playwrights use today and generally always have. What Aristotle was delineating in this construct was, in the final analysis, the nature of theatre itself, the substance of the art of theatre. The basic substance of this art—as indeed of all the arts—is a constant which defines the art form. What changes through the years is the emphasis given to one or the other of these elements—to their strength, validity, truth, or effectiveness. Hence we have arising what seem to be a variety of forms or types, and then we give this different combination of elements a new name; we call it a new "form," or structure. These Aristotelian "necessities" are, as it were, a basic biological organization, like the head, torso, legs, and arms of the human body. They make up the organism which is theatre. The human organism has, over several millennia, been operated upon by a variety of stimuli to effect changes in both its outward appearances and in its group functions. Just so has theatre suffered various kinds of "sea change" under various kinds of pressures. The very fact that it is an *organism*, a living thing, has predicated growth and change. A mere glance around the world of art (such as one might make in a museum or an art gallery, for instance) will demonstrate that theatre is not alone among the arts in exhibiting change and growth—and sometimes decline and death.

Form, then, is *structure*, the relationship of the various parts to each other and to the whole. Mode, on the other hand, is an attitude, a point of view, the artist's way of looking at the world. Any art product—musical composition, painting, sculpture, building, poem, novel, or play—reflects the point of view of its creator, his orientation and reaction to the world about him. He draws his materials from that world: people, places, things, and ideas. He selects his materials on two bases: (1) what will be viable for use in the particular art form he is creating; and (2) what will be expressive of his point of view. The first of these will determine primarily which of the arts he will use: sonata, portrait, lyric, historical novel, or melodrama. The second will determine how he handles his materials, how he disposes and arranges them, how he interprets them, how he colors them. The results then can be said to have a *form* and a *mode*.

The mode influences not only the choice of subject matter, but the relationships and the use of all of the six elements of drama: Thought, Fable, Character, Dialogue, Melody, and Spectacle. It is most closely related to Thought, since Thought itself is closest to the dramatist and directs his choices in the other elements, both as to materials to be used, the ways of using them, and the relative importance of the various elements in the final performance. Dramatic poets in the age of Pericles had only three choices of form: tragedy, comedy, and satyr play. And the mode was one: classicism, conditioned by the intellectual climate of the time which stressed the golden mean and the reasonable man. Changes in society and in ways of thinking about the world have multiplied from that time to this and so have dramatic modes. The classic mode has expanded to include naturalism, realism, selective realism, and satire. The romantic mode has been added, functioning as an entity in its own right, with subspecies of impressionism, expressionism, constructivism, theatricalism, and others.

Obviously, the pressures operating for change in the theatre came from the changing world about it, for theatre (perhaps more so than the other arts) is no more nor less than the reflection of the society which produces it. Theatre is, perforce—by its very nature—more audience-oriented than the other arts; there is simply no performance if there is no audience. One may speculate that playwrights write for "an ideal" audience, and no doubt this is sometimes true, and even necessary, when a specific production of a given play is neither feasible nor possible. But the evidence of history, if not even the nature of the medium itself, is against this kind of "posting letters into a dream." From the beginning of time to the present moment playwrights have written for audiences whom they either knew firsthand or envisioned exactly. Theatre is a public art; if it ignores its public it ceases to exist. Just as Sophocles wrote for the citizens of the Athens he knew, Molière wrote for the court of Louis XIV, Shakespeare for the populace of London, and the current crop of off-off-Broadway playwrights for the particular segment of the population who frequent their playing places. The kinds of plays all these and their legions of fellow playwrights have produced have been inexorably conditioned by the character of the audiences for which they were intended. The level of sophistication, of learning, of taste; the hopes, and desires, and fears; the predilections, possibilities, and practices of those "out front" have always been of primary concern in theatre. That the playwright and all theatre workers are people of their own time, conditioned by their particular world, goes without saying. But the influence of the audience on theatrical forms and modes is a directly traceable and potent influence.

If one were to treat this subject exhaustively, one would emerge with a voluminous intellectual and social history of Western

Figure 4–1

The Cleveland
Museum of Art
*In classic Greek times
the population of
Athens came to the
Theatre of Dionysus
to experience both
tragedies and comedies.*
(Collection of the
Educational Department)

civilization, in which theatre would be but a small part. Such a task is beyond both our capacity and our intention. We shall, therefore, take a stance in the theatre itself, as if it were the center of the wheel, and look out to the perimeters and along the radii to identify the contributing elements. That there were many more than the composition of the audience is quite true. All areas of human knowledge, a great many technological and mechanical discoveries as well as philosophical and artistic ideas, had their influences, at least in miniature. Chiefly as these new areas of knowledge and accomplishment became the property of audiences as well as artists did they affect theatre. We shall keep our sights on the theatre, and refer to specific ideas and movements only as they affect the writing of plays and their performance.

One additional clarification may prove useful before we embark on this task. We have discussed the nature of *mode* as a contributing factor in theatre; we should also explain its fundamental dichotomy—classic and romantic. In the old folk tale "The Emperor's New Clothes" you have a capsule illustration of the classic vs. romantic modes. The remark of the little boy, "Why, he has nothing on," is the statement of a classic mind which sees what *is* rather than what might be. The other spectators have the romantic temperament: seeing whatever it is they would like to see, rather than what is. To use another metaphor: the classic eye looks through lenses of clear glass; the romantic eye uses tinted lenses. True it is, of course, that even clear lenses can be so ground as to give a distorted picture of reality, and the tinted

Figure 4–2

Festival Theatre,
Stratford, Ontario
The Oedipus Rex *of
Sophocles is one of the
most famous of Greek
tragedies, here
re-created by Sir Tyrone
Guthrie with something
of the awesome mood of
its original production.
See also 6–3.*

lenses can be anything from rosy to a very dark shade of gray. The extension of the metaphor will simply indicate that dramatic mode is no simple thing, and that the permutations could become endless. But we must start somewhere.

The classic mind in theatre tends to think in terms of what can be contained in a play which is to be given in a particular theatre for an audience which it envisions exactly. The Fable employed is likely to be the climactic section of a longer narrative, using as a point of attack an event close to the climax. It has unity of time and place as well as unity of action. It is not only such a play as *Oedipus Rex* which has only one locale (before Creon's palace), and a length of time in the playing close to the time used in the events which transpire, and a single line of action with few characters, but also such a play as Arthur Miller's *The Price*, which takes place in a large attic, covers about two hours in time, and has a total of four characters.

The romantic mind, on the other hand, seems always straining to burst the boundaries of theatre. His Fable is likely to be episodic, beginning at the early stages of a narrative, with an early point of attack, multiple incidents in the development, probably a subplot, many scenes in several locations, and maybe years of time compressed into the "two hours' traffic of the stage." Shakespeare's *Antony and Cleopatra* has 38 scenes in 7 geographic locations, with 34 named characters plus extras, and a space of time a few years in the telling. O'Neill's *Marco Millions* has 12 scenes, ranging from Italy to China and points between, with 33 characters, and several years in the telling.

Dialogue, Mood (Melody), and Spectacle in the romantic mode are likely to be extravagant, poetic, rapidly changing, and pageantlike. In the classic mode the dialogue will be likely to be spare, even when it is written as poetry (the Greeks), the mood consistent and sustained, and the spectacle only what is germane or absolutely necessary. Classic is a Greek temple, a sonnet, a one-set, three-character play; romantic is a Gothic cathedral, an epic poem, an extravaganza. We draw the extremes; there are shades of gradation in both modes.

FORM AND MODE IN CLASSIC TIMES:
THEATRE AS RELIGIOUS FESTIVAL

Ancient Greece was the first society in the history of the world to state that "man is the measure of all things." Even its gods were very human, with prejudices, predilections, and pettinesses often found in everyday people. But they also had more than a touch of greatness about them, even as man himself did. The glory of man was his mind, which saw the world whole and all its parts related. No portion of it was beneath notice; the Greek curiosity was boundless. The whole natural universe was studied and from the study was derived the principle that the physical world is intelligible, that there are order and first principles. Man as a natural phenomenon, as a physical being, was worthy of respect, and the cultivation of the body was an important part of Greek culture. Man's mind was a reflection of the principle of order implicit in the universe; by it he ordered his own existence and that of his society. Discipline of mind and the love of truth, discipline of the body and freedom of spirit were the hallmarks of the classic temper. Nothing human was omitted from their consideration and investigation; practically all areas of study which we still follow originated with the Greeks.

Figure 4–3

*Greek New Comedy
was riotous and
inventive, as this
bas-relief of a Greek
New Comedy scene
suggests.*

The very wholeness of their vision meant that they also recognized the urges of passion, the drives of instinct, the existence of
boundless ambition, and excess. Apollo, entity representing the
golden mean, had engraved on his temple at Delphi the words,
"Nothing to excess," probably as a reminder of the ever present
Dionysian extreme. The drama, of course, was devoted to the
worship of Dionysus, the god of wine and of fertility. But here
the curiously logical and complete Greek mind showed its interesting dichotomy. Greek tragedy could, in a sense, be the illustration of the Appolonian dictum, for the excesses contained therein
are always subject to implicit reprimand, and the ending of the
tragic Fable always involves a restoration of equilibrium. Even
the form of tragedy is controlled, logical, and clear. Greek
comedy, on the other hand, is freer in form and excessive in
action—the implicit representation of the Dionysian spirit. In
addition, Greek comedy takes its subject matter from everyday
life: political events, social problems, family relationships, the
abuses of the law, the futility of war. Each is treated with a clear-
eyed realism and lack of cant that expose the situations for what
they are. From the synthesis of classical tragedy and comedy we
derive today the outstanding characteristic of great literature in all
periods: rich humanity and formal beauty.

Theatre in classic Greek times was part of a religious celebration.
It developed from ritual, and at its apogee had many formalized,

ritualistic characteristics. The actors were priests of Dionysus, and the performances were given at seasonal festivals in honor of the god. The most prestigious of these, the Great Festival of Dionysus at Athens, was given annually in the spring. Plays to be performed were chosen in competition and prizes were awarded for the performances. The plays for which we remember Greek drama today were performed at this festival—those of Aeschylus, Sophocles, Euripides, and Aristophanes. Since the occasion was the greatest holiday of the year, lasting for the better part of a week, all businesses were closed and everybody— the populace of Athens and the hordes of visitors—attended the festival events. Long before dawn on performance days, people lined up at the entrances to the Theatre of Dionysus at the foot of the Acropolis, waiting to be admitted. They brought their lunches, their cushions, and their sunhats; the atmosphere was like that of a country fair or a great picnic. They found spots to their liking on the benches, which lay in curved rows up the slope of the hillside, and faced the huge circle (65 to 90 feet in diameter) of hard-packed earth lying at the foot of the hill within the curve of the seats. Beyond the circle lay a long, low house with three to five sets of double doors in its facade, the middle one grander than the rest and bigger. It served as a backing to the orchestra circle and as the place of entry or retirement for the chief actors. The space between the so-called *scene house* and the banked seats on either side served as an entrance for both the audience and the members of the chorus in the plays. The whole structure was completely open to the skies and the weather; hence the settings of the Greek plays are almost invariably outdoors, "before the palace." When a flute player entered and took his place at the altar in the center of the circle, the performance was about to begin. A hush fell over the 17,000 or so people on the benches, as they settled down for several hours of watching and listening.

What they witnessed had many of the qualities of ritual about it: poetic speech, patterned movement, music, chanting and singing, exotic costuming. And the stories presented in these terms were ones they knew and loved—chiefly the old tales of the House of Atreus from the (to them) legendary period of the Trojan Wars. Most of the audience knew how the action would turn out, and who the characters were, so they could concentrate their attention on the new embodiment of the old tale which was transpiring before them. (Though it is probably likely that the further one gets from Periclean times the less the audiences knew about these materials, since Aristotle, in the *Poetics*, states that "the familiar plots, though familiar to only a few, delight everybody.") It was interesting to see how each poet would use his Chorus, that transformed vestige of the dithyrambic tradition. There were fifty of them in Aeschylus' *The Suppliants*, entering from the parados to the orchestra circle in stately movement and singing—a stunning opening to the show. They are, of course, the daughters of Danaus, about whom the story is told. In *The Persians*, a smaller group of chorus members impersonated Persian Elders to open the play with song. But in *Seven Against Thebes* and in *Agamemnon* the play opens with a speech by a single character, Eteocles in the first, the Watchman in the second; and the respective choruses do not enter until later, Theban Women in the former, Argive Elders in the latter. And in Sophocles' *Antigone* there is a whole exciting conversation between Antigone and her sister, Ismene, before the Chorus, as Theban Elders, enters. So there was always something exciting to watch for. Once in, of course, the Chorus remained in view for the whole performance, now moving in graceful rhythms to the music, song or chant, now standing in precisely arranged groupings to witness, with the audience, the actions of the named characters, now taking part in that action. And when the entire action was completed, they left in a kind of recessional. Terrible events occurred here: Oedipus putting out his eyes when the terrible truth of the Sphinx's curse was revealed to him through his own prodding, Orestes killing Aegisthus and his mother, and being pursed by the Furies, Medea killing her children in her rage against Jason. But the awful events themselves took place behind the closed great doors—one could imagine how it was—and then there was the surprise of the doors opening so you could see the results of the bloody deeds. And the performers wore masks—great heads, really, so they were somehow abstracted, and bigger than life with their thick-soled boots, padded bodies, and long, flowing gowns. In this way, the actors were more clearly visible in the very large theatres, as the hero lived through his contest with fate and found his measure as a man.

As the majestic stories move from beginning to end (usually three connected plays following each other) the audience agrees with a delighted shiver to the statement, for instance, of the Chorus at the end of Oedipus: "We must call no one happy who is of mortal race, until he hath crossed life's border, free from pain." For what they have seen—experienced—is the very image of life itself in all its fullness: birth, growth, maturation, decay, and death; a great swell of movement, climax, and decline; a mighty rhythm that they recognize and of which they stand in awe, here encompassed, unified, and made clear. That was Greek tragedy: stupendous, satisfying, and somehow invigorating, a fitting tribute to the great Dionysus, the god of fertility—the life principle.

Immediately following the presentation of the three tragedies, each from 60 to 90 minutes in length, the playing area was virtually inundated by a horde of men dressed as satyrs who performed the satyr play, required by convention for reasons of religious conservatism from the pen of the tragic poet whose plays had just been performed. The satyr, of course, was sacred to Dionysus—a mythical man-beast, supposed companion of Silenus and Dionysus. The satyr play was a kind of burlesque of the preceding tragedy, and the dance of the satyr chorus was wild and abandoned. "Yes," it would seem to say, "we know that the grand design is serious, but here and there in the corners is a lot of fun." Life is irrepressible.

Later that day, or on a succeeding day, the festival performance would be a comedy, like *The Acharnians* of Aristophanes. Here the chorus is 24, as against 15 in the usual tragedy, and divided into two groups of opposing sentiments. The comedy is always fun, because the subject matter is largely invented by the poet and so is new to the audience. Dicaeopolis, Aristophanes' "hero" in *The Acharnians*, has a delightful point of view: he makes a private peace with the Spartans. When he is brought to task for this and condemned to die, he borrows the clothes of tragedy from a reluctant and lugubrious Euripides and pleads his cause so well that he is let off. Since the story is new to the audience, more events must be presented so they can follow the story. When Dicaeopolis emerges triumphant at the end of a series of incredible adventures it is the triumph of the little man, the indomitable spirit which overcomes all manner of obstacles, a series of crises of not-quite-major proportions. His cleverness wins out and we leave him on the crest of his triumph. This is Greek comedy.

Elsewhere and outside the religious festivals, the Greek in classic times might have been amused by the *phylakes*, fugitive presentations of dramatic materials somewhat like vaudeville sketches or comic turns, with much emphasis upon physical activity and practical jokes. But we know these only by hearsay and the evidence of vase paintings, so they remain elusive.

Here, then, is the dichotomy of dramatic forms developed and played in classic Greece as a part of the worship of Dionysus: the tragedy with its compression, its agony, and its struggle against Fate; and comedy (of which the satyr play might be said to be a kind), ribald, discursive, matter-of-fact, and everyday, exhibiting the hero's triumph over the kinds of obstacles that abound in the ordinary world: obtuse neighbors, cunning tradesmen, vainglorious acquaintances, and carping relatives. The mode, also, is what we have called *classic* in both comedy and tragedy: the clear-eyed perception of the world as it is. The characters are *real*—drawn from presumed history in the case of the tragedies, and from everyday life in the comedies. The action is compressed and contains nothing that cannot quite naturally be played in the theatre used. Indeed, it is from the nature of Greek theatre that we derive the very terms tragedy, comedy, and classic mode. But even in these clearly marked distinctions there is the seed of what will later flower into the "wandering and bastard Muse" of the satiric mode. It lies in the raillery and derision with which Aristophanes treats many of his characters, and in the Platonic dictum that comedy should be used to "correct" abuses. Such a "corrective" aim is always that of the satirist, and his elusive presence can be discovered in many ages and forms of theatre. He is the child of the classic mode and appears chiefly in plays which are in this mode, although here and there he makes a brief appearance in plays of the romantic mode, like the figure of Malvolio in *Twelfth Night*.

The theatre of ancient Greece was classic in mode, tragic and comic in form, and religious in its reason for being. The forms and the mode of ancient Greece were adopted completely by the Romans; but there was absolutely no connection between Roman theatre and religion. It was a *secular* theatre, the first the Western world knew. It emphasized the comic form, in every way taking over, not the Old Comedy of Aristophanes which was too stringent and ribald, but the New Comedy of Menander. (Of these

Figure 4–4

*The predominant
theatre of the Middle
Ages was derived from
the stories of the Bible,
as this multi-scened
detail of Memling's*
The Passion *suggests in
its painted
representation.*

we will speak more at length in Chapter 7.) The examples of
tragedy from Roman times are poor and thin, but there was one
characteristic in those of Seneca which was different from those
of the Greeks: he introduced to the sight of the audiences horrible
scenes and ghosts—and that innovation would have fruit in the
Renaissance.

FORM AND MODE IN THE MIDDLE AGES:
STILL A PREDOMINANTLY RELIGIOUS THEATRE

As everyone who is aware of anything is aware, the Greek civilization was swallowed up by the Roman, which in turn sickened
and died in the fifth century A.D. After another five hundred or
so years, a kind of theatre is operating again in Western Europe.
Again it is religiously inspired, but now it is for the glory of the
Christian God. Its birth and growth is completely unconnected
with the glory that was Greece; it is an autonomous development.
It lasts for about four hundred years.

Its intention is frankly didactic: to teach the mystery of the
soul's salvation. Its development was a slow accretion from a

85

THE DEVELOPMENT

OF DRAMATIC FORMS

AND MODES

simple dramatization of the resurrection incident in the life of Christ to a lengthy series of stories covering the whole literature of the Bible, from Genesis to Revelation. By the middle of the thirteenth century, the whole cycle is being given on Corpus Christi Day at the beginning of June. By this time, also, performances have generally left church property and church jurisdiction and are under the supervision of the craft guilds (in England), or other specially designated groups of laymen. The performers are not professional actors (except in Spain); they volunteer their time and resources annually to this great religious festival. The method of production is unique. Each episode is presented on a wheeled and roofed platform, or wagon (in England and Spain), which travels in succession to previously designated spots in the cathedral town, where an audience is gathered to watch. Or the episodes are performed successively on a long narrow platform backed by representative setpieces (mansions) from which the performers emerge (France), or in the town square (Germany, Switzerland), where the requisite mansions have been erected in locations around the open space. One after the other the episodes succeed each other: The Creation, the Fall of Man, Cain and Abel, Abraham and Isaac, Noah's Ark, etc., etc., through the Birth of Christ, His life, the Crucifixion, the Resurrection, the Ascension, etc., to the Last Judgment—the whole plan of salvation. The theology is sound, for the all-powerful medieval church sees to that. But the traditional Biblical characters are often given endearingly human traits: the pathetic questionings of Isaac as his father prepares to sacrifice him, the naggings of Noah's wife as she cannot comprehend his building of the ark. And these necessary characters are often supplemented with invented ones that have their roots in contemporary medieval society: Mak and his fellow shepherds, for instance, in the famous *Second Shepherds' Play*.

The costuming is symbolic and often gorgeous: gold faces on the angels and wings, gloves for God and Herod (since gentility always wore gloves in those days), horns and hair and tails for the devils. The stage effects are as realistic as ingenuity can make them: the bush burns for Moses, the loaves and fishes multiply for Christ, and the Hell-mouth spouts smoke and flame. Nothing is left out that can possibly be presented. Each episode is complete within itself, and yet there is a grand arc of unity in the whole

Figure 4–5
New York Pro Musica
The Play of Herod
(here in a modern
production directed by
Noah Greenberg) was
one of the most popular
plays of the Middle Ages.

cycle—the complete plan of salvation, from the Fall of Man to the
Last Judgment, made graphic and moving by the immediacy of
theatre. Some parts are very serious, others extremely comic, and
the audience enjoys it all. They sit for hours as the pageantry
passes before their eyes; at least once a year they "read" the Bible.
The effect must have been somewhat like a De Mille Bible epic
in the modern days of motion pictures, except that then the actors
were live and the episodes clearly divided, and the entire presentation was motivated by a deeply religious faith as interpreted by
the Roman Catholic Church.

These *cycle plays* were the dominating theatrical form of medieval times. Their performance continued in Spain well into the
eighteenth century, although by that time they had pretty well
disappeared elsewhere. The Oberammergau Passion Play and the
Passion plays of Brittany, Mexico, and various other parts of the
world today are vestiges of this medieval event. The play structure encompassed tragedy, comedy, and farce and reconciled
them all within the grand design, sometimes even within a single
episode. So great was the teaching power of the cycle play that

Figure 4–6

The Oberammergau Passion Play still survives as a vestige of the medieval cycle plays. Here is the judgment scene from the 1886 production.

dramatic technique was put to work in other kinds of materials: *saints' plays* and *morality plays*. The lives of the saints were detailed in the former; in the latter, abstractions like Gluttony, Pride, Good Deeds, etc., were animated and set to acting out their typical characteristics, as in the play *Everyman*. These, too, were didactic in intent and could be given on much less grand occasions than the great Corpus Christi celebration, since they were much shorter and self-contained. For purely social occasions, *folk plays* like *Robin Hood*, or *farces* like *Maistre Pierre Pathelin* might be performed, and these, which had no connection with theology and were purely secular in intent, were the forerunners of the secular theatre art of the Renaissance.

In the cycle plays, the saints' plays and the moralities, medieval society found a perfect vehicle for instructing the largely illiterate populace in church doctrine: the overriding importance of the Church as the sole avenue through which nobles and peasants alike could achieve the Paradise for which this earthly life was but a preparation and a prelude. Almost without exception the art works of whatever kind in the Middle Ages are anonymous; individual personality counted for nothing; the group effort was the whole, and all for the glory of God.

From this discussion of the plays of the Middle Ages, it is easy to see that neither classic forms nor classic mode had any progeny in these times. Even the short folk plays and moralities were discursive and episodic, often ranging over wide areas of time and space, often with a multiplicity of characters. And certainly the predominant form (the cycle play) had these characteristics in abundance. What was *born* in the Middle Ages was the romantic mode and the possibilities of romantic forms; what finally *died* was religious theatre.

SECULAR THEATRE: THE TRIUMPH OF INDIVIDUALISM

With the spread of the secular spirit which marked the Renaissance came a concomitant reemphasis upon the dignity and worth of the individual, his abilities and infinite potentialities. This growing emphasis was reinforced by the entry of Greek ideas into the collective consciousness, and the uneasy alliance was begun between Greek humanism and Christian theology which has persisted almost to the present day. From this point forward, until nearly the end of the nineteenth century, Man was the measure of all things. What he was, how he conducted himself, what his goals were—the details of these generalizations changed somewhat, but the center was on Man. The full flowering of the Renaissance brought forth a bewildering fecundity of ideas, and a richness of artistic creation which adorned the living world, now the center of man's attention instead of the life to come. Theatre was a part of that world, and to the repertoire of medieval drama were swiftly added romantic tragedy, romantic comedy, the chronicle play, the pastoral, the Senecan tragedy or revenge play, the satiric comedy, the improvised comedy, the intrigue comedy or "cloak and sword" play, the comedy of humors, and the rogue play—a veritable avalanche. None of these, of course, were instantaneous creations, like Minerva springing full-armed from the head of Jove, but developed rather rapidly from incipient beginnings in earlier times, reaching their full identity in the late fifteenth, the sixteenth, and the early seventeenth centuries.

The predominantly romantic mode of the English Renaissance was an inheritance from the Middle Ages. It affected the forms of tragedy and comedy to such an extent that *romantic comedy*

89

THE DEVELOPMENT
OF DRAMATIC FORMS
AND MODES

Figure 4–7

Seattle Repertory
Theatre
*The history, or
chronicle, play
developed in the
Renaissance as the direct
descendent of the holier
"histories" of medieval
times. Here is a scene
from one of the most
famous of these
chronicles, Shakespeare's
Henry IV, Part 1.
See also 1–1. Directed
by Allen Fletcher.
(Bill Houlton)*

and *romantic tragedy* became generic terms used by critics to designate a particular form of theatre from that day to this. It also affected the rise of the *history play*, or chronicle, whose subject matter was determined by the swelling tide of nationalism which was a concomitant of the Renaissance. These chronicle plays, like the *Henry* and *Richard* plays of Shakespeare, like *Las Mocedadas del Cid* of Guillen de Castro which detailed events in the lives of national historical figures, were a kind of live history text which, consciously or not, touted the advantage of being English or Spanish. The instrument was at hand to make plays of history. If the cycle plays performed the "history" of the chosen race, could not the new secular heroes be given life in a similar way? Was not the episodic structure of the cycle play, its mixture of serious and comic effects just the thing for these materials? So you have a Falstaff in *Henry IV*, and a very loose and extended plot structure.

In Spain, the influence of the romantic mode from its cycle plays led to a particular manifestation in Renaissance times. Quite uncritical glorification of the intrepidity of the hero in overcoming all manner of obstacles is the characteristic of the Spanish "cloak and sword" plays, like Lope de Vega's *Madrid Steel* and Tirso de Molina's *Deceiver of Seville*, in which intrigue, mistaken identities, secret love affairs, and the doings of a flamboyant aristocracy, presented in a swift succession of scenes, stressed action and accomplishment. They were the "westerns" of Renaissance Spanish theatre, the Errol Flynn vehicles of the Renaissance stage.

But one of the distinguishing characteristics of the Renaissance was an acquaintance with the classical writers of Greece and Rome. The resurgence of interest in the classic writers engendered a spate of Senecan or *revenge plays*. (Senecan texts had been preserved from Roman times in the medieval monasteries.) Some, like Kyd's *Spanish Tragedy* had a single line of action with no subplots—the Aristotelian prescription. But the particularly English heritage of *seeing on stage* whatever was presented as part of the action led to the adoption of Senecan playwriting practices rather than those of the Greeks who debarred violence from the sight of the audience and reported it by messenger. In parts of France, Spain, and Italy in particular, however, reams of plays with classical tragic themes used both the Senecan and the Aristotelian principles of construction. They make for rather dreary reading today. The revenge motif (an individual "getting even" for real or imagined wrongs) was an ubiquitous one, used in many kinds of plays, and sublimated in such a one as *Hamlet*.

The medieval abstractions of the morality play descended into the Renaissance in the *comedy of humors*, like Ben Jonson's *Every Man in His Humour*. But now the emphasis is upon the man and his predominating characteristic, for which he is aptly named. *Volpone* is a case in point, where the type-named characters clash in a social situation, and each arrives at his just deserts. Though this kind of play owes something to the classic comedy with its stock characters, in England at least it is closer to the old morality than to Menander, although the handling of the material is in the classic mode. In Italy, however, playwrights like Machiavelli (in *Mandragola*) are closer to the stock figures of the Greek writer of new comedy, Menander, and of the Roman "comedians" Plautus and Terence, no doubt because the Italians generally were more aware of the classic heritage than those further removed, geographically, from its epicenter. *Mandragola* might be called a *rogue comedy*, as might also *The Alchemist*, since they detail the triumph of a cunning rogue who wins out by being a little sharper and cleverer than his fellows—a somewhat equivocal application of the power of individualism. On the other

Figure 4–8

One of the great tragedies in the romantic mode is King Lear, here with Frank Silvera playing the title character. See also 3–4. (George E. Joseph)

Figure 4–9

The Max Reinhardt Archive, SUNY, Binghamton

This scene from Max Reinhardt's production of A Midsummer Night's Dream *shows the conclusion of the rustic's presentation of their play to Theseus and Hippolyta. See also 3–8.*

Figure 4–10

University of Iowa

Mandragola is a rogue comedy of the Italian Renaissance, here in a setting reminiscent of stage design in that period. Directed by Edward Sostek, designed by A. S. Gillette.

Figure 4–11

*A 17th century
commedia dell'arte
company performing in
an open-air theatre in
France. (From an old
print)*

hand, viewed as *satiric comedy* (and both these plays can be considered in this light), they have a salutary effect in exposing pretension to reveal truth, which function is the purpose of satire.

Immensely popular too in the Renaissance, and rising to a high order of excellence in artistry was the improvised comedy, the Italian *commedia dell'arte*. Somewhat akin to the comedy of humors, in that each of the personages possessed an overriding characteristic, and perhaps obscurely descended from the old Roman mimes in which the stock characters each wore a distinguishing mask and costume, the *commedia* presented a gallery of characters with a particular given name—Arlecchino, Pedrolino, Il Capitano, Il Dottore, Pantalone—who maintained that name with its accompanying mask and costume throughout a series of adventures outlined by scenario but largely improvised by the performers. There has never been a time in the history of theatre when improvised comedy rose to such heights as in the Renaissance. These performers were incredibly skilled, the best of them, and thus stand as examples for the phenomenon introduced once more by the Renaissance—the professional theatre person who could be respected for his skill in his chosen work.

THE DEVELOPMENT

OF DRAMATIC FORMS

AND MODES

Figure 4–12

University of Arkansas
A modern production of
The Servant of Two
Masters, *done in
commedia style.
Directed by Norman
DeMarco, setting by
Preston Magruder.*

But the best of the kinds of plays appearing as entities in the Renaissance were the *romantic tragedies* and the *romantic comedies*, so called. (The labels we have attached ex post facto to distinguish them from "classic" forms.) *King Lear* and *A Midsummer Night's Dream*, say, might be paradigms, or *Dr. Faustus* and *Friar Bacon and Friar Bungay*, or *The Duchess of Malfi* and *A Shoemaker's Holiday*. Free-ranging, encompassing many scenes, with the action covering various times from a night to a number of years, with many characters and usually a subplot, they are reminiscent of the episodic structure of the medieval cycles and reflect unerringly the broadranging interests and heterogeneous character of the period in which they were first performed. Great characters, by force of will striving toward the goals they set themselves—these are what we find in the comedies as well as the tragedies. To become undisputed King of Scotland, or Lord Mayor of London; to acquire in one's lifetime all the knowledge in man's ken, or simply to marry the person of one's choice— these are the goals to be achieved by individual striving. In the tragedies the visible goals are not accomplished, but something else is substituted for them—generally self-knowledge. In the comedies they are, because the obstacles are not so profound and the goals not so wide. Into the further nature of tragedy and

Figure 4–13

Institute for Advanced
Studies in the Theatre Arts

*A scene from Racine's
Phèdre, perhaps the
greatest of the neo-
classic tragedies, with
Mildred Dunnock as Oenone
and Beatrice Straight as
Phèdre. Directed by Paul-
Émile Deiber.
See also 6–4.*

comedy we will inquire in later pages; suffice it to say here that
when we turn back now to the Renaissance plays it is to these
romantic tragedies and comedies we first look as being the most
typical of the time and the most meaningful for today.

The episodic inheritance is particularly apparent in the plays of
Christopher Marlowe, where only the dominating character of the
hero—Tamburlaine, Faustus, or Barrabas—tie the events together.
Shakespeare, on the other hand, had learned from the classic
sources with which he was acquainted at either first- or secondhand that Plot itself had an inherent form which would make
plays more interesting and more comprehensible to an audience.
So in his best work he combines the multiplicity of scenes and
characters inherited from medieval drama with the careful development of plot derived from classic sources to make a new and
wonderful entity: the romantic comedy and the romantic tragedy.
Because of the subsequent history of performance and criticism
of his plays we tend to forget that he was a master at plotting.
No doubt (except for the history plays, where the actual events
took precedence over arrangement) he started always from plot.
That he was, in addition, a master at characterization makes
many a critic and copier lose sight of his basic skill in plotting and
emphasize his characters to the exclusion of plot.

One other kind of romantic play reached intimate perfection in that early Renaissance: the *pastoral*, as exemplified by Guarini's *Il Pastor fidi*, or Tasso's *Aminta*. These are graceful gestures of a sophisticated society playing artfully with the love motif in an outdoor setting of beneficent nature. The characteristics of the form were absorbed into other kinds of plays, and the pastoral as an entity in itself quickly disappeared.

There is, of course, in the romantic play no unity of time and place, and it was just this lack that caused the French critics of the late seventeenth and the eighteenth centuries to criticize Shakespeare so severely and to delay so long in accepting his genius. For the French by that time had forgotten their own roots in the medieval theatre and had transformed their drama into a neoclassic one. For that matter, even in England in the eighteenth century (its own neoclassic period), Shakespeare was "regularized" when presented on the stage; i.e., tidied up, with comic scenes removed from the tragedies, since by their inclusion was violated unity of action, as the neoclassic critics thought. The mixture of comic and tragic in Shakespeare is simply, again, his inheritance from the medieval cycle plays, not a conscious choice on his part to "relieve" the intensity of the tragedies for his audiences. If anything, the so-called comic scenes *heighten* the tragic intensity.

But by the time the great French playwrights attained their stature, unique influences had been operating and had their effect in France alone. One of the most erudite and skillful minds in history, that of Cardinal Richelieu, had not only conceived and brought to pass a strong French nation, but he had also established the Académie Française, arbiter of language and literature. And on the throne was Louis XIV, who outlived Richelieu by a couple of ordinary lifetimes, and who was an arbiter absolute himself. Logic, decorum, rule, and taste joined with the natural French love of reason and practicality to turn the attention of the literati, and in turn of the theatre-going public, away from the profusion of romantic comedy and tragedy to a starker, more compressed style. Neoclassicism, it called itself, and at its best it produced in tragedy Racine's *Phèdre* and in comedy Molière's *Le Misanthrope*. In the former, incidents are few as are characters; there is no elaborate stage spectacle and very little indicated physical movement for the actors. The place of the old Greek

chorus is now taken by an invention of the eighteenth century—a single character called the *confidente*. The verse is precise and correct, and there are many long speeches. But the atmosphere is that of a volcano about to erupt; the pressure builds inexorably until the top blows off and Phaedre and Hippolyte lie dead. The very restrictions seem to increase the tensions; the struggle is within the soul of Phaedre, who is all the time fully conscious of her sins and almost, but not quite, strong enough to conquer her sinful emotions. *Phèdre* is a paradigm of the neoclassic tragedy as *Le Misanthrope* is of the comedy. Only a stable social order, with mores clearly understood and generally accepted, can produce this kind of play, for its action shows the progress and the fate of Alceste, who by his prideful superhonesty violates the canon of good sense and is deserted by his friends—the fate which he richly deserves. Only a playwright who deeply understood and loved mankind in all its varieties and idiosyncrasies could have produced this play, which depends for its effectiveness on the balance between the misanthrope and his social group, a balance which teeters back and forth until Alceste makes his last ridiculous

Figure 4–14

APA-Phoenix Company
*Célimène and her
friends in the
APA-Phoenix
production of Molière's
The Misanthrope.
See also 11–30 and 11–31.*
(*Van Williams*)

mistake and loses Célimène. Here, as in the tragedy, there are no extraneous characters, the plot is tightly knit, and the suspense dependent upon the clash of character on character.

The classic mode reanimated in France in the seventeenth century had production techniques totally different from those of the classic Greek era. The theatre was a roofed-over structure requiring interior lighting, which fell equally on audience and actors. The largest part of the audience of some 1500 or so stood or sat facing the stage, which was framed by a proscenium arch. Perhaps 50 or so wealthy and titled patrons sat on benches on either side of the stage itself, perpendicular to the edge of the stage. The acting area was thereby reduced to a square of about 20 by 20 feet, and scenery was simply a painted backdrop perhaps supplemented by two or three pairs of side wings. Under these conditions, it is easy to see that the pageantry and spectacle of the Greek theatre was impossible. The functions of the chorus in the ancient plays, particularly as they served to bring out the inner musings of the chief characters in exchange of dialogue, were taken over by individual *confidentes,* as Oenone functions in *Phèdre* and Narcissus in *Britannicus.* Physical action was at a minimum, and the reporting by messengers of events supposed to have taken place off stage was not merely a convention adopted from the ancients, but an absolute pragmatic necessity. Extravagant gestures were not only frowned upon, they were impossible, and the audiences delighted in long, virtuoso speeches by the individual characters. These virtuoso speeches they called *tirades.*

No doubt, the very restrictions of the staging caused the writers of neoclassic tragedy to use the inner tensions of their characters as the prime source of conflict. Though the actors wore no masks, and were arrayed in costly and formalized court dress, their economy of movement and controlled intensity of speech must have given much of the same impression of formal beauty that ancient audiences felt in witnessing the Greek tragedies.

In the comedies also, the same economy of plot and character prevailed—notably in those of Molière. But, as in the classic comedy, the personages were drawn from the immediate society, as the miser, the misanthrope, or the ridiculous precious ladies. This application of the classic mode in form with the classic perception of character made for a new thing in comedy—the best

Figure 4–15

Carnegie-Mellon
University
*This scene from a
modern production of
Farquhar's* The Beaux
Stratagem *successfully
conveys the atmosphere
and feeling of this late
Restoration comedy.
Directed by Bernard
Engel, settings by
Charles Dox.*

the world has known. It is the classic clarity of vision used by a perceptive and sympathetic genius which makes the Molière comedy so outstanding. The classic conception of man as the measure of all things put character at the center of Molière's work and made it the best in comedy. The particular French atmosphere of the mid-seventeenth century, which stressed the order, decency, and decorum innate in the classics and coupled it with a highly sophisticated society glad of the chance to demonstrate its "sweet reasonableness" after the preceding period of civil and religious wars, was particularly beneficent to the growth and flowering of the finest theatre the French have known—their golden age.

When the English in the Restoration and the early eighteenth century tried to use the French neoclassic principles, their tragedy became *heroic drama*, like Addison's *Cato*, full of bombast and sententious speeches, and the comedy, while brilliant in its kind, was rather the *comedy of manners* than that of character. Such

99

THE DEVELOPMENT

OF DRAMATIC FORMS

AND MODES

plays as *The Way of the World, Love for Love,* and *The Country Wife,* for instance, written primarily for the narrow audience of court society, do not so much probe characters as they violate good sense, but rather delineate a select society where the fumbler violates good taste, as it has been accepted by that society.

The latter half of the eighteenth century brought a greater democratization to theatre audiences; royal patronages were withdrawn and theatres had to survive on the beneficences of new theatre audiences, freshly arrived from the country or newly affluent from commerce or trade. The stern agonies of the noble Cato were as foreign to most of this audience as were the pretensions of Lady Wishfort; new kinds of plays were in order. George Lillo's *The London Merchant* admirably filled the bill. George Barnwell served as a warning to all apprentices not to be led astray from good morals and good business practices; while Mr. Thorogood, his employer, served in the opposite capacity as a good example. Here is *bourgeois drama,* specie—*domestic tragedy,* with characters drawn from the same middle class of which the audience was composed, demonstrating in broad terms the acceptable and unacceptable modes of behavior, with the unacceptable ending in ruin. Here is a kind of new didacticism in the theatre, generally implicit but often explicit. In fact, Diderot, the French critic and sometime playwright, extolled theatre as a perfect vehicle for inculcating mob virtue and was a great admirer of *The London Merchant.* He became a firm advocate of this seemingly realistic domestic tragedy and extended his interest as well to the *genre serieux,* or *drame,* or *comédie larmoyante,* as it was variously called—that type of play in which characters from ordinary life go through a series of trials that almost overwhelm them but, in the end, by virtue of their fortitude or a stroke of luck, things turn out well for them, or at least not disastrously. These plays are written in prose, the language of everyday; the costuming, of course, is contemporary with the play, and the settings tend to be detailed. The domestic tragedy maintained its identity for some time; Lessing, the renowned German critic, wrote a very popular play in this form, *Miss Sara Sampson.* But more popular with the increasing audiences were the *drames,* where one could look forward to a happy ending in spite of past tribulations, and where virtue was always rewarded and villainy got its just deserts.

The *comédie larmoyante* moved into the nineteenth century and became, towards its end, the *melodrama*, filled with incident and spectacular scenery, broadly drawn characters so that the "good guys" and the "bad guys" could be easily identified, and always the poetic justice ending with rewards and punishments meted out in exact proportions as they were deserved. Succeeding generations of new theatre audiences everywhere in the Western world thrilled to the perils and satisfactions of this dramatic form in the theatre until the movies came along and showed that they could do it better and cheaper. They are still doing it.

Beginning in the eighteenth century, the heretofore fairly clear-cut distinctions between comedy and tragedy as form and the classic and romantic as mode break down, and form and mode seem to pursue separate paths. Much of the predominant playwriting of the century was highly romantic in its content; i.e., in Mood and Language the world as one would wish it to be, as well as in its form; i.e., in Fable incidents cumulative in effect and widely ranging in time and space. But in Character and Spectacle there was a definite development of that classic mode which sees things as they are and as they can be contained in theatre: what John Gassner calls "Classic Realism" (*Form and Idea in Modern Theatre*).

Let us be clear about one thing: there was realism in staging practices long before the mode of realism became pervasive and of prime importance to the total work of theatrical art. And the disparity between realistically dressed characters and spectacle and far-from-realistic plot and personages detracted from the artistic worth of the productions. The violation of probability in Plot and Character in such plays as Cumberland's *The West Indian* and Steele's *The Conscious Lovers*, for instance, make them incredible to twentieth-century audiences, although their contemporary audiences saw the action as idealized in both instances—as what *ought* to happen (hence desirable and pleasing) rather than what probably *might* happen in the given circumstances (hence real and believable).

Perhaps the first tentative movement toward realism was made about midway in the eighteenth century, when characters from middle-class society were introduced into serious drama, like George Barnwell and Miss Sara Sampson. Characters from the immediate social milieu, of course, had always been used in comedy, except perhaps in the *commedia*, whose characters, by virtue of their costumes, masks, and type-names, were abstractions from reality rather than *real*. But, as we have seen, the eighteenth-century *drame* brought people from ordinary walks of life into serious plays. But this was "token" only; the drawing of those characters and the situations through which they went were hardly realistic, nor was their dialogue.

But the very tendency to use in serious plays characters from ordinary walks of contemporary life had realistic influences in another way. Now the characters were wearing costumes that befitted their supposed stations in life, and the stage appurtenances began to be more factual as well. From 1800 on, in France, in Germany, and in England, the wing-and-back-shutter system of dressing the stage gradually metamorphosed into the box-set. There is some evidence that sets of parallel wing flats were joined together by another flat on the diagonal to form a section of wall at the Mannheim Court Theatre as early as 1804. In 1811 we find Goethe complaining about the "box-set" in his autobiography. In 1834 the innovative English producer Planché was reported as using a stage "entirely enclosed" in a production at Drury Lane, and in 1841, when Mme. Vestris did her famous production of Dion Boucicault's *London Assurance* at Covent Garden, not only were the sides of the stage shut up to form rooms with real walls, but those walls had doors with knobs and moldings, and the stage furniture was real and practicable. The whole production eventually appeared in New York, box-set and all.

At the very same time (first half of the nineteenth century), there was a tremendous reaction against the neoclassicism and the "tearful comedy" of the preceding years which took the form popularly known as the Romantic Revolution. Surprisingly in France, the bastion of classicism in both form and mode, appeared Victor Hugo, whose *Hernani* at the Comédie (1830) used the expansive scene of the romantic mode, the hero willing his own destiny, and the succession of stirring events in cumulative form and poetic language. He had been preceded by Goethe and Schiller in Germany, and would be followed by Dumas and (late blooming example) the Rostand of *Cyrano de Bergerac* (1898). The counterpart of these renowned romantic dramatists in the popular theatre were the melodramas of Pixérécourt, which had

Figure 4–16

Tufts Arena Theatre
Our American Cousin,
*a typical 19th century
comedy. Lord
Dundreary, center, was
a very popular stage
character. His name was
given to a certain style
of whiskers.*
(Duette Photographers)

grown by degrees and become separate from the *drame* of the
mid-eighteenth century by the process of adding thrilling scenes—
coups de théâtre—for their own sakes to the even line of development of the *drame*, by making the unpleasant characters more
evil and the good ones more virtuous, and by complicating the
staging to an overwhelming picture with many tricks and moving
parts designed to surprise, delight, and thrill. This was the theatre
of the boulevards in Paris when Hugo conquered the Comédie
with a play much like those of his lesser regarded contemporaries.
In both "boulevard" and "Comédie" plays, scenery is an integral
part of the production and not a mere background; to remove the
set would make the play unintelligible, a fact which does not hold
for the Shakespearian play in which the stage dressing is largely
immaterial. The fact that Hernani was an outlaw, as had been
many of the heroes in the German romantic drama (not excepting
Goethe and Schiller), was another mark of its romantic mode.
Freedom as a way of life is romantically enshrined in the rebel,
the outlaw.

   The world as one would wish it to be in some grander, freer
age; characters as one would wish them to be in some idealized

THE DEVELOPMENT
OF DRAMATIC FORMS
AND MODES

society; adventurous action, lavish spectacle, whether of group action or scenery or both—all these are typical of the romantic mode. Escapist? Perhaps, but certainly not necessarily. The most typical product of the romantic mode in the present day is, of course, the Broadway musical, but the romantic mode is evident as well in other theatre movements which occurred in the twentieth century. Before we consider those, we must look at the predominant modes and forms as the theatre moved into that century.

FORM AND MODE IN THE AGE OF SCIENCE:
THE REAL AND THE SUPERREAL

The outstanding characteristic of Western civilization in the last hundred years has been the growth of its devotion to science. Prior to 1850 that body of knowledge which we call science was known as "natural philosophy," a term completely discredited today. The scientist has become the world hero; the "scientific method" has been exalted to a position approximating omnipotence. Not only discoveries and developments in science, but so-called "scientific thinking" has reduced the role of the individual, in some cases to total extinction, and has turned world attention away from the infinite possibilities inherent in the individual to the fragmentation not only of his personality but of his relationships. Psychology and sociology have investigated in minute detail various aspects of human activity on the personal and social level, and have been largely responsible for the decreasing emphasis upon a *willed control* of his destiny and his environment by the individual. Not only is God dead in the present world, but man, made in His image, is also reduced to a bundle of neuroses, drives, and frustrations which he only dimly understands, and over which he has no control. Science has become god; observation, experimentation, and the worship of the Fact for its own sake have become a way of life. Man is no longer the center of the universe, but a problem to be solved, a specimen under a microscope, a bit of matter to be analyzed in the laboratory, a statistic to be dealt with in complicated computations. What happens to theatre—that most man-centered of all the arts —in such a world?

It all began simply enough, but the repercussions have been enormous. In the latter half of the nineteenth century, the luxuriousness of the romantic mode, its prodigality in situation and character increasingly made it become inimicable to the ordered logic of the French mind by and large. (The Englishman and the German have no such problem.) The great wave of the romantic mode was shortlived in France; by the last half of the nineteenth century it was being replaced by the "well made" plays of Sardou, Scribe, and Dumas *fils*. They were classic in construction, but highly romantic in content. In England, in the 1860s and 1870s, the Bancrofts and their associate, the playwright Tom Robertson, did a whole series of plays that not only used the "doorknob" realism of setting, but concerned themselves with contemporary problems: *Society, Ours, Caste, Play*, and *School*. By the last quarter of the century, realism in Spectacle had been completely accomplished; the physical world the audiences saw on the stage had its parallel in real life.

In both France and England, the personages of the plays were largely drawn from the same circles as those of the audiences; the plays were almost exclusively written in prose and the language of everyday speech. The point of attack is late in the action. The earliest of these plays is in five acts with the first devoted to exposition, the second and third to complication, the climax comes at the third-act curtain, and the fourth and fifth acts comprise the dénouement. Scribe and Sardou brought the form to perfection; indeed so much so that plot and the complication of situation took precedence over all the other elements in the play. When, toward the end of the century the five-act construction gave way to a three-act one, the climax conventionally came at the end of the second act.

What was it, then, that Zola and Antoine did in the 1880s that causes us today to speak of them as if they were "the fathers of realism?" What they did was to violently dislocate the life view of the artist so that he looked at the world in a new and different way. They diverted attention from middle-class materials and genteel behavior and focused it on "the beast in man" as Zola said, stressing his affinity with the other orders of nature in the spirit of scientific observation—hence the term *naturalism*, which is often applied to this kind of realism. In the excess of his zeal, as well, Zola championed the jettisoning of Plot entirely, since the very idea of a beginning, a middle, and an end is antithetical, he thought, to what one observes in nature. (He was wrong, of course, for nothing is more "natural" than birth, growth, and death.) What was good about the movement, however, was that it did insist upon *observation*, upon accurate rendering of speech and action (Antoine revolutionized acting styles), and upon bringing into the theatre materials which had heretofore been circumscribed. The just proportion of all the elements of drama, with the dramatist's eye fixed on the real world, led to the perfection of the mode in the plays of Henrik Ibsen, who is more rightly called "the father of modern (realistic) drama" and whose plays are among the few judged "great" in the canons of theatre.

Impressed with the method of science which made its great leap forward subsequent to the publication of Darwin's *Origin of Species* in 1859, and disgusted with the romantic and melodramatic theatre fare of his contemporary society, Emile Zola, in the 1870s had called for the incorporation of the scientific method in the writing of plays and in their production. Life should be presented on the stage, he said, in the meticulous detail, the formlessness and indirection that it has in the "real world." The dramatist should be a scientist, objectively observing, making no comment, giving no direction. (In other words, he trades in his prerogatives as an artist for the dubious distinction of becoming a scientist.) Fortunately for theatre, Zola was no playwright, but his strictures did influence not only a number of writers, but also the whole theatrical mode called "realism," which we will consider in more detail in following chapters.

The formlessness which Zola advocated would have had its logical conclusion in the annihilation of theatre art. (Or perhaps we should say that it has had its logical conclusion in the modern Andy Warhol movie, in which for six hours an audience contemplates the spire of the Empire State Building.) The most salutary effect of his criticisms was to turn the attention of playwrights and producers to materials hitherto largely neglected: submerged sections of society, and social problems. The *problem play* (drama of ideas, *pièce à thèse*) is a modern dramatic form taking its impetus from the scientific mode. Its best representatives are the plays of Henrik Ibsen and George Bernard Shaw. In such plays as Ibsen's *Ghosts*, *A Doll's House*, and *An Enemy of the People*, and Shaw's *Mrs. Warren's Profession*, *Major Barbara*,

Figure 4–17

Arena Stage,
Washington, D.C.
*One of Shaw's idea
plays,* The Doctor's
Dilemma, *as produced
by Arena Stage,
Washington, D.C.*

and *The Doctor's Dilemma,* for instance, the social problems of venereal disease, the position of women, water pollution, prostitution, the manufacture of arms, and the abuses in medical practice are explored. By their very nature, Thought is the most important element in problem plays; the other elements are subordinate to it. Indeed, Shaw was so anxious that his thesis be not missed or misunderstood that he wrote lengthy prefaces to almost all his plays, and Ibsen frequently wrote about the problems with which his plays dealt. Luckily, the audience in the theatre is not subjected to these prefaces and comments; what it sees is the play itself, the dramatic action unfolding before it as a lived experience. Though in these mentioned plays the subject matter, or what the play is about, are social problems drawn from the contemporary society, each has a larger frame of reference. Thus *Ghosts,* for instance, is not merely about venereal disease, but is an action concerned with how a marriage forced by convention yields the bad fruit of which the disease is the evil symbol, and the prostitution dealt with in *Mrs. Warren's Profession* stands for the larger idea that society itself forces people to prostitute themselves in some way. Both Ibsen and Shaw used controversial contemporary social problems to deal with ideas concerning man's

107

THE DEVELOPMENT

OF DRAMATIC FORMS

AND MODES

Figure 4–18

Purdue
Professional Theatre
*The epitome of the
realistic mode is evident
in this scene from a
revival of Chekhov's*
Uncle Vanya. *Directed
by Joseph G. Stockdale,
Jr., setting by Jerry
Williams.*

perennial problem of adjusting to his world. These *idea plays* tend toward the classic form and are wholly within the classic mode, that clear-eyed perception of the world as it is.

Another effect of scientism on playwriting was in the production of the *mood* or *environment* play, like those of Chekhov and Maeterlinck. These approach closer to Zola's precept of relative formlessness, for the plotting of a succession of events, the tying and untying of a knot, seem almost totally absent. Of the two, it is Chekhov who maintains his identity as a realist (hence to a degree, in the classic mode) because he used an impressionistic technique similar to that of the impressionist painters in building up his canvas of meticulously realized small strokes to create a sense of "livingness," a pervasive Mood. And, in their form (which is not really formless but a new thing under the sun), they constitute the beginning of a new form—modern tragicomedy—which we will discuss in Part III. Since Chekhov, the mode of classic realism has been a persistent one in theatre. The realist playwrights, by their skill in handling their materials, by the clarity of their vision as they observe particular worlds, and by their skill in character delineation, create plays which will live long beyond the immediate times which produce them.

The essence of the realistic mode is its application to all the elements of drama in just proportion and harmony. One can find examples of the realistic mode everywhere in theatre, from the nineteenth century to the day after tomorrow. It is the world as it presents itself to our eyes and our ears, its details selected and arranged, of course, according to the governing Idea of the playwright, but having *verisimilitude* for the audience, seeming factual and true to them. Though the tracing of the realistic mode in theatre in all its intricate detail and manifestations might often seem to prove nothing more than that what is one man's realism is another man's romanticism, still the concept is constant and recognizable. The difficulties occur when it is applied exclusively to one or the other of the necessary dramatic elements while the rest are in another mode entirely. This violation of unity of effect is what bothers us as an audience and makes us less than satisfied that what we are seeing is a work of art.

In modern times, realism as a mode is most frequently found in the form of comedy, although it also occurs in tragicomedy, that widespread modern form. But almost as soon as modern realism appeared in the theatre, there were reactions against it and a shifting toward the romantic mode. An embryonic romanticism is to be found in even such seemingly realistic plays as Ibsen's *The Wild Duck*, which Karl Guthke calls a "tragicomedy." Here the bird and its capture, life in the converted garret, and death epitomize the illusions by which several of the characters live and how they are destroyed when the illusions are shattered. This play, as well as *Ghosts*, *The Master Builder*, and *The Lady From the Sea*, can be viewed as the unfolding of a realistic dramatic action. Yet all of them, as well, seem to invite the audience to find private meanings in the imaginative substrata below the level of the logical action; there is a symbolism inherent in each. One intuitively grasps rather than clearly understands a hidden meaning, as one does with his *Peer Gynt*. Ibsen's latest plays, like this early one, move toward the deintellectualization of the drama and make it subject to private interpretation rather than clear and precise in its statement.

To some extent we might say that all plays have symbols in the very fact that they are imitations of life, as Aristotle would say. But when the symbol stands out as a symbol intentionally, and the playwright means to build effects by symbols, we say the play is *symbolic*. The young Maeterlinck, who called *The Master Builder* "somnambulistic drama," quickly embraced symbolism and wrote several plays of "spiritual action" where that which is seen and heard on the stage is not the reality, but the symbol of a life beyond the stage life, a kind of Poe-world, in the misty midregion of Weir. Maeterlinck, perhaps more philosopher than playwright, called for a "static theatre," devoid of action, in which the dialogue would simply imply an action somewhere beyond the visible stage, and where the music, light, and setting would reinforce a mood of dream-likeness and unreality. In *The Intruder*, *Pelléas and Mélisande*, and *The Bluebird* the characters seem like somnambulists "who are a little deaf and are being continually awakened from a painful dream," as he puts it. His aim is to evoke the invisible, the intangible, the subconscious, the unintelligible. It is the *inner action*, the action *behind* the visible action that he is aiming to show. He later became somewhat disenchanted with these experiments in "static theatre." See his essay, "The Modern Drama": ". . . the sovereign law of the stage, its essential demand will always be *action*. . . . And there are no words so profound, so noble and admirable, if they lead to no action, bring about no decisive conflict, or hasten no definite solution." (D. C. Stuart, *The Development of Dramatic Art*, p. 634.)

Strindberg, admirer of Maeterlinck, took a step further away from the real world into the realm of *expressionism*, where the personages on the stage are not just symbols of something beyond themselves, but abstract ideas personified as human beings. The predominant treatment as dream and fantasy puts these plays in the romantic mode. In his *To Damascus* the character of The Unknown subdivides and meets himself in different phases of his own entity: as Caesar, as the madman, as the beggar. In Evreinov's *Theatre of the Soul* the stage setting is a pulsating heart, and the actors impersonate the Rational Entity, the Emotional Entity, and the Subliminal Entity in conflict over various Concepts of the Dancer and the Wife, which are also personalized. The technique is somewhat reminiscent of the old medieval morality which personalized abstractions, but in the morality the action was real in a real world (as in *Everyman*), whereas in the expressionistic play there is no pretense at surface reality; expressionism is subjective, dealing with *inner* reality. One of the central characters in Ernst Toller's *Masse-Mensch* is The Nameless One, who is described as The Spirit of the Masses. Three of the nine scenes, as Toller describes the play, take place in the woman's mind—"she is the protagonist, the only character in the play who has a name,

Figure 4–19

Arena Stage,
Washington, D.C.
*Scene from the
production of the
expressionist play,* The
Adding Machine. *Mr.
Zero, the protagonist,
is seated in front, with
his head bowed.*

Sonia Irene." She projects through a dream medium "her horror of capitalistic control, of proletarian warfare, and her pity for its victims." In Elmer Rice's *The Adding Machine*, the protagonist's name is Mr. Zero, and his friends are Mr. One, Mr. Two, Mr. Three, and Mr. Four. The antagonist is The Boss. In the expressionistic play, light, sound, movement, color, and mass are instruments of explicit use, along with the abstracted entities of character, to build the Fable and project the dramatic action. Expressionism reached its apogee in Germany immediately following World War I, but its principles and its techniques have widened the possibilities of theatre ever since.

Vsevolod Meyerhold, that incredibly fertile genius of the pre-Stalin Russian theatre, was also caught up in the current of Maeterlinckian antireality. As early as 1905 he was saying (Marc Slonim, *Russian Theatre*, New York: Collier (Macmillan), 1961, p. 184): "The time has come to attempt to stage the unreal, to render life as perceived in fantasy and visions." Primarily a director, he went through a period of symbolist allegiance, then of expressionist, and finally arrived at what he called "constructivism," in which the actors used a system of "biomechanics" or overt physical movement over, under, and around a setting consisting of ramps, steps, ladders, poles, arcs, and platforms—reality stripped to its fundamental structures and arranged to offer the possibility of movement in space which would make explicit in action the various emotional states of the characters and their relationships to each other. Meyerhold was not a play-wright, and there is no drama particularly written as a "constructivist play." But he prefigures the point of view of the absurdist playwrights when he says that words are "but an embroidery on the canvas of movement." Slonim describes Meyerhold's famous production of Crommelynck's *The Magnificent Cuckold*, given in 1922, in the following terms (p. 247):

The comedy, which lampooned a miller who looks for his wife's lover and makes all the male population of the village pass through her bedchamber, was by no means a revolutionary subject, but Meyerhold used it in order to test his latest innovation, biomechanics. The stage was completely denuded, no curtains, no rafters, no backdrops. It was occupied by a mill-like construction (by Lyubov Popova) with platforms, stairs, a viaduct, and inclined surfaces. On this truly constructivist stage, actors in blue overalls ran, jumped and moved like acrobats. Instead of "true emotions" they presented movement and acted like athletes, exhibiting all sorts of physical exercises with the exactitude and inventiveness of drilled professionals.

Meyerhold was the implacable enemy of reality on the stage. He felt that theatre was an art which should free one from the materialism of life; it should be food for the spirit. In his views and in his stage practices he influenced not only future directors but future playwrights as well. For he insisted throughout his life that the theatre should be "theatrical." At a typical Meyerhold performance the audience was never allowed to forget that it was in a theatre; it was expected to participate with the actors in a conscious game of make-believe in a fully lighted auditorium from which the proscenium arch and the front curtain had been abolished.

If the playwrights of dream and fantasy plays keep insisting that audiences look further *within* a character, the *epic play* goes to the opposite extreme. The inside of the head is forbidden territory; indeed it is even forbidden the audience that it get "inside" the play. It must figuratively stand aside, observe, and *think* about what it is observing. And to make sure that it does not lose itself in the action, or believe in the characters as characters, the play-wright will interrupt the action for a comment or explanation by a noninvolved performer, or quickly insert a kind of parenthetical

Clever is not he who
never makes mistakes.

Clever is he who knows
to correct them at once.

incident, or a direct address to the audience in his own person by
one of the performers, or a strip of film, or placards. The epic play
is a dramatic form chiefly practiced by Bertolt Brecht but also
used by Thornton Wilder and some few others. A dramatic action
is sustained; there is generally a recognizable plot; the actors
usually function on two levels: as characters in the play and as
actors performing the play, i.e., as themselves. Brecht's *A Man's a
Man* and Wilder's *The Skin of Our Teeth* are examples. The
mode of production for plays of this kind is what has been named
"theatricalism."

John Gassner, in his *Form and Idea in Modern Theatre* (New
York: Holt, Rinehart and Winston, 1956) would contain all nonrealistic theatre in the term "theatricalism." But it seems to me
that we are on more tenable grounds when we apply that term to
the particular permutation of the romantic mode which, in its
way of seeing and saying declares that we are frankly in a theatre
and experiencing something written and staged with no pretense
that it is real. In all of these the audience is frankly brought into
the performance by one or more characters as it is directly ad-
dressed. The style is often called *presentational*, as opposed to
representational; i.e., the performers are presenting a story, or a
series of scenes or actions during which the audience is taken

Figure 4–20

Carnegie-Mellon
University
*Epic theatre style for a
production of* The
Measures Taken. *Masks
and the illuminated
legend are typical
Brechtian characteristics.
Directed by Eric Vos,
setting by Frederick
Youens.*

THE DEVELOPMENT
OF DRAMATIC FORMS
AND MODES

directly into the performance, as opposed to the kind of situation where the performers seemingly do not recognize that an audience is present but play through a representation of an action while the audience watches. Asides and soliloquies are longstanding techniques of the presentational style; newer departures are those used in the plays mentioned above. Clifford Odets' *Waiting for Lefty* (1935), in which the whole theatre becomes a union hall and some of the performers speak from the audience space is another technique. This technique of including the audience in the performance directly, as it were, i.e., making the whole theatre into performing space, is one which has developed in the present day into what its practitioners call "environmental theatre." We will deal with it at some length later on. Giraudoux's *Electra* (1937) has a character called The Gardener who, on stage by himself, speaks directly to the audience; Robert Bolt's *A Man for All Seasons* uses a character called The Common Man for the same purposes. It is not only to say frankly to an audience, "we are in a theatre, as we both know, and this is not real life" that the theatrical mode is employed, but also it involves the audience more directly in the performance. It can be effective; if overdone it is alienating, for audiences *are not* performers any more than a church congregation is the priest. Again, as John Gassner puts it (*Form*, p. 175), "The aim of theatricality is to create a new reality—*a reality of art*—on the stage."

Another form largely developed in the age of science is that of the *documentary play*, like Rolf Hochhuth's *The Deputy*. Speciously factual, it makes a selection from recorded history, using so far as possible the words of its sources, and arranges these in sequential fashion. Presumably nothing about the play is invented; it has the air of truth and tends to be classic in both form and mode. Yet obviously the playwright makes the selection of the bits and pieces he uses, and the play can very well be a case of special pleading. The type has some ancestry in the history and chronicle plays, but in those the events only were used, and the words invented by the playwrights. The current documentary play, on the other hand, owes more probably to documentary films, and television programs, and journalism than to the earlier form.

Finally, we might say that the one other dramatic form developed in the age of science is the so-called *antiplay*, which con-

Figure 4–21
The Balcony, *Genet's*
modern anti-play. See
also 9–6.
(Martha Swope)

sciously rebels against all hitherto existing theatrical forms. It is
chiefly noted for its rejection of Language as an element of theatrical form. Genet, Ionesco, and Beckett are its chief apostles, and
behind them Artaud and Alfred Jarry. Its mode is generally (if
somewhat erroneously) called "absurd." It has developed over the
last few decades, primarily since World War II. It is influenced by
the modern philosophy of existentialism and the movements of
surrealism and cubism in painting. It also has a relationship to the
principles of the expressionists, who tried to make visible and
tangible in stage terms the inner states of human beings. What is
different about the absurdists is their apparently negative point
of view. Theirs is a partial vision, special, and the glasses are very
dark-tinted indeed. But it is a pervasive mode in modern theatre.
We will discuss it at some length in Part III, Chapter 9.

No theatre in the history of the world has been so rich in the
possibilities of dramatic form as the present. All of these we have

115

THE DEVELOPMENT

OF DRAMATIC FORMS

AND MODES

mentioned, from first to last, are still available to us, and new forms will no doubt continue to be developed. Some of those which had primacy in the theatres of other days would hardly be used again—heroic tragedy, perhaps, or the revenge play, the pastoral, or Aristophanic comedy, or the medieval cycle play. But melodrama, tragicomedy, farce, romantic comedy, tragedy, and romantic tragedy are still viable forms and available for use. So, too, are the basic modes: the classic and the romantic. Their application will be different in plays written in the present day, as we have briefly seen above, and as we will explore more in depth in the pages to follow. The theatre, of course, has been entirely secular in intent since the Renaissance; some religious plays have been written from time to time, but they are the exception rather than the rule.

Thus, in this discursive consideration of the modes and forms, we have filled in a few more spokes of the wheel whose perimeter is the world and whose center is the theatre. By this time all of us must certainly be convinced, with Marshall McLuhan, that the Gutenberg technology is indeed outmoded, that knowledge is not linear, but circuitous, centripetal, centrifugal; and that theatre is certainly all of these. How many ways are there to approach it? Many. Many. And each adds a modicum to the whole, to the convoluted unity which is theatre. After a brief pause in the next chapter to consider the conventions of theatre, we shall proceed in Part III with another approach—that through a consideration of the nature of the predominant genres: tragedy, comedy, their lesser relations, and some newer forms.

5

Conventions

The art of theatre—as indeed all the arts, as well as society itself—exists as a possibility and an entity because of certain conventions. A convention in the theatre is simply an agreement between the audience and those producing and/or performing the play that, for their mutual benefit, they will agree to accept certain devices not because they are real or natural, but because their purpose is not only acceptable but necessary to the realization of the theatrical work of art. The theatrically naive craftsmen in *A Midsummer Night's Dream* were not aware of certain theatrical conventions, hence they spent a great deal of time worrying about how to show moonlight, how to accomplish a wall, and whether or not the ladies in the audience would be "affrighted" by the lion. Their solutions to these problems are extremely funny to us because we know—as Shakespeare's original audience also knew—the conventions that govern these eventualities. Washington Irving made good comic use of his yokel Jonathan's ignorance of theatre conventions when he has Jonathan describe his first theatre experience in terms of his being an unwilling but interested "peeping Tom" at the doings of some mysterious family who lived in a strange house where one wall was missing. Theatre could not exist at all were it not for a series of conventions; i.e., illusion-making devices which the audience accepts for the sake of the illusion.

For convenience, we may divide theatrical conventions into two kinds: those that have always obtained (by and large those necessary for the art to exist at all), and those which have changed with the changing times. A knowledge of the former will aid in the understanding of the art as a whole. A knowledge of the latter is indispensable to an understanding and a just appreciation of any given theatrical event. Conventions of either kind, in order to be accepted by audiences, must be necessary, effective, appropriate, and unmistakable. They must be founded upon things or ideas with which the audience is familiar so that the agreement to accept them will be instantaneous and will seem logical. Above all, they must observe a certain decorum; i.e., a suitability to the occasion of their use. It is to the acceptance of theatrical conventions that Coleridge's term "the willing suspension of disbelief" most aptly applies.

The basic conventions of theatre are easily enumerated. In order for the art to exist at all we agree that Nicol Williamson is Hamlet for the duration of the play, that Olivier is Archie Rice, that Judith Anderson is Medea. We know perfectly well that in the real world these three actual people are far from the personages they represent. What is actually occurring is a psychological substitution. The audience, its imagination stimulated by the action and speech of the person on the stage, automatically translates the pretense of the stage into the realities it is designed to suggest. All theatrical conventions work in this way, as indeed the total art of theatre itself. We know that, in truth, the stage Oedipus does not put out his eyes, that the stage Willie Loman does not die in an automobile accident, that the stage Hamlet is not really slain. But through our imagination we translate the mimicked action into a *real* action and agree to believe it. Theatrical performance is in itself a convention.

The theatre is a world of pretense; it lives by conventions. These agreed upon falsehoods, these permitted lies, these "lies like truth" which are necessary to the existence of theatre function not only to enlist the collaborative activity of the spectator's imagination, but also to elevate the action from the specific to the general, as Thornton Wilder says. The latter function is the more important. It is the very fact that a recognized and recognizable player is impersonating Archie Rice or Medea or Hamlet that "releases the events from the particular" (i.e., from involvement with the real or actual) and lets the action stand for all similar actions everywhere at all times and in all places. This process is a kind of generalization into truth and universality. The convention of impersonation (character in action) is at one and the same time the device that enlists the sympathies of the audience by its specificity, and lends "aesthetic distance" which allows the audience to ob-

Figure 5–1

Festival Theatre,
Stratford, Ontario
*The convention of
impersonation is here
illustrated as Alec
Guinness dies in the
stage character of
Richard III. The death
itself, of course, is
another convention.
(Peter Smith)*

serve, to meditate, to consider, and to conclude. It engages the
audience subjectively so that they *feel with* the characters; it en-
genders in the audience that objectivity which leads them to think
about the characters and the action. Only children and the very
naive (as we mentioned above) assume that actors *are* the characters they represent. Adults know better; they agree to the lie
so that they may apprehend a larger truth.

When we consider the play itself we are confronted with another
convention. We generally see a whole action with a beginning, a
middle, and an end, and we accept the compression of time and
action to be natural. We have always accepted the passage of
time to be whatever the playwright says it is. In the Greek theatre
the choral odes marked the intervals between the actions of the
episodes; in the Elizabethan theatre a momentary clearing of the
stage between scenes marked whatever time division was required; in later periods, act divisions, the dropping of a curtain,
or intermissions marked time intervals, and it is not unusual to

Figure 5–2

Museum of Modern Art
*Lighting and scenery
are conventions. In
Mielziner's sketch for
Yellow Jack, the canvas
walls of the set are
accepted as solid, and
the directed electric
light streaming through
the windows is accepted
as sunlight.*

find in modern programs the information that a lowering of the lights in the first act (or whatever) indicates that a period of time has passed. As for time of day, we accept that—and always have —conventionally. Elizabethan plays were played in daylight. If an actor carried on a lantern or a torch, it was night. Or he might simply say, "How sweet the moonlight sits upon that bank"— and it was moonlight for the audience. Today we accept without question the fact that a stage bathed in blue light, upon which every actor is visible to us and to each other, is imaginatively a stygian blackness in which the various actors cannot recognize each other. Stage time is often compressed in its presumed passage. If note is made in the action that the time is "now noon," for instance, we think it not strange that it should be "four o'clock" on stage when our watches tell us that only half-an-hour has really elapsed. We take no note of how much time it would actually take for a stage character to exit on a given errand and return; we accept the exit and entrance as dramatic necessities whenever they occur in the action. Years can pass in stage time and we think it not strange; stage time is truly relative to the action.

Stage speech is another convention that has always been with us. The audience needs to hear all the words, so even in the most

Figure 5–3

Carnegie-Mellon
University
*In this realistic stage
setting for* A Touch of
the Poet, *the "fourth
wall" is removed to
allow the audience to
participate in the
action. Directed by
Mordecai Lawner,
settings by Theodore
Woods.*

intimate scenes the performers speak with a volume out of all
proportion to the actual circumstances, and it seems right to us.
Also, no matter what the circumstances of the stage action, lines
are generally delivered toward the audience. It is part of the director's business to see that this happens as naturally as possible. If
one character on the stage must whisper something to another
character, the farthest reaches of the audience hears what he says,
but another actor not five feet away from the speaker does not
hear him *because he is not supposed to,* and we believe that he
has not. Though most people in real life would simply enter or
leave a room as the action dictated, we think it not strange that
the actor on the stage delivers a line as he enters and has another
to mark his exit. We accept the language we hear as true and
right for the performance in hand, although we know that even
in Shakespeare's day everybody outside the theatre didn't speak
in poetry. Heightened language has always been a convention of
theatre and still is today, even in this prose age. What two tramps
of their evident incapacity would *really* talk like Vladimir and
Estragon while waiting for Godot? What "family man" like Mr.
Antrobus in *The Skin of Our Teeth?*

Stage gesture is another convention. While the audience knows
that in the real world the various gestures of people they meet

121
CONVENTIONS

Figure 5–4

Festival Theatre,
Stratford, Ontario
*The convention of stage
gestures—larger and
more definite than in
real life—is illustrated
by this trial scene from
The Merchant of Venice.
See also 11–24 and
11–25.*

may be indiscriminate, unselected, and often unmeaningful, they
demand the opposite of stage gesture: that it be well chosen and
meaningful in the context of the play. Further, it must be "big
enough" to "read" in the audience; i.e., often exaggerated over
what a similar gesture might be in real life. In both speech and
gesture, of course, the stage differs from the movies, for the latter
medium can register on the film the most minute of gestures and
the most quiet of vocalization. That the stage conventions of
speech and gesture are not transferable to the movies was nicely
illustrated in recent years in the filmed version of Olivier's great
Othello done for the Chichester Festival and preserved on film;
his performance, on film, seemed overdone and embarrassingly
"ham."

Overt stage action as well as individual gesture is also a matter
of convention. Sword play is carefully staged to *seem* real, as are
wounds and deaths. The audience accepts the seeming reality of
the gunfire at the opening scene of Shaw's *Arms and the Man*
because such acceptance is necessary to motivate the entrance of
Bluntschli. They agree to accept the pretense that the actors are
really consuming those tremendous meals which are often a part
of the action of plays, even though they rationally know that the
human beings who play the parts of the diners could not continue
to do so in reality for performance after performance. Important
conversations and actions on stage almost invariably take place
down stage and center (where they are most visible and audible

Figure 5–5

Purdue
Professional Theatre
*Stage fighting is a
carefully arranged
convention, as in this
scene from* Romeo and
Juliet. *See also 6–5 and
13–15. Directed by
Joseph G. Stockdale,
Jr., setting by Stuart
Wurtzel.*

to all of the audience) even though in nonstage conditions such a relationship of persons to surroundings might be quite unnatural. It is, of course, the business of the actors and directors to make this stage necessity *seem* natural by the preceding and subsequent movements.

The scenic investiture, too, has always been one of the theatrical conventions. In the classic Greek theatre the scene house was taken for a palace by the audience if the actors said it was, or a temple, or a cave, or whatever was necessary for the action. In Elizabethan times the essentially bare platform stage could be anything from an Athenian wood to "the vasty fields of France," so long as the imagination of the audience was stimulated by the dialogue and the actors to accept it as such. The Elizabethan audience even willingly set the stage in their imaginations if a placard reading "The Forest of Arden" was hung on one of the stage pillars. The audience of the original production of *School for Scandal* accepted without question the seeming entrance of the actors through the walls of the set, because the stage was set at that time with wing flats, and there were no actual doors except in the proscenium arch. Indeed, the whole development of changeable scenery hinged upon the acceptance of rather radical conventions, which obtain even today. We do not transplant trees, or bushes, or flowers, or build real houses on the stage. The painted canvas flats, borders, and set pieces are "read" as such by audiences. And there have been many periods in theatrical

Figure 5–6

New York Shakespeare
Festival's Delacorte Theatre
*A strip of cloth moved
to represent the ocean
waves—a convention of
the Oriental theatre—is
used here in a
production of* The
Tempest. *Directed by
Gerald Freedman.
(George E. Joseph)*

history when structures or objects not even faintly resembling natural objects were conventionalized to represent them. Oriental theatre is replete with such conventions. A fan in the hands of a Chinese or Japanese actor may be a sword, a dish, a pen, a knife, or *whatever he uses it as.* Two chairs and a table make a mountain to be ascended; two flags with a wheel painted on each become a chariot; a painted cloth on two sticks is a city gate. Only enough suggestion is used to stimulate the imagination of the audience. The conventions of the Oriental theatre are many and traditional. Their effect is marvelously childlike and imaginative, abstract and aesthetic. Western theatre since the 1920s, when there was an upsurge of interest in Oriental theatre, has greatly profited from the aesthetics of the Oriental theatre.

Theatre conventions are a game which the audience agrees to play with the actors and their acting space. Greek audiences accepted men playing the women's roles; Elizabethan audiences accepted boys in similar roles. The Greek chorus could be old men, young men, young women, a throng of citizens, or whatever was needed for the purposes of the play. On the Elizabethan stage a handful of people could be opposing armies by the simple expedient of entering from opposite doors and meeting at or passing the center of the stage. In modern musical comedy, the facile singing and dancing chorus can be juvenile delinquents, society spectators at Ascot, cabaret waitresses, or whatever the imagination of the audience is called upon to make them. When a leading character has a revelatory conversation with a maid, a servant, or an almost depersonalized chorus, audiences accept these conventions because the information conveyed in them is necessary to their understanding, even though common sense tells them that in ordinary circumstances such conversations would not take place. In plays presentational in style they also accept the convention of the aside and the soliloquy, because these reveal the inner states of the characters speaking to an extent that the stage action does not; both aside and soliloquy are not even conventionally accepted in representational plays. How many people outside the world of theatre read a letter aloud as they are writing it, or when they receive it? Stage characters always do. How many family groups, gathered for an evening of conversation move every few minutes to different seats? Stage families usually do.

Some conventions were peculiar to particular ages in the theatre and disappeared entirely at later periods rather than changing in form as those we have hitherto discussed. We no longer agree to accept men or boys playing women's roles, except as a joke to which we are privy, as in *Charley's Aunt*. The gloves which were the mark of station for God, kings, and prophets in the medieval cycle plays are a lost convention, although the nobles of Shakespearian plays almost invariably wore gloves. The elevated shoes, padded costumes, and masks of the Greek convention have totally disappeared today, even in modern revivals of the plays in which they were used. Sir Tyrone Guthrie's use of masks in his Stratford, Canada, production of *Oedipus Rex* some years ago was a stylistic innovation for the purposes of that performance only, as was their more recent use in the Minnesota Theatre Company's *House of Atreus*. The "heroic feathers"—ostrich plumes in the coiffure or on the hat—which actors and actresses wore in the tragedy of the neoclassic period did not outlive that time, nor did the "cloak to go invisible in" which was a convention of the Elizabethan theatre. The eye patch which completely disguised the eighteenth-century actor, although he otherwise looked just as

Figure 5–7

Minnesota
Theatre Company
*In classic Greek times,
actors wore masks and
men played the women's
roles, as here, in the
Minnesota Theatre
Company's production
of* The House of Atreus, *directed by Sir Tyrone
Guthrie. Douglas
Campbell plays
Clytemnestra.*

he did before is no longer a viable convention. Nor will we any longer accept a Julius Caesar in the full-bottomed wig of the court of Louis XIV, or Cleopatra in stays, beribboned skirts, and powdered wig. Nor do we expect stage vistas to have an upward sloping (raked) stage, as they did in the Renaissance and for a long time afterward. But the modern period introduced conventions of its own. The "fourth wall" convention in realistic staging asks the audience to believe that all the principal pieces of furniture in a room are arranged to face one wall, and that wall is not there—it is invisible so that the audience can see the action. We are not disturbed by the flood of electric light which follows upon a stage character's turning the switch of a lamp or a wall switch. We accept that an actor is actually playing a piano if he sits down to do it, even though the music comes to us over amplifiers from backstage. When a telephone on stage rings loudly enough to be heard in the farthest reaches of the house, and a stage character answers it, carrying on a conversation of which we can hear only one side, we accept that he is talking to an actual person on the other end of the line, and if his words are carefully enough composed by the playwright we can even gather the substance of the conversation. New and untraditional plays often introduce conventions of their own, like Nagg and Nell in the ashcans of *End-game*, and we accept even these because the action of the particular play makes them necessary and appropriate.

Figure 5–8

New York Pro Musica

In medieval times, actors impersonating angels wore gloves, halos and wings, as here, in The Play of Daniel.

So long as any convention is suitable to the occasion for which it is put to use, the audience will accept it and imaginatively make it into whatever it needs to be. All theatre audiences are aware of the limitations of the stage and conventions are a necessary part of that limitation. But whatever conventions are used must *seem* appropriate; they must be unmistakable and effective. The transaction that takes place between audience and players is enhanced by their mutual acceptance of such conventions, and certainly plays of past times cannot be fully understood and appreciated without a knowledge of the conventions which were in use at the given time of the play.

III
The Predominant Genres

6

Tragedy

How many kinds of plays there are will depend, as Elder Olson points out, on whether you are a "Lumper" or a "Splitter." The extreme position of the latter is that of Benedetto Croce, who in his famous article in the eleventh edition of the *Encyclopaedia Britannica* says that every play is unique, and hence there are as many *kinds* as there are *plays*. The extreme of the Lumper position is reached by such a one as Walter Kerr, who, in his book called *Tragedy and Comedy*, allows that there are only *two* kinds: tragedy and comedy. While it is true from one point of view that every art work is a unique creation, yet there are similarities—principles—observed to be at work in various genres. Every play, like every statue, building, musical composition, or painting, is a *construct*, consciously created by the artist, using and arranging those elements we have heretofore discussed. His personal sensitivities, his point of view, his social milieu, and his received tradition will all have a bearing upon his choices and his arrangements. Whether we will or no, historicity is inevitably attached to any consideration of dramatic form. But, just as in the world outside the theatre constants have existed since the beginning in spite of many and various changes, so in the theatre itself. Of these, tragedy is one.

A mystique exists in Western culture about the dramatic genre called tragedy. Since its beginnings in ancient Greece, tragedy has always been held in the highest esteem in Western theatres; the writers of tragedy have always been considered worthier than those whose chief concern was with comedy, and the "worth" or "vitality" of a given age has often been judged on its ability or nonability to produce great tragedies. One of the popular critical stances of our own age, for instance, is that which bemoans "the death of tragedy." Part of this value structure, of course, devolves from the fact that tragedy reached a perfection of form at a somewhat earlier date than comedy, and it was the genre used by the great geniuses of the classic theatre: Aeschylus, Sophocles, and Euripides. The value judgment of the ancients on their theatrical forms has been continuously agreed with down through the centuries, and the volume of words written *about* tragedy since then is in almost infinite excess of the aggregate total of the tragic plays themselves. Our constant preoccupation with the term points at least to an indication that, whaever it is, it is inextricably bound up with the life of the race; tragedy is somehow a vital part of what it means to be human.

For my own part, I must admit that, over the years, I have been somewhat at a loss to understand the seemingly universal confusion about what is tragedy and what is not. I have stood aghast at the ever lengthening literature which debates the subject, at the impressive list of critics, pundits, professors, and playgoers who have wondered aloud and in print about it. For it has always seemed to me eminently clear and unarguable. Tragedy is a matter of life and death: "Life and death upon one tether, And running beautifully together." It is life lived in the shadow of death, death experienced in a triumph of life. It is the tension and the paradox from which arises beauty and exaltation. It is the triumph of the human spirit which fights against all odds for an idea in which it believes, and sinks to glorious defeat with head still high and fist raised against the lowering heavens. It is concerned with no small or mean ambition but with truth itself, whatever that may be—the truth that makes one free, so that death becomes a fulfillment, a magnificent final chord. The "virtual future" of every man (to use the phrase Susanne K. Langer assigns as the province of drama) is death, and he knows it deep down whether he admits it or not. And he yearns for a life style which he can explain in somewhat the same terms as Thoreau used in speaking of his sojourn at Walden: "I went to front only the essential facts of life, [so that] when I came to die [I would not] discover that I had not lived." Tragedy elucidates these confrontations. No one wishes, with J. Alfred Prufrock, to measure out his life in coffee spoons. If he does, he is somewhat ashamed of the wish and longs for the grand gesture, the concentrated *living*—Walter Pater's "sixty to the minute"—which enables him to be reconciled to his

Figure 6–1

Museum of Fine Arts, Boston

Tragic mask from classic times, about 400 B.C.

"virtual future," so that the inevitable death with which his little life is rounded can be met, perhaps even overcome, so that a part of his essentiality, his meaning, survives his physical death.

It is thus that tragedy is rooted in nature—in the nature of man. Political and social structures, metaphysical and ethical systems evolve and change. The paradox of life and death is seen in various configurations in various times and places. And the theatre, being of all art forms the most lifelike, mirrors forth these varied configurations. But at any given moment its tragedies can tell us of man's deepest concern and how he deals with it. Other genres, of course, are also means of dealing with man and his world, but none cuts so deep and so vitally as tragedy; it is the ultimate truth of man's existence: "Let her paint an inch thick, to this favour must she come." Other genres explain away, evade, or ignore "this favour," or try to turn it into something else—a very human gesture. But to this favor must we all come, and that is the secret of our agelong love affair with the genre of tragedy. It is also a basic part of the reason why we cherish *Antigone*, *Hamlet*, *Phèdre*, and *The Master Builder* and go to see them again and again and again, even though we don't write plays like that anymore.

So the literature about tragedy proliferates: the birth of tragedy, the death of tragedy, the idea of tragedy, the essence of tragedy,

the tragic hero, tragic themes, tragedy and the theory of drama, the definition of tragedy, tragedy as a view of life, etc., etc. *ad infinitum*. Thus it has been and, from the outpourings of the modern press, one would guess that thus it will always be. The subject is inexhaustible. One need only stake out a portion of the terrain, and he is off and running. How does one find a path through this critical woods? Or, to switch metaphors, how does one discern the forest faced with all these trees?

One begins, of course, with the work of art itself, as Aristotle did, and develops a substantive definition which is descriptive rather than prescriptive. Hence, if a play is (as we have described it above) a construct including theme or thought, plot or fable, character, language or diction, music or mood, and spectacle, then we should be able to consider a tragic play in the light of these factors and find some constant regardless of historical time and geographical place. That will be our definition of tragedy, as experienced in the theatre. Then we will try to see how the modes (themselves a product of particular emotional climates and inclinations) affected the production of tragedy for the theatre and so produced the varying embodiments of the genre.

The Thought, or governing concept, of tragedy is always one of some magnitude or seriousness, according to the value judgments

of the period in which it is written. In ancient Greece, the tragedies dealt with the replacement of the blood feud by rule of law,
with the nature of the *polis*, or with the conflict between duty to
one's state and to one's family. In Elizabethan times, the great
human motivations came in for scrutiny: ambition, jealousy,
gratitude, love. In Racine's France, the conflict between love and
duty was uppermost; in modern times it is man versus himself,
his environment, or heredity, or his sense of futility, or loss of
identity. But it is always a life and death struggle.

The Plot, or Fable, of the tragedy has one unalterable characteristic whatever its material—the inevitability of the catastrophe.
The plot may be simple or complex, its action concentrated or expansive, its setting single or multiple. But the ending must be a
necessary result of the action as shown; it must be implicit in
what Oscar Mandel calls the "original configuration." The very
action taken from the outset must have within it the seed of
destruction, and that seed must grow organically and inevitably
to the flower of tragedy. Fortuitous circumstances, accidents, or
the possibility of alternatives have no place within this rigorous
construct; there is no "way out." Antigone must bury her brother,
while Creon must uphold the civil law; Phaedra's passion for
Hippolytus must consume her; once Macbeth has set his foot on
the ladder of absolute power there is no turning back. One of our
basic dissatisfactions with *Romeo and Juliet* as fully realized
tragedy is its air of fortuitousness: *If* Friar Laurence's messenger
had not been prevented by his accidental stumbling into the
plague, *if* Romeo had arrived a few minutes earlier at the tomb,
if, if. Perhaps the eighteenth-century producers were right to play
this play with a happy ending, including a reconciliation of the
warring families as a result of the "scares" they had been through.
The action of a true tragedy is a *necessary* one, the ending
inevitable.

The Characters of true tragedy are those that excite our admiration or, as Oscar Mandel puts it, "our earnest good will." Aristotle
was quite explicit in his description of the tragic protagonist:
"a man whose character is good (though not preeminently just
or virtuous), whose misfortune is brought about not by vice or
depravity but by some error or frailty." Succeeding critics crystallized this statement into the hallowed "theory of the tragic
flaw," which harmonized well with the Christian philosophy con-

cerning the sin of pride, and pride was equated with the Greek *hubris*, said to be the outstanding characteristic of the classic hero. So in this field—as in so many others—Renaissance and post-Renaissance humanism effected a reconciliation of Greek and Christian thought. But the majority of these critical structures extracted the character from the world of the play and dealt with him as if he were a reality in the real world. Since he is manifestly a creation of the dramatist, and exists only within the action of the play, he cannot be considered apart from it. He is a *dramatis persona*, a mask of the play, a represented human being effecting and being affected by represented situations and incidents in the total construct. As one surveys the long list of *persona* usually designated "tragic heroes" in our Western culture, from Oedipus to John Proctor, the chief characteristic that emerges (and which causes our admiration) is not particularly pride, but *commitment* —the wholehearted giving over of oneself to a chosen line of action. (Was Shakespeare questioning this concept of the tragic character through Hamlet? In his movie version Olivier undoubtedly thought so, for he made it "the tragedy of a man who could not make up his mind.") The commitment, within the action of the play, makes for a short but intense simulated life which must end in death, actual or symbolic. The tragic hero "burns with a hard, gem-like flame." That is why we call him a hero and admire him. Most of us are moderates, acclimated to compromise, choosing to define "self-realization" as the process accumulated and lived through over a long period of time—"the full life," "the completed life," etc. The celebrated Golden Mean of the Greeks was a moderate vision in this sense; the "flaw" of Oedipus, Antigone, and Medea was to choose intensity and hence brevity over moderation and hence longevity. But the tragic hero "really lives," we say, comparing his fictional state of single-minded devotion with our own real state of distraction and small compromises. He is a *hero;* most of us are *moderates;* some of us are *fools.* Hero and fool are both singleminded, committed. The difference lies in the reason for commitment. The hero is committed to a value system which is the counterpart of that held in esteem by the consensus of his fellow men; the fool is committed to an idea or an action which has little or no value for his fellow men, and the issue of his action is laughable or pitiable, but never admirable.

Life itself may, on occasion, present us with tragic heroes: Alexander, Jan Hus, Thomas More, Lincoln, Woodrow Wilson, each carrying within himself the seed of his own destruction: the inability to compromise upon the point of his crucial commitment. But each of these actual lives is so "fuzzed over" with minutiae, with actuality, that the line of action is not clear. The art of the theatre *selects* the pertinent details, and *arranges* the tragic pattern, and the "poor shadows" on the stage become more real than life itself. The tragic hero lives intensely, feels greatly, has an enlarged capacity for joy and for pain, is "larger than life-size," hence memorable, hence admirable, hence satisfying. Observe there is no mention here of social or economic station. The tragic hero is not *necessarily* a king or a great man, but only thus limited when the milieu of the playwright limits the characteristics we have mentioned to persons in exalted stations. We shall see later how social conventions affected the depiction of tragic heroes on the stage.

The Language of tragedy may be poetry, or it may be prose. The choice here, too, depends upon the accepted convention of the time in which it is written. For a very long time in the Western cultural tradition, poetry was the only form in which plays could be written, and playwrights were called "dramatic poets." But, in the eighteenth century, for various reasons, that convention began to change; the twentieth century is often called "the age of prose." Today plays written in poetry are rare indeed. But, whether prose or poetry, the language the playwright chooses for his tragedy is elevated and serious; it is particular and vivid; it is often eminently "quotable." The point we made above in the discussion of Language in plays in general is particularly applicable here: the characters speak not as their counterparts in real life probably would (if, indeed, such counterparts exist), but as one would wish they would *ideally* speak, if they could. Although, as anyone who knows anything at all about theatre would freely confess, particularly in the present day, it is perfectly possible to have an effective stage presentation with little or no emphasis upon the beauty and fitness of language, tragedies depend for a large part of their effect upon the playwright's facility in its use. There is a peculiar fitness in this situation: as tragedy is the highest expression of man's view of the would, so language is the most highly developed of his skills, the tool which is most

uniquely human. It is almost impossible to conceive of great tragedy without great language, and the tragedies of past times tend
to comprise the heart of the great literatures. Sophocles, Shakespeare, Racine, Goethe—you have only to name them to realize
this fact. Facility with words is no small part of their fame. But
one must remember that every word of dialogue the playwright
sets down is meant to be spoken by a character he has conceived.
Moreover, it must also be remembered that the language of
theatre is not simply words or text, but words in situations, last
actualizations of the action, integral and undetachable from the
whole construct. So the speeches must seem native to each character, must be the expression of *his* thoughts and the reflection of
his character and not the playwright's. Because so often the words
are memorable, we tend to quote out of context and, for instance,
ascribe a misanthropic point of view to Shakespeare through
Macbeth's "tomorrow and tomorrow" speech without realizing
that here it is not Shakespeare speaking, but Macbeth, at the end
of a long, disastrous action. Such examples could be multiplied
almost indefinitely.

The fifth element that marks tragedy as a genre is Mood (a
possible interpretation, as we have seen, of Aristotle's Music, or
Song-making). The mood in tragedy is serious yet exhilarating,
disastrous yet hopeful, a storm ending in calm. Many critics have
pointed out that the province of tragedy is the action which details discord ending in reconciliation, or rebellion ending in the
restoration of equilibrium. And innumerable treatises have dealt
with the Aristotelian "pity and fear" which tragedy is said to
"purge"—the familiar "catharsis" of the classical dictum concerning the purpose of tragedy. It is unfortunate that the fragmentary manuscript which has come down to us from the first
critical theorist does not contain the elaboration of the "purgation
idea" which he promises, and generations of critics have specu-
lated in the light of their own predilections; one may opt for
metaphysical, ethical, political, social, or psychological explanations. But again, in spite of (or perhaps *because* of) these critical
accretions, one must refer again to the *felt experience* of tragedy
in the theatre. Even this, of course, will vary with the social
and psychological orientation of a given audience—the mood of
tragedy in George Lillo's London was quite different, say, from

that in Shakespeare's Globe or in Racine's Paris. There are conceived tragedies that stand the test of time and those that do not. There are bad tragedies and there are good ones. Tragedies as we have known them have elicited a wide variety of emotions: despair, triumph, indignation, horror, resolution, submission, fear, melancholy, pity, and myriad combinations of these. But the grave physical and spiritual suffering which is always the lot of the tragic protagonist gives us pleasure in the theatre. How? Because it is transmuted into art which, as Oscar Mandel says (*Definition of Tragedy*, p. 85), allows us "to ventilate our passions in safety"—a statement which is not very far removed from the Aristotelian "catharsis" whether argued from medical, psychological, or ethical grounds. But the pleasure of tragedy witnessed in the theatre is more than this. It is compounded of a satisfaction that one has encompassed a complete and serious action, a cycle of being; one has become intimately acquainted with a represented human being who has lived fully and intensely through his commitment to an irrevocable course of action; one has enlarged his understanding and his sympathies with respect to the state of man in the universe. This is the mood of tragedy: pleasure through pain. Theme, plot, character, language, and *mise en scène* all contribute to mood, as indeed mood is affected by all these other parts, not only of tragedy, but of the *play* as a form. Again, analysis must only lead to synthesis.

Finally, it is possible to interpret *Mise en scène*, or Spectacle, as *what is represented on the stage*, the "scenario" as opposed to the playscript. Here Aristotle is no sure guide. He tends to dismiss spectacle as "the least artistic and least integral to the art of poetry." (Chap. 6), and goes on to say that "the power of tragedy . . . is felt even apart from representation and actors." Many centuries of literary critics who have divorced dramatic literature from theatrical representation would agree with him. But as were they, so too was he dealing largely with playscripts in the formulation of his *Poetics*, rather than with actual performances in the theatre. The most elementary theatre experience, however, proves to any perceptive member of an audience that the play is more than what one reads. In the theatre itself (which is where the play belongs), it is not at all what one reads; it is what one *sees* and *hears*. To experience theatre one need not be literate (although it helps). We hear the tale of Haemon's suicide, then see his body as it is carried on stage. We watch while the plebeians of Rome reenact the assassination of Caesar on the hapless poet, Cinna, and the mirror image extends and enlarges the horror of the original murder. We see the stricken Macbeth put off the borrowed robes of kingship and reassume the garb of the soldier while he says, "Yet will we try the last," and in spite of his evil we thrill to his courage. We see Phaedra sink to a chair, and the visual image reinforces the weight of the despair which we hear in her words. We see Hedda Gabler fondle the pistol and prophesy her end. What we see is as important as what we hear. In the great plays of our received tradition, the spectacle is implicit in the dialogue; stage directions and descriptions are unnecessary. In these latter days, when all manner of suspicion is being cast upon the spoken word, the playwright must, perforce, include much explanatory material which is not spoken on the stage but which is necessary for the performance. Sometimes, indeed (and not solely in the present day), a play which is a sorry thing in the words of dialogue written down can be electric in the theatre.

In one manner of thinking, spectacle is an immutable part of the play as form, not an embellishment, not an inferior or less important factor. It is this when conceived of as the *living through* by actors of the action conceived by the playwright; without it there is no play. If, however, we limit its application to scenic representation—set and costume, properties and lights—then indeed the complexity or simplicity of all of these is open to infinite variations, and what one sees of these inanimate objects on the stage will depend upon the historical period of the supposed action and/or the conception of the director in staging the play. At a minimum, there must be a space for acting adequate to the demands of the play; at a maximum, the stage dressing must not overwhelm the actors. We shall see in the following pages how the complexity or simplicity of the idea of events transpiring on the stage varied from age to age in the theatre.

What, then, is tragedy as a genre? Few concepts of Western thought have been so repeatedly defined. Here are some representative definitions:

Tragedy, then is an imitation of an action that is serious, complete, and of a certain magnitude; in language embellished with each kind of artistic ornament, the several kinds being found in separate parts of the play; in the form of action, not of narrative; through pity and fear effecting the proper purgation of these and similar emotions.

—*Aristotle, The Poetics, Chapter 6, 360–322* B.C.

A tragedy is the imitation of the adversity of a distinguished man; it employs the form of action, presents a disastrous dénouement, and is expressed in impressive metrical language.

—*Scaliger, Poetics, 1561*

We ought, in tragedy, before all things whatever, to look after a greatness of soul well expressed, which excites in us a tender admiration. By this sort of admiration our minds are sensibly ravished, our courage elevated, and our souls deeply affected.

—*Saint-Evremond, Of Ancient and Modern Tragedy, 1672*

From the stage we are not to learn what such and such an individual man has done, but what every man of a certain character would do under certain given circumstances. The object of tragedy is more philosophical than the object of history.

—*Lessing, Hamburg Dramaturgy, No. 19, 1769*

Tragedy absorbs . . . music . . . then puts beside it the tragic myth and the tragic hero. Like a mighty titan, the tragic hero shoulders the whole Dionysiac world and removes the burden from us . . . tragic myth . . . delivers us from our avid thirst for earthly satisfaction and reminds us of another existence and a higher delight.

—*Nietzsche, The Birth of Tragedy, 1871*

The general law of the theatre is defined by the action of a will conscious of itself; and the dramatic species are distinguished by the nature of the obstacles encountered by this will. . . . If these obstacles are recognized to be insurmountable, or reputed to be so, as were, for example, in the eyes of the ancient Greeks, the decrees of Fate, or, in the eyes of the Christians, the decrees of Providence; as are, for us, the laws of nature, or the passions aroused to frenzy and becoming thus the internal fatality of Phaedra and of Roxane, of Hamlet or of Othello;—it is tragedy.

—*Brunetière, The Law of the Drama, 1894*

From the point of view of the playwright, then, the essence of a tragedy, or even of a serious play, is the spiritual awakening, or regeneration, of his hero.

—*Maxwell Anderson, The Essence of Tragedy, 1938*

I think the tragic feeling is evoked in us when we are in the presence of a character who is ready to lay down his life, if need be, to secure one thing—his sense of personal dignity. . . . tragedy, then, is the consequence of a man's total compulsion to evaluate himself justly.

—*Arthur Miller, Tragedy and the Common Man, 1949*

Tragedy . . . is not a spectacle of evil; it is a spectacle of a constant and inevitable relation between good and evil, a dramatic representation of a law of values.

—*H. A. Myers, The Idea of Tragedy, 1956*

A work of art is tragic if it substantiates the following situation: A protagonist who commands our earnest good will is impelled in a given world by a purpose, or undertakes an action, of a certain seriousness and magnitude; and by that very purpose or action, subject to that same given world, necessarily and inevitably meets with grave spiritual or physical suffering.

—Oscar Mandel, A Definition of Tragedy, 1961

Tragedy . . . is a chosen destiny in a public cause for order, a victory which restores balance and is a consummation.

—Raymond Williams, Modern Tragedy, 1966

In all of these definitions, however diverse in expression, a few things stand out: Tragedy in the first place seems always to assume somehow or other that human life is meaningful and valuable. Secondly, it seems always to indicate that however complex man may be, he possesses a will, that in some sense that will is free, and that, further, he is in some sense responsible for his actions. And finally, tragedy seems to assume that over and above man there exists some superhuman power, or force, or moral order, or fate, or destiny. Hence tragedy is concerned with the problem of evil, which is an everlasting and eternally mysterious question, and says that man wrestles with the question, suffers pain and sometimes death, but is not defeated, because his life is *meaningful*.

Classic Tragedy

Armed with the assumptions detailed in the preceding section, we are ready to consider the major manifestations of the genre called tragedy over the wide spectrum of Western theatre history. Hopefully we will be able to see in what embodiment particular times and places experienced tragedy in the theatre. It must be obvious from the foregoing that one must begin in classic Greece, from whence tragedy itself arose. We will then proceed to neoclassic France, to the romantic tragedians of England and Germany, and thence to modern times. We shall in each instance consider sources, means, and effects, while bearing always with us the idea of the form of the play *qua* play.

The origins of classical tragedy are, at the best, speculative. Aristotle, our best source of information on the subject, says merely that at first both tragedy and comedy were "mere improvisation," that tragedy "originated with those who led off the

Figure 6–3

The Max Reinhardt
Archive, SUNY,
Binghamton

*Photograph of a Max
Reinhardt production of
Sophocles'* Oedipus Rex.
See also 4–2.

dithyramb," and that it "advanced by slow degrees as men developed each new element that came to light; having passed through many changes, it found its natural form, and there it stopped." (Chap. 3) What those "new elements" were, and what the nature of the "many changes" one can only guess. We do know, however, that from prehistoric times in Greece, great choruses of men chanted, at the important religious festivals, dithyrambs in praise of the gods, chiefly Dionysus. Legend has it that Thespis, the leader of a rural Icarian dithyrambic chorus, about the middle of the sixth century, B.C., separated himself from his fellows and, with his single voice, posed questions which they answered. Thus, so the story goes, was acting born, and the dramatic form separated from the epic. The "many changes" probably include the widening of the subject matter beyond the boundaries of Dionysiac legend to include many other characters and stories, and the actual *impersonation* of characters. Aeschylus is supposed to have added a second actor and cut the size of the chorus; Sophocles is said to have added the third actor. Now we are on firmer ground. Aeschylus' play *The Suppliants* (circa 492 B.C.) has a chorus of fifty maidens who carry the burden of the action, and, although the cast of characters lists three men, at no time are more than two on stage at the same time; probably only two actors took these roles.

Throughout the entire period of Greek tragedy, until it ceased to be written, the Chorus remained a part of the presentation. Therein lies its uniqueness. In two of the remaining tragedies, both by Aeschylus (*The Suppliants* and *The Persians*, 472 B.C.), the first voices heard are those of the Chorus, hence it is assumed that these belong to the period before tragedy had reached "its natural form." All the other extant tragedies follow a set division into certain definite parts. First comes the *prologue*, which may be a monologue (as in *Agamemnon*) or a dialogue (as in *Ajax* and *Antigone*), and forms a short introductory scene, briefly acquainting the audience with the requisite information concerning the dramatic situation of the play. Then comes the *parados*, the first appearance of the Chorus, singing and dancing as they enter. They remain "on stage" at it were, until the conclusion of the play. After the opening choral song comes the first *episode*, which closely approximates an act or scene in a modern play. Another choral ode, now called a *stasimon* succeeds the first episode, and so on through the piece until there are four or five episodes with their accompanying *stasima*, and the play closes with the *exodus*, at the end of which the Chorus leaves the stage. Occasionally a *stasimon* is replaced by a *commus*, which is a lyric passage sung by an actor or actors together with the Chorus. The chorus parts are usually divided into *strophe* and *antistrophe*, sometimes followed by an *epode*. On occasion the Chorus divided into halves and spoke responsively. In the later plays of Euripides, the *stasima* seem little more than choral interludes, but both Aeschylus and Sophocles, and sometimes Euripides, seem to use the Chorus as the background of public opinion against which the action of the play is projected, as the vehicle whereby the poet can make clear the universal significance of the action, or as a body of interested commentators on the action. But always the Chorus is *there*. To understand its presence, one must not only be aware of the development of classic tragedy out of the dithyrambic chorus, but also of the nature of the "playhouse" in which these tragedies were performed.

We have already, to some extent, described this "playhouse."

It was a great, open-air theatre, whose heart was the *orchestra* of packed earth, the focus of attention because it was where the bulk of the performance took place. It was traditionally descended from the old dithyrambic "dancing place." In earliest times audiences placed themselves more or less comfortably on the hillsides contiguous to the *orchestras* to watch the performances; at the apogee of classical theatre times, so renowned an architect as Lycurgus regularized this hillside seating by designing concentric circles of stone benches which bordered about three-quarters of the orchestra and ascended the hillside, with special seating (stone chairs with backs and arms) down front and center for the priest of Dionysus and the special state guests. The *scene house* facing the audience on the opposite side of the orchestra usually represented just what it was: a house of some kind—a palace or a temple, and the stories of the plays transpired outdoors because the theatre was outdoors. As we have seen, actors entered and exited into the scene house and often changed character masks and costumes therein, so that the three of them could play all the characters the playwright had invented. In contradistinction to the Chorus, the actors wore beautifully contrived masks which fit over the entire head and were larger than life-size, boots with thick soles to make them taller, and long-sleeved, high-waisted gowns to increase the illusion of height. No attempt was made to depict events other than what might plausibly transpire before a palace or a temple; messengers brought news of removed events, and if it became desirable for the audience to see the issue of events which took place *inside* the building, like the murder of Agamemnon, the great center doors were opened and a wheeled platform was pushed out with the death tableau upon it, and pulled back in again, the doors closing, when its point had been made.

Theatre and play form developed together, a natural growth, with complementary strengths and weaknesses. In a theatre of so great size, large effects were the only ones which could register with the audience—the mass movement and mass chanting of the Chorus, the deliberate enlarging of the size of the actors by mask and costume, their measured movement and gesture. The full sweep of this grand movement cannot be achieved in our modern theatres; one needs to go to Epidaurus where each summer in the ancient theatre the Greek National Theatre does the old plays in an approximation of the ancient style. (Although they do not use masks, the make-up and wigs are heavy and stylized.)

Though the nature of the events and the actions represented were "natural" in that they did not exceed the nature of their surroundings, the productions were in no respect what we would call realistic. They were always given as a part of the great religious festivals (particularly the Great Dionysia of Athens), and an altar stood in the center of the *orchestra* circle. In addition to serving as the place from which the flute player usually performed, it was sometimes also used as a "stage prop" in the action of the play. (It was, for instance, the rock to which Prometheus was bound.) The Chorus, costumed alike, were the Elders of Thebes, or the Young Women who were friends of Electra, or Corinthian Women who knew Medea. They were always men, as were the actors, even when their *dramatis persona* was that of a woman. (Only men participated in the public life of ancient Greece; and, of course, since actors were Priests of Dionysus, they must be men.) No attempt was made, other than in costuming, to pretend that they were women; their voices and their movements were their own, and not falsetto nor dainty. The whole was a grand design, telling the stories which were the cultural heritage of the people, chiefly the legends of the House of Atreus and the happenings in the Trojan War. Because the stories themselves were known at least in outline by many of the spectators, the performance wasted no time in unnecessary exposition, opened the action near the climax of the story, and moved swiftly to its end. Since the persons portrayed were legendary figures and gods, the fact that they were larger than life-size in actual appearance on the stage was fitting, albeit their exaggerated size was probably dictated by the fact that they needed to be seen clearly in the very large theatre. They spoke in carefully structured poetic forms, sometimes moving to chant and to song—this, too, a means to clarity and audibility. They were *representative* men whose actions were public and significant, who moved within an ethical structure recognized and honored by playwright and public alike. On these great festival occasions, everyone was reminded of his heritage, of his duty to the gods and to the state, the while he was moved emotionally by the awesome events transpiring before him, the beauty of the poetry and the pervasiveness of the music. It was a *total* theatrical experience.

Greek tragedy was deeply rooted in the Greek society, in materials and in manner of presentation; it grew and developed with that society. It is the plays which were largely written in the fifth century B.C. that Aristotle, in the fourth century B.C., studied and wrote about. From them he derived the principles that he enunciated in the *Poetics*. The best of these plays, he said, had a single, integral plot, covered a small span of elapsed time, and had but one setting. The single action represented was more interesting when it was *complex* rather than *simple*; i.e., when it contained *reversal* or *discovery*, or both, as the fortune of Oedipus reverses itself from good to bad, and he discovers the truth about himself. The plot was always most important, and the whole thing had ethical substance because the chief characters were kings and great men whose actions affected the *polis*. For this reason, too, the actions had magnitude of import but concentration in the presentation. There were no extraneous incidents; the tying and the untying of the complication had a clear beginning, middle, and end. The end proceeded from necessity or probability, and even though the poet took his actions and characters from known stories, he selected and arranged his incidents to give this necessary effect. Through this artistic arrangement poetry gains its precedence over history, in that its actions acquire a quality of universality, and render things "apparent without teaching." What Aristotle described was a shared and collective experience, at once indistinguishably metaphysical and social, a mature form, emanating from and touching at every point a mature culture and hence not transferable. At the same time, however, it became the tradition of Western culture: "We are all Greeks"—but with a difference.

Neoclassic Tragedy

By the time we get to seventeenth-century France, wherein Neoclassicism produced the store of great French dramatic literature, the ambience of tragedy had changed. The tidal wave of the Renaissance had washed over Europe, and the landscape had been considerably altered. The Greek dramatists had been rediscovered and printed in the original as well as in translation, as had Aristotle's *Poetics*. The zeal of the Renaissance humanists had transmuted the empirical observations of Aristotle into im-

Figure 6–4

The Living Theatre
*A production by Julian
Beck's company of
Racine's* Phèdre. *See
also 4–13.*
(Alix Jeffry)

mutable rules. The new popularity of the pagan Roman writers had elevated Horace to an eminence equal to that of Aristotle, and intervening critics produced several treatises on tragedy which are amalgams of Aristotle and Horace. It was the latter who insisted that the only right form of tragedy was five acts, that the chorus is a necessity, that proportion, good sense, and decorum are mandatory, and that plays are written and performed for "pleasure and profit." In the sixteenth century, several critical treatises had been published and widely circulated and discussed: Daniello (*La Poetica*, 1536), Sebillet (*Art poetique*, 1548), Minturno (*Arte Poetica*, 1563), Scaliger (*Poetices Libri Septem*, 1561), Castelvetro (*Poetica d'Aristotele*, 1570), and Jean de la Taille (*Art de la tragedie*, 1572). Through them one can trace the petrifaction of the Aristotelian principles into rules: High kings and the ruin of great empires form the proper stuff of tragedy (Daniello); the elapsed time of performance should be not less than three hours nor more than four (Minturno); an "unhappy issue" is not essential to tragedy—it is enough if the play contain "horrible events" (Scaliger); the time of the representation and that of the action represented must be "exactly coincident" and the scene must be restricted to "that one place alone which could be visible to one person" (Castelvetro); the "true and only end of tragedy is to move and arouse keenly the passions of each of us" (Jean de la Taille).

Practical playwrights, at the same time, were turning out a wildly varied series of plays, seemingly in complete ignorance of the theorists' rules. Then came the end of the Valois kings, the consolidation of the nation under the Bourbon, Henry IV, and its rise to stature through the reign of his son, Louis XIII, and his intrepid minister of state, Cardinal Richelieu. After conquest, rebellion, turmoil, and wars, everyone desired and sought peace and order and right reason. The intellectuals and aristocrats of France seemed deliberately to begin setting everything in order, from the social structure to the language itself. Richelieu set up the Académie Française in 1636; the Comédie Française was established by Louis XIV in 1680. Between those two dates, by many a "white paper," preface, summary, opinion, and such, the path of French playwriting was charted, announced, and circumscribed. The "dramatic poets" (for so they called themselves) considered that they were *classic* dramatists, and refer constantly to the precedents of the great Greek writers of tragedy. As a matter of fact, much of their work had superficial resemblances to the ancients. But the whole is by no means neo-Hellenic; it would be difficult to point to a given individual work which could be so designated. The reasons are not hard to find.

The world of which theatre was the reflection in seventeenth-century France was a very different world from that of the ancients. There was no *polis* in the Greek sense of the word, no *demos*, no deep metaphysical or mystical ambience, and absolutely no connection whatsoever between theatre and religion. One of the developments of the Renaissance, as we noted previously, had been the secularization of the arts, literature and theatre no less than painting and sculpture. Though another of its characteristics had been the individualization of the human being as distinct from society in general, this point of view acquired a curious emphasis in the court of Louis XIV, who said "L'état, c'est moi." The statement was both figuratively and literally true. The court and the aristocratic society which surrounded it were the only significant members of the social whole, the center around which the whole world swung. That tight little society saw itself first of all as *reasonable*, i.e., functioning entirely on the level of reason in its personal, ethical, and political life. Descartes had just deduced existence itself from thought; the rationalistic philosophy invaded all areas of human activity, including theatre. Francis Fergusson calls the neoclassic playwrights in France the Theatre of Reason (*The Idea of a Theatre*, Princeton, N.J.: Princeton University Press, 1949). Life was a social game in aristocratic circles then, played by rules which everyone accepted and understood. Inevitably, this decorum, this *gloire*, this *pompée*, this exquisite self-consciousness was reflected in the theatre.

From the ancients, whom they explicitly espoused as models, they took characters and subject matters, not only Greek but also Roman. Phaedra, Iphigenia, Andromache, Pompey, Cinna, Horace, Polyeucte, Bérénice, and many more classical figures move through their stories on the French stage. Occasionally there is a Biblical figure, like Athalie, or a legendary one like El Cid, but only occasionally. The French saw the classical personages not primarily as representative (as the Greeks did) of mankind, but as representations of the life of the mind, of the triumph of reason, and the rightness of aristocracy. They also took from the Greeks, as passed down to them by intervening critics, a solidified concept of the Unities of Time, Place, and Action, so that the effect of the plays is one of high concentration with few incidents and few overt *deeds*. The famous controversy over Corneille's *Le Cid* contains the paradox of its condemnation for violating the unities and its praise for strengthening the aristocratic order as Roderigo triumphs in choosing duty over love. The Greek chorus, so alien in concept and so misunderstood in use, they replaced with a series of nurses, attendants, and pedagogues attached to the noble personages; these secondary figures functioned (as they inferred the Greek chorus had functioned) as narrator, transition, prophet, advisor, or sounding-board. Only once was a chorus sucessfully used—the young women in Racine's *Athalie*. The five-act structure, as prescribed by Horace, was inviolate.

In many superficial ways, then, the neoclassic playwrights copied

THE PREDOMINANT

GENRES

the ancients. But the inner life of the plays was entirely different, and the performance of them in the theatres also utterly so. In a closed room, in a closed situation, elegantly dressed characters explore themselves and their reactions in minute detail, the conflict generally centering upon the opposition between love seen as personal desire and duty seen as social and/or political obligation —just the topics endlessly debated *outside* the theatre in innumerable drawing rooms and salons. It is the debate of a self-conscious and self-satisfied society, sure of its mores and confident of the triumph of "right reason." Almost any of Racine's plays can be used as illustration. The suffering is internal, within the minds of the characters; it is revealed in long speeches somewhat like arias, but the revelation is decorous, well-reasoned, and controlled. Physical movement, except for exits and entrances, is at a minimum, so much so that the necessity for Phaedra to sit at the point where she is weighted down by her passion has huge reverberations in the theatre. Incidents are vigorously selected and refined, so that the whole becomes an abstract moment of experience. Bérénice, for instance, is nothing more than a series of dialogues: Antiochus and Arsace (his *confident*) talk; Arsace returns to say that the Queen will shortly arrive; she enters and she and Antiochus engage in a duet as it were; and so on for the rest of the play until at the end Titus reasonably concludes that his duty to Rome is more compelling than his love for Bérénice; she agrees and departs. The only necessary stage decorations are two doors—not even a chair. These plays are timeless and placeless, needing little indication of accoutrements of reality and making no use of them. *Phèdre*, probably the most popular of these plays with non-French-speaking audiences (though an almost instant failure when it was first produced), is one of the few that ends in death for the protagonist; rationality should be able to work things out to avoid complete catastrophe, and if the original story demands that it end in death, then justify it on rational grounds, demonstrate how "the slightest evil is severely punished," and see that "the very thought of crime is made as horrible as the commission of it." (Racine, Preface to *Phèdre*, 1677.)

So exquisite is the poetry of these plays that every French schoolboy knows long passages of them "by heart"; so intricate is the interplay between meter and rhyme and word choice that they are well-nigh untranslatable. Audiences unacquainted with French can have little idea how much of the action is implicit in the words, their rush and ring, their nuance and implication. To unaccustomed eyes the playing of these plays is static, unadorned. The excitement is an inner tension.

In the plays of Corneille, even putting *Le Cid* aside, there is somewhat more overt action. That is perhaps because the strict garment of French Neoclassicism sat somewhat uneasily upon him anyway, but also because his chief subject matter was from the Roman past, where he found the political orientation more congenial. George Steiner (*The Death of Tragedy*, p. 56) says that no other dramatist in the Western tradition had such a sure grasp of the tragedy of politics as did Corneille: ". . . words carry us forward toward ideological confrontations from which there is no retreat. This is the root tragedy of politics." Again it is words which are paramount: words—that ultimate tool and weapon of rational man, that epitome of the neoclassic (but not neo-Hellenic) theatre of seventeenth-century France, its "Golden Age."

Romantic Tragedy

Some conception of the richness of the Renaissance is quickly apparent when one notes how the same basic impetus led to widely differing phenomena. As early as 1516, Sir Thomas More was writing his *Utopia*, and by 1539 there was an English Bible. Greek was studied at Oxford as early as 1500; several playwrights, including Shakespeare's contemporaries Ben Jonson and Marlowe, were products of the New Humanism as graduates of Oxford and Cambridge. The giving of plays in the classical style was a part of the accepted curriculum at these two universities, as well as at the Inns of Court. England had been a national entity with a firm and powerful monarchy for more than a hundred years before France achieved that state. The Wars of the Roses had ended the last great civil strife in England in 1485, and though there was a flurry of uncertainty after the death of Edward Tudor in 1553, and sanguinary horrors under Bloody Mary, the great Queen Elizabeth was crowned in 1558, and she proved a worthy daughter to her redoubtable father, Henry VIII. The Queen herself was a child of the Renaissance, proficient in Greek as well as Latin, and in French, Italian, and Spanish as well. Her long reign (to 1603), her unwavering Protestantism, and her toleration of religious dissenters prevented the catastrophes that ripped France and Germany asunder. She was "Gloriana," undoubted Queen, "with the heart and stomach of a king," in control of matters foreign and domestic, with a sharply appraising eye and a keen intellect that chose her assistants when and where she needed them for the good of the only real love she ever accepted—England. And England loved her in return. All the established orders of society, from peasant to lord, hailed her. She was no less England than Louis Bourbon would be France a generation later. Why then stands there an unbridgeable gulf between the great dramatic achievement of England and of France—a gulf so wide that succeeding centuries have scarcely bridged it, and almost nothing is more foreign to the inheritors of Elizabethan England than the plays of Corneille and Racine?

If, indeed, theatre is a reflection of the world which produces it, then the English world was a very different one from the French. For the action of the English plays is wide-ranging over time and space, the Plots are infinitely involved with often subplots and counterplots, the Characters give voice to a full range of emotions and use explicit actions, the Language is varied and often employs prose as well as verse in varying kinds, and there is often an intermixture of comic scenes in the tragedies. The plays are, in short, in the romantic mode rather than the classic and make a new thing under the sun. Just as in Greece and in France, this new thing comprised the body of the greatest dramatic literature in the language and, in this case, perhaps the greatest the world has ever known. The truth of the matter is that classic principles of dramaturgy never really took root in the soil of England. The native growth was strong and vigorous, and the infusions of classicism administered by the schoolmen and the Continental *aficionados* like Sir Philip Sidney, did no more than perhaps graft a superficial blossom or two on the native vegetation. Comparatively self-assured from the beginning of the sixteenth century, the English intellectual climate allowed for the slow growth and development of native forms, which assimilated along the way foreign influences of varying kinds without losing their identity. About the only major playwright who practiced in the classic mode was Ben Jonson, and all his erudition and argument could not woo his friend Shakespeare to do the same. Even the covey

of "University Wits"—Marlowe, Peele, Greene, and Nashe—
quickly gave up the classic mode which had been taught them at
the universities when they came up to London and began writing
for the popular theatre.

The Theatre, built by James Burbage and opened in 1576, as the
first building in England constructed for the sole purpose of performing plays, adapted conventions for playing that had a long
native history. Traveling companies of players had, for many
years, erected platforms in the inner courtyards of inns to play
for the standing audience in the yards; the more exclusive patrons
gathered in the galleries that surrounded the yards. Even before
that the English public was accustomed to watching the great
medieval cycle plays as they stood around platforms in the open
air. So the theatre that Burbage built was an open space surrounded by roofed galleries, with a platform stage jutting out into
the yard from a tangent of the surrounding building. Members
of the audience stood in the yard or sat in the galleries, as their
inclinations (and their pocketbooks) indicated. They were of all
walks of life, from the one-penny standees to the aristocracy in
the expensive lords' rooms partitioned off from the galleries
nearest the stage. The stage was partially roofed over with a
canopy supported by two columns and brightly painted on the
underside. It was called (symbolically if you like) the Heavens,
and the space underneath the stage was called the Hell. The stage
floor itself had one or more traps and was backed by a portion
of the main building which was reserved for the actors. It probably had a kind of alcove at stage level which functioned as an
"inner room" in the plays, a balcony just above that, and probably another at the third level where the musicians played. It
certainly had two doors leading from the backstage area, one on
either side of the "inner room." The only stage decoration was
that of the house itself.

There are certain analogies between the Greek and the English
playhouses but absolutely no direct influences from one to the
other. This playing space developed to meet the needs of the
players and the audiences; and it strongly influenced the kinds of
plays written to be performed in it. There was no front curtain,
so *Hamlet*, for instance, must end with a stately procession to
clear the stage of all the dead bodies strewn about. There were
few or no bits of stage dressing to give the illusion of place, so

Figure 6–5

Festival Theatre,
Stratford, Ontario
*The duel scene in
Romeo and Juliet, in
period costumes neither
Elizabethan nor modern.
See also 5–5 and 13–15.
(Douglas Spillane)*

the words of the players must paint an imaginative picture: "How sweet the moolight sits upon this bank." The stage space was fluid and undifferentiated, so scene followed scene by the simple device of one set of actors exiting at one door while another entered at the other door. The curtain closing off the "inner room" was opened at the beginning of scenes in which a character had to be "discovered," and then the action moved to the large open stage. "Aboves," like the balcony scene in *Romeo and Juliet*, were played from the gallery above the inner room. Language, painting imaginary pictures in the minds of the spectators, largely carried the burden of settings. But the movements of the actors were detailed and specific, and their costuming was rich and elegant, after the fashion of the day. Sword play, battles, deaths, dances, songs—all were "realistically" presented, and the "grave trap" in the stage floor was opened to present such scenes as that of the Gravediggers in *Hamlet*. This was a "panoramic" stage, as Alan Downer calls it, as compared to the "focused" classic stage; and the drama presented on it was one of aggregation rather than of isolation.

Figure 6–6

Minnesota
Theatre Company
*Sir Tyrone Guthrie's
production of* Hamlet,
*in stylized but non-
period dress. See also
2–3.*

As experienced in the theatre, the English tragedies seem very different indeed from the Greek or the French. For one thing, the audience need have no prior knowledge of the story; the action is cumulative, and all circumstances, characters, incidents, and knowledge pertinent to the world of the play are explicitly given in the course of its performing. It is as if the dramatist and the players were creating a complete world in all of its detail, with nothing left out. It is a concrete, complex, and multisided world, which seems to explore all the possibilities of human nature. Its richness can be almost overwhelming, as when, for instance, one comes to decide how *Hamlet* will be *played.* His proposed action is clear and simple—to kill Claudius, as directed by the Ghost of his father. But before that action is completed, his own nature and the nature of the state of Denmark are explored in rich detail. Macbeth, too, has a simple action: to be undoubted King of Scotland, as prophesied by the witches. We see the beginning of his action: first doubt, then quick confirmation of the possibility of the prophecy as he becomes Thane of Cawdor. His courage as a soldier is taunted by his wife as she urges him to seize the

Figure 6–7

Milwaukee
Repertory Theatre
Othello *performed in
traditional costume.
Directed by Robert
Benedetti.*
(*Gene of Aida*)

opportunity to become King by murdering Duncan; he is sustained through the evil consequences of that evil deed by the enigmatic prophecies concerning his birth and the woods of Dunsinane, and by the time he meets his deserved death at the hands of Macduff we have explored in shivering detail the whole nature of evil in a dramatic experience direct and immediate, an action felt and vivid from beginning to end. So vivid, indeed so lifelike, so detailed are the tragedies of Shapespeare that we have to keep reminding ourselves that they are a *fabrication* (Solon accused Thespis of "telling lies"), a construct imagined and put together by the mind and hand of one man. That verisimilitude to which we respond is the result of art, of selection and arrangement of materials and details. The play is a *made thing*, whether springing from the intuitive genius or the acquired skills (or both) of the playwright as he observes his world and meditates upon its nature and its meaning.

So it is possible to extract from the richness of Elizabethan tragedy the principles of the construct. As from the beginning of the genre, we can consider the nature of the action or conflict, the stature of the protagonist, and the breadth of the theme or Thought; we can note the contribution to the whole of the "embellishments" of Language, Mood or Music, and Spectacle. But throughout such analysis we must remember—as always—that the whole is greater than the sum of all its parts, and that the artistic creation itself is more important than its critical analysis.

Elizabethan theatre was a *secular* theatre, with no direct connection to religion, but Francis Fergusson, in *The Idea of a Theatre*, suggests that it was "as central to the life of its time as an ancient rite," by pointing out in detail the "ritual" scenes in *Hamlet*. It is an ingenious and provocative exercise, rich in implication and demonstration. The idea of theatre as ritual is a popular one these days, but what is germane to our argument here is that the Elizabethan tragedies presupposed a given world order, just as the Greek tragedies did. There are given ethical imperatives as well as an accepted social heirarchy. In the received tradition, man stood midway between the angels and the lower orders of creation, and God was over all. Each man had his allotted place: the human social structure was a reflection of the divine order of the universe. Order and life were divine principles; their disruption the evil which caused pain and suffering. In keeping with the Renaissance emphasis upon the infinite capacities of the individual human being, the Elizabethan tragedies (particularly Shakespeare's) explore the limits of man's action in this universe. So the breadth of the Thought is almost limitless, and, I suppose, in a sense religious, although not theological.

Because the accepted social scheme implied that kings, generals, and noblemen were best equipped in thought and feeling to carry out this exploration, being men of large capacities, the protagonists in the tragedies meet with Aristotle's description that they be men "whose character is good (though not pre-eminently just or virtuous) . . . whose misfortune is not brought about by vice or depravity, but by some human error or frailty." The Elizabethans were not writing to Aristotle's prescription (they largely did not know it) but to the demands of a total scheme that we call by the name of "tragedy." The Characters in these plays are always seen against a given background, they react with a given world, the action of any given play is never a private action but a public one with implications for the total world of the play. The particularity of the presentation of the major figures in these plays (and very often of the minor ones in Shakespeare), gives the impression that "character is all"—they seem so *real*; but a closer inspection (or perhaps a broader objectivity) clearly places them within the framework of the whole. Plot and Character are so closely intertwined and so mutually detailed in these plays that they are almost inseparable and proof of the futility of the argument concerning whether plot makes character or character makes plot. In any event, the action as it proceeds in, say, *King Lear* or *The Duchess of Malfi*, has the same necessity, or inevitability (although it is considerably more complex) than one observes in the ancient tragedies. The stories begin far ahead of the climax, there are many more incidents and complications, but the climax is reached, and the dénouement follows. The Plot has the beginning, the middle, and the end upon which Aristotle insisted.

The Aristotelian "embellishments" are likewise there: Diction, Music, Spectacle—not because these plays were following any "rules," but because these factors are indigenous to the nature of the play. The language of the Elizabethan tragedies is largely poetry—and some of the most magnificent poetry ever written in English. We have already mentioned how quotable much of it is. But from a theatre point of view, the important thing to observe is that those magnificent speeches are also integral parts of the characters and the action, that the lines of the play spring from the situations and the orientations of the personages. The Porter is no less vivid and exact with his few lines than Macbeth is with his many. The Porter, of course, speaks prose, which is fitting for his station in life and for his state of being at the moment he speaks. We no longer argue about whether this scene belongs in the play; it is both structurally and emotionally necessary at this point.

Of songs there are many in these plays; music was dear to the hearts of Elizabethans, and the language itself is music. As for the spectacle, we have already dealt with that in some detail in our discussion of the staging. It only remains to say that the acting was more factual, more "real," had more verisimilitude than did that of the Greek theatre, yet at the same time it was not "naturalistic," but, as befits the material with which it worked, somewhat larger than life-size. Men looked and acted like men on Shakespeare's stage, and the boys who played the women's roles were evidently very believable women.

One of the reasons for the avalanche of commentary on this period of theatre history (and it is indeed gargantuan in total bulk) is that the richness of detail embroidered on the structure of the plays allows for endless exploration; it was by these details that the romantic dramatists of the post-neoclassic period were led astray. Triggered by the perceptions of Lessing in his critiques called *Hamburg Dramaturgy* (1769), German writers turned from the aping of French Neoclassicism to consider the earlier English plays. Shakespeare they found more congenial than Corneille and Racine. What they saw was not the hard core of his structure but the multiplicity of his incidents and the colorful completeness of his characters—the "technique of the curiosity box," as Goethe characterized Shakespeare's plays. So he wrote *Goetz von Ber-lichigen* (1773), with forty-one speaking characters and fifty-four changes of scene. It is a vast panorama composed of many incidents and subplots, with a noble hero who dies at the end. Schiller produced *The Robber* (1781), glorifying the freedom in the eventful life of his hero. The full force of eighteenth-century romanticism swept over Europe in the early years of the nineteenth century, and for the theatre its credo is best embodied in Victor Hugo's famous Preface to his play, *Cromwell* (1827) which called in ringing terms for the complete abandonment of rules and precepts in the theatre in favor of "the general laws of nature . . . genius which divines rather than learns" with no prescriptions save those which are inherent in the subject which the writer freely chooses. For Hugo, as for these post-Rousseauian writers in general, nature was sublime and stormy, filled with the violent, the unexpected, and the irrational, and the plays they wrote reflected these images. The hero now can be noble only if he follows his own particular vision, rebels against confining civilization, and lives intensely under the open sky. Hugo's *Hernani* is the outstanding example of the type. The language of the play is elevated and extravagant, the incidents crowded and eventful, the plot intricate. One would be hard put to derive a feeling of necessity or inevitableness about Hernani's final demise, but the journey is an exciting one, not so much when the play is read, but certainly as it is experienced in the theatre. An example which is closer to our knowledge is that of Rostand's immortal *Cyrano de Bergerac* (1898) which Coquelin played with such bravura when it first was produced, and which many actors and audiences since have loved. The action is really rather incredible and more than a little sentimental, being centered almost completely in the character of the hero, but the sweep and movement of the scenes is infectious, and it is a hard heart indeed who does not shed a tear for Cyrano's demise at the final curtain. Life is not like that, of course, in spite of the Romantics' appeal to nature; but wouldn't it be grand if it were, even for a short time? The mood these plays generate is a very far cry indeed from *Oedipus* or *Hamlet*; the concentration is upon flamboyant personality rather than upon a significant, public action, and the province of tragedy is thereby diminished. Cyrano does, however, have his deep commitment; he does bring his destruction upon his own head, through his own willed actions, and we are satisfied. We do not pity him; we admire him, and we call him a tragic hero. From Shakespeare to Rostand is a long road, but the way is clearly marked.

Modern Tragedy

A number of critics would say that there is no modern tragedy, that tragedy is dead. Some say it died after Shakespeare, some would place the funeral after the great French tragedies. But they are looking in the wrong places for the wrong things. Certainly no one should expect modern playwrights to produce Greek tragedies, or French, or Elizabethan, nor even Romantic; we live in a different world. And certainly our consideration of the three great periods of tragedy is demonstration enough that *no* theatrical period ever repeats itself; there are wide differences among the great three, as there must be, since the theater of any given period reflects the world in which it exists.

Now, if there is one characteristic about our present world concerning which critics of any caste whatsoever agree, it is that it is "fragmented." The term has an infinite number of applications, but in theatre its impact is demonstrably clear. As Francis Fergusson puts it, the great mirror that Shakespeare held up to nature has been fragmented, and the implication is that we can never put the pieces back together again. Here we must observe that if there is anything the human race must have learned in its long ascent from savagery, it is that there is no use in crying over spilt milk or lost worlds. Besides, the great tragedies of those lost worlds we mourn are still vital in today's theatre, as the programs

Figure 6–8

Theatre Collection,
New York Public Library
The Weavers, late 19th
century tragedy in the
realistic mode.

of innumerable playhouses can attest. So we must ask ourselves what principle keeps them alive, why playhouses still draw large audiences for *Oedipus Rex, Antigone, King Lear,* and *Hamlet.* I suggest that we have already considered more than one principle thus far. It may not be amiss to summarize them here: (1) Tragedy demonstrates the capacity of men to suffer in what they and others conceive to be a great cause; (2) The result of this suffering can be an expanded consciousness, an enlightenment; (3) Tragedy explores the mystery of being human and tries the conception to its limits; (4) It treats this life-and-death matter with appropriate seriousness and completeness; and (5) The catastrophe it demonstrates is not only inevitable but inherent from the beginning of the action, just as death is inherent in the moment of birth. All tragedy is in some sense ironic, and the development and present popularity of the genre called "tragicomedy" (which we will discuss in detail later), is but the extreme of the ironic point of view.

It is true that the compact and fairly homogenous worlds of Sophocles and Shakespeare—even of Racine—no longer exist, but to say that therefore tragedy is dead seems to me particularly short-sighted. Surely some of the fragments of that great world mirror whose destruction Professor Fergusson laments still reflect an image of man not unlike, in its essentials, that which the whole did in earlier times. Darwin, Freud, and Marx (chief culprits in the fragmentation, one would assume from the laments of modern Cassandras), have created other reflections, as have many other influences on modern man. But tragedy is *not dead*. It is sometimes crowded out by other genres, and certainly it wears a different costume in the present-day theatre. But its being is unmistakable, and its continuing presence still, as always, makes for some of the most satisfying theatre experiences to be had.

How has the costume changed, and what dress does Melpomene wear today? The first ancient trapping to disappear was the king's crown for the hero. As early as 1731, George Lillo was writing in the Dedication prefixed to his tragedy *The London Merchant*, that it was manifestly foolish to suppose that "Princes, etc." were the only persons liable to fall into misfortune through some frailty or misjudgment; so his hero is a London merchant—apprentice, rather (appropriate to the age when business acumen was beginning to be greatly admired). It's a somewhat sententious and bleak play (modern audiences would not believe it), but it had widening repercussions. It led Diderot in France to develop the *drame*, serious bourgeois drama, and Lessing in Germany to write *Miss Sara Sampson* (1755), in which the catastrophe is believably inevitable, once the reader can get beyond the didactic and sentimental speeches which it contains. The major difference to be marked here is that these "modern" (for the eighteenth century) tragedies took their protagonists from the world of the eighteenth century and not from a preceding one, as had Shakespeare, Racine, and the Greeks.

At the same time that Melpomene lost a crown, she also lost the trappings of poetry, for the writers named above wrote their "bourgeois tragedies" in prose, a language they felt (and rightly) was much more suited to their characters and subject matter. It is not a very supple prose as we would judge it, but the use of prose for entire dramatic works was then in its infancy. As it developed artistic uses, primarily through the novel, it became a

Figure 6–9

Purdue
Professional Theatre
Of Mice and Men,
dramatized from
Steinbeck's short novel,
becomes a modern
tragedy in work clothes.
Directed by Joseph G.
Stockdale, Jr., setting by
Jerry Williams.

potent instrument in the theatre as well, and continues so to the present day.

The tragic hero reached further down the social scale in 1837, when Georg Büchner wrote *Woyzeck*, which is about a man from the lower classes led irrevocably to his doom by the great passion of his life. Then, in the last two decades of the nineteenth century, came Ibsen with *Ghosts* (1881), *Rosmersholm* (1885), *Hedda Gabler* (1890), and *The Master Builder* (1892); Hauptmann with *The Weavers* (1892); and Strindberg with *Miss Julie* (1888). The twentieth century opened with Yeats' *Deirdre* (1906) and Synge's *Riders to the Sea* (1904). Then came O'Neill with *The Hairy Ape* (1922), *The Emperor Jones* (1921), *Beyond the Horizon* (1920), and *Mourning Becomes Electra* (1931); Elmer Rice with *The Adding Machine* (1923); Garcia Lorca with *Blood Wedding* (1933) and *Yerma* (1934); and Arthur Miller with *The Crucible* (1952), not to mention *Death of a Salesman* (1949). The list is by no means exhaustive. Yet as late as 1949 we find this same Arthur Miller feeling constrained to write a defense of the use of "the common man" in tragedy. And in the 1930s Maxwell Anderson deliberately turned to poetry to revive the "dying" art of tragedy, presumably because tragedy, he thought, needed verse to make it live. Fortunately, his *Winterset* (1935) is an authentic tragedy in spite of the meter.

Figure 6–10

Museum of Modern Art
*The final scene of
O'Neill's* Mourning
Becomes Electra, *as
sketched by Robert
Edmond Jones.*

It is impossible, of course, for us to analyze here all the individual modern tragedies which have been written and continue to be written. We cannot even list them all by name. But we can point to some common characteristics, and differences, and perhaps see how some of the plays came to be the way they are.

It is not, of course, as Elder Olson points out (*Tragedy and the Theory of Drama*) the *natural* or *real* subject matter which makes tragedy (or comedy, for that matter), it is the *conceived* subject matter—the *dramatic conception*, "and the kind of art which is exerted to realize it." The scientific impetus of the late nineteenth and the twentieth centuries has been in many ways inimical to tragedy, in that it stressed observation and reportage rather than the insightful conception of an action for which observation and reportage can then be supporting materials. The so-called "scientific point of view" (with us since Darwin) is not the *creative*, since the scientist generalizes only upon the greatest number of individual cases available, whereas the artist/dramatist must find a *general* truth in each case. Among modern playwrights, Ibsen perhaps more than any other illustrates this point. Caught in the web of the realistic mode, imbued with the fever for social change, he nevertheless succeeded in seeing the falseness in relationships, in society, and in the conditions of man which he presented as symptomatic of a general condition. His

Figure 6–11

Lincoln Center
Repertory Company
*García Lorca's
brooding poetic tragedy,
Yerma, as produced by
the Lincoln Center
Repertory Company.
(Martha Swope)*

heroes challenge to the death the existing compromising world order while having within themselves a destructive inheritance from that order; the action is necessary and tragic. Even within the shackles of a minutely detailed realism of setting he succeeds in associating an explicit image of life with the material objects best able to denote and dramatize this image: the steeple in *The Master Builder*, the flagpole in *Lady from the Sea*, and the "vine-leaves" image in *Hedda Gabler*, the orphanage in *Ghosts*. Each has ambiguous, symbolic, and metaphorical implications which make it a dramatic symbol. Much of the power and universality of Ibsen lies in this capacity for universalization. When this capacity is lacking, then realism becomes a tyranny, and tragedy flies out the window.

Another movement in modern tragedy has been an increasing personalization or individualization of the action (our heritage from Freud). It is one of the ironies of modern theatre that Eugene O'Neill once remarked in conversation, "I am not interested in plays which are merely about the relation of man to man.

I am interested in nothing except the relation of man to God"
(Krutch, *"Modernism" in Modern Drama*, p. 118). For he is
frequently the dramatist of the casebook, conceiving actions
where isolated persons clash and destroy each other, as in *Long
Day's Journey into Night* and *Mourning Becomes Electra*, plays
which become peculiarly private tragedies in spite of the author's
intent, particularly in the latter, to use a wide canvas. But in others
of his plays he does succeed in demonstrating the determination
of his heroes to find in the universe something besides themselves
to which they can belong: Yank in *The Hairy Ape*, Ephraim
Cabot in *Desire Under the Elms*, Josie Hogan in *A Moon for the
Misbegotten*. These are tragic heroes. In Tennessee Williams,
who on the whole has probably created the most intensely personal gallery of characters in modern drama (although his plays
more generally belong to the genre of tragicomedy than to that of
tragedy), the most successful show these characters struggling for
something outside themselves: Amanda Wingfield in *The Glass
Menagerie* and Blanche in *A Streetcar Named Desire* are fighting
for human dignity and worth, however poor their weapons.
Blanche, particularly, is struggling against being reduced to an
animal and having her world reduced to the animal level; she ends
in madness. Human beings cannot be dignified if they are regarded
as animals. The conceived action of a tragedy must somehow
stretch beyond the private and the completely personal; it must
mean more than simply "the Mannons are having a bad time
of it."

A third tendency of modern tragedy is that which sinks the
individual in the mass and, following Marxist tendencies, conceives the dramatic conflict in class terms. Perhaps the earliest
play to do this is Hauptmann's *The Weavers* (1892), where the
explicit struggle is between workers and "management." The
expressionists of the period immediately following World War I
often wrote in this vein: Elmer Rice's *The Adding Machine* is one
example. Others are Ernst Toller's *Masse Mensch* (1921), and
Georg Kaiser's *Gas J* and *Gas JJ* (1918–1920), in which indus-
trialism crashes to destruction. Odets' *Golden Boy* (1937) shows
the sensitive talented protagonist being led to his destruction by
economic pressures. Even Anouilh's *Antigone* (1944) glorifies the
stand of the protagonist against bureaucratic oppression. The

Figure 6–12

New York University
*Maxwell Anderson's
modern tragedy,*
Winterset, *which plays
poetic language against
starkly realistic sets and
costumes. Directed by
William Vorenberg,
designed by Stephen
Palestrant.*

stand of the Marxists in general, however, tends toward optimism in that the economic ills can be cured by revolution and the triumph of the workers. Brecht, whose works could not be called tragedies, is their most able spokesman. And, in a way, the Fabian socialism which is the underlying theme of so many of the plays of G. B. Shaw (in no way either a writer of tragedy) is a kind of Marxian solution. The very emphasis of Marxist thought on the collective rather than on individual action tends to lead playwrights of this persuasion to comedy, tragicomedy, and other forms rather than to tragedy, but the Marxist influence is discernible and active in modern tragedy.

The fourth major influence on modern thinking—existentialism—we will deal with later in our consideration of new forms. Here it might be salutary if we tried to summarize, in terms of Aristotle's "necessities," the form of modern tragedy.

The Thought of modern tragedy has been influenced by the three great streams of discovery and statement (end products of the investigative mind of reasoning man) called Darwinism, Marxism, and Freudianism. If we can be forgiven an almost unpardonable oversimplification, we might summarize their influence as follows. The first says that man's life is entirely shaped by his social and physical environment, that he lives in a world where survival belongs to "the fittest"; i.e., to the biologically strong, to the ruthless. The second poses the same question of survival but equates it with economic warfare, where the individual is caught in an historical movement which pits the have's against the have not's. The third turns the struggle for survival inward and makes man the victim of his inner drives, the libido and the ego. But whether the playwright is primarily concerned with one or the other of these concepts, his construct puts man at the center of the theatre, where he has always been—struggling desperately to express himself, to find a meaning for his existence, to commit himself to something larger than himself, to find his true nature and give his life some meaning. So, in spite of the fragmentation which Professor Fergusson deplores, the essential reflection given back by the broken pieces is, in modern tragedy, what it has always been in the tragic mirror. The lights are a little lower, the reflection is a little dimmer, less hopeful, and less distinguishable —but *present.*

The Plots of modern tragedy, no matter what the conventions through which they are expressed, do have a recognizable protagonist and an antagonistic symbol of some sort, though it may be inner, economic, or environmental. Since the loosening of form which came with the beginning of the twentieth century, it is not always easy to identify the old, standard Exposition, Rising Action, Climax, and Descending Action, but a surprising number still contain the ironic reversal which Aristotle so long ago elucidated, and there is almost invariably present a causality of incident linkage. Mrs. Alving, at the moment of seeming triumph in her struggle to realize the "joy of life," is ironically faced with the truth of her son's fatal illness; each of the succeeding incidents in Arthur Miller's *The Crucible* is plausibly linked in a causal relationship. The action of modern tragedy does not always lead to the death of the hero, but then that end was never invariable in tragedy.

The realistic vogue had its effect on the Characters of modern tragedy, as we have seen. Perhaps it has even blinded us somewhat to the true nature of the genre in that it has (by comparison with the kings and princes of the received tradition) made us feel that Willy Loman, Ephraim Cabot, The Bride in *Blood Wedding,* and Yank were too close to us in time to render them larger than life-size. But writers of modern tragedy have increasingly been reaching into the past for archetypal figures. O'Neill tried it in

Figure 6–13

Dartmouth University
*Peter Shaffer makes a
modern tragedy from
historical materials in
Royal Hunt of the Sun.
Note the use of a raked
stage and masks in this
production. Directed by
Errol Hill, designed by
Rolf Beyer. See also 10–21.*

Mourning Becomes Electra with the use of the Civil War era; the French writers (and Hauptmann as well) have used again the classic stories of the Trojan Wars; Arthur Miller goes back to the Salem witch trials for *The Crucible*; Peter Shaffer explores an uncharted country and time in *The Royal Hunt of the Sun*; Robert Bolt uses the great and tragic figure of Thomas More in the highly successful *A Man for All Seasons*, and Ronald Ribman sets *Ceremony of Innocence* in the eleventh century. The "distancing effect" of these time lapses have aided audiences in seeing the archetypal nature of the characters and the actions. But it is even possible to retain in the mind's eye modern "figures against the sky" in their memorable moments on the stage of tragedy: Hedda Gabler fingering the pistols, the Emperor Jones pursued by The Little Nameless Fears, Yerma joyless at the festival, Willy Loman departing for his last fatal ride, Jerry and Peter on the bench in Central Park—all struggling human beings declaring to the death their humanness. The modern tragic protagonist is more generally *man alone*; stripped of his traditional place in a set hierarchy and an accepted social scheme, he fights a lone battle, usually an *individual* rather than a *public* one.

The Language, or Diction, of modern tragedy is almost exclusively prose, as language in the theatre in general has been for a long time now. It has seemed somehow devalued in many of the

Figure 6–14

The American
Place Theatre
*Ronald Ribman's recent
Ceremony of Innocence
is another tragedy
written in modern times,
although its scene is
historical.*
(Martha Holmes)

plays, because the social status of the characters (if the language is to have credibility) has not been such as to allow elevated speech. But Garcia Lorca has found a way to have his Spanish peasants speak poetry; the eulogy over Willy Loman's grave is certainly poetic prose, and the modern French writers in particular exhibit the facility with language which has always been the mark of French playwrights. The new dramatists (as we will see later) tend to denigrate the use of language, but it is interesting to note that even in the most recent work of Harold Pinter (not a writer of modern tragedy, to be sure, but of tragicomedy primarily), critics have consistently praised his use of language, that most human of all human activities.

Mood is colored by the intellectual currents we have discussed above and made tangible on the stage by the combination of the factors of Plot, Character, and Language, combined with Spectacle. In the realistic tragedy the mood of striving against obstacles is enhanced by the factual stage setting, the furniture against which people collide, the stifling effect of heavy drapery and clothing. In the nonrealistic modes, sounds and settings abstract these "obstacles" in varying ways to body them forth on the stage.

Modern tragedy has had open to it a wider variety of treatments —of modes—than any preceding. Ibsen, of course, uses the mode

Figure 6–15

Theatre Collection,
New York
Public Library

Arthur Miller's Death
of a Salesman *is one of
the most frequently
discussed of modern
tragedies. Note the use
of platforms of varying
heights in Mielziner's
set. See also 11–22.*

of realism almost exclusively; as does O'Neill in *Desire Under the Elms*. But O'Neill also ventures into expressionism (*The Emperor Jones, The Hairy Ape*), and the stage settings have varied from the most detailed to the most abstract, for here too the possibilities are endless.

Thus, while modern tragic theory has largely insisted that modern tragedy is not possible, tragic art exists. While determinists reduce man to a victim, and nihilists insist that existence is nothing more than futility and frustration, the *lived experience* of man sees a larger picture. Evil cannot exist unless there is good; man gets what he pays for and pays for what he gets; the core of life is double; neither groundless optimism nor pointless despair is a realistic view of life. Tragedy *is* this *lived* experience; it is pain, evil, and suffering *lived through*, and it is affirmation. Even after so much suffering, and so great a death, life comes back; life ends the play. "Life and death upon one tether, And running beautifully together." Even Giraudoux, in 1941, could say of tragedy that it "affirms a horrible link between humanity and a

Figure 6–16

One of the most powerful and effective of tragedies written in modern times is A Man for All Seasons. *(Friedman-Abeles)*

destiny greater than the human destiny. In tragedy, man is pulled away from his quadruped's stance on all fours by a leash which holds him upright, whose rule he is ignorant of, whose tyranny he knows by heart" *(Bellac and the Theory of Tragedy)*. Modern tragedy, as tragedy always has, details man's search for a *meaning* to his existence, that meaning to be found through suffering and possible death.

Tragedy is by no means the whole of our modern theatre; but then it never was the whole of any previous theatre. From Sophocles to Shakespeare and Racine are more than two thousand years, from Shakespeare to the present day less than five hundred. Some critics, like Nietzsche, insist that great tragedy appears only in a period of settled calm and optimism. Others, like Alvin B. Kernan using the same phenomena, "prove" that it occurs in a period of turbulence, just preceding massive change in the social structure. To say that the modern theatre has produced no *great* writer of tragedy is true. But it does not then follow that tragedy is dead. When and if our undoubtedly *great* tragic drama appears it will certainly not be like that of the Greeks or the Elizabethans, or the French, because it will be the mirror held up to our world, not theirs. Meanwhile, we have O'Neill, and Giraudoux, and Garcia Lorca, and—yes—Arthur Miller to comfort us and to show us many dimensions of the state of being human.

7

Comedy

Comedy is the second great persistent genre which, in some form or other, has been a part of Western theatre since its beginning. Tragedy has been, and often still is, discussed as an entity—as though it existed by, of, and for itself alone. Comedy, on the other hand, is seldom thus discussed. It is more frequently talked of as the reverse of tragedy: tragedy is serious, comedy is funny; tragedy has a sad ending, comedy a happy one; the chief personages of tragedy are of high degree, those of comedy of low estate; tragedy is exalting, comedy entertaining. Few are the writers who "explain" comedy in ways other than as a reflection of or comparison with its generally more respected fellow traveler. What tragedy is not, then comedy is. It has been so from the beginning. In the mutilated *Poetics* which has come down to us, Aristotle seems to spend very little of his time on comedy; his mention of it is peremptory and somewhat condescending. He says that "there are no early records of comedy, because it was not highly valued," and "it was a long time before comic dramas were licensed by the magistrate; the earlier comedies were produced by amateurs." (Chap. 5) Whether in the lost portions of his manuscript there was any comprehensive treatment of comedy is the argument of scholars and for our purposes fruitless. Even a glance at the roots of theatre in primitive societies reveals that it grew in the soil of tragedy; the dramatic concerns of prehistoric man are matters of life and death. Comedy was a comparatively late and bastard form which insinuated itself into the deeper concerns of social groups as Man's inimitable (though occasional) high spirits bubbled up when he became more at ease in his environment. One does not laugh when one is worrying where the next meal is coming from, or from whence the next blow of Fate will descend.

Historically, matters high and holy were Man's first concern, and he was deadly serious about them. The origins of comedy are obscure; one can only speculate about them. Perhaps the first comic touches were inadvertent: the grimace of an inept dancer who inadvertently failed to keep up his part, or stumbled, and the audience was well enough disposed to laugh. Perhaps appreciative laughter was excited by the ridiculous gait of a successful hunter imitating the bear he had conquered as he regaled his well-fed comrades in the feasting following the hunt. The propensity of the audience to laugh at what it considers comic has engaged the attention of critics, philosophers, and more lately psychologists for a very long time indeed, and more often than not discussions of comedy concern themselves with the nature of laughter and what causes it rather than the nature of comedy itself. Over the wide stretch of time it would appear that man has, while enjoying laughter and the comedy which caused it, been rather ashamed of the whole business, relegating comedy to a lower order of excellence than tragedy, for instance, and then trying to justify it on rational and didactic grounds as his critical faculties developed. Less care also seems to have been given to the preservation of comedies: Aristophanes is the only classic writer of ancient Greece whose comedies have been preserved (eleven of them) in their entirety; Menander was for a very long time represented only by fragments, except that the Roman writers, Plautus and Terence, from whom many scripts have descended, frankly wrote in imitation of him. Pre-Christian critics sometimes tried to fit comedy into the frame devised for tragedy, as when we find in the *Coislinian Tractate* (2–4 cen. B.C.) the following definition:

Comedy is an imitation of an action that is ludicrous and imperfect, of sufficient length, in embellished language, the several kinds of embellishment being separately found in the several parts of the play, directly presented by persons acting, and not given through narrative; through pleasure and laughter effecting the purgation of the like emotions. It has laughter for its mother. [Lane Cooper trans.]

It was not just the writers of the Christian era who insisted that comedy, like the Scriptures, be "profitable for reproof, for correction, for instruction in righteousness." Plato, in his *Philebus* (c. 360–354 B.C.) seems to be insisting that the mixed pain and pleasure one experiences "at a comedy" is the result of the exposure of the vice of self-ignorance, and John Tzetzes says (*First*

Figure 7–1
Museum of Fine Arts, Boston
Comic mask from classic times.

Poem to Aristophanes, c. A.D. 1110–1180) of Cratinus, predecessor of Aristophanes, that "to the pleasure of comedy he added profit, attacking evil-doers, and chastising them with comedy as with a public whip." The latter, of course, may be simply a medieval "reading into" Cratinus of the moralism of the critic's own age, but the ideas of enlightenment and improvement through the dramatic form of comedy have persisted for a very long time. This particular *effect* or "final cause" (to use an Aristotelian term) of comedy in the theatre is one with which we at the present day may and indeed have argued. But more germane to our present line of argument are the other "causes"—material, efficient, and formal. In other words, what is the nature of comedy as a construct in the theatre? What are its materials and means? How are these shaped to form the genre we call comedy? That, in general, any lived experience is instructive for the normal human being can go without saying. The deriving of pleasure from such lived experience in the theatre is not solely the prerogative of comedy, for as we have seen, a deep and intense pleasure is the result of the experience of tragedy as well—as indeed of all valid art experiences (or there would be no art).

The criticism that sees comedy as impossible of discussion except in relation to tragedy has some truth on its side. Comedy does not seem to be able to exist except in a society whose value structure has been crystallized, whose ideas and ideals are apparent and real. And we have seen that tragedy has operated in this very sphere, dealing with moral issues, ideas, and ideals.

Tragedy, therefore, would seem to be seminal, comedy somewhat post facto. Medieval audiences would not have dared to laugh at Noah's wife if they were not perfectly sure that Noah was completely right in his unquestioning obedience to God's command. Molière's audience would never have laughed at the misanthrope if the values reflected in the society of which he is a part were not undoubtedly approved. Those infamous three men on a horse would not be funny at all if their audience did not accept without question the values of home, job, and wife for which the greeting-card verse-writer, butt of their humor, stands. There are critics today who say that comedy is as equally impossible to us as tragedy, since we have no settled and widespread value system.

Of the purgative function of comedy we need say little except that it certainly does *not* involve the purgation of pleasure and laughter, or audiences at comedies would leave the performances in a sober frame of mind indeed—and we know that they generally do not. Laughter, however, according to modern Freudian theorists, does serve to discharge from the depths of our social selves our fear and hatred of the foreign, the different. It also, they say, harmlessly deflects aggressions which acceptable social behavior keeps suppressed: the unconsummated wish to strike one's mother-in-law is realized by seeing an actor on a stage do it to his stage mother-in-law; the desire to trip up the smooth-talking egoist of our acquaintance is fulfilled by our seeing the circumstance worked out on the stage. In this way, comedy has a psychologically purgative effect.

There is also some truth in the long-held didactic point of view that comedy is "profitable for correction, for instruction." No doubt the ubiquitous presence of the satiric mode in many comedies has led to this point of view. For, as we have seen, the satiric mode is that point of view of the playwright that seeks to expose follies and abuses. But no mode can substitute for form (although it can *influence* form). And satire is not inclusive enough to account for the whole of comedy. Do we learn by *Twelfth Night* that it is unwise of girls to pretend to be boys, or from *An Italian Straw Hat* that we ought not to leave straw hats hanging on bushes in parks, or from *Summer of the Seventeenth Doll* that manual workers are unstable in affairs of the heart? The amount of learning that goes on as the result of experiencing comedies in the theatre is in many cases, if not in all, implicit and not explicit; hardly anyone ever goes to theatre of any kind expecting to learn something, anyway.

The whole truth about comedy is not to be found in any of these partial truths. But two more observations may be in order before we try to see the nature of the Aristotelian "necessities" in the genre of comedy. The *social* nature of comedy is unquestioned and unquestionable. Just as a joke is not a joke unless there is someone to hear it (few people tell jokes to themselves; the sharing is most of the fun), so comedy presupposes a social group, both on the stage and in the audience. Suffering can be individual; fun is shared. Comedy is also a mature expression. Just as it reaches its best in mature civilizations, it is best practiced and understood by the mature. Unless especially gifted, young actors are notoriously unable to handle comedy; young children are humorless for anything except the broadest grotesqueries, at which they will laugh if they are not frightened. Maturity brings a scale of values and a deepened knowledge of the world which give comedy its best materials and its point of view. Comedy at its best is, to subvert the Shavian phrase, wasted on the young. In how many college classrooms have I had to defend Molière and the Restoration writers! But to understand them—and comedy at large—is a very maturing process. Let us proceed with our inquiry.

The Thought of comedy is not concerned with the dreadful doubleness of man's existence, with the vital issue of life and death, of death in life and life in death. It celebrates only life; it rides on a wave of sheer vitality. Its impetus is the Shavian Life Force, hence its immemorial emphasis upon the sexual impulse, bodily functions, physical characteristics, and a line of action which takes its protagonists over and around obstacles towards success, towards celebration, towards the establishment of a new or the reestablishment of an older and more desirable order. So marriages and festivals—symbolic or actual— are the immemorial "happy endings" of comedies. A more balanced (perhaps a more *truthful*) representation of man's existence must include the fact of death (hence, probably, the higher esteem he has always accorded to tragedy). But comedy has its own truth. It is the truth of Fortune rather than of Fate, the truth of finiteness rather than infinity, the truth of compromise and limitation rather than that of commitment and idealism. Comedy is practical, not visionary;

objective (both in the sense of detached observation and in that of working for a particular limited goal), not subjective; human or subhuman, not superhuman. Comedy is a reflection of the world as it is, not as it might be. Hence it is chaotic, disparate, episodic, full of compromise, full of surprises, taking the bad with the good, eminently social rather than individual.

The facets of comedy are myriad, as life itself is marvelously diverse and unpredictable. It includes lampoon, invective, verbal wit, caricature, farce, parody, burlesque, humor (in the Jonsonian sense), satire, irony, fantasy, manners, customs, mores, villainy, aspiration, failure and accomplishment, love and malice, generosity and avarice—all the afflictions a tyrannous nature can bestow upon mankind, and all the joys man can wring from nature and the world in his multifarious dealings with them. So it is open-ended, contingent, ethnic, anarchic, a sheer balancing act celebrating vitality. It looks at man and his Destiny and regards the whole business as a mere spin of the wheel of Fortune—now up, now down, but clinging on for dear life. There is no metaphysical world in comedy. Moral judgments of good and evil are largely outside its view, except that, as mentioned above, it has at its core the idea of contrast to an ideal value structure accepted by a particular society or social group. It is primarily concerned with "how to get along" in the world with expedience, with compromise. Its debates are not of moral issues and ideas, generally speaking, but of social behavior and the unwisdom of folly. Its ambience is an *amoral* one. As we look at the various kinds of comedy in later portions of this chapter we shall see how the contingencies and fortuitousness of given circumstances in the real world influenced the Thought of specific comic dramatists.

As one considers the Plots, or Fables, of the comedies which have appeared and are appearing on the world's stages, there would seem to be a bewildering diversity. What is revealed upon closer inspection, is not diversity but a perpetual repetition, a continuing "sameness." The most universal comic plot in the world is "boy-meets-girl; boy-loses-girl; boy-gets-girl," and a very great proportion of the theatre's comic dramatists have used this as a basic plot line. The image of life inherent in the union of the sexes is a universal comic symbol, an insistence upon the on-goingness of existence, not only from the individual point of view of self-fulfillment, but from the point of view of the continuity of the race, the perpetuation of the social whole. From Menander to Murray Schisgal this action has been repeated, in every age and clime, and the ending—explicit or implied—is that they "live happily ever after." It is the paramount story-line in romantic comedies such as those of Shakespeare; it wears its rue with a difference, though still of prime importance, in the Restoration and eighteenth-century comedies; it is the very stuff of the musical comedy stage of today. In many other comedies the "boy-meets-girl" fable, while integral, is subordinated to the importance of the "blocking" characters and their idiosyncrasies: Plautus' *Miles Gloriosus*, Molière's *The Miser*, John Cecil Holm's *Three Men on a Horse*. But the interest of these blocking characters cannot wholly obscure the basic action, and the play ends in a marriage and/or reunion or celebration.

The other comic fable, ubiquitous but not quite so universal, is that of ambition—the desire of an individual or a group to acquire more prestige, more money, more *something* than they have, and their devising of ways to accomplish these ends. Very frequently the *desideratum* is beyond all normal expectation; frequently the desirer is peculiarly unfit to obtain his desires; often he accepts a compromise or a substitute. The end is the same: feasting and celebration. From Dicaeopolis in Aristophanes' *The Acharnians* to Molière's *Bourgeois Gentilhomme* and beyond, this striving and compromise have been an integral part of the comic scene. The comic hero never dies; even in the old folk plays a doctor stood by to administer life-giving pills to the downed hero.

Characteristically, *complication* receives the most emphasis in the development of the comic plot. The *climax* and the *dénouement* are likely to come in a rush, all near or at the end, with a surprise, discovery, revelation, or recognition that sets everything right and is cause for celebration. Young Marlow in Goldsmith's *She Stoops To Conquer* finds that the girl he is *supposed* to marry is the one he *wants* to marry, and that the confusion has been precipitated by Tony Lumpkin's practical joke. Giraudoux's *Madwoman of Chaillot* triumphantly rids Paris of its potential despoilers in a tremendous *coup de théâtre*. Duke Theseus abrogates the unjust Athenian law on marriage to pair off the lovers satisfactorily in *A Midsummer Night's Dream*. The subtitle of Goldsmith's play is "The Mistakes of a Night"; the word mistakes could almost be taken as a synonym for comedy: mistaken

Figure 7–2

Festival Theatre,
Stratford, Ontario
*Falstaff, the paradigm of
comic characters,
cavorts in* The Merry
Wives of Windsor.
*Directed by Michael
Langham.*
(Douglas Spillane)

interpretations of actions and situations, mistaken identities—
these are the very stuff of the comic plot. Another characteristic
is that of "doubleness": the story of Rose and Lacy in Dekker's
The Shoemaker's Holiday is paralleled by that of Ralph and Jane;
there are two sets of lovers in Molière's *The Miser* and four in
A Midsummer Night's Dream, five if you count Pyramus and
Thisbe. Subplots abound in comedy—complications are funny in
their own right; they are "inherently absurd" as Northrop Frye
points out ("The Structure of Comedy" from *Anatomy of Criticism*, Princeton University Press, 1957). Comic plots are most
frequently episodic. Since complication and surprises are inherent
qualities, no one asks for logical unfolding development. The
most that one requires is that in retrospect the action should
seem logical within the given circumstances of the play. That is
another reason why the comic dramatist so frequently uses
doubleness —if you are inclined not to accept a single instance or
happening, the fact that it is paralleled or reflected in a similar
instance or happening within the same sequence of events will
probably persuade you to accept it. *Exposition* in the comic plot
is generally held to a minimum, and revealed at strategic spots
throughout the action. The term *inevitability*, which figures so

Figure 7–3

Front Street Theatre
Murray Schisgal's Luv
*is a recent redeployment
of an ancient and
continuing comic
plot-line.*

large in the tragic plot, has no applicability in comedy. We know
that there will be a happy ending, and our interest is maintained
in observing the manipulations of the dramatist to bring about
that desirable end. No matter what the complications, *life* must
triumph in the end; the despoiler must be spoiled, the blocking
characters got round, revelry must go forward—and more often
than not those characters who have impeded the party prepara-
tions (so to speak) are finally incorporated into the party.

Often the Characters in comedy are not highly individualized;
often they represent *types*: the hypocrite, the miser, the braggart,
the pedant, the fop, the profligate, the vain, the inept, the buffoon,
the "fall guy." As Albert Cook points out in *The Dark Voyage
and The Golden Mean* (1940), the comic character almost never
represents the norm, which laughs at him and expels him from the
given, "normal" society. Molière's misanthrope is a classic example. Even Falstaff, marvelous comic creation that he is, must
be expelled from the normal, necessary society of the court of
Henry V. (The plays in which he appears, with the exception of
Merry Wives of Windsor, of course, are not comedies, but histories; he is, however, a paradigm of the comic character, and has
been so considered since the moment he was created.)

Figure 7–4

Hunter College, CUNY
*It is Grandpa
Vanderhoff in* You
Can't Take It with You
*who lives in our
memories. Designed by
Charles Elson.*

As pointed out above, these abnormal types are usually the blocking characters in the line of the play's action, but they are responsible for most of the fun of the play. The prevailing convention of the *commedia dell'arte* could be a metaphor for universal comic action and characters: The "masks"—Il Dottore, Il Capitano, Harlequin, Brighella, Pantalone, and so on—set up obstacles, schemed, connived, changed courses, or were duped, while the *inamorata*, the *unmasked* young lovers, went a straight path to each other and were united in the end. They were the norm, the embodiment of the life principle which must triumph in comedy. Often they were rather colorless characters, but the *commedia* could not exist without them. This comic pattern, in spite of changes in details, is a constant one. Who remembers the names of all those young lovers in Plautus or Molière or even in *You Can't Take It with You?* It is the Braggart Warrior, Harpagon, and Grandpa Vanderhof who live in our memories. Through these departures from the norm the audience intuits that norm, while at the same time vicariously enjoying the rebellion against the norm implicit in these stage characters. Comedy not only laughs at the follies and foibles of society but also functions as a release from its strictures and as a corrective for its abuses.

We have no intention of implying here that all characters in all comedies are one- or two-dimensional, for this is by no means true. In farces, where the emphasis is primarily upon events and actions, detailed characterization is at its minimum and Plot is more important than character. (No one probes the inner motives of either of *The Odd Couple* or wishes to.) But there are other kinds of comedies. The characters of the comedies of manners, like *The Way of the World* and *The Country Wife*, are fuller, more explicitly detailed; and we feel that we know them better, even though they are representatives of social types in a severely circumscribed society. And comedy like that of Molière is fundamentally founded on character, fully revealed in the action of the plays. In comedy, as well as in tragedy, we tend to value higher those dramatic constructs which reveal character to as full an extent as possible. Indeed, in the social comedies, character takes precedence over plot, as it does in Molière. Gustave Lanson, the French critic, has pointed out (*The Drama Review* [*JDR*] 8:2, Winter, 1963) that plotting per se is the least of Molière's concerns, and he is not very good at it. But what makes him "the first jester of France," if not indeed of the entire world, is his creation of inimitable characters. The key is probably in the explanation Athene Seyler (the English actress) uses in talking about the acting of comedy: that comedy must be "founded on truth and on an understanding of the real value of a character . . . it is only when one thoroughly understands a person that one can afford to laugh at him." (Seyler and Haggard, *The Craft of Comedy*, New York, Theatre Arts Books, 1947, p. 11.) She then goes on to explain the root of comedy as being "lack of balance, distortion, over-emphasis or under-emphasis, and surprise." (p. 16) Each of these appears in the comic character so that he is seen "a little out of proportion," but the knowledge of his truth is basic. There lies Molière's strength, and the strength of Falstaff, and of any other comic character whom we cherish.

It is true, however, that specific differences in age, station, class, nationality, dress, and physical endowment play a larger part in the comic action than in the tragic. Indeed, a whole body of comic literature concerns itself with the generation gap—youth against age. And how effective as a character would Falstaff be if he were not so fat? Or M. Jourdain if he were not so obviously a *nouveau riche*? Or Lord Dundreary if he were not so British upper class? Or Aguecheek if he were handsome and accomplished? Comedy exploits these differences, and its gallery of portraits is an infinitely varied one. Comedy makes no *moral* judgments; its milieu is *social*. "Here," it says, "are all manner of people; look about you and see if what we show is not the way they are. See how people behave under the slings and arrows of outrageous fortune. You may judge if you like; I merely show and

Figure 7–5

*Trygaeus on his beetle
in a recent revival of
Aristophanes'* Peace.
(Kenn Duncan)

tell." The comic dramatist always draws his characters from the
society in which he lives; comedy is always contemporary. He
may, like Shakespeare, set his scene on the seacoast of Bohemia,
or in the environs of Athens, but the characters are his contemp-
poraries, not legendary, not historical, but fabricated out of the
world he *knows*—and that is more than half their fun. "Comedy,"
says Aristotle, "is an imitation of lower types": i.e., those orders
of society, those kinds of actions which are revelatory of the human state but "not accompanied by pain or injury" (*Poetics*,
Chap. 5), since the object is to give pleasure and to cause laughter.

The Language of comedy exploits practically the whole gamut
of verbal wit: puns, invective, derision, raillery, burlesque, and
sarcasm, as well as understatement, hyperbole, bad grammar, and
malapropisms (all contrasts to the normal, or ideal, language);
not, indeed, all of these in every comedy, but however many the
particular construct demands or can bear. But no series of jokes,
each individually funny, can make a play. Almost every Broadway
season sees at least one misguided comedian who seems to think
so. (Cf. Woody Allen's *Play It Again, Sam*, 1968.) For Language
is simply *one* of the factors in the construct called a play, and
whatever words the dramatist assigns to his characters must be
believable for that character in that particular action or situation,

must grow from and contribute to the total comic rhythm of the entire presentation. Basically, as Elder Olson points out (*The Theory of Comedy*), there are two kinds of comic diction: that which makes the speaker himself comic, and that which makes persons other than the speaker comic. The first includes absurd characteristics of speech itself: faults of enunciation, grammar, or dialects (all departures from the norm or accepted modes of speech). It also includes inflated language, or bombast, as when the speaker uses a level of speech too formal for its content. Here also are those speeches which are too prolix, like that of Arnolphe in *School for Wives* as he explains to Agnes why she is to marry him instead of the young Horace, or too concise, as when Lady Bracknell, in *The Importance of Being Earnest*, comments that Jack Worthing's having lost both his parents "looks like carelessness." (Though the seat of this particular joke could be said to have a moral base: that one should think more of parents than to make this understatement.) Finally, this first kind of comic diction includes those speeches and speakers which accidentally "unmask" an action, such as revealing the true feelings of the speaker, or insulting while trying to compliment, or revealing the emptiness of boasting even while the boasting continues. The second kind of comic diction—that which makes persons other than the speaker look ridiculous—range from the harsh and obvious use of invective, sarcasm, and derision through the gentler raillery and burlesque to banter and ironic statement. That is, it may directly state, or indirectly imply, incongruencies. But, in any event, language is, as we have said, simply one of the devices of the comic dramatist, and frequently the *action* of the comedy (the thing *seen*) is of more importance than the language (the thing *heard*), particularly in farce.

As we discuss the Mood of comedy, we are inexorably led to a brief consideration of the *comic* itself. For comedies have included all manner of naturally disastrous events: war, pillage, murder, rape, and insanity, as well as a host of other minor disasters. Indeed, one of the more delightful of modern comedies, Joseph Kesselring's *Arsenic and Old Lace* (1941) includes not one but twelve murders. The secret, of course, lies in the treatment, in the mood engendered in his audience by the playwright. All the *signs* he uses in the play—speech and action—indicate that *in these circumstances* the matter is not to be taken *seriously*, that *in this case* there is a disjunction of values, that those things which in other circumstances would have value (good or evil) are here of *no value*, and that, in any case, the personages involved in *this* action are distorted, out of proportion, lacking balance. Or they have not made the normal distinction between fact and fantasy; they are acting out what normal people (like us) would suppress. A particular kind of *depreciation* is involved; both person and action in comedy are shown to be not only not the object of serious concern but also the absolute *contrary* of serious concern. *Born Yesterday* (1946) is a good comedy because (among its other comic devices) the things which in other circumstances we would value—money, position, power—are herein shown to be the absolute contrary of serious concern. The capacity of comedy for the disjunction of values makes it very often anarchic, revolutionary, and salutary and is probably responsible for the statements of critics that comedy is objective and intellectual as compared with the subjectivity and emotionality of tragedy.

Spectacle, if we conceive it as the *thing seen* rather than merely the stage dressing, is of infinite importance in comedy, for the forms of *visual* humor are many: harmless incongruities, ludicrous perceptions, grotesqueries, slapstick, practical jokes, caricatures, and cartoons. These appear not only in the settings and costumes, but also in the movements and physical appearance of the performers. The very person of Falstaff is funny, being such an exaggeration of the norm; the sniffles of Tyson in *The Lady's Not for Burning* are incongruous with his position as mayor and father; the chocolates in the ammunition box of Bluntschli in *Arms and the Man* are ludicrous because he is a soldier; the character of Throttlebottom in *Of Thee I Sing* is a caricature of the office of Vice-President. The examples could be multiplied indefinitely. The cluttered stage of *You Can't Take It with You*—snakes, cats, candy, printing press, typewriter, easel, and all the other accoutrements of that highly disparate family—is comic in and of itself, even before the action of the play begins. The ridiculous disparity of Petruchio's costume as he comes to his wedding with Kate is a necessary part of the play's action. The ass's head of Bottom is a visualization integral to the action of *A Midsummer Night's Dream*. Also part of the spectacle of comedy are the innumerable chases, hidings and discoveries, beatings, and fallings down that have filled the comic stage since the

Figure 7–6

New York University

*One of the most durable
and famous of anti-war
comedies is
Aristophanes'
Lysistrata. Not only
historically, but also
intrinsically, it is at
the very roots of
comedy. Directed by
Hedy Peters, designed
by Stephen Palestrant.*

beginning of time. Even the scenery "acts" in many comedies: chairs and ladders break, kettles drop, walls quiver, roofs cave in, lights misbehave. Colors in the settings and costumes are often exaggerated and sharply contrasted, and shapes and lines pushed somewhat out of normal. Spectacle, then, in comedy is inherent in the individual actor: appearance, grimaces, gesture, movement, and costumes; in the total stage movement: groupings, actions, the use of props and sets; and in the setting itself, and all of these are integral to the comic effect. Only in plays where the action is confined to the clash of character on character (like Molière's) is the setting a mere background and not an "actor" in the performance. But, of course, in these the scenario, as opposed to the setting acquires added importance.

Thus the comic dramatist, by a certain selection and ordering of the elements of the play, produces for an audience a life experience which generally creates a feeling of euphoria, or well-being, or satisfaction, which may range from gusty and uproarious guffaws to the "thoughtful laughter" which George Meredith would allow as the only province of comedy. If we were to hazard a definition, we might say that "Comedy is the imitation (in the

Figure 7–7

Wayne State
University
*Farce is the oldest and
most persistent of comic
forms. Here, in a
modern revival of* A
Flea in Her Ear, *the
essence of farce is
evident in the
exaggerated actions of
the characters.
Directed by Richard
Spear, settings designed
by William Rowe.*

Aristotelian sense) of an unserious action, whole and of sufficient magnitude, with pleasing language suited to its several parts, enacted, not narrated, which affords a contrast to an ideal and a relaxation of concern by annihilating the causes of concern."

Depending upon the kinds of materials (action and characters), the ordering of these, and the emphases which reveal the playwright's point of view, comedy has generally been conceded to have several types. Not all those which have, over the years, been individually named have viable distinctions, but several are autonomous and ubiquitous enough to need treatment here. Farce is perhaps the most persistent and universal of all forms of comedy; burlesque (travesty and parody) one of the rarest. Falling between these extremes of occurrence are romantic comedy and social comedy (including comedy of character and comedy of manners, which is sometimes called high comedy). Some classifiers would add several more subspecie: satirical comedy, sentimental comedy, rogue comedy, comedy of humors, comedy of wit, comedy of intrigue, and comedy of ideas. But we shall see, as we consider the major categories, that all of these are subsumed under the larger designations. Comedy has been such an ever present genre in the theatres of the world and throughout recorded history that the extreme "splitter" position could make a new category for every time and place. Such a task would be manifestly impossible here and also supremely foolish.

Figure 7–8

Cleveland Playhouse
*The hilarious disguises
and discoveries of
Charley's Aunt make it
one of the most
effective of farces.
Directed by Mario
Siletti.*

Perhaps because three of the major types—*farce, burlesque,* and *social comedy*—often contain satire, often (as it were) exist in the satiric mode, comedy has traditionally been said to "castigate follies and vices." But romantic comedy eschews satire altogether, and given farces and social comedies can and do exist outside the satiric mode. Only burlesque is totally contained within it. Satire and comedy are not interchangeable or identical. The first is a mode, the second a form. Let us now see how the process of comedy works in the major types.

Farce

In many categorical listings, over periods of many years, farce is, time after time, called "the lowest form of comedy," or "low comedy." Such a designation has accrued to farce for many reasons, few of them tenable, the chief probably being that character delineation in depth is at a minimum in farce, and we have always been a character-oriented people. Also, physical actions—pratfalls, beatings, slapstick, and such—are more usual in farce than in other comedies, and we have always tended to denigrate physical activity as compared with mental agility. Finally, farces are likely to contain more and broader jokes on sex than other comedies, and our received culture nominates these as "low" in our scale of values. Thus we have had, for centuries, a kind of *apologia* for farce, even though—all the while—it has been tremendously enjoyed by countless audiences in the theatre. Farce is not "the lowest form of comedy," it is simply one of the types; the earliest and most persistent.

Farce is the ultimate in the *reductio ad absurdum*; its generic force is the ridiculous; its object is laughter. From the ancient Greeks who witnessed Aristophanes' first comedy to the latest "uproarious play" on Broadway, the aim of farce has been constant: to arouse laughter. It has sometimes hit other targets as well, as Aristophanes often did, but the first Thought has been the laughter. Aristotle says that comedy was at first "mere improvisation" by those who "led the phallic songs." Presumably they "at first compos[ed] invectives" while the "graver spirits . . . were making hymns to the gods and encomia of famous men." It was Homer, says Aristotle, who "first laid down the main lines of comedy, by dramatizing the ludicrous instead of writing personal invective. His *Margites* bears the same relation to comedy that the *Iliad* and the *Odyssey* do to tragedy." (*Poetics*, Chap. 4) To our sorrow, the *Margites* has long since been lost, but the Aristotelian message is clear. Comedy, from the first, has *made fun* of the serious pursuits of society by showing them to be *unserious*, by taking away the grounds of their seriousness. All eleven of Aristophanes' extant plays do just this. His method is that of the rhetorician, translated to dramatic means. He makes a statement, recommends a course of action, then shows the results of that action. That first comedy, *The Acharnians*, can be used as illustration. It says, "If you are tired of war, as Dicaeopolis is, conclude your own peace, as Dicaeopolis does, and these are the results which will follow." The conventional structure of Old Comedy is the perfect vehicle for this method: the *prologue* announcing the intention, the *parados* or entrance of the Chorus, the *agon* or the argument about putting the intention into effect, the *parabasis* or direct address of the Chorus to the audience, the *episodes* or illustrations of the results, the *stasimon* or choral song, and the *exodus* of the Chorus, the ending. The Plot is not consecutive and cumulative, the action not probable or believable in the "real" world. Trygaeus, in *Peace*, flies to heaven on the back of a dung beetle to ask the gods for help in ending the Peloponnesian War. Euelpides and Peithetairos in *The Birds* establish a new *polis* midway between heaven and earth because they are completely disgusted with the prevailing mania for litigation in Athens. The methods are manifestly absurd, the action is improbable, the whole sequence of episodic situations ridiculous. But the audience makes its own *inferences* in retrospect, that war itself is ridiculous no matter what anyone says of it, and that real work and service to the community are of much more worth than politics and litigation. Thus, much of Aristophanes is satiric in effect, and his targets are politicians, writers, military men, even the gods themselves. In fact, each of his plays is somewhat like a dramatic cartoon, containing metaphors which debase and make absurd the given target, just as newspaper cartoons do today. The trick is to preserve enough likeness to the target so that it is recognizable to the audience. Needless to say, in farce of this kind the Characters need be no more than two-dimensional, and are not; the Language is rife with puns and witticisms; the Spectacle, or visual image, is of paramount importance; and the Mood or Music is quick-paced and full of surprising changes. Aristophanes is unique. He has no faithful followers, although many of his techniques, even many of his specific "jokes" have traveled long and far. The lampooning and caricature of specific people, the parody and travesty of situations and styles, the satire of mores and accepted beliefs, even specific visual and verbal jokes (Socrates in a basket—Falstaff in a basket; Philocleon in the chimney saying "I am the smoke going up"—the chicken thief in the henyard saying "Nobody here but us chickens") have been used over and over again from age to age.

But Aristophanes and Old Comedy were succeeded by Menander and New Comedy—and farce was never quite the same again. (Scholars designate a transitional period called Middle Comedy, but there are only ephemeral traces of it.) The exigencies of the aftermath of the Peloponnesian War evidently had something to do with eliminating the expense of the Chorus in comedy, and certainly the statute banning the representation of actual persons in the comedies to be performed had a profound effect. For New Comedy, as we find it in Menander and the Roman dramatists Plautus and Terence (who copied him), differs greatly from that of Aristophanes. The Plot is now the one we know from innumerable copies down through the ages: a young man and a young woman are prevented from marrying because she is a foundling, but the action discovers her to be a long-lost, well-born and hence eligible person. Sometimes there is a recalcitrant father like the *Curmudgeon* of Menander, who is made amenable by his rescue from a well into which he is fallen. Sometimes there is a blocking character like the *Miles Gloriosus* of Plautus who wants the girl for himself and has to be unmasked by a series of tricks. The plot line is now generally carried through from beginning to end in a more consecutive fashion: exposition, complication, discovery (or climax), and celebration (or dénouement). There is still generally a prologue, and characters still, on occasion, directly address the audience as the chorus did in the *parabasis* of Aristophanic comedy, and the plays generally end with an invitation to the audience to join in the rejoicing. Like the tragic plot, that of comedy now consists in the "tying and untying of a knot," even though what is stressed is the tying, and the untying is more frequently the metaphorical Gordian slashing, a surprise development. Action is still paramount, intrigue and counterintrigue abound. It will always be so in farce.

The Characters have now become not actual personages but entirely invented *dramatis personae*, who are representative of particular ages, stations, or character traits: old men, young men, slaves, married women, virgins, courtesans, parasites, etc., with differentiations within the types—clever slaves, stupid slaves, benevolent old men, stupid old men, lascivious old men, and so forth. So perceptive was Menander's observation of his world and its people that the representative men and women he created for the stage possessed characteristics of such universality that most of them became prototypes for generation after generation of stage personages to follow. Sheridan Whiteside in *The Man Who Came to Dinner* is a modern curmudgeon; Groucho Marx is the modern braggart, Tony Lumpkin the type of conniving servant, although in Goldsmith's play he is a member of the family. All are hoist on their own petard, in true farce fashion. Right along through history these recognizable characters have been appearing; *Maistre Pierre Pathelin* is a medieval conniver who is finally foiled; *Charley's Aunt* is the center of a more recent and equally hilarious comedy of errors and mistaken identity. From first to last in farce *things* have a way of making trouble for *people*: the well in *The Curmudgeon*, a needle in *Gammer Gurton's Needle*, the hat in Labiche's *An Italian Straw Hat*, greeting-card verses in

Figure 7–9

National Theatre
of the Deaf
Sheridan's The Critic
*is a delightful 18th
century burlesque. See
also 10–20.*

Three Men on a Horse, spaghetti in *The Odd Couple*. And always *visual* humor is of the utmost importance in farce.

It would hardly profit us here to trace its historical descent in detail from classic times to the present, for, although the milieu of the material has changed, the basic ingredients have not—the invention of absurd situation; the exaggeration of character; the mocking, cynical, amoral, indifferent tone; and the emphasis upon visual effects. Since Menander, the hyperbolic *probable* (in contrast to the improbability of Aristophanes) has more consistently been the scene of farce; the personages and the settings are at least nominally of the real world, however exaggerated. And, from the beginning, pace and timing in the playing have been crucial. The conception of farce requires a particularly antic frame of mind; the writing of it a peculiarly unabashed eye and an inventive mind; the playing of it both physical and mental agility as well as an unerring sense of timing. It is one of the most challenging of all the forms of drama.

Figure 7–10

Dartmouth University
Patience *is an example
of the burlesque
techniques of the late
19th century Gilbert
and Sullivan. Directed by
Henry Williams.
(Pierce Studio)*

Burlesque

Burlesque, as we have noted above, is a type of comedy which lies entirely within the satiric mode, as farce frequently does. Burlesque is a parasitic art. It cannot exist without the original. But it is a merry parasite, like mistletoe, even though its purpose is the basically satiric one of pointing out excess to effect correction. It has two forms: parody and travesty. The former ridicules the style of the original, departing from the subject matter; the latter retains the original subject matter and throws the style overboard. To do either the writer of burlesque must be exceedingly familiar with the actual work or style, must understand it on an intellectual level, and must appreciate it on an artistic level. Then he can choose the salient points about which he would talk.

Burlesque has a long tradition. The satyr plays given after the performance of a tragic trilogy in the Greek classic theatre were burlesque. The Vice in the medieval moralities was a burlesque caricature of the Evil One. The Pyramus and Thisbe sequence in *A Midsummer Night's Dream* is a particularly successful bur-

Figure 7–11

Hunter College, CUNY
*George Bernard Shaw
burlesques the
extravagances of
romanticism in his*
Arms and the Man.
*Designed by Charles
Elson. See also 1–7.*

lesque of tragedy. And Shakespeare himself has been burlesqued innumerable times, as for instance in Barbara Garson's *MacBird!* of recent infamy. Sheridan's *The Critic*, Buckingham's *The Rehearsal*, and Fielding's *Tragedy of Tragedies; or, the Life and Death of Tom Thumb the Great* are outstanding eighteenth-century examples. In the nineteenth century, John Brougham in America and Gilbert and Sullivan in England successfully followed this perilous art. Shaw's *Arms and the Man* (1894) burlesques the extravagances of romanticism. In the twentieth century, Philip Moeller burlesqued classical history in such a play as *Helena's Husband;* George M. Cohan burlesqued melodrama in *Seven Keys to Baldpate;* Kaufman and Ryskind burlesqued American politics in *Of Thee I Sing;* and off-Broadway has, in recent seasons, made a good thing of burlesquing the early days of movies, with *Little Mary Sunshine, Curley McDimple,* and *Dames at Sea.*

The mechanism of burlesque is the mechanism of comedy: the elimination of grounds for concern, the annihilation of the *seriousness* of the original, the disvaluation of value judgments, the reduction to absurdity. Cartoon, caricature, lampoon, derision,

Figure 7–12

Festival Theatre, Stratford, Ontario

Ben Jonson's The Alchemist *is a comedy of humors with character names reminiscent of the medieval moralities. Directed by David Giles, designed by Kenneth Mellor.* (Douglas Spillane)

incongruity, and inversion—all these are, at one time or another, a part of burlesque. The type requires a knowledgeable audience if the full impact of the presentation is to be enjoyed (although it is true that such burlesques as those of Gilbert and Sullivan, for instance, can and do have viable lives in the theatre long after the "originals" have been forgotten), and an even more knowledgeable writer. No wonder that, compared with the number of comedies extant, those which are burlesques are so few in number.

Social Comedy

Still, to some extent, within the satiric mode lies social comedy. But (like farce in this respect) not all social comedies are satirical. Indeed, many of them can be so read only by the eye of the beholder, as some people would read Restoration comedy, and Molière. To do so is to impute a moral and ethical motivation which consorts ill with what we know of these dramatists, even when some of their plays themselves might seem to be somewhat satirical. But that is another story. What do we mean by "social comedy," and how does it differ from farce and burlesque?

We have said earlier that social comedy includes what is often called *comedy of character* and *comedy of manners*, and that the

THE PREDOMINANT GENRES

Figure 7–13

This old print shows a court performance of The Imaginary Invalid *with Molière in the title role.*

latter is sometimes called *high comedy*. The distinctions are fairly easily made, and the development not hard to follow. The change from Old Comedy to New was essentially a change from personal satire and robust humor to a socially based comedy; i.e., the personages of the drama were no longer mainly recognizable as particular individuals, but as representations of types prevalent in the real world. From an emphasis on the political side of the *polis* and the ramifications thereof as evidenced in Aristophanes, the emphasis moved to the human side, to family and other inter-personal relationships. What comedy existed in the Middle Ages (*Maistre Pierre Pathelin, The Wandering Scholar from Paradise,* the comedy sequences in the cycle plays) stressed the *social station* of the protagonists and antagonists, and the *commedia dell'arte* derived its masks from various social stations and its subject matter from its social milieu. An interesting parallel de-velopment in England is the *comedy of humors* produced by Ben Jonson around the turn of the seventeenth century. Based partly on the medieval concept of the four "humors" which were thought to govern human behavior (blood, phlegm, yellow bile, and black bile), and partly on the classic types (Jonson was a dedicated classicist), and using type names out of the medieval moralities (Face, Mosca, Corbaccio, etc.), he exposes comic figures who are "abnormal," by reason of having succumbed too completely to one facet of character, and thus rendered themselves absurd. The comedy of humors displays the typical comic attributes of lack of balance in the characters, distortion from normalcy or well-roundedness, and overemphasis upon one facet or trait. Where the leading character is a scoundrel, like Volpone or Face, the play is sometimes called a *rogue comedy*.

Further refinement of characters, more specific attention to their interaction, produced the social comedy called *comedy of character*, of which Molière is the supreme practitioner and very possibly the universal master of comedy for all time. Interestingly enough, he began as a writer of farces, replete with chases, beatings, disguises, and all of the farcical claptrap, as in *Les Fourberies de Scapin*. He had been a close student of both the French and the Italian commedia, knew and admired the "masks," and used their essences frequently in his own creations. But as his skill grew he came to realize that there were other ways to deal with character, other and perhaps better ways to expose selected characters to situations which would throw into relief their peculiarities and demonstrate their ridiculous incongruity with sane social standards. The high social consciousness of his particularly select world fostered his venture. "There is more to a man than his skin, that we should touch him" social comedy—and Molière— seem to say. Nothing is necessary for these plays but the people in them: for the exhibition of character and of human relations all that is needed is an opportunity for social intercourse. Scenery is detachable and unimportant—an interior, an exterior, a couple of doors, a chair or two—and it need not change at all during the course of the action. For the action is concentrated, the existence of the characters arrested at a point of time; they have no personal history, only a social context. They have only such traits as are absolutely necessary to the play, and their language is generally unadorned and straightforward. Even the story line, the plot, is comparatively unimportant; its only function is to reveal character in situations most conducive to the most penetrating revelation.

Alceste in *Le Misanthrope*, Orgon and Tartuffe in *Tartuffe*, M. Jourdain in *Le Bourgeois Gentilhomme*, and Harpagon in *L'Avare* exist in a given social context, and the situations in the

Figure 7–14

Purdue
Professional Theatre
*The total world of this
particular social comedy
is gathered in this
group portrait of the
characters in Tartuffe.
See also 1–2 and 3–5.
Directed by Joseph G.
Stockdale, Jr.,
designed by Robert
Williams.*

plays are for the sole purpose of revealing their characters. In *Le
Misanthrope*, generally conceded to be the best of Molière, there
need be very little physical action of any kind; it is almost completely a "conversation piece." *Tartuffe* contains at least two
"bits" of more overt movement: the hiding of Orgon under the
table to overhear the Tartuffe-Elmire conversation, and the shack-
ling of Tartuffe by the King's emissary at the end. It is character
which matters, and the "interpretation" usually applied to Molière
is that he is, through his characters, revealing the folly of a violation of good sense. He himself seems to support this idea when
he writes in the *Preface to Tartuffe* (1669): "To expose vices to
the ridicule of all the world is a severe blow to them. Reprehen-
sions are easily suffered, but not so ridicule. People do not mind
being wicked; but they object to being made ridiculous," and he
ends that essay by quoting the Prince of Conde's remark that no
one objected to another playwright's piece which "makes game
of Heaven and religion, about which these gentlemen care very
little," while they did object to *Tartuffe* because "Molière's makes
game of them; it is that which they cannot tolerate." Molière's
great plays, in the constant tradition of comedy, destroy the
grounds of presumed serious concern and tellingly caricature a

Figure 7-15

Minnesota
Theatre Company
Congreve's Way of the
World *is a supreme
example of the comedy
of manners, or, as
Charles Lamb would
call it, "artificial
comedy." Directed by
Douglas Campbell.*

Figure 7–16

University of Iowa
*The Country Wife is
another of the
Restoration comedies
of manners which also
uses the device of
disguise. Directed by
David Knauf, designed
by John Kasarda.*

Figure 7–17

Milwaukee
Repertory Theatre
Oscar Wilde's The
Importance of Being
Earnest *rates as a
comparatively modern
comedy of manners, and
the director's concept
in this revival makes
it modern in dress.
See also 3–2.
(Gene of Aida)*

whole gallery of people who violate the canons of good sense, a criteria arrived at by the consensus of a given society. That the canons of good sense with which Molière is concerned are not peculiar to his contemporary world, but generally held by civilized society everywhere, gives his plays a universality and permanence that lesser playwrights lack. No less important is his deep and sympathetic understanding of man in society, and his most meticulous observations of what the social milieu means in human terms. In his astute social consciousness, keen wit, common sense, and capacity for serene amusement he almost single-handedly established the most prevalent form of modern comedy, and his copiers are legion.

One further step of refinement produced the *comedy of manners*—that type of social comedy usually designated "high." It is high in sophistication but narrow in range, with a strictly selected focus. Whereas the comedy of character tends to look upon society as the aggregate of collective human experience, and the "good sense" which it espouses as the collective sanction are the virtues of sanity and reason, the comedy of manners conceives of society as the refined product of conscious artifice embodied in Fashionable Society, and its emphasis is upon the manners nominated as "good" by that Society in playing its game according to its rules. "You have good taste if you like what I like," says the denizen of this narrow world, and "It's how you play the game—whatever the game in progress may be." In this world, correctness of deportment has very little to do with either individual personality or common human impulses. The social amenities are of central importance; the *mode of living* is the essential occupation. They are the best examplars whose impeccable taste, brilliance, and wit most grace the game. Only the most leisured and affluent society, of course, can afford such a game, and it was the leisured and affluent society of the Restoration Court which produced the most brilliant examples. Nothing has touched them since for sheer virtuosity, except perhaps Oscar Wilde's *The Importance of Being Earnest* (1895), Noel Coward's *Private Lives* (1930), and S. N. Behrman's *End of Summer* (1936), or Terence Rattigan's *O Mistress Mine* (1944). Philip Barry's *Holiday* (1929) and *Philadelphia Story* (1939) have much of the same feeling, but in each the virtues of *real* work in a real world are at least introduced.

Figure 7-18

Purdue
Professional Theatre
Shaw's Misalliance *is a*
social comedy in the
mode of realism.
Directed by Joseph G.
Stockdale, Jr., designed
by John Boyt.

The supreme example of the comedy of manners is, without question, Congreve's *The Way of the World* (1700). That "way" and that "world" are never in question; no morality or criticism is involved; its scale of values are completely accepted. Mirabell and Millamant are perfect sophisticates to whom the social graces are matters of supreme importance. The game must be played even as each recognizes the truth and depth of feeling for the other; the delightful scene of the marriage contract maintains the perfect skill of socially acceptable behavior even while it reveals the truth and passion underneath. Other characters in the play fail to keep this perfect balance and make themselves ridiculous: Lady Wishfort, Petulant, Witwoud, Fainall, and Mrs. Marwood.

The comedy of manners is a highly rarified and specific type; only the Restoration period has multiple examples in the plays of Congreve, Wycherley, Etheredge, and Farquhar. Sheridan's *School for Scandal* (1777) is a late-blooming example, and those mentioned above are other isolated incidents. Setting is of little consequence to these plays, since the players of the game are the only important items, except that those written and performed after the high tide of realism in the theatre have been done with meticulously realized and lavish settings. Needless to say, they are usually caviar to the general public who look upon them as trivial, if not inconsequential.

A special niche in the halls of social comedy is reserved for George Bernard Shaw, whose long career in the theatre was constantly influenced by his early allegiance to Fabian socialism and his avowed iconoclasm and intellectualism. He was a great admirer of Ibsen, particularly as the Norwegian treated social problems in his plays. But Shaw's dramatic genius was purely comic. From the earliest to the latest of his plays he deals comically and ironically with subjects more frequently dealt with outside the theatre: war (*Heartbreak House*, 1917, and *Back to Methuselah*, 1921), patriotism (*The Devil's Disciple*, 1897), economics (*The Millionairess*, 1935), religion (*Major Barbara*, 1905), prostitution (*Mrs. Warren's Profession*, 1894), health (*The Doctor's Dilemma*, 1906), and many others. His point of view is almost invariably challenging, his writing rigorously intellectual, and his characters just sufficiently lacking in balance, just sufficiently distorted to be truly comic. And the surprise, which is always an essential element of comedy, is to be found in most of his plays: the ending of *Major Barbara*, for instance, or that famous epilogue to *St. Joan*, which puts it indubitably in the comic genre. Because the effectiveness of the action in Shaw's plays often depends solely on language, his plays are sometimes called *comedy of wit*, because of the "problems" with which he often deals they are sometimes designated *comedy of ideas*. But whatever particular labels may be applied, the more than fifty plays which comprise his work have been a constant ornament to the genre of social comedy and a constant delight to theatre audiences.

Romantic Comedy

All the types of comedy we have discussed thus far can appear more or less frequently within the satiric mode. Romantic comedy never does. It is the child of the Renaissance, and had its most brilliant progeny in the comedies of Shakespeare with few successful examples since. J. L. Styan calls it "humorous comedy" (*The Dramatic Experience*, p. 99), and that nomenclature will help us to fix it in the hierarchy of comedy. Elder Olson insists that none of Shakespeare's fourteen "so-called" comedies except *The Merry Wives of Windsor*, *The Comedy of Errors*, *Love's Labour's Lost*, *A Midsummer Night's Dream*, and *The Taming of the Shrew* are *really* comedies (*The Theory of Comedy*, p. 89), and cer-

Figure 7-19

Northwestern University

Shakespeare's Comedy of Errors *takes its plot from Plautus and is sometimes played in Roman dress. In Shakespeare's own day it would have been played, as here, in Elizabethan costume. Directed by Lee Mitchell, setting by Mary Griswold.*

Figure 7-20

Hanover College

Twelfth Night is a good example of Shakespearean romantic comedy, and the character of Malvolio has joined the universal gallery of great comic characters. Directed and designed by Tom G. Evans.

tainly from the premises he adopts, the judgment is justified. The solution lies in the fact that the generic term *humor* is a larger and more inclusive one than *comic*, and romantic comedy is humorous comedy. The classic inheritance of New Comedy dictates a mode which operates in the *real* world, which sees unabashedly the foibles and follies of mankind, and tends to exaggerate and/or expose them. It is rational and logical; it is concentrated and specific. James K. Feibleman says (*In Praise of Comedy*, p. 183): "In classical comedy the ideal of the rigorous logical order is unqualifiedly demanded by the criticism of actuality. No sympathy is felt for the extenuating circumstances which render that goal difficult of attainment." The romantic, on the other hand, "tends to relax a little from the uncompromising demand for the logical ideal, and to identify its interest somewhat with the irrevocable uniqueness of elements flowing by in historical order." Romantic comedy belongs to the realm of Humor rather than that of the Comic, which is, nevertheless, included in the larger term. Perhaps one more quotation will suffice on this point. In his *Essay on the Idea of Comedy and the Uses of the Comic Spirit* (pp. 72 ff.), George Meredith epitomizes Humor thus:

If you laugh all around him [the ridiculous person], tumble him, roll him about, deal him a smack, and drop a tear on him, own his likeness to you, and yours to your neighbor, spare him as little as you shun, pity him as much as you expose, it is a spirit of Humor that is moving you. . . . The Humorist of mean order is a refreshing laugher, giving tone to the feelings, and sometimes allowing the feelings to be too much for him; but the Humorist of high has an embrace of contrasts beyond the scope of the Comic poet.

Though this essay, as a whole, has much in it that one could quarrel with today, Meredith has here caught the essential difference between the Comic and the Humorous. The latter is a larger term and includes an element of sympathy and understanding not contained in the former. Romantic comedy also, as Feibleman intimates and Northrope Frye explains ("The Argument of Comedy," *English Institute Essays*, 1948, Columbia University Press, *passim*), has an attitude about it which identifies its interests with lost or perishable actuals; it is, as Frye says, associated with the "green world," in a sense the *ideal* world, and moves between it and the "normal world."

In these two basic ways, then, romantic comedy differs from the

Figure 7–21

Hunter College, CUNY
*Romantic comedy
written in the 20th
century is exemplified
by Christopher Fry's*
The Lady's Not for
Burning. *Designed by
Charles Elson.*

other types: its informing spirit is Humor, and its scene is larger. Professor Frye goes on, in his admirable essay, to suggest that the "drama of the green world" descends from dramatic tradition which includes folk ritual like the St. George Play and the mummers' plays, the Feast of Fools, and other folk festivals, in which the theme is "the triumph of life over the wasteland, the death and revival of the year." Thus it is *life* which is celebrated in romantic comedy, the wave of sheer vitality which is the characteristic of comedy of whatever kind and at whatever time, and the canon of Shakespearian comedy cannot be excluded.

It is not only Shakespeare who has written this type of comedy; John Lyly and Robert Greene were there before him, and after him Oliver Goldsmith, J. M. Barrie, A. A. Milne, William Saroyan, J. M. Synge, Christopher Fry, Dylan Thomas, and Thornton Wilder. Even O'Neill's *Ah, Wilderness!* and Anderson's *High Tor* belong here. As always with comedy in general, the given subject matter shifts with shifting tastes from age to age, and in romantic comedy, the particular temperament of the dramatist has been of more than usual influence. This type requires a combination of graceful poetic sentiment and a lively awareness of the lapses from reason that such a sentiment is heir to. Such a balance is not easily achieved, as the plethora of sentimental plays in the history of drama will attest.

Romantic comedy shares with romantic tragedy a Plot which is complete, complex, and cumulative in a pattern of increasing suspense. It tends to be narrative, and somewhat descriptive, with

Figure 7–22

Theatre Collection,
New York
Public Library

*This famous scene
from Thornton Wilder's
Our Town shows that
romantic comedy need
not depend on stage
decoration for its
effects. (Vandamm)*

all necessary action given in the play. Its story starts long before the climax, its action is wide-ranging, there are likely to be many scenes in several disparate places, although Fry's *The Lady's Not for Burning* (1948) and Saroyan's *The Beautiful People* (1941) achieve their effects with compression of both time and place. On the other hand, Wilder's *Our Town* (1938) ranges over time, space, and eternity in locales specified by only the most rudimentary of settings. In *The Skin of Our Teeth* (1942), he uses a wide stretch of time with only two changes of setting: the Antrobus home and the Boardwalk at Atlantic City. Styles of production, of course, as they occur in historical setting, have influenced the treatment of time and space in romantic comedy, but the typical romantic "spaciousness" or "freedom" is generally present. And, as comedy in general usually does, romantic comedy ends with a triumph, a celebration, a wedding, or at the very least, a *hopeful* outlook. Because of its emphasis upon plot complication, its wide-ranging scene in time and space, the type of play usually designated *intrigue comedy* belongs as a specie of romantic comedy. The most typical of these are the plays written by Lope de Vega in the Spanish Golden Age.

The Characters of romantic comedy embrace all kinds and types: Malvolio, Sabina, Bottom, Emily, Rosalind, Thomas Mendip, Isabella, etc.—both "normal" and "abnormal." The normal characters—like Emily, Olivia, and Rosalind—are presented with gentle, sympathetic compassion which sets the "norm" as to what human creatures *should be* (and occasionally are). The abnormal

209
COMEDY

Figure 7–23

APA-Phoenix Company

George Kelly's The Show-Off *is a modern addition to the gallery of great comic personages.*
(*Van Williams*)

characters—like Malvolio, Jacques, and Mayor Tyson—are abnormal only as they depart from the accepted norm posited in the individual play, and are excluded from that accepted norm in the play's action. The scheme of existence in romantic comedy, while often remote from common reality, is true to human nature as observed by a tolerant, gently critical eye. The character portrayals are—it must be understood—not falsifications but based upon deliberate and special selection, just as such selection is basic to other types of comedies. If they sometimes seem to inhabit a dream world, this propensity is no more than most of us exhibit in our own dream worlds which we create from our own desires.

The Language of romantic comedy is sometimes verse, sometimes prose, but always poetic, as befits its untarnished, unsophisticated, and frequently childlike (in the sense of "wonder") characters and themes. As mentioned above, its Spectacle is wide-ranging, and its Mood one of graceful sentiment, lighthearted gaiety, and genial laughter. Caustic satire and serious censure have no place in its charitable spirit of good humor, and are, in the action of the plays, expelled from good society. It moves in an atmosphere of sheer fun and delight in the unconscious absurdities of agreeable human nature.

Figure 7–24

University of Arkansas *Beggar on Horseback derives much of its comic power from its expressionistic technique. Directed by George Kernodle, settings designed by Clay Osborne.*

The genre of comedy ranges from the sharp and caustic satire inherent in Aristophanes' portraits of Euripides in his plays to the still observant but genial picture of humanity that is present in the plays of Saroyan and Wilder. Each of the types that we have discussed here (except perhaps that of Aristophanes and the *commedia dell'arte*) are and have been in use by playwrights since its inception. One of the difficulties of dealing with comedy as a genre is the seemingly bewildering number of different kinds of comedies. As we have seen, this profusion hinges upon the fact that life itself is very diverse, chaotic, and profuse; comedy is the reflection of that life. But the ordering mind of man tends always to arrange the disorder of nature, and what we have tried to do here is to show that even that antic disposition which is comedy has an order and arrangement.

It seems advisable again here to reiterate that every play, of whatever type or genre, is an individual construct, and our intent is not to set up a dormitory of Procrustean beds wherein separate and always unique creations must be pulled and slapped to fit the labels. Comedy, being in every age and clime so sensitive to its social milieu and so dependent upon it, has myriad configurations. It is particularly susceptible to changes in customs and mores and thus is, in many ways, the most ephemeral of dramatic

Figure 7–25

Purdue
Professional Theatre
*Born Yesterday is one
of the most effective
and enduring of modern
comedies. Directed by
Joseph G. Stockdale, Jr.,
designed by Jerry
Williams.*

forms. Nothing is so stale as yesterday's joke. But human nature is everywhere and at all times more alike than different, and insofar as comedy takes its materials from this universal phenomenon it will continue to be vital, whatever its date of birth. What we have tried to do here is to show some bases for the dramatist's selection and arrangement of his comic materials, and the effects to be achieved by that process. Thus we have added one more spoke to the wheel whose center is theatre and whose rim is the world. Now we proceed to another.

8
Mixed Genres: Melodrama and Tragicomedy

Thus far we have dealt with the two great dramatic genres: tragedy and comedy. Each had their origins with the beginnings of theatre itself and each has been the subject of much critical discussion through the ages. We have acknowledged that there have been wide applications of the words *tragic* and *comic* through the ages, and that even their present meanings are applicable to a wider span of human experience than theatre alone. But since the subject of our entire discussion is theatre as an art, and the object of our inquiry an understanding of that form of art, we have talked chiefly about what constitutes the theatrical art forms called tragedy and comedy. We have seen that, although materials and points of view have varied from time to time, each of these tends to be a homogeneous and mutually exclusive dramatic form.

We have now to deal with two genres which are *mixtures* of tragedy and comedy: melodrama and tragicomedy. Throughout almost the entire historical existence of tragedy and comedy, there have also been plays which could not be regarded as either the one or the other. Since these two structures seem to contain within themselves all possible artistic approaches of the artist to his world, anything that lay outside has seemed to the theorists mere mixtures and obviously inferior. Both tragicomedy and melodrama have, until very recent years, been terms of derogation applied to plays which, their critics felt, succeeded (for one reason or another) in *not* being either tragedy or comedy. But audiences enjoyed them anyway, and they kept on being written. At the present day, both theatregoers and critics have achieved emancipation from traditional dicta, and theorists have engaged themselves in the rehabilitation and the analysis of these heretofore "bastard" forms. A "poetics" of each is emerging and, while not yet fully constituted, has advanced far enough to remove the connotations of denigration that have long hovered round these two mixed genres. Although it was Plautus who first used the term tragicomedy in the prologue to his *Amphitryon,* and critical arguments have raged over its applicability in practically every century since, we shall begin our discussion with melodrama, a term which did not come into use until late in the eighteenth century. We do this because, in today's theatre, the older term has much more applicability than the newer. It seems, therefore, much more sensible to dispose first of the somewhat more easily understood, and in many ways the much simpler term.

Melodrama

About the year 1780, the word *melodrama* was applied to two really opposite kinds of theatrical performance. In Germany it was used to designate a passage in an opera which accompanied spoken words with music. In France, *mélodrame* meant a musical passage intended to convey a character's emotional state while he was silent. The practice had been first used by Rousseau in his monologue, *Pygmalion* (1775). It was not until 1800 that it appears on the playbills of Guilbert de Pixérécourt in Paris to designate the new theatrical form of a highly moral plot accompanied by music, ballet, combats, processions, and intricate scenic effects which universally came to be called melodrama. By the time it became thus officially designated, no new ingredients remained to be discovered, and those which were used in varying combinations could trace a long line of descent. The conflict of virtues and vices in symbolic form goes back at least to the medieval moralities, and the ranting, tyrannical Herod of the cycle plays is a prototype of one of melodrama's villains. The distressed heroines, revengeful ghosts, domestic agonies, inflated language, and physical sensations of much Elizabethan playwriting (*The Spanish Tragedy, Titus Andronicus, The Jew of Malta, The Yorkshire Tragedy,* and *Arden of Feversham*) were just the kinds of things that melodrama would later use to good effect. Then, in the eighteenth century came sentimental comedy, bourgeois tragedy, the Gothic novel, and Goethe and Schiller. The first developed as a reaction against Restoration comedy, the second as a reaction

Figure 8–1

New York Shakespeare
Festival's Delacorte Theatre
*Ancestors of the
melodrama are plays
like Shakespeare's*
Titus Andronicus, *with
its extravagances of
action and character.
Directed by Gerald
Freedman.
(George E. Joseph)*

against neoclassic tragedy. Both, to suit the tastes of their wider middle-class audiences, are full of ringing moral sentiments, of pathos and distress designed to wring tears from their audiences. The characters are benevolent fathers, uncles or guardians, generous heroes, beautiful orphans who turn out to be heiresses, loyal friends, confounded villains, serious and honorable lovers, etc. Steele's *The Conscious Lovers* (1723), Lillo's *The London Merchant* (1731), and Cumberland's *The West Indian* (1771) are but three of a host of these. They influenced the *comédie larmoyante* of La Chausée and the *drame bourgeois* of Diderot, Mercier, and Sédaine in France, which possessed the same characteristics. The early appearance of the Romantic Revolution in Germany was heralded by Goethe's *Goetz von Berlichingen* (1773) with its idealized brigand chief fighting against tyranny, and Schiller's *Die Räuber* (1782) which set a character pattern of a falsely accused hero of noble birth, a suffering heroine in captivity, and a cold-blooded villain in a castle.

Meanwhile, Horace Walpole had written and published *The Castle of Otranto* (1765), which he said sprang from a dream; it contains a haughty tyrant, a brace of innocent maidens, a mysterious knight, an unacknowledged heir, and, of course, the castle.

215

MIXED GENRES:

MELODRAMA AND

TRAGICOMEDY

Figure 8–2

National Museum, Weimar

The discursive and wide-ranging romanticism of Schiller's Wallenstein *also influenced the development of melodrama.*

It had the first great success of the novels latter dubbed Gothic, from the antique architectural backgrounds which were characteristic. (Horace Walpole had spent many years creating himself "a little Gothick castle" on the Thames at Strawberry Hill.) The popularity of this novel, plus the literary respectability bestowed upon brigands and such by Goethe and Schiller, led Mrs. Radcliffe, an otherwise blameless married Englishwoman, to write *The Mysteries of Udolpho* (1794) and Matthew Gregory Lewis to write *The Monk* (1796), perhaps the two most popular novels ever written in the Gothic style.

The mixture of high-flown morality, inflated rhetoric, tender sentiments, extremes of character, thrilling music, spectacle, blood, violence, and emotional agony which had appeared in the popular sentimental drama, the brigand plays of the Germans, and the Gothic novel was exactly the combination to thrill and excite the hordes of "citizens" who thronged the new theatres of Paris in the days of the French Revolution. The addition of a little revolutionary ardor, such as appears in the theatre pieces of Tréogaste and Villeneuve in the early 1790s, assured their success, and the

Boulevard du Temple (later nicknamed the Boulevard du Crime) became the world capitol of this new theatrical genre. Pixérécourt's first production, *Selico, or The Generous Negroes*, first appeared in 1793 and was typical of the "dialogued pantomimes" that filled the theatres of Paris for several years. In them were always found ghosts, caverns, cells, conspiracies, battles, and riots. Mostly they were collections of formless scenes, interspersed with music and dancing, but Pixérécourt (a man of considerable personal refinement and learning), determined that scenery, music, lighting, and the movements of the actors should not be left to chance but should be made integral parts of the plays. He had his first big success in 1797 with *Les Petits Auvegnats*, and then in the next three years with dramatizations of two sensational novels by Ducray-Duminil, the second of which, *Coelina, ou L'Enfant du Mystère*, was named "melodrama" on the playbill. Declaring that he presented plays for those who could not read, he went on to write or adapt a hundred and twenty different melodramas in the next thirty-eight years, insisting always that he aimed at a totally unlettered populace.

It was a translation from Pixérécourt, made by Thomas Holcroft, that first appeared in England at Covent Garden on November 13, 1802, billed as melodrama and called *A Tale of Mystery*. Significantly, this production was given at one of the three patent houses (the other two were Drury Lane and the Little Theatre in the Haymarket), and throughout the century the patent theatres continued to play melodramas—new ones written especially for them, and old ones which they stole from the minor theatres. A contributing factor to the burgeoning of melodrama in England was the old Licensing Act of 1737, which had confined the performance of "legitimate drama" (regular comedy and tragedy) to the patent houses, although they could also play anything else they liked. Legitimate drama shortly came to be interpreted as covering the spoken word, and theatres other than the patent houses, if they wished to give public performances, were confined to music, spectacle, and dumbshow. Recurring difficulties of legal discrimination between legitimate and illegitimate drama gradually allowed the nonpatent houses to add increasing numbers of passages of spoken words to their productions, but the emphasis remained on music, spectacle, and action—all attributes of melodrama. The patent privileges were not actually abolished until

1843. By that time the principal melodrama theatres in London had been built, and the abolition had little effect on either their finances or their repertory. They had found out that the greater part of the potential theatre audience in London preferred illegitimate to legitimate drama. Everywhere— in England, France, Germany, and America—melodrama was the genre most frequently performed during almost the whole of the nineteenth century. It drew the largest audiences, filled the most theatres, and engaged the largest number of actors, not excepting even Edwin Booth and Henry Irving. It reached its peak of popularity about 1880 and since has been in a long, slow decline (although it has never entirely disappeared) on the stages of Western theatres. Let me repeat that phrase—melodrama *in the theatre*—when we speak of a decline. For at the present moment, one could name dozens of movies and many times that number of television shows which perpetuate the genre for today's viewing public.

What manner of genre is this ubiquitous phenomenon in theatre? James L. Rosenberg justifies it on aesthetic grounds as "direct, pure perception," and hence the *highest* form of theatre which, being a "physical place" whose materials are flesh and blood and whose means are public mimetic representation, has as its end "to make us . . . more meaningfully alive"; melodrama has "visceral," not "cerebral" impact, and hence embodies this principle in its "purest form." ("Melodrama," in Robert Corrigan, *The Context and Craft of Drama*, San Francisco: Chandler, 1964.) The argument is cogent, perhaps even particularly sympathetic today, when so much experiment is going on in "visceral" theatre, but one needs to ask the question whether man is totally visceral and not at all cerebral. The question answers itself through an even cursory look at the fame of the best of melodramas as compared to plays embodying a more balanced view of life.

In any event, however, melodrama was—and is—a widely popular genre, and it behooves us to understand the "what" and the "how" of it. "Melodrama must build on a firm foundation of absolute certainties and immoveable verities," says Michael Booth (*English Melodrama*, p. 181), and this is the clue to both its nature and its structure. Its "absolute certainties" are that virtue will be rewarded and evil will be punished; its "immoveable verities" that generosity, courage, industry, honesty, chastity, humility, and repentance will always triumph over cupidity, connivance, cowardice, cruelty, pride, sin, and sex. And the conflict of the vices and the virtues is presented in cartoon style—exaggerated and unmistakable, in black and white. The appeal to the emotions is direct, and is underscored by musical accompaniment, either in songs or background music, the effectiveness of which in inducing emotional reaction is attested to by the scoring of innumerable movies. The melodrama makes its points broadly and unequivocally; there are few hesitations. The battle lines are drawn, the conflict ensues, and the triumph is inevitable. It is, as Eric Bentley says, a "spontaneous, uninhibited way of seeing things . . . drama in its elemental form" (*The Life of the Drama*, New York: Atheneum, 1964).

Action is the life of melodrama; *events* are of overriding importance. The *what* happens is far more important than the *to whom*, or the *why*, because the persons and the reasons are foreordained by the imperatives of the genre. The issue is never in doubt; members of the audience can thrill with impunity to the direst of circumstances, the most heroic of escapes, the most grandiloquent of stances, perfectly safe in the knowledge not only that they are watching a play, but also that in the world of this play (as distinct from the actual world), neat poetic justice will prevail.

We have seen that in tragedy, the conflict is *within* man; in melodrama it is *between* man and man, or man and things. This oversimplification into polarities and opposites was typical of the popular nineteenth-century mentality, and it is to the same phenomenon that melodrama (although not usually so called) appeals today. Melodrama, Professor Krutch says, "satisfied the simple souls of its audience which are neither philosophical enough to question its primitive ethics nor critical enough to object to the way in which its neat events violate the laws of probability." (Joseph Wood Krutch, *"Modernism" in Modern Drama*, p. 124.) There is no intent in melodrama to bring the hero to a point of self-discovery or recognition; repentance and remorse (two recurring phenomena in the melodrama of crime and fallen virtue) were usually brought about by external phenomena such as exhortations, dreams, lost children, mothers, wives, or sweethearts. The fundamental issue is not the reordering of self, but the readjustment of the individual in his relations with others. Certain unshakeable moral preconceptions underlie the whole melodra-

Figure 8–3

Theatre Collection,
New York
Public Library
East Lynne *was one of
the longest-running and
most popular of 19th
century melodramas.*

matic structure: the sanctity of the family, respect for one's elders, especially parents, and the preservation of the chastity of unmarried women are almost universally the motive forces for plots.

The actual materials of Plots varied as the popular interest was caught by varying subject matters. M. Willson Disher, in his breezy book *Melodrama: Plots That Thrilled* (New York: Macmillan, 1954), talks about fifteen or more popular subject matters: detective stories, murder puzzles, spy stories, "profligate" stories, "Magdalen" stories, business ventures, crime stories (chiefly "gentlemen crooks"), low-life stories, and several others. Professor Booth, in the book already mentioned, categorizes in more orderly fashion: Gothic and Eastern melodramas, military and nautical, domestic, and sensation. All possible sources of materials were used in nineteenth-century melodrama: novels were dramatized as fast as they were written; history was rifled for material; sensational news was made into plays; even plays themselves were frankly reworked time and time again. There were, for instance, an uncounted number of *East Lynne*'s, in many guises, on the stages of America, England, France, and Germany throughout the century. Repetitions with minor changes should be no news to us: the typical product of Hollywood is a cogent instance, to say nothing of the television series.

Now, the penchant of melodrama for action, for spectacular happenings and the breathless piling of incident on incident might

Figure 8–4

The Octoroon, *by Dion Boucicault, had many of the attributes of the "sensation" melodrama.*

give it a superficial resemblance to farce. But a second thought will easily point the difference. Melodrama is completely *serious;* farce, being a type of comedy, is *unserious.* It is true that some melodramas, like Campbell's *The Forest Oracle* (1829), had comic subplots, and that most of them had one or more comic characters in the persons of servants, workmen, precieuses, pedants, and so on; but the main line of action was *always* serious in intent. That is presumably why numbers of critics, from time to time, have called melodrama "the lowest form of tragedy." The difference, however, between *The Ticket-of-Leave Man* (1863) —or any other melodrama, for that matter—and *Oedipus Rex* is neither qualitative nor quantitative but *substantial, formal.*

The scheme of the action in melodrama is basically unvarying, as we have seen. And the Characters must, of necessity, be definitely and clearly divided into "the good guys" and "the bad guys." (We are familiar with the pattern from the ever popular Western movie and/or television show.) In the main line of action, the hero and the heroine are "the good guys," and the villain is "the bad guy." Generally, all other characters in a given play—fathers, mothers, relatives, friends, acquaintances, servants, etc.—are lined up behind either of these, with the preponderance of numbers accruing to the hero and heroine. The villain makes up in diabolical cleverness what he lacks in numerical superiority.

MIXED GENRES:

MELODRAMA AND

TRAGICOMEDY

Central to the typical nineteenth-century melodrama is the beseiged heroine—a Doris Day character—whose vicissitudes are not only impossible but often preposterous. Her chief problem is invariably to protect her virginity, or, having lost it, to expiate that cardinal sin in agonies of remorse. Sometimes the effort is too much for her, and she dies at the end of the play, usually in the arms of the forgiving hero or some other interested person. The idea of feminine chastity was, in the nineteenth-century, conceived to be not only the cornerstone of "domestic felicity," but the very foundation of society itself—hence its popularity as a basic ingredient in the melodrama. If the heroine were a married woman, then this chastity became fidelity to the marriage vow, and its violation the cardinal sin. This chastity/fidelity was the essence of "femininity," the most desirable attribute for the heroine. Even Joan of Arc explained in John Daly Burke's play *Female Patriotism* (1798) that though her "love of liberty" steeled her to action, it did not change her "timid, soft, and virgin" nature. In addition to this all-important core of characterization, the heroine of melodrama is courageous, sensitive, understanding, careful of the duty and love due her parents or guardians, and tender with children and old people, the very foundation of right and truth. Scoundrels are often advised to find their reformation in marriage to a "good woman," and she was often the "guardian angel" of the hero or other male character. But she also had to be patient and long-suffering—and fleet of foot! For one of the imperatives of the melodrama is that the hero and heroine should be separated early in the action, at which point she begins to suffer: she may be spurned by the hero, cursed by her father, left alone and starving in a garret with a brood of children, pursued through dark woods by bandits, forced aboard a smuggler's ship, chased across a frozen river by bloodhounds with her baby in her arms, or trapped in a burning building. Needless to say, she escapes these perils through her own endurance and by the intervention of the hero, always at the last moment, when suspense and tension have been built to the highest possible point. It is this fair and virtuous heroine who is the emotional center of melodrama; around her swirls the storm center of the action.

The hero of melodrama is allowed a little more latitude than the heroine. If he is a husband and has been "led astray" by drink, cupidity, or evil companions, he can be brought back to rectitude by the good offices of the heroine. Temperance and other reform-oriented melodramas are of this type. The criminal hero (and there were some, like Jimmy Valentine) must be at heart a Robin Hood and must repent his evil ways. But the more usual hero of melodrama is a handsome young man of action and courage, eternally devoted to his sweetheart or his wife, with miraculous physical prowess that enables him to survive fires, shipwrecks, earthquakes, prisons, knifings, or whatever other natural or un-natural disasters assail him as he attempts to foil the villain and rescue the heroine. In the military melodramas his outstanding virtue is patriotism, although this is invariably coupled with his virtuous love for the heroine.

In spite of his centrality, however, the hero is more acted upon than acting. The prime mover of the action in the melodrama is the villain, who pursues the heroine, connives to discredit or kill the hero, and keeps thinking up "dastardly plots." He is strong-minded and bold, grim, determined, and immensely evil. In the earlier melodramas he is a bloodthirsty villain: a pirate, highway-man, swashbuckler, renegade. Later he could be a smooth-talking, saturnine, elegantly dressed *roué* of no less evil proportions. He sometimes has as accomplice a shifty, cowardly, half-comic per-sonage who occasionally foils his plots at the end of the play and goes over to the side of Good. Another of his companions, partic-ularly in the later melodramas, is the adventuress or "bad woman," who is always elegantly dressed, probably smokes ciga-rettes (the hero always smokes a pipe), and attempts to seduce the hero. She always comes to a bad end: exile, prison, or death. The motivations of these villains are generally obscure, and only the sketchiest of reasons are ever enunciated in the plays: extreme avarice, or ambition, or desire for revenge. But the very lack of specifics makes his total baseness more spine-tingling to audi-ences: they can supply their own motivations.

Aside from this essential triangle—heroine-villain-hero—melo-drama had other stock characters: old man, old woman, comic man, comic woman, and sometimes children. The chief use of the older characters and the children is to heighten the pathos of the action. Fathers are far more prevalent than mothers, and some-times it is they who protect the heroine from the villain while the hero is off trying to clear his good name, or in prison unjustly, or exiled for equally wrong-headed reasons. Mothers are usually dead but "of sainted memory." Aunts, guardians, grandmothers, however, are usually alive and mostly used to issue warnings, enunciate moral platitudes, and be quite inactively "on the side of good." Comic men sometimes protect the heroine during the enforced absence of the hero; they are generally also "on the side of good." Comic women are aligned to the comic men and usually allow for a passage of dialogue that is commonsensical and natural in contrast to the high-flown sentiments and diction of the major characters. There is no confusion of characterization in melo-drama—each character is what he seems to be, and he is consis-tent from beginning to end. These are dream people in a dream world—not the world as we know that it is, but as we might hope it could be. Melodrama is "transcendently true," says David Grimsted (*Melodrama Unveiled*, p. 233), in that it pictures a world "the way it ought to be," which is "at least as real as actuality, and more to be talked about."

This idealization is reflected in the Language of melodrama, for the characters in the main story line speak a formal, inflated language full of inversions, circumlocutions, and metaphors. Listen to Sir John Trevanly in Fitzball's *The Inchcape Bell* (1828), as he looks at the picture of his dead wife and kidnapped son: "Ever, on the anniversary of this fatal day—a day of misery to the wretched, heirless Trevanly, my soul turns with a new yearning to yon lineaments. Oh, my sainted wife—my lost, lost boy, worse than dead, torn from me in a fatal, unguarded hour! Ah, when will my torn, lacerated heart have ceased to remember, to deplore ye! Must I still live, live on despairing? Hear me, Heaven!" Or to the heroine who has been evicted from her home by the villain, in W. S. Foote's *Bitter Cold* (1855): "I spurn the reptile whose venomed sting has poisoned the peace and happi-ness of a cheerful home! Become thine? Never! Were that loved husband *guilty* I would still be to him a true and honest wife. Go! Leave me, and the curse of an insulted, injured woman rest upon thy head! Hence, begone!" She is speaking for hundreds of typical heroines of melodrama. The glittering generality is always sub-stituted for the precise term: spacious mansions, costly viands, beauteous finery, sweet babes, angelic creatures; or, on the other hand, foul fiends, basest beasts, dishonored faces, and lewd women abound in melodrama. *Elevation* was the aim. The "low" characters, on the other hand, were permitted to speak the language of everyday, as in the delightful exchange between the low comedy lovers in William Dunlap's *The Archers* (1796):

Cecily: I shall like you the better for it as long as I live—if you're not killed.
Conrad: Why, you should like me better for dying for my country.
Cecily: Should I? Well, may be I should; but somehow I shall never like a dead man as well as a live one.
Conrad: Well, I don't know but that your taste is as well founded as your politics.

This dichotomy of style is consistent with the melodramatic conception: the implicit division between the ordinary and the extraordinary. The inflated language of the principal characters is, of course, the easiest part of melodrama to burlesque, and in the early twentieth century, when the typical nineteenth-century melodrama was falling on evil days, there were many such burlesques, especially of the older plays which had been on the boards for three generations. From about 1875 on, one finds not quite such a sharp dichotomy in the levels of usage of language, and only its rudiments in modern melodramas like *The Petrified Forest* (1935). But one need only think of the adventure and historical epics of movies, such as those starring Douglas Fairbanks, Errol Flynn, and Stephen Boyd, to see that the melodramatic conventions of language are still with us.

We have already mentioned that Music was from the first an integral part of melodrama, and its use was to set or underscore a mood. Sad and weary music for suffering heroines, agonizing music for the deaths of children and old fathers, threatening music for the villain, mysterious music for scenes of conspiracy, horrible music for ghosts, clashing music for storms, and joyous music for reunions of separated lovers. In the earlier melodramas, each character had a special musical chord or phrase that was heard each time he entered, and often speeches were underlined or punctuated by musical chords or passages. Cinema, as it largely took over the whole structure of melodrama in the early twentieth century, kept the musical accompaniment and enlarged its use; even today there is hardly a movie made which does not use some music on its sound track. The music of melodrama helped that genre to go straight to its physical and emotional point, appealing

Figure 8–5

Theatre Collection,
New York
Public Library
Sadie Thompson of
Rain *is typical of the*
"wicked woman"
heroine of one of the
types of melodrama.
(Vandamm)

directly to the most elemental feelings of its audience, without pretension and without intellectuality.

Precinema melodrama presented on the stage incredibly complex Spectacle. In *Pauvrette* (1858), the big scene is set down thus by the playwright:

Large blocks of hardened snow and masses of rock fall, rolling into the abyss. . . . The avalanche begins to fall—the bridge is broken and hurled into the abyss—the paths have been filled with snow, and now an immense sheet rushing down from R. entirely buries the whole scene to the height of twelve or fifteen feet, swallowing up the cabin and leaving above a clear level of snow—the storm passes away—silence and peace return—the figure of the Virgin is unharmed—the light before it still burns.

Part and parcel of the appeal of melodrama were these "sensations": buildings falling or on fire, locomotives crossing the stage to appear again in the distance crossing a bridge which collapses, ghosts rising and crossing the stage, shipwrecks and burnings and sinkings, rescues from drownings, escapes from castle prisons, earthquakes, landslides, appearances and disappearances. Intricate stage machinery was needed for these effects, and often a particular effect invented by a given theatre was "stolen" by a rival

Figure 8–6

*Melodramas are still
occasionally popular
and effective on the
stage, as is the new
Child's Play.
(Martha Swope)*

house and another play written by the staff dramatist to incorporate it. Pixérécourt was particularly fertile in the invention of
these effects, then a number of English mechanics took precedence, to the point where English theatres, in Victoria's time,
were famous worldwide for their "trick work." Needless to say,
these "special effects" were exactly what the movies could do
more effectively—and ultimately more cheaply—than the stage.
But there had always been a specie of melodrama not dependent
upon "sensations": crime plays, plays about the sins of society,
and cup-and-saucer dramas; and when the cinema took over the
spectacular and sensational melodramas, the stage continued with
these other kinds: *Night Must Fall, Tobacco Road, The Desperate Hours, Dial "M" for Murder, The Bad Seed, Rain,* and *The
Little Foxes.* In plays such as these, the scene is more realistic,
with the stage effects limited to night, storm, mysteriously opening doors, crashing windows, and "specials" like the mysterious
hatbox in *Night Must Fall.* But the plot and characters are typically melodrama: there is no question about who is the villain, and
suspense and surprise are rampant. Their purpose is no less
"thrills and chills" than the older, more spectacular plays.

In the world of melodrama there is no moral ambiguity; sin is

Figure 8–7

*The acrid taste of
Duerrenmatt's* The
Visit *makes it a
typical tragicomedy.*

the product of character rather than of society; the issues are clear-cut and direct; characters are presented "whole" without equivocation; music underscores the direct emotional appeal; the visual effects are stunning, the length and pace of the scenes short and rapid. It has, as Mr. Rosenberg says (Ibid., p. 244), "no inhibitions . . . Man Alive in a Universe of Danger . . . with Death always just offstage, waiting in the wings." This statement might almost be a direct description of the James Bond movies.

Tragicomedy

In contrast to melodrama, modern tragicomedy is of moral ambiguity all compact. Sin (if indeed such term exists) is not the product of character but of society, of environment, of all kinds of extrapersonal influences. It is a much more intricate theatrical statement and has had a longer and more involved history.

Plautus' rather apologetic statement was "I shall mix things up; let it be a tragicomedy." It is the first appearance of the term; the Greek writers had not used it. What Plautus mixed up were characters: upper-class persons and lower-class ones. Tragedy was the province of the former, comedy of the latter; their mixture needed apology and a new mixed term. Though Plautus seems to have invented the term, because he did not think it proper "to make it entirely a comedy wherein kings and gods ap-

Figure 8–8

In Who's Afraid of
Virginia Woolf? Edward
Albee uses the
tragicomic form in the
realistic mode.
(Friedman-Abeles)

pear," his mixture had been present in theatre from its beginnings. Horace in his *Ars Poetica* (ll. 220 ff.) notes the difficulty of the Greek *satyr* play which was a hybrid of tragic and comic subject matter, but he does not use the term tragicomedy. Nor does Aristotle. Certainly the tragicomic mixture is to be found in the great cycle plays of the Middle Ages: serious actions alternating with comic ones, comic characters mixed in with serious ones, as in that universal paradigm of the cycles, the famous *Second Shepherd's Play.*

In the Renaissance, authors of the canon of religious plays written "after Terence," and generally called "the Christian Terence," named their plays tragical comedies or comical tragedies, and in 1502, the secular Spanish play *Celestina* is subtitled *tragicomedia*. Renaissance theorists had difficulty with the term; both they and the writers of plays recognized that there were the aesthetic wholes of tragedy and of comedy, but that there was also a hybrid form that lay somewhere between the two, or that was a mixture of the recognized forms. This hybrid exhibited one or more of the following characteristics: mingled high and low characters, mixed styles of tragic subject matter written in familiar language or the reverse, comic and serious incidents in a single play (Sidney's "hornpypes and funerals"), and a serious and potentially tragic action with a happy ending. The issue was complicated by the many plays which drew their subject

Figure 8–9

Minnesota
Theatre Company
*Chekhov was the first
great playwright to
synthesize the
tragicomic form, as in
The Three Sisters.
Directed by Tyrone
Guthrie, designed by
Tanya Moiseiwitsch.*

matter from historical sources (hence *real* and *true*, hence *tragedy* by Aristotelian precept) but which, in their actions, had these mixed characteristics. Elizabethan England solved the problem largely by calling these plays histories to distinguish them from right tragedies and right comedies.

By the end of the sixteenth century in Italy and France, the term tragicomedy was applied to almost any play which dealt with serious subject matter, followed the neoclassic rules of unity of time, place, and action, and had a happy ending. By the third decade of the seventeenth century, the English were also applying the term to romantic tragedies with a happy ending. English writers never conformed so specifically to the neoclassic rules of dramatic composition, much to the disgust of Philip Sidney and Ben Jonson who unsuccessfully tried to establish (the first by criticism, the second by playwriting as well) the classic ideals in England. By the end of the seventeenth century, and throughout most of the eighteenth, tragicomedy was a term of opprobrium designating "a Mixture wholly monstrous and unnatural," of either a haphazard putting together of mirth and gravity in a

Figure 8–10

American
Conservatory Theatre
*The stasis and realism
of Chekhov's plays are
mirrored today in those
of Harold Pinter, such
as* The Caretaker.
(Bill Houlton)

single play or the union of two plots—one comic and one serious
—in the same play. This is the period when Shakespeare's plays
were "regularized" in performance; i.e., excising what was considered comic material from the tragedies, even though Samuel
Johnson defended him by an "appeal to nature," wherein the
comic and the tragic is mixed. The tenor of the age was, of
course, for "nature methodized."

So thoroughly did the neoclassicists discredit the term tragicomedy that the mixed drama which continued to be written had
to find new terminology. Diderot decided to call it *le genre
sérieux*, as something "between comedy and tragedy," because
tragicomedy can only be "a bad kind." Mercier called it *drame*.
Others applied the term *comédie larmoyante*, or tearful comedy,
to the species detailing the vicissitudes of middle-class life which
ended fortunately for the protagonists. Anyway, by the old definition of *mixture*, even melodrama is tragicomic.

At the same time that new terms were being devised for an old
mixture, and that the comic scenes in Shakespearian tragedy were
beginning to be explained as "heightening the tragic effect," the

MIXED GENRES:

MELODRAMA AND

TRAGICOMEDY

Figure 8–11

Lincoln Center
Repertory Theatre
*Mood dominates the
plays of Tennessee
Williams, as in* Camino
Real, *in the recent
production at Lincoln
Center.*
(*Martha Swope*)

German critic Lessing (*Hamburg Dramaturgy*, No. 70, 1769)
began to formulate what eventually became the modern theory
of tragicomedy. In essence he says that, although it is the province
of art to sort out for us the multifariousness of nature and direct
our attention to particular objects and sensations, there are those
phenomena where "gravity provokes laughter, sadness pleasure or
vice versa, so directly that an abstraction of the one or the other
is impossible to us." Tragicomedy (Lessing does not here mention
the term) is indeed a mixture of tragic and comic effects, but the
nature of the mixture is crucial. Not an *alternation* of effects but
a *simultaneity*, a *fusion* is the key—comic and tragic *at the same
moment*, without detriment to either. Ionesco says, "The comic
is tragic." It is seeing things with a "double vision," with "one
weeping and one laughing eye," a "tragicomic fusion" wherewith
"the tragic is more tragic and the comic is more comic," as Karl S.
Guthke says (*Modern Tragicomedy*, p. 59). This synthesis is particularly congenial to twentieth-century modes of thought, which
stress a sense of interdependencies within a continuum, the mo-
dality of relationships, and the difficulty of isolating particular
events or determining their meanings. Tragicomedy has "come
of age," and gained respectability as a dramatic genre.

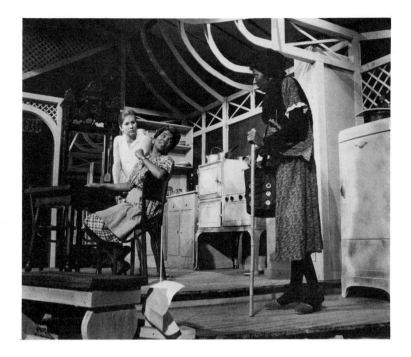

Figure 8–12

Marymount College
*Carson McCuller's
Member of the Wedding
is a typical modern
tragicomedy. Directed
by Marietta Battaglia,
designed by Elmon
Webb. (Gonda Studio)*

It is not that the double vision, the weeping and the laughing eye bent upon the same object, the fusion of effect has not hitherto been apparent in theatre. One need only contemplate Shakespeare's *Troilus and Cressida* to see its affinity to *The Visit* or *Who's Afraid of Virginia Woolf?* The same *acrid taste* is derived from all three—they all have the same "final cause," or *effect* to use Aristotle's term. In fact, as J. L. Styan points out (*The Dark Comedy,* pp. 22 f.), the antiromantic subject matter of Shakespeare's play, its showing of the disintegration of social and personal values, its ugly imagery, its deliberate confounding of the audience's reactions "anticipate amazingly those changes in convention more commonly met with in twentieth century drama." The use of the term tragicomedy here could go far to solve the persistent problem of Shakespeare's "bitter comedies."

But it is from the turn of the twentieth century on that tragicomedy as a genre exhibits gathering strength and pervasiveness. The plays of Chekhov are prime examples. That Chekhov himself called them "comedies," and that Stanislavsky, who first directed most of them, regarded them as "tragedies" (or at any rate serious and not comic) attests the ambivalence which is one of the hallmarks of tragicomedy. Unfortunately perhaps for both

Figure 8–13

Hunter College, CUNY
Though the setting is that of pre-classic times, Giraudoux's Tiger at the Gates is a tragicomedy in the modern sense of the word. Designed by Charles Elson.

artists, the term "tragicomedy" had no critical currency at the time. The mode of Chekhov's plays is, of course, realism, and the action seems to proceed quite naturally, in completely natural surroundings, and through entirely believable characterizations. But the elements of that seeming reality are most artfully selected and arranged. Plot, in the sense of sequential and/or causative arrangement is almost nonexistent. The three Prozorov sisters want to go to Moscow and don't go; Madame Ranevsky doesn't want to sell the cherry orchard but does. There are no great decisive deeds; in fact, very little happens as the result of conscious decisions on anybody's part—things simply develop in the course of time passing. None of the characters are heroic-size, and very few of them fool-size. They are for the most part indecisive, misguided, poorly informed, frivolous, sadly gay or gaily sad, living out their stage lives in a welter of minutiae, boredom, and inactivity.

Chekhov, however, circles his limited actions so constantly, gives his characters so many multiple signs from so many points of view, that the *lived time* of each play is completely real and satisfying. Ivanov and Uncle Vanya begin to be the antiheroes that tragicomedy will later feature, and the almost static action will lead to the stasis of Harold Pinter's *The Caretaker*. Plot and character function in the service of mood; the Chekhov plays are the first in a long line of plays which, for want of a better word,

234

THE PREDOMINANT

GENRES

Figure 8–14

The London Theatre
Workshop
*Brendan Behan sees
with the double vision
of tragicomedy in* The
Hostage. *Directed by
Joan Littlewood.
(Friedman-Abeles)*

are often called "mood plays." Included in these are plays of Tennessee Williams, O'Casey and Synge, Carson McCullers, Osborne, Pinter, Ghelderode, and many others. Writing in 1953, the playwright John Van Druten said (*The Playwright at Work*, Boston: Writer, Inc., pp. 36 f.):

If there is a new-born creature in the theatre of the past thirty years, I would say that it is the play of mood, the play whose main quality—far more important than its story or plot—is the maintenance and communication of a certain mood, through which the entire action is presented.

To a greater or lesser extent the Mood in all of these is the acrid, bitter-sweet one of tragicomedy, the ambivalent yes-and-no, the fusion of serious and comic, the weeping and the laughing eye. Aside from the careful symphonic structure to be observed in Chekhov's plays, sound itself is of utmost importance, from the whistle of the train that is bringing Madame Ranevsky home to the sound at the end of the play which Chekhov describes thus:

A sound is heard that seems to come from the sky, like a breaking harp-string, dying away mournfully. All is still again, and there is heard nothing but the strokes of the axe far away in the orchard.

Specific directions concerning musical accompaniments and sound cues are frequently found in the playscripts of this genre. Williams is notorious for his close attention to this matter, quite aside from the fact that his ear is particularly attuned to the music

Figure 8–15

University of Missouri
*Christy Mahon of
Synge's* Playboy of the
Western World *is a
typical tragi-comic
hero, as is also
Pantagleize. See also
1–4. Directed by
Larry D. Clark.*

Figure 8–16

The Living Theatre
*Though the mode is
symbolism, the form is
tragicomedy in
Strindberg's* The Ghost
Sonata. (*Alix Jeffry*)

of language, which he uses superlatively. O'Casey counterpoints the foxtrot and the waltz in *The Silver Tassie*; the jazzy music in *A Taste of Honey* and *The Hostage* in itself counterpoints the action. The effect is always *double*—comic and pathetic at the same time. The tensions set up in audiences by the tragicomic techniques can be destructive; if pushed too hard by playwright and performance, especially if the mood is too grim, an audience will find relief in laughter no matter how irrelevant. An exceedingly nice (i.e., precise) sense of balance is needed in both the writing and the performing.

Chekhov, of course, was writing at the apogee of the realistic mode, and the Spectacle in his plays is complete realism. Modified realism—at any rate verisimilitude—continues to be the mode of tragicomedy. By and large, recognizable places, even though multiple settings (like those in *Summer and Smoke* and *The Member of the Wedding*) are the rule. And personages with all-too-human characteristics, like Christy Mahon, Stanley Weber, and Jimmy Porter people these plays. The tragicomic hero, however, invariably embodies the dichotomies of body and mind, being and mask, ideal concept and reality, intention and fulfillment; he is often the antihero. The end of the action in a tragicomedy is as often a question as an answer.

Just as comedy and tragedy as genres have been subject to different modes in their long existence, so too has tragicomedy, even in the comparatively short period of time since it reached its apotheosis at the beginning of the present century. It has appeared in the mode of symbolism in such a play as Strindberg's *The Ghost Sonata*; in the mode of the Maeterlinckian "static drama" in Pinter's *The Caretaker*; in the mode of expressionism in Toller's *Masse Mensch*; in the theatricalist mode of Tennessee Williams's *The Glass Menagerie*. It has appeared in the representational style of Osborne's *Look Back in Anger* and the presentational style of Arthur Miller's *A View from the Bridge*. It includes the metatheatre of Pirandello and the epic theatre of Brecht.

No matter what stage scenarios these modes have required, the tragicomic form is present and recognizable. The Plot structure may be episodic, as in Brecht (*The Caucasian Chalk Circle*, *The Good Woman of Setzuan*, and *Mother Courage*), with the episodes loosely tied together by an overarching statement, or meaning, and frequently interrupted by presentational episodes. Or it may be progressive and cumulative, as in Duerrenmatt's *The Visit*, where the arrival of Madame Zachanassian sets off a causative chain of events. But in either case, exposition in the usually accepted dramatic sense is likely to be at a minimum, the complication rapid, and the dénouement puzzling. Sometimes the performance simply stops, as it does in Pirandello's *Each In His Own Way*, with no resolution of the conflict in sight. Sometimes the action is a simple series of reversals as it is in Synge's *The Well of the Saints*, where the blind old man and the blind old woman get their sight then lose it again, exclaiming, "The Lord protect us from the Saints of God." In Sartre's *No Exit*, the four characters simply arrive in the closed room and talk—that's all the action there is. In other words, the tragicomic dramatist exercises a great deal of freedom in departing from the received tradition of plotting.

Characterization, too, varies widely but it has one constant—these are recognizable human beings. They are generally not particularly admirable, but they are *recognizable*; i.e., not grotesques or abstractions. Pirandello's philosophical preoccupation with the nature of reality leads him, in his metatheatrical plays at least, to insist that they are "characters," or *dramatis personae*, and not *people*. And they do tend to lunge on to the scene with no preparation whatsoever, as his six characters march to the stage during the *staged* rehearsal of the acting company gathered in the theatre. This technique allows Pirandello to explore several layers of reality and illusion. And in Brecht's polemical plays he tends to make his characters dance on puppet strings, as does Gayly Gay in *A Man's a Man*. He has good reason for that, however, in the demonstration he is giving of how one man can be made into another. But mostly the characters of the modern tragicomedy are sufficiently detailed to be believable, and mostly the dramatist's intent is to have them accepted as *real* people, as in Jack Richardson's *Gallows Humor*, or Anouilh's *The Waltz of the Toreadors*, or Williams's *Sweet Bird of Youth*. The chief characters of these plays are seldom heroes in the received sense of the word but often bungling mediocrities who hope rather than act, but whose very individual and contradictory details give them a kind of universality. Ghelderode's Pantagleize, whom we have described earlier in this book, is a typical tragicomic hero.

These characters practically never die at the end of the action; much of the tragicomic force comes from their necessity to live on, no matter how dull or meaningless or contradictory their projected lives might be.

The Dialogue of these plays has verisimilitude—it is such as might reasonably issue from the characters who speak the words. In fact, the non sequiturs and circumlocutions of Aston and Davies in *The Caretaker* are so vividly "right" for those characters that one can only marvel at Pinter's skill in dialogue. No less skillful and revealing is the dialogue of John Osborne's *The Entertainer*, in which Laurence Olivier played so memorable an Archie Rice. The poetic cadences of Tennessee Williams in *The Night of the Iguana* or *The Seven Descents of Myrtle* are everywhere evident, yet there is sufficient differentiation to make each character's speech peculiar to him. The characters do not talk "nonsense" as those in the plays characterized *absurd* usually do; within the boundaries of the conceived characters in these plays, the dialogue "makes sense."

Of Mood and/or Music we have already spoken in some detail above, and of Spectacle we need only say that modern tragicomedy accepts and uses the dramatic conventions of whatever mode the dramatist chooses. There is no attempt to deny the theatre as theatre. In the realistic mode the spectacle is self-contained, and the audience observes. In the various mutations of the theatricalist mode, the play makes varying degrees of direct contact with the audience and draws them in to the theatrical experience in franker, less suble ways.

Thus modern tragicomedy comprises a recognizable genre. Perhaps when we have lived with it a little longer and have developed more of a perspective toward it, we will see that those plays now generally (and incorrectly) called *absurd* should also be subsumed under its rubric. But at the present reading it would seem to preclude those theatrical phenomena which use the grotesque in their aesthetic form, and whose philosophical content is the existential absurd. Pirandello, I know, sits rather uneasily here; but the aggregate of his accomplishment is more like that of his fellows here than it is like that of Artaud, Beckett, and Ionesco, even though the fecundity of Pirandello's genius supplied the newer playwrights with many inspirations. At any rate, it is somewhat ironic (a fitting stance for tragicomedy) that the nutshell

Figure 8–17

Minnesota
Theatre Company

*Pirandello wrote
tragicomedies before
the term gained critical
respectability, as here,
in* Enrico IV.

Figure 8–18

Carnegie-Mellon
University

Brecht's Mother
Courage *is a good
example of the
tragicomic protagonist,
in both her speech and
her actions. See also
10–13. Directed by
Word Baker, designed
by Charles Dox.*

Figure 8–19

Lincoln Center
Repertory Theatre

*The epic theatre style
of Brecht's* Caucasian
Chalk Circle *heightens
its effectiveness as
tragicomedy.*

Figure 8–20

The dichotomy of expressions on the faces of these characters in Pinter's The Homecoming *epitomizes the double vision of tragicomedy. (Friedman-Abeles)*

Figure 8–21

University of Arkansas

The gay-sad mood of Anouilh's Thieves' Carnival is typically that of tragicomedy. Directed by Cleveland Harrison.

Figure 8–22

Rosencrantz and Guildenstern Are Dead *might in many ways be said to sum up the essence of tragicomedy, having not one, but two anti-heroes. (Martha Swope)*

statement to epitomize this genre was made by Ionesco: ". . . the tragic is comic, and the comic is tragic." In other words, the tragicomic fusion makes the tragic more tragic and the comic more comic. But it was Pirandello who said that, like Machiavelli, he laughed "to provide an outlet for my painful tears."

9

New Forms

If a theory of modern tragicomedy (whose plays have been with us as individual creative acts for a long time now) has yet to be successfully formulated, how much less likely are we to be able to formulate a theory for the new theatre, whose plays did not appear in any quantity until the 1950s! For criticism is always *a posteriori*—after the fact. If there is anything that we have learned from a glance at critical theory from Aristotle to the present day it is that any formulation *must* be based on the analysis of *particular* theatrical constructs as they were *played* in a given theatre; critical theory must be descriptive, as Aristotle's was. How accurately such descriptive postulations can be applied to the new forms of theatre is a very moot point indeed. Of the few attempts that have so far been made in this direction, one of the earliest, and probably still the best, is Martin Esslin's *The Theatre of the Absurd*. It is perhaps the most comprehensive and detailed critique of the new theatrical genre, but its basic approach is admittedly philosophical, including in its consideration all those modern dramatists who come under the rubric described by Camus:

A world that can be explained by reasoning, however faulty, is a familiar world. But in a universe that is suddenly deprived of illusions and of light, man feels a stranger. His is an irremediable exile, because he is deprived of memories of a lost homeland as much as he lacks the hope of a promised land to come. This divorce between man and his life, the actor and his setting, truly constitutes the feeling of Absurdity.

[*Le Mythe de Sisyphe, Paris: Gallimard, 1942*]

By 1964, George Wellwarth, in *The Theatre of Protest and Paradox*, was presenting a group of new French, German, English, and American writers whose "similarities consist of a common theme (protest) and a common technique (paradox)." But this "commonality" includes such disparate dramatists as Ghelderode, Ionesco, Brendan Behan, John Osborne, Duerrenmatt, Adamov, Pinter, Albee, and Jack Gelber. It is true that a quantity of "protest" underlies the work of all these (and the others which he writes about), and that there is some "paradox" involved in the theatrical constructs which they produce. But within the framework of the plays themselves as aesthetic entities one is bound to see more differences than similarities in the *oeuvre*, say, of Pinter and Ionesco, or Osborne and Adamov. Of the above-named playwrights we would consider only Ionesco and Adamov belonging primarily to the new genre we will try to analyze here, and the others primarily writers of tragicomedy as defined in the last chapter. The reasons, we hope, will be forthcoming as we proceed here with what must—in any event—be a tentative criticism.

The difficulty of synthesizing the movement of avant garde drama of the past twenty years is apparent in the variety of names applied to it. In addition to the two mentioned above, it has also been called "The Theatre of Panic" (Arrabal), "The Theatre of Cruelty" (Artaud), "The Comedy of the Savage God" (Yeats), "The Theatre of Assault" (Peter Brook), "Theatre of Disruption" (George R. Kernodle), and "Ritual Theatre" (Jerzy Grotowski and others); no doubt this list is not exhaustive, and other terms are still being invented and applied. What to call the theatrical construct (beyond the generic terms *play* or *performance*) that appears in these various "theatres" is a conundrum. The most popular designation at the moment would seem to be *antiplay*. A more positive nomenclature remains to be invented. But, if we cannot now "name" this genre as we could heretofore designate Farce, Comedy, Melodrama, Tragedy, and Tragicomedy, we are in no worse position than our forebears who (as we have seen) had difficulties of nomenclature upon the appearance of new forms. We can, at any rate, trace the development of the new genre, mark its distinguishing characteristics as *play*, and point to the means it uses and the effects it achieves. So we shall (hopefully) begin to see that there is indeed a new dramatic genre abroad in the world of the theatre, whatever its name.

The subject of the present chapter—*New Forms*—is ultimately ironic, because if there is one thing upon which all varieties of "new theatres" and all persuasions of "new playwrights" are agreed (and both seem to make fetishes of uniqueness and disagreement) it is that *dramatic form does not exist*. It disappeared in a great explosion in 1896, although it took almost two generations before a significant number of practicing playwrights and theatre people realized that fact, and it may take considerably longer before the general public is aware of it. "So heavy is the hand of dead tradition!" would be the remark of New Theatre devotees concerning this particular "cultural lag." What seems to be happening, of course, is that a new genre is being added to those already available to the theatre. Whether or not it will prove autonomous and durable is, as Thornton Wilder might say, "still very much an open question." In the meantime, we can perhaps gain some insights by a closer consideration of the phenomenon.

A second common characteristic of the New Theatre (the first is the annihilation of *form*, as mentioned above) is the seeming violation of *probability* as it is and has been known in other genres. As Elder Olson points out (*Tragedy and the Theory of Drama*, op. cit., p. 49), there are four kinds of probability: common natural, conditioned natural, hyperbolical, and hypothetical. Each is dependent for its acceptance on the dramatic process of which it is a part and is inherent in the various dramatic forms. Common natural probability appears most frequently—but not exclusively—in the realistic mode; it embraces those circumstances and actions which an audience will accept without question or preparation as having verisimilitude. What appears on stage is "lifelike" or "just like it is"; the recognition is instantaneous. Conditioned natural probability is that which most frequently appears in tragedy. Here circumstances and actions are accepted without question if there seems to be sufficient *cause*.

Hyperbolical probability is that which is recognized as being an exaggeration, but which contains an apparent element of truth, such as is usually the province of farce and the entire domain of melodrama. Hypothetical probability, which includes fantasy, is predicated on some such statement as *"if* there were fairies, they would act like this," or, *"if* the Devil could assume human form, this is what he would be like," or, *"if* animals could talk, they would talk like this." In the plays of the New Theatre, parents live in ashcans, a heroine has three noses, a man makes love to a

Figure 9–1

Lincoln Center
Repertory Theatre
*The caricatures
intended by Jarry for
Ubu Roi are apparent in
this scene from the
Yugoslavian Atelje 212
revival of the play
presented at The
Forum.*

pig, everybody of all generations and sexes in a family are named "Bobby Watson," a corpse keeps growing and consumes all the space in a house, and arms and legs drop off live people. Probability seems to have been discarded along with form. Actually, the way in which these manifest impossibilities are *used* by a given dramatist can be a measure of his skill and success. They can even be turned into *probabilities* if the *given circumstances* make a correspondence between them the *actual* impossibles and probabilities already accepted within the play itself. In Ionesco's *Amédée*, the spreading death-in-life of Amédée and Madeleine is established and accepted, so that the hideously growing corpse simply becomes its visualization. In Rochelle Owens's *Futz*, on the other hand, the "hero's" fornication with the pig seems gratuitously thrown in for shock value because the given circumstances of the play establish this guileless fool without it, although a perhaps more generous interpretation of the play's action might point to the playwright's espousal of more liberal sexual mores.

But we must get back to that explosion of 1896 and its repercussions. The event that we are talking about is, of course, the opening, on December 10 of that year, of Alfred Jarry's new play, *Ubu Roi*. It was presented by Lugné-Poë at the Théâtre de l'Oeuvre, and King Ubu was played by Gémier. In line with

THE PREDOMINANT

GENRES

Figure 9–2

Marymount College
Jonesco's The Bald
Soprano *brought to
immediate notice a new
theatrical form.
Sets designed by
Michael Hampshire.*
(Daniel Berry)

Jarry's wishes (and in consonance with the needs of the play), the setting was neutral, with the rapidly shifting scenes announced by printed placards. The *dramatis personae* were gross and obscene caricatures, the language frequently scatological. King Ubu is greedy, cruel, treacherous, cowardly, and dirty. Having killed Wenceslas, King of Poland, he usurps the throne, consigns all nobles to the "disembraining machine," confiscates all money, and finally escapes by sea the vengeance of the Emperor of Russia and Bougrelas, the rightful heir to the throne. The effect is brutal and anarchic, but what incensed that first-night audience was the language; the revolutionary significance of the play was lost on all save a few, like Yeats who is reported to have said (on observing the performance), "after us [poets like himself], the Savage God."

In an essay in the *Revue Blanche* following the presentation, Jarry wrote:

I intended that when the curtain went up the scene should confront the public like the exaggerating mirror in the stories of Madame Leprince de Beaumont, in which the depraved saw themselves with dragons' bodies, or bulls' horns, or whatever corresponded to their particular vice. It is not surprising that the public should have been aghast at the sight of its ignoble other-self, which it had never before been shown completely.

[*Tr. Barbara Wright, Ubu Roi, New York: New Directions, 1961, p. 174*]

Figure 9–3

Cherry Lane Theatre
*Beckett's ironically-
titled* Happy Days
*epitomizes the informing
thought of the new
genre in theatre.*
(*Alix Jeffry*)

When Sacha Guitry, the popular actor, said of the play, "It is not related to any other form of literature," (Ibid., p. v.) he was as close to the truth as any of Jarry's contemporaries were able to get. Jarry himself died of acute alcoholism at the age of thirty-four—eleven years after that momentous first night; his increasingly antisocial behavior and flamboyant perverseness had alienated all but a few of his friends and acquaintances. What was regarded by many as "a school-boy prank" faded from memory, except for the influence it, and Jarry's other writings, had on the avant garde movements in painting, literature, and music which were known by the names of Fauvism, Cubism, and Dadaism.

Ten years after Jarry's death, Apollinaire produced *Les Mamelles de Tirésias*, a grotesque vaudeville for which he invented the term "surrealist," defining it in the Preface to the printed play as a new kind of "imitation of nature," such as "When man wanted to imitate the action of walking, he created the wheel, which does not resemble a leg. He has thus used Surrealism without knowing it." (*Oeuvres*, Paris; Pléiade, p. 866.) Though the later application of the term Surrealism to art took a different turn, Apollinaire himself was one of the group of painters, poets, and dramatists who were at that time trying to find ways to express the "truth" behind the surface of reality. (The current involvement of painters in the theatre phenomenon called Happenings is a somewhat

Figure 9–4

University of Arkansas
Albee's The American
Dream *negates all the
accepted ideas of the
cult of individualism,
which is brought into
question by the new
theatre forms. Directed
by Cleveland Harrison.*

parallel situation, there being many crossings-over and mixtures of art forms in experimental productions.)

Twenty years after Jarry's death there opened in Paris the Théâtre Alfred Jarry, founded by Antonin Artaud and Roger Vitrac; it lasted for two seasons. And in 1938 there was published in Paris a slender volume called *Le Théâtre et son Double* which was a collection of various of Artaud's writings on the theatre. It is a distillation of his personal philosophy, his experiences in the theatre (he had been actor and director on the stage, actor in the movies), and his dream of what the theatre should and must be. Its impassioned statements synthesized a being and a direction implicit in the work of Jarry, Apollinaire, and the other "experimentalists," and it became the gospel of the New Theatre after World War II. Artaud was interested not in the reform of theatre, but in a complete revolutionary transformation. Like Jarry, he was an active iconoclast, convinced that all logical systems, all social conventions, all received traditions were futile and dangerous. He saw theatre as a means of expressing rebellion against the condition of man's helplessness in an implacably hostile universe—the point of view that would be later formulated in non-theatre terms by Camus; protest and defiance are the appropriate response to the hostile universe.

In this series of essays, manifestos, letters, and notes, Artaud cries out for "no more masterpieces"; the tyranny of the *word* is to be abolished, and the theatre returned to the "magical mimesis" of gesture. We must discover "the pure theatrical language" which is "plastic and physical" and which makes "space speak." It must be a "theatre of cruelty" by means of which "all the perverse possibilities of the mind . . . are localized" so that the action of theatre impels men "to see themselves as they are," for thus only "it causes the mask to fall, reveals the lie, the slackness, baseness, and hypocrisy of our world." This cruelty is not the harshness of man to man, but the cruelty of the cosmos, where "the sky can still fall on our heads," a "kind of higher determinism" where "evil is permanent." The themes of this new theatre must be "cosmic, universal," must deal with "this elementary magical idea." It must "abandon psychology" and "induce trance," that is to say "an atmosphere of hypnotic suggestion in which the mind is affected by a direct pressure on the senses." The spectacle is to offer "a marvelous complex of pure stage images," a "poetry in space," wherein language becomes but one of a complex of expressive media, and "a play composed directly on the stage, realized on the stage" is not inconceivable. In this theatre "the spectator is in the center and the spectacle surrounds him." Through sound, light, and "the dynamism of action" the sensitivities of the spectators will be "put in a state of deepened and keener perception." I have here extracted and arranged those elements of Artaud's discursive work which were in varying ways and to different degrees utilized by the new playwrights and theatre workers. Paul Arnold (*TDR* 22, p. 21) has pointed out that the philosophical basis for Artaud's whole theory (viz., that the complete liberation of evil forces—even beyond the libido— would bring about the good) is an "obvious philosophical, psychological, and historical error." But we are more concerned with the theatrical implications of his statement and the seminal ideas it promulgated for such writers as Beckett, Ionesco, Adamov, Genet, and so on, and such performance concepts as the Polish Lab Theatre, the Living Theatre, The Open Theatre, the Performance Group, Café La Mama, and the work of Peter Brook and others. *The Theatre and Its Double* has been an immensely significant document—perhaps *the* most significant for theatre—thus far in the twentieth century.

Now, the disillusion and the evil omnipresent and visible of which Artaud speaks can be found in the plays of many of his contemporaries: those of Cocteau, Giraudoux, and Sartre, those existential writers whose plays belong to the genre of tragicomedy. It was not until after World War II that experimentation in the new form outlined by Artaud got under way to any extent, and not until the fifties that it reached theatrical viability and significance, primarily in the plays of Eugene Ionesco, Samuel Beckett, and Jean Genet. The larger number of Ionesco's plays makes him the most ubiquitous and exemplary of the new dramatists, even though the well-deserved worldwide fame of Beckett's *Waiting for Godot* has made that play perhaps the most significant of any written in the new genre. Between the ending of the war and the appearance in 1950 of Ionesco's first play, *The Bald Soprano*, Genet, Arthur Adamov, and Jean Tardieu had tried their hands and minds in this mode of expression, but Ionesco's genius brought it to perfection. Let us see if we can analyze its characteristics.

Since, like any other play, these are intended for performance in the theatre—indeed hardly exist without performance—it is possible to approach them through the old Aristotelian "necessities" of Thought, Fable, Characters, Language, Music or Mood, and Spectacle. We have seen that these necessities are all the possibilities there are for a play, and by inquiring into the why's and wherefore's of them in the work of these new playwrights, we can perhaps judge if we have, indeed, a *new genre*, or merely some aberrant branch of a long established one.

It goes almost without saying that the Thought that informs all of these plays derives from a particular intellectual climate fairly widespread in the twentieth century, and intensified by World War II—particularly by the development and use of the atomic bomb therein. It is a denial of Individualism with its concomitant structures of moral and social values, coupled with the philosophical hypothesis that "God is dead," and that rationality—reason—(itself a product of the growth of Individualism) is an untenable concept. Unfathomable "dark forces" rule the world and "not to have been born" is best. But having, through no act of volition, become a part of the dehumanized and fragmented world, a person simply endures its senselessness, making random gestures into the void. As always, the best plays informed by this Thought make it a *lived experience*, and not merely a statement or a

Figure 9–5

Festival Theatre, Stratford, Ontario

The actualization of nothingness is the achievement of Beckett in Waiting for Godot. *(Douglas Spillane)*

Figure 9–6

Events and characters are not logically structured in such a play as Genet's The Balcony, *but are seen in a kind of kaleidoscopic fashion. See also 4–21. (Martha Swope)*

Figure 9–7

APA-Phoenix Company

Time is telescoped in Exit the King, *in which the descent to death becomes a lived experience in the theatre. (Van Williams)*

Figure 9–8

Nagg and Nell in Endgame *spend their stage lives in ashcans.*

Figure 9–9

Yale Repertory Theatre

The epitome of character fluidity in the new theatre forms is evident in Transformations, *performed at the Yale Repertory Theatre.*

Figure 9–10

New York Shakespeare Festival Public Theatre

Characters are de-humanized automatons in Vaclav Havel's The Memorandum. *Directed by Joseph Papp. (George E. Joseph)*

demonstration, as does Ionesco's *The Chairs* (1952), and Beckett's *Happy Days* (1961)—an ironic title if there ever was one. All the inheritance of the culture of individualism—optimism, faith in progress, family life, togetherness, physical fitness, euphemistic skirting of the ultimate facts of the human condition—is negated, as in Edward Albee's *The American Dream* (1959). This is "dark comedy" indeed, the "comedy of the Savage God."

With such an informing Thought, it follows "of necessity" that Plot or Fable in these plays is practically nonexistent. Disbelief in rational processes precludes a causative sequence of events, a "tying and untying of a knot." Many of these plays are one-acts, probably because the longer form is so implicitly sequential, and it is very difficult to actualize "nothingness" for an extended period of time. Beckett, of course, does actualize nothingness most successfully in *Waiting for Godot*, although even this two-act play is shorter than most of those we have been in the habit of calling "full-length." Most of these plays are static in the sense that each is *pure act*, a closed situation with no past and no future. Exposition and dénouement have no place in such a scheme; climax does not exist in the usual sense of the term. These accoutrements of the more conventional genres are sometimes replaced by a mounting tension, built by a variety of visual and auditory means, which ends in a kind of explosion.

In Ionesco's *The Lesson* (1951), for instance, the increasing tempo and unintelligibility of the dialogue, the worsening toothache of the pupil, and the increasing agitation and physical movement of the professor culminate in the murder of the pupil by the professor. Even in plays like Genet's *The Balcony* (1956) where there are many personages and seemingly much activity—even a revolution going on somewhere outside in the city—the events are not structured in logical fashion but seen as in a kaleidoscope or a hall of mirrors. There is very little sense of articulated time, of elapsed time in this kind of play, and even where a sense of time passing is integral to the meaning of the action, as in Ionesco's *Rhinoceros* (1960), it is a compressed and distorted time. Logical time as it appears in the rational world is violently dislocated in many of these plays, as in *Exit the King* (Ionesco, 1962) were the stage action represents half-a-lifetime's journey to the grave. More generally, the sense of logical time passing is not present at all in these plays—there is a timelessness and often a placelessness about them, such as is more usual to a dream or a fantasy. It is Beckett who takes this sense to its ultimate in *Waiting for Godot*, where time seems to stand almost absolutely still.. The annihilation of time is a difficult achievement, because the very nature of an action involves elapsed time, but these playwrights come close to achieving this impossible feat in most of their plays unless, of course, the very core of the play is *time passing* as in *Exit the King*.

Given the informing Thought, and the substitution of tensions and/or states for Plot, it again follows—"of necessity"—that Characters are not drawn in the sense of being "characterized." I suppose that the nearest descriptive term for the drawing of these *dramatis personae* would be "caricature." Certainly Madame Rosepettle, Amédée, Clove, Chantal, Jack and Jacqueline (to name but a few of many) are not what we have come to call "fully rounded characters," whom we can acknowledge as being lifelike. They have some affinity to the characters in the medieval morality or to those in the "comedy of Humors" in that they are *extractions* or *epitomes* or *essences* of one or a selected few of the multifarious traits which "real" human beings possess. Often, too, they are *exaggerations*, in the clown sense, as are Vladimir and Estragon in *Waiting for Godot*. Some of them are true grotesques, like gargoyles or other travesties on human physiognomy, as Hamm and Clove, and Nagg and Nell in Beckett's *Endgame*, as Roberta II in Ionesco's *Jack, or the Submission* with her nine fingers and three noses, or as the motel keeper in Claude van Itallie's *Motel* is a huge puppet.

Frequently they have no names of their own but are: the Young Man, the Old Woman, the Official, the General, the Man, the Woman, the Soldier, the Young Cowboy, Senator One, Witness One, Senator Two, Witness Two, and so on. In this propensity they are somewhat reminiscent of characters in some of the expressionist dramas, like Elmer Rice's *The Adding Machine* (1923), and the generalization is done for somewhat the same reason—to *depersonalize* the character, except that in the expressionist plays the technique tends to *universalize* the characters thus treated, whereas in these plays it seems to render them chiefly more insignificant (which, I suppose, is another form of universality). Characters seem often to hold their identities very tentatively and to change into animals (as in *Rhinoceros*), or into another identity, as the Martins turn into the Smiths in *The Bald Soprano*, or everybody turns into somebody else in *The Balcony*. Or they are completely dehumanized automatons, as in Vaclav Havel's *The Memorandum* (1965). These varied presentations of character largely reflect the underlying premise of New Theatre playwrights: that human beings have, in our world, become *devalued* as human beings; that personal identity is nonexistent.

So, too, has Language been devalued in our world (and in these plays) and is useless (or almost so) as a means of communication. The classic, and frightening example, is the cliché-ridden, senseless "conversation" of *The Bald Soprano*, which is repeated in kind in *The American Dream*. It is language run riot in an age of mass communication so that it no longer means anything at all. The increasing unintelligibility of the Professor's speeches in *The Lesson*, and the wild incomprehensibility of Lucky's great monologue in the first act of *Waiting for Godot* are other good particular examples. But even less flamboyant examples than these illustrate the same propensities. Language is useful, as Artaud insisted, only as one of the forms of sound, as the lovers in Tardieu's *Lovers in the Metro* (1952) move to their own word music "Un, deux, trois, amour, Un, deux, trois, toujours," or express their bewilderment: "Yes I you!/I you never, me!/Yes, you me!/It's you who/Me who what?/When then?/Nowhere/Where then?/Never." No significant statement can be made in language, as the mute Orator proves at the end of *The Chairs*. Since language is itself incomprehensible and useless for communication it is just as well to invent another system of putting words together, like *Ptydepe* in *The Memorandum*, in which characters frequently converse in words like these: "My colleagues sometimes ylud, kaboz pady el too much, and at the same time they keep forgetting that etrokaj zenig ajte ge gyboz." Verbal nonsense, as Martin Esslin has pointed out (*Theatre of the Absurd*, pp. 240 ff.) has been around in our culture for a very long time indeed, but always before it was the aberrant which served to reinforce the norm. Its present use in these plays is nihilistic and horrifying because in conjunction with the nonplots and noncharacters it becomes a reinforcement for the dark view of the world projected in these plays.

Since Language is devalued in substance and in use, it follows that Spectacle acquires an immense and overriding importance—

not the décor only, but the total scenario, or thing seen on the stage—the appearance, gesture, and movements of both persons and things. Beckett took the denigration of words to its ultimate in two short plays called *Act Without Words I* and *II*, where only the action of the figures in the plays has any communicative value. King Ubu, cheerfully dumping nobles down the trapdoor to the debraining machine, the Professor knifing the Pupil, Choubert being forced to swallow hunks of stale bread in Ionesco's *Victims of Duty* (1953), Grandma being consigned to the sandbox, Jonathan pouring his huge collection of stamps and coins over the limp body of Rosalie, and the routines of the hat and the shoes in *Waiting for Godot* are all forcible visualizations not dependent on words. Sometimes what begins as an ordinary action is pressed relentlessly to its extreme, as when the timid little voyeur in Tardieu's *The Keyhole* (1955) asks a woman to undress and she not only takes off all her clothes but proceeds to take out her eyes, pull off her lips, strip off her flesh until only the skeleton is left. The scenery "acts," too: the huge, growing corpse in *Amédée*, the chairs and their proliferation, the growing pile of furniture in *The New Tenant* (Ionesco, 1957) which swallows up the man, the corpse and the voracious plant in Kopit's *Oh, Dad, Poor Dad, etc.* (1960), the "studios" and their accoutrements of props and costumes in *The Balcony*, the collapsible stage setting and papier-mâché dummy in *Motel*. In many of these plays the impression is that "things are in the saddle and ride mankind"—a completely calculated effect and a very important part of the total construct.

In these plays, Music, or sound, is likely to be on an elemental level and used for emotional effect. Noises, cries, explosions, and the sonorous qualities of words, as well as specific instrumental effects become a part of the total theatre in which, as Artaud wrote in 1938: "violent physical images crush and hypnotize the sensibility of the spectator," and in which "the sonorization is constant."

Whether or not the choices these dramatists make in the various elements of the play form constitute a new genre is finally for future critics to decide, when time has sifted the effectiveness of the present representations. Readers of this book will surely participate in the formulation of critical theory for these new plays, and perhaps one of them will make the final definition which has

Figure 9–11
Cherry Lane Theatre
The second character in
Krapp's Last Tape *is a*
tape-recorder.
(*Alix Jeffry*)

thus far largely escaped statement. These dramatists are themselves fond of calling their productions *antiplays* or *antitheatre*,
and Ionesco has one of his characters (D'Eu in *Victims of Duty*)
speak what amounts to their manifesto:

The theatre of my dreams would be irrationalist. . . . Inspiring me with
a different logic and a different psychology, I should introduce contradiction where there is no contradiction, and no contradiction where there is
what commonsense usually calls contradiction. We'll get rid of the principle of identity and unity of character and let movement and dynamic
psychology take its place. We are not ourselves. Personality does not
exist. Within us there are only forces that are either contradictory or not
contradictory. . . . The characters lose their form in the formlessness of
becoming. Each character is not so much himself as another. . . . As for
plot and motivation, let's not mention them. We ought to ignore them
completely, at least in their old form, which was too clumsy, too obvious
—too phony, like anything that's too obvious—No more drama, no more
tragedy: the tragic's turning comic, the comic is tragic, and life's getting
more cheerful.

Having dealt in the foregoing discussion with the material, efficient, and formal "causes" of the new drama, it remains but to
say a word about the final cause, or effect. It is a peculiar and
limited view of the world which says that the human situation
can be wholly equated with hopeless anguish, that the alienation
of man is complete, and that revolt is useless. If every human
activity is no more than an exercise in futility, why even write
plays? Perhaps the definitive statement is made in what is prob-

Figure 9–12

In Genet's The Blacks *characters are masked to destroy their individuality. See also 12–4. (Martha Swope)*

ably the best of all these plays, *Waiting for Godot*. It is a play about *waiting; Godot is anything for which one waits.* In its balanced structure of two acts, each ending identically (Well, shall we go?/Yes, let's go./*They do not move.*); with Vladimir and Estragon and Pozzo and Lucky neatly balanced as two pairs and as two individuals within the pairs; with several passages where silence is importantly balanced with speech; in the balance of quiet and active, ridiculous and serious, it is as if Beckett were making visible and audible in the dramatic act the precarious balance between hope and despair, between humanism and nihilism in the present world. What can we do? We can *wait.* No positive act is possible in his philosophy; the dramatic expression (which, by the way, he calls "a tragicomedy in two acts") is definitive.

With the emergence of this genre (if it *is* a new genre), we can —to some extent—characterize the various genres according to which of the Aristotelian necessities it most stresses. We may end up here with a violent distortion, for it is perfectly true that the thought content or the intention of the playwright is the organic and seminal germ which accounts for and directs the relationships perceived among the elements in any given play. To characterize form by an extracted organic strand is, of course, a wide generalization, and exceptions could be instantaneously proffered for every statement. But it may prove useful in gaining perspective and food for thought. In tragedy, then, the predominantly im-

Figure 9–13

Purdue
Professional Theatre
*Persons are treated as
things in* Oh, What a
Lovely War! *Directed
by Joseph G. Stockdale, Jr.,
designed by Robert Williams.*

Figure 9–14
New York Shakespeare
Festival Public Theatre
The chief character of
Huui, Huui *is a complete
nonentity, and his life
is meaningless.
Directed by Joseph Papp.*
(George E. Joseph)

Figure 9–15

New York Shakespeare
Festival Public Theatre
In Hair! *music and
sound effects achieve
paramount importance.
Original production,
directed by Gerald Freedman.*
(George E. Joseph)

portant unit is the Thought: "Man gets what he pays for, and pays for what he gets." In melodrama it is Plot: the intricate "tying and untying of the knot." In comedy it is Character: the whole panorama of humanity in both its ridiculous and admirable qualities. In tragicomedy it is Mood: the bitter-sweet mixture of honey and myrrh, of sad and gay at the same time. In this new genre it is Spectacle: nonhuman and nonliterary, where man is a "thing" and there is no sense nor logic. Such a category is obviously too pat and too easy, but stressing the Spectacle of the New Theatre does allow us to follow, briefly, two new theatrical phenomena which grow out of Artaud's manifestoes and which characterize experiments in theatrical production at the present time: happenings and what, for want of a better word, we might call "environmental theatre." Each, to some extent, is the ultimate extension of the nonplay, but they arrive at this goal by different means, by rather opposite techniques.

The central power of the best of the new plays is that of the poetic image, the intuition in depth brought to life in dramatic metaphor which confronts an audience and moves it by power and aptness. Not discursive logic, not linear arrangement of informational signs, but a kind of *total environment* making its impact in prelogical ways is its strength. Yet, in spite of protestations to the contrary, it retains its viability as *play* and is contained in the architectural structure of theatre.

Happenings, on the other hand, are more likely than not to be performed *outside* the theatrical structure, and there are those who would not include them as a part of theatre at all. They are, however, an extension of theatrical means and a form of experimentation in theatrical form which deserves some notice. The name itself is unfortunate because it implies haphazard happenstance, lacking preparation, planning, and form. In truth, the theatrical events which have acquired this name are anything but haphazard and spur-of-the-moment performances. The name derives from the title given to one of his early works of this kind by Allan Kaprow—18 *Happenings in 6 Parts* (1958–1959), which was the end result of a period of development, exploration, and trial and a discrete entity in its own right. So new is the entity called a happening that its form is still volatile, and only Jean-Jacques Lebel in France and Michael Kirby in the United States have done any considerable assessment and criticism of it.

The impetus for its development in the United States came from the fields of art, music, and dance; as time went on some theatre people were drawn into the experimentation and production. One of its forebears was the impudent Dada movement in art circles about the time of World War I, which merged into the much more important and influential Surrealist school in the 1920s. Dada, a word picked by chance out of the dictionary, was used to name the activities of the poets Tzara, Ball, and Hülsenbeck, and the sculptor Jean Arp who presented sketches ridiculing contemporary culture and conventional behavior in the Cabaret Voltaire in Zurich. The movement spread to Paris, Hanover, and New York and drew in other artists and writers, including Max Ernst, Marcel Duchamp, Schwitters, and Breton. It was iconoclastic and nihilistic in intent and activity. Surrealism (the word first appearing in 1924) had the positive intent of governing entirely by the workings of the subconscious mind the entire content and creative principle of a work of art. The means to be used, in art as well as literature, were to be "automatic." André Breton became its chief spokesman, and its most outstanding representatives were Max Ernst and Salvador Dali. The automatic and subconscious aspects of surrealism led, in turn, to the abstract expressionism of Jackson Pollock, William de Kooning, and Mark Tobey, in which the *process* of the painting becomes more important than the product, the *doing* rather than the *thing done*—a point of view which is prevalent in the happening. Continuing experimentation by artists such as Rauschenberg, Tinguely, Oldenburg, and Kaprow led to collages of found materials, then to action collages, then to environments, then (particularly by the last two artists named) to the complete involvement of artist, objects, and viewers in the presentation called a happening.

Another parallel line of development comes through dance and music. About the same time that the Dadaists were active, the dancer Mary Wigman was eliminating music and interpretation from many of her dances, and Rudolf von Laban, a dance theorist and teacher in Hungary (Wigman had once studied with him), was attempting to synthesize laws of movement based on everyday life. The modern dance movement in general, developing in the years since then, has been away from the traditional two-dimensional, picture-frame stage of classical dancing and toward the three-dimensional use of space-movement for its own sake rather than for the telling of a story, and an extension of the natural movements of the body. The great exponent of modern dance however—Martha Graham—retains an emotional continuity in her presentations, which led Merce Cunningham to break away from her group and begin experimenting with dance movements organized by chance methods and without story or consistent characters. Paul Taylor and Ann Halprin explored the relationship of movement to environment, and the latter particularly, in this experimentation, discovered audience involvement to an intense degree.

John Cage, the composer, approaching performance from his own point of view, abandoned traditional harmonic structure in his compositions, experimented with chance methods, and the noise music of the earlier Italian Futurists (supplemented by practices of the Dadaists) in which the noises of machines, bells, sirens, cans, keys, rattles, falling objects, and so on, along with silence itself (which Cage says can never be absolute). In 1952 he presented at Black Mountain College a "simultaneous presentation of unrelated events" which included the reading of a lecture, the playing of a piano and a phonograph, improvised dance, and movie projections, with the events taking place within and around the audience who were seated on chairs distributed in four equal wedge-shaped areas facing a center free-space, with wide aisles and space surrounding the outside of the grouped chairs.

In the early 1950s, there was much cross-fertilization of ideas by personal association among dancers, artists, and musicians, particularly in New York, and (as we have mentioned above) the first presentation called a happening was given there by Allan Kaprow in 1958–1959, although similar presentations had been given by Kaprow and others in the years immediately preceding. In the years immediately following, both Kaprow and Oldenburg presented happenings in Europe, and avant-garde artists there began the creation of their own events, calling them, as had been done here, happenings. The first European happening, according to Jean-Jacques Lebel (*TDR* 41, p. 104), was given in June, 1960, in Venice.

The "aesthetic" of the happening has been most exhaustively detailed by Michael Kirby in the Introduction to his *Happenings: An Illustrated Anthology*, in which he defines the happening as "a form of theatre in which diverse elements, including nonmatrixed

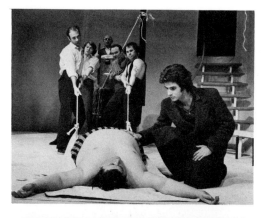

Figure 9–16

The American
Place Theatre
*The Theatre of
Cruelty is nicely
epitomized in the
inhuman action of George
Tabori's* The Cannibals.
(Martha Holmes)

Figure 9–17

Royal Shakespeare
Company
*The action of Marat-
Sade transpires in a
madhouse. See also
10–10. Directed by
Peter Brook.
(Tom Hollyman)*

performing, are organized in a compartmented structure" (p. 21).
The perils of defining a form so new and so obviously volatile are
apparent in his immediate exceptions of some recorded presentations, but the given definition is eminently useful in trying to
understand what a happening is.

The *form of theatre* indicates an event which takes place generally in space not originally planned as theatre space: galleries,
lofts, stores, halls, courtyards, houses, basketball courts, swim-
ming pools, parking lots, city streets, parks, fields or almost any
found space that can be adapted to the needs of the given
presentation. About the only rule governing the selection of space
is that it should be such as will allow audience involvement either
by active participation in the events or by being placed physically
in their midst. The *diverse elements* are literally anything that has
visual, auditory or tactile appeal. Allan Kaprow even presented an
Eat (1964) in the old Ebling Brewery caves in the Bronx, during
which the primary appeal was gustatory. A basic premise of the
happening is that as many appeals as possible shall be made
simultaneously. Platforms, stepladders, mattresses, cargo nets,

Figure 9–18

Purdue
Professional Theatre
*We are all performers,
but the world is crazy,
so we ought to* Stop the
World. *Directed by
Joseph G. Stockdale, Jr.,
designed by Joseph
McArdle.*

chairs, tables, boxes, inner tubes, lawnmowers, brooms, barrels, automobiles (whole, demolished, and in parts), as well as various kinds of cloth hangings in strips and expanses, and plastic, foil, and paper in all manners of treatment from shreds to sheets are selected and arranged for their visual and tactile properties. (The list is not exhaustive; it is obvious that absolutely anything can become a part of the environment of a happening.) Also any kind of noise or music-making instruments may be used, along with movie projections of film or slides.

Kirby's *nonmatrixed performing* simply means that any human beings involved in the happening are there by virtue of their "natural" qualities (appearance, movement, etc.) rather than by virtue of any assumed "acting" or "characterization." In fact, many of the creators of happenings deliberately did not use trained actors in order to avoid such "artificiality." The *organized in a compartmented structure* means a lack of continuity, logic or sequence in the presentation through its time span; that when more than one event or activity are transpiring simultaneously they have no integral relationship but are discrete entities;

Figure 9–19

Negro Ensemble
Company
Song of the Lusitanian
Bogey *is an outstanding
example of the black
experience in the
theatre. (Bert Andrews)*

that there is no such thing as focus or major point of interest demanding the attention of the entire audience at a given moment.
The idea is somewhat like that of a circus, where multiple activities are taking place at the same time: acrobats on the high wire,
equestrians in the center ring, the lion tamer in another, a juggling
act in another, and the clowns everywhere. (Except that in a
happening there is no assumed character like that of the clown,
and the audience is integrated within the performance.)

Various principles are at work in the happening: message complexity, multifocus, chance technique, and a playing with modes
of perception, aside from the universal audience involvement on
the level of release from the individual's usual mode of behavior.
Whatever message the creator has in mind—and the artist usually
has in mind a meaning in a symbolic or suggestive sense—is a
part of the process of the presentation and forces upon the receiver (the audience) the necessity for sorting out the multiple
stimuli to make a pattern meaningful to himself; or he can choose
not to do so. There are no scripts as such; the artist-director,
having conceived an idea, makes a sketch (as Kaprow did for
Eat), or a diagram (as Ken Dewey did for *City Scale*), or a kind
of plot—a brief descriptive listing of the prepared environments
and the actions to be presented in each. Since the action in a
happening is, as Kirby says, "indeterminate" (sketched out but
not plotted in detail), and all the elements of whatever kind are

Figure 9–20

Karamu Theatre
In Day of Absence
some of the black
performers impersonate
whites by the
impressionistic use of
face paint.
(Reuben Silver. AJDART
Archive)

"alogical" (having no reference whatsoever to logical structures, even as *illogic*), the presentation is open-ended and impossible of identical repetition. Even with the rudimentary guidelines of sketch, diagram, or scenario, several of which have been published (see *JDR* and Kirby's book), the presentation can only be described post facto and not repeated, since there are so many variables in both the planned elements and the audience.

Happenings might be said to be a literal expression of McLuhanism: the involvement of people in their environment of multifocused complexity. American happenings would seem to be a kind of celebration of that complexity, a "psychical intent" to "give back to artistic activity what has been torn away from it: the intensification of feeling, the play of instinct, a sense of festivity, social agitation." (Lebel in *JDR* 41, p. 103.) They demonstrate "the principle of stage-audience integration, the preeminence of artistic creation over rational examination, the importance given to mood and environment." (Ibid.) It might almost be Artaud talking. But Lebel would add to the necessities of the happening an explicit political and social content of radical opposition to the "power structure," and the advocacy of "the structural transformation of human relationship." He says that in this respect European happenings differ from American. In any event, the happening is in no way representative of what McLuhan calls the Gutenberg technology of linear perception; it is

Figure 9–21

Red, White and Maddox
*is a pseudo-documentary
with satirical intent.*
(Joy Gainer)

Figure 9–22

Lincoln Center
Repertory Theatre
*Presumed
"documentaries," like*
In the Matter of
J. Robert Oppenheimer,
*have been developed in
recent years.*

Figure 9–23

Arena Stage,
Washington, D.C.
The Great White Hope,
*another "documentary,"
moved from its premiere
at Arena Stage to a
large Broadway
production.*

based on the prelogical perceptions of pre-Renaissance man, a sensory experience with multiple appeals. Some of the artists who began the movement are no longer active in it; and the French participants seem to have directed their energies into what Lebel calls *liberation theatre* (the student revolt, street theatre, and guerrilla theatre). But the San Francisco Dance Workshop continues its activities begun by Ann Halprin, Kaprow continues to stage happenings in many localities in the United States and abroad, and many other entrepreneurs are entering the field. No doubt additional creative and critical ideas will be forthcoming. In very recent years there has been an avant-garde emphasis on what are called mixed-media presentations, which are chiefly combinations of visual and auditory elements (dance movement, projections, and films, with various kinds of instrumentation and noise/music). They are in the nature of happenings, and while they may not in every respect adhere to Kirby's definition, they are a part of the experimental movement.

More closely allied to theatre itself, because it originated with theatre people almost exclusively, is the second avant-garde movement which we have loosely called *environmental theatre.* It, too, is an application of some of the Artaudian principles, particularly that which calls for a *metteur en scène* (producer, director, author) who would create a new theatre. The Polish Lab Theatre, the Living Theatre, and The Open Theatre are the longest enduring and perhaps the outstanding examples, the first the creation of Jerzy Grotowski, the second of the Becks, the third of Joseph Chaikin. Each has, at some point, expressed his indebtedness to Artaud's ideas. Others are Eugenio Barba's Odin Teatret in Denmark, The Performance Group in New York City, The Firehouse Theatre in Minneapolis, Café La Mama, and Theatre of the Ridiculous, to name only a few. The earliest in point of time is the Living Theatre, which has been in more or less continuous operation since 1951; the next is The Polish Lab Theatre which opened in 1959; Chaikin began The Open Theatre in 1963. Each has its distinguishing characteristics as well as some basic similarities; among them they encompass the whole of the concepts and practices to be found in this particular theatre style.

Each began as a reaction against traditional theatre and accepted modes of production. Julian Beck and Judith Malina (Mrs. Beck) decided in the late forties that they would secede from the New

York theatre scene and start a theatre of their own. Their first production was in 1951—Gertrude Stein's *Faustus Lights the Lights* at the Cherry Lane Theatre in Greenwich Village. Chaikin, by his own admission, was a Broadway success-oriented young actor who, after playing Gayly Gay in a Living Theatre production of Brecht's *A Man's a Man*, gave up his notions of being a Broadway star and opened an acting workshop in 1963 which produced its first plays as The Open Theatre early in 1964. Grotowski, once a "commercial" actor in his native Poland, opened his "laboratory theatre" in 1959 in a small, provincial Polish town, Opole. In talking of his aims, he says:

In the first place, we are trying to avoid eclecticism, trying to resist thinking of theatre as a composite of disciplines. We are seeking to define what is distinctively theatre, what separates this activity from other categories of performance and spectacle. Secondly, our productions are detailed investigations of the actor-audience relationship. That is, we consider the spiritual and scenic technique of the actor as the core of theatre art.

[*JDR 35, p. 60*]

Chaikin defines the goals of his theatre in somewhat similar terms:

To redefine the limits of the stage experience, or unfix them. To find ways of reaching each other and the audience. To encourage and inspire the playwrights who work with us. To find ways of presenting plays and improvisational programs without the pressures of money, real estate, and other commercial considerations which usurp creative energy. To develop the ensemble.

[*JDR 26, p. 191*]

And Julian Beck has said concerning the aims of the Living Theatre:

Life is not suspended in the theatre. The actor breathes, the spectator lives. In the theatre life is intensified. . . . We seek a style of acting that will produce revelation. . . . A performance is an act of love in which the playwright, actor, and theatre artist expose themselves, body and spirit, under ordeal, at great risk, to produce catharsis and enlightenment for an anonymous audience.

[*JDR 18, p. 199*]

Difficulties with the Fire Department caused the closing of the Cherry Lane Theatre after the Becks had presented six different productions there. After an interval, a loft theatre and then another converted space enabled them to add some fifteen more plays to their production list before insolvency and defiance of the Internal Revenue Service led to the closing of their theatre, a short-lived imprisonment for Beck, and the removal of the company to Europe in 1963. They returned briefly to the United States in 1968–1969. Theirs is a history of recurring money problems, of almost constant poverty, but of absolute commitment to an ideal. Their lives, their work, and their hopes are a single thing: the theatre in which they believe. During the years of moving about Europe the company became a kind of commune, and dedication to their own community is the outstanding characteristic of its members. In addition to performing plays which they liked written by "outside" playwrights, they early began to "create" plays of their own. (They had performed Jarry's *Ubu Roi* at the Cherry Lane in 1953.) First they "transformed" scripts to their own particular style of playing, and then they began building performances out of group discussions and the trying-out of ideas. Both processes were evident in the four plays they brought back from Europe. They played Brecht's *Antigone* and their own version of the Frankenstein story, along with *Mysteries and Smaller Pieces* and *Paradise Now*, the latter two being complete constructs of their own.

Almost from the beginning the Becks declared themselves revolutionaries opposed to the power structure of Western society and politics; they have commendably persisted in this point of view, not only in their theatre statements but in their mode of living. Theirs is a theatre with a definite philosophical commitment which works through movement and sound (speech being primarily considered as *sound*, not discursive speech) to create images which will surround and involve audiences and move them to action. Stefan Brecht, the philosopher, in a long and involved article (*TDR* 43, pp. 47–73), analyzes their ideology as consummated in their performances: "An association in which the free development of each is the condition of the free development of all." He finds both virtues and flaws in their acting out of this principle. Essentially he says that the necessities of theatre ("the theatre is not life," *Irwin Silber*, Ibid., p. 86) are that such spontaneity does not "create its form; the grandiose harmony of these Passion plays is to the eye evidently not the organic life of free personalities in interaction but the conjoined product of directorial genius and of the self-sacrifice of a membership." But, on the other hand

Figure 9–24

Allan Kaprow, a leading artist in the development of happenings, preparing for 18 Happenings in 6 Parts, 1959. (© 1970 by Fred W. McDarrah)

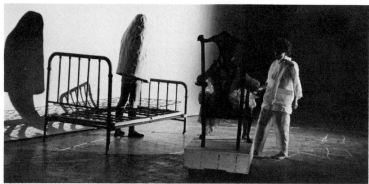

Figure 9–25

The presentation of Robert Rauschenberg's Linoleum Happening. (© 1970 by Fred W. McDarrah)

Figure 9–26

Pageant Players

Street theatre has developed in recent years to a popular activity stressing freedom of form and "found" audiences. (© 1970 by Fred W. McDarrah)

The performers' real or apparent excitement is projected and transmitted, the acoustics, kinetics and optics are designed to excite as are rock and roll or marches. The subject matter is inflammatory: pursuit and co-ercion, violence and death, creation and resistance, the taking of risk—the anarchist revolution, miraculous, is a gambler's compendium of risks. The thesis presses all this on us as our own life-and-death concern.

It would appear that the Living Theatre might be called "the theatre of the revolution."

Not so politically oriented, and less peripatetic in its operation, The Open Theatre has succeeded in developing playwrights of superior quality as well as in exploring new dimensions of the art of acting. Plays are "made" through the process of interaction and exploration between a practicing playwright and a body of actors. The playwright provides a "form," i.e., an idea, an action, or a theme, and the actors improvise, selecting their own language, building their own relationships. Any given situation may be tried in a variety of ways; actors may change roles frequently. At the end of a given work period, the playwright goes off and writes down the dialogue. Integral to the process is the acting technique called transformations, a kind of game in which, at a given signal, an actor changes roles: i.e., from being the interviewer he becomes the applicant, or vice versa. Or actors are "sent in" to replace other actors in an ongoing scene in ongoing characters. The em-phasis, in this way, is always kept on the *action* rather than upon the developing psychology of the characters, upon the *theme* or underlying idea rather than upon the sequential or logical pre-sentation of scenes. Chaikin has said, "We're interested in a theatre of illusion and mystery, not one of behavioristic psy-chology." (*JDR* 26, p. 196) The "forms" suggested by the play-wright may be death, sanity, war, old age, etc. There is little discussion per se; the acting company attack the theme in *action:* in speech and movement directly. A choreographer is a part of the group and helps the actors explore the limits of movement and matters of rhythm. Playwright and actors work in a free inter-change, a sharing of experience, attitudes, abilities, and ideas.

What results are plays like Megan Terry's *Viet Rock* (1966) or Claude van Itallie's *America Hurrah!* (1967) and several others. The method of working eventuates in a play whose unity lies in its idea and its effects (this might well be called "a theatre of effects") as Artaud stated theatre should be. The structure is not one of acts and scenes but rather one of a succession of *action blocs*, which may have some kind of associational relationship or may be entirely disassociated. The "transformations" keep the audience from identifying with an actor as a character and jolt its sense of reality; it is a kind of theatrical cubism in which the ongoing *idea* remains paramount. The attempt is always to involve the audience directly, to confront them with their own aliveness in a world of change. "A sense of being alive now, in this room, in this place. We are alive here," says Chaikin. ". . . a sense of community and mortality. A confirmation of the mutual mortality of the people in the room. If you go to a play you must participate in it; you may or may not like it." (*JDR* 43, p. 144) Thus The Open Theatre is devoting itself to *the act* and its mutual effect upon performer and audience; it is concerning itself with the basic fact of theatre and finding new ways to deal with it.

Perhaps the most famous of these groups is The Polish Lab Theatre, whose guiding genius is Jerzy Grotowski. Profiting by a state subsidy since its beginning, it has not been plagued with financial problems and has had the enviable leisure of concentrating on artistic concerns. Grotowski and his associates, in their exploration of "what is distinctively theatre" (stripping away the glamour of lights, sound, scenery, costumes, and make-up) have decided that it is the set of transactions that takes place between actors and audiences, and that the actor is a kind of mystic votary who must be infinitely skilled in reaching and communicating to the deeply overlayed, prelogical consciousness of modern man. Thus the theatre becomes a modern secular ritual dealing with archetypal symbols of myth, image, and *leitmotiv* in which everyone participates according to his abilities. "Not to show the world as separated from the spectator, but, within the limits of the theatre, to create with him a new world," says Ludwik Flazen, Grotowski's prime associate. (*JDR* 27, p. 158) The actor gives himself completely to this endeavor, developing his physical capabilities so that he can do incredible feats: using his facial and bodily muscles so exactly that he can change his appearance from character to character without the use of make-up and acquiring the ability to concentrate his psychical energies so that his performance is an elevated and trancelike expression concentrating on purely vocal or physical effects. Words can be pure sounds as well as a means of intellectual communication;

parts can be exchanged during performance; actors can meta-morphose from one character to another or even to a *thing* like a telephone or a typewriter. Everything which is art is *artificial;* any means of expression is permitted so long as it is justified by the logic of the production, has been deliberately chosen, and composed within the whole. Plays of any kind are simply blue-prints to be explored, changed, recomposed, or transposed in order to discover and present the archetypes which form the basis of the communion between actor and audience. *Dr. Faustus, The Constant Prince, Akropolis,* and *Hamlet* are re-created with the original text functioning simply as a score which may be edited, confronted, or brought into consonance with the experi-ence and being of actors and audiences. Thus the text becomes the order and structure which disciplines the search for spon-taneity and creativity. "Searching for spontaneity without order always leads to chaos," says Grotowski. (*JDR* 41, p. 45)

The playing space is fluid, with the actor-audience relationship subject to change from play to play or even within the same play. But the relationship must be *organic* and inherent in the play per-formed. A mere whisper or touch by an actor to a convenient spectator is pure cheating and trickery; the spectator's role at a theatrical performance is to be a spectator—a concerned and involved spectator, but a spectator, not an actor. So in *Dr. Faustus* they are invited guests, sitting around a long table, to whom Faustus appeals in order to make an analysis of his life; the events appear in flashback. In *Akropolis,* whose action takes place in a concentration camp (as the Lab Theatre interpreted it), the spectators are seated on chairs throughout the room and the actors treat them as if they were ghosts from another world, totally irrelevant and incomprehensible as the actors go about their assigned tasks, yet by their very presence adding to the sense of congestion and the limitation of space which is basic to the con-cept. In *The Constant Prince* the audience is separated from the actors by a high fence over which only their heads protrude; the action is seen as if taking place in a medical amphitheatre, or a bullring. "It is not essential that actors and spectators be mixed," says Grotowski, "the important thing is that the relation between the actors and the spectators in space be a significant one." (*JDR* 41, p. 43) Environment is to serve the only significant and unique function of theatre—the transactions that take place between

Figure 9–27

The Polish
Laboratory Theatre
*A highly stylized
fantasy, Akropolis,
blends Biblical themes
and Greek heroes in
20th century reality.
Here two concentration
camp prisoners re-enact
the Biblical story of
Jacob wrestling with
the Angel of the Lord,
under the direction of
Jerzy Grotowski.*

actor and audience. This changing relationship demands a new kind of theatre—a *space* which can be brought to the service of the presentation.

Richard Schechner, the American critic-teacher-director, has attempted to set up a series of "axioms" which characterize environmental theatre (*JDR* 39, pp. 41–64):

1. The theatrical event is a set of related transactions among and between performers, members of the audience, production elements and the space in which the performance takes place.
2. All the space is used for performance; all the space is used for audience.
3. The theatrical event can take place either in a totally transformed space or in "found space."
4. Focus is flexible and variable; it may either be multi-local, or single (the traditional).
5. All production elements speak in their own language, either in harmony or in counterpoint; contradictory statements are not ruled out.
6. The text need be neither the starting point nor the goal of a production; there may be no text at all.

This is the New Theatre, in which past literature becomes material available for present creativity which "builds around and through it" to enter into a communion of actor and audience on the subject of their mutual life and mutual mortality.

THE PREDOMINANT
GENRES

Figure 9–28

*An early production of
The Living Theatre,
The Collection, brought
them some fame.
(Friedman-Abeles)*

Before closing this chapter on new forms in the theatre, it might not be amiss to point out here the presence and nature of two types of theatrical phenomena briefly mentioned above: *street theatre* and *guerrilla theatre*. Both are designedly confrontational and revolutionary in intent. The former is the name given to the presentation on urban streets of a dramatic piece (skit, morality, political farce) written expressly for or adapted to that purpose. It is short in length (five to ten minutes or less in playing time), incisive in statement, using contemporary themes of political or social import. It is acted on the street itself, or on a platform or flatbed truck, and the performers themselves gather the crowd. In production style it is related to the medicine shows of the old West and the travelling *commedia* troupes of earlier vintage. In purpose it is allied to the "agit-prop" plays of the American thirties. It is frankly aimed at arousing the audience to action by confrontation. The Bread and Puppet Theatre, the Teatro Campesino, the San Francisco Mime, the Pageant Players, and Spirit House are examples of troupes engaging in this kind of theatre activity.

Guerrilla theatre is even more politically oriented and revolutionary. Its practitioners distinguish it from street theatre by calling it "theatre which pretends not to be theatre"; i.e., a

Figure 9–29

The Living Theatre
*Julian Beck in Avignon,
France, demonstrating a
scene from* Paradise
Now *to some of the
company members.*
(© 1970 by Fred W.
McDarrah)

planned event which takes the spectators off-guard by acting as if
certain things were true, and ideally never revealing their staged
qualities. Any chosen locale is the playing space—from street
corner to convention hall—and the production style is as realistic
as possible. The aim is to radicalize the unsuspecting audience by
representing social and political abuses as detailed and extreme
actualities. If the audience, by chance or by design, later finds
out that it has been "conned," it is doubly upset—once by the
event itself, and once by the discovery. Hence, say its practitioners, people are sensitized to abuses and hopefully persuaded to
correct them. Few theatre groups operate in this way: The American Playground, the National Liberation Front, the State Department Interventionists, the Yippies. Guerrilla theatre operates
as guerrilla warfare. Both it and street theatre are frankly didactic
and political, at the cutting edge of today.

Thus we have encircled theatre from various directions: the
play itself, ways of seeing, and the predominant genres, with a
brief consideration of the new ways which are being tried to spin
the old wheel whose rim is the world and whose hub is the
theatre. We shall next attempt a consideration of the artists who
make theatre: actor and director, playwright, designer, architect,
and critic. We shall try to see how these members of a community

function for themselves, in relation to each other, and for the whole of theatre. Though we take out parts for consideration and inspection, we must remind ourselves again that the part is not the whole; it is a deeper and truer understanding of the whole at which we aim in examining the parts.

Figure 9–30

The Open Theatre

Eve bites the apple in The Serpent. Created by Claude van Itallie in collaboration with The Open Theatre under the co-direction of Joseph Chaikin and Roberta Sklar. (Photo courtesy of Roberta Sklar)

IV
The Artists of the Theatre

10
Actor and Director

It might seem, from our previous preoccupation with forms and modes, that the written word of the dramatist is the most essential part of theatre. Certainly in the received tradition of literature this impression cannot help but be made; for centuries our only way of preserving the ideas and statements of past times has been through the written word. But theatre is a NOW proposition; it is created—and always has been—in the now, in the present. Playscripts (as we have been saying from the beginning) are essentially and always blueprints for performance, including the action conceived by the playwright. They can be admired as literature, but they do not become *theatre* until they are performed. And the one essential for performance is the actor. Indeed, as we have said over and over again, the core of theatre is the actor-audience relationship. With it there is theatre; without it there is none. This is the only absolutely and always present factor. Theatre is made where an actor meets an audience and with it *lives through* an experience in which both are interested and involved.

The actor and director constitute the *living component* of the theatre art; the designer and architect supply the *environment*; the playwright and critic supply *the words*, the ideas, the philosophy, and the form. It follows, then, that since theatre is the art form of *virtual life*, the living components are the most essential; without them theatre does not exist. In that seminal time of ancient Greece from which our Western theatre sprang, actor, director, and playwright were one and the same human being, and he was musical director, designer, and choreographer as well. Thus Aeschylus functioned, and Sophocles as well; they controlled all the effects that were to be produced in the performance. In the long stretches of time since then, the various components of the theatrical art have been separated out, and today each is generally realized by a separate functionary working in close cooperation with his fellow artists. Occasionally, one individual will achieve success in a dual capacity: Laurence Olivier, Jean-Louis Barraúlt, and John Gielgud are renowned as both actors and directors. Even less frequently is there an individual, like Peter Ustinov, who is actor, director, and playwright. Rarely now does a playwright direct his own work, and almost never does either actor or director completely design the production or write the playscript. How this situation came about is an interesting development.

From the very first, the function—and the problem—of the actor has been that of *impersonation*. Even the primitive actor impersonated: a buffalo, an island, growing corn, a successful hunter, etc., and he almost invariably used mask and costume to help him submerge his own personality and assume the characteristics of the person or thing impersonated. His aim was to *seem* to be what he was *pretending* to be and to make his audience accept the impersonation. Down through the long history of acting, impersonation remains the central problem. And the essential dichotomy might be expressed by the terms *presentational* or *representational*. That is to say, the basic argument that has endured concerning acting (aside from whether it is an *art* or a *craft*, something *native* or *acquired*, *inspired* or *learned*) is whether the actor should include his audience in the frank statement that *he is an actor assuming a role*, or that he should seem to be really *living* the role which the audience observes and hence be unaware of their presence. These antipathies have been present as possibilities from the beginning, and the constantly recurring "reforms in acting" that dot theatre history swing like a pendulum between these poles. The intellectual climate of a given period, and the nature of the material with which the actor worked in that period have determined the point of the arc receiving collective sanction. Those actors who most fully met this collective sanction are the "great actors" of their time. So there is a long and continuous history of acting; the history of directing as a separated function is much shorter, and generally confined to modern times.

In the homogeneous society that was ancient Athens, men were citizen-soldiers, philosopher-kings, actor-poets—truly all-round

individuals, with every faculty ideally developed to its utmost. And the theatre was spokesman for this centrality, a part of religious festival. The theatre had supposedly developed from the exploit of Thespis in separating himself from the dithyrambic chorus to speak separate lines, and it was natural that such a poet-actor was central to the theatre. Euripides was censured, not only because he did not act in his own plays, but also because he sought the aid of Iophon, son of Sophocles, in preparing music for his productions. Since the poet was the *maker*, he operated in all areas of the construct: speaking the lines, training the chorus and the musicians, setting the *mise-en-scène*. But even then—the minute Aeschylus added a second actor (said to be Cleander) to the Thespian "one," the office of *actor* became separated from the other functions. For obviously this second actor was not the prime *maker*, but one of the elements in the making, who was to dispose himself as the chief actor-poet required. By the fourth century, when the great tragedies were no longer being written,

Figure 10–1

Metropolitan
Museum of Art
*Statuette of a Greek
tragic actor.*
(*Rogers Fund, 1913*)

Figure 10–2

Metropolitan
Museum of Art
*Terracotta statuette of a
Greek comic actor,
probably 4th century*
B.C. (*Rogers Fund, 1913*)

the actor emerged as the most important single entity in theatre; it is the classic "age of great acting." There was even a society, or guild, organized for his benefit—the Artists of Dionysus—which functioned to protect his interests, regulate his working conditions, and set standards of payment. New plays were still staged by their poets, but the bulk of the repertoire was from the writers of the past. And here the actors took charge, the most respected in a given company being the actor-director (although the term did not exist).

In Roman times the same situation prevailed: Plautus staged his own plays and sometimes acted in them (he had been an actor before he began writing plays), but actors had a separate and recognized function. Roman times have given us a name second only to Thespis as a renowned and legendary actor—that of Roscius, friend to Cicero, who was not only made a freeman but knighted for his skill. Though Plautus in early Republican times had been a freeman, actors in the Roman Empire were generally slaves, owned by patrician households, and trained in performance by a master who literally had the power of life and death over them. (The same system prevailed in the serf companies of nineteenth-century Russia.) In both Hellenistic times and Roman times, actors were professionals, in that acting was their way of life and the means whereby they made a living. The debate concerning method of acting was not a concern in classic times, because the nature of the materials with which the actor dealt required a formal, presentational style. And the masks and costumes which the actors wore underlined this style. No one watching Nicostratus perform Oedipus assumed that he *was* Oedipus, and neither did he. But he was no mere reciter of lines. He filled the lines, the mask, and the costume with as much emotional content as was possible; the actor Polus is said to have used the urn containing the ashes of his son to induce in himself the proper emotion while he was playing Electra mourning over the ashes of her supposedly dead brother.

In medieval times acting was an almost solely amateur and part-time pursuit. There seem to have been some practitioners of a ragged and bankrupt professionalism throughout the Middle Ages in the persons of jugglers, mimes, and troubadours; some historians believe them to be the discredited descendents of Roman actors. But since the predominant theatrical form in medieval times was that of the great cycle plays, the productions being done by settled communities, the participation of the wandering, outcast professionals is dubious, or at least sporadic and occasional, the exception rather than the rule. Since the great cycles originated in the church, their production was, for a long time, done under church supervision. There is a delightful manuscript, called the *Concordia Regularis*, dated A.D. 965–975, in which Ethelwold, Bishop of Winchester in England, gives minute instructions about how the Easter playlet shall be staged. It is probably our first *regiebuch* in English, and the good bishop one of the first directors of record in the language. He directs that the opening lines of the playlet should be sung "in a medium voice of dulcet pitch," and that the three "brethren" playing the Marys at the tomb of Christ should enter "slowly, in the manner of seeking something." As such primitive and early episodes developed into a whole series of plays given on one or more days, the actors were laymen who performed as a part of religious duty and (in England) for the honor of their guilds.

On the continent, where the shows did not travel as they did in England and Spain, the complications of performance necessitated a "director" of sorts. The famous Jean Foquet miniature of the playing of "The Martyrdom of St. Apollonia" pictures a priestly figure, baton and book in hand, face alert and interested, obviously directing the action of the crowded scene. And the equally famous Luzerne prompt book names Renward Cysat, city clerk of Luzerne, the director, and gives sketches for the arrangement of the city square for the two days of performance. From old guild and town records, we know that rehearsals were held prior to performance; and from the scripts themselves we deduce that no little skill was demanded of the actors.

By Shakespeare's time, theatre was produced by companies of men and boys (to play the women's parts) who stayed together for years of playing, and who were organized somewhat after the fashion of the craft guilds, with masters, journeymen, and apprentices. The boy apprentice lived in the house of his master and learned from him the skills necessary to his craft of acting: declamation, singing, dancing, and the playing of one or more musical instruments. Shakespeare was an actor (though never a really renowned one) and his own director. But primarily he was resident playwright for his company, whose chief actor and star

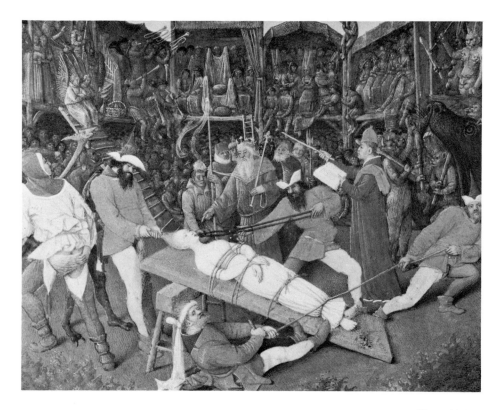

Figure 10–3

Portion of Fouquet's medieval miniature depicting a performance of the Martyrdom of Saint Apollonia. *The clerical regisseur stands with book and baton in hand in the midst of the performance.*
(*Photographie Giraudon*)

was Richard Burbage. Almost all the great leading roles in Shakespeare's plays were written for Burbage to perform. The leading actor of the rival company was Edward Alleyn, who first created the great roles of Marlowe's plays. From the evidence of the plays and from contemporary comments, we gather that actors then were incredibly proficient in voice production, and admired for playing to each other and maintaining a characterization throughout the length of a given play. But the platform stage, the universal recognition that boys played the women's parts, and the convention of the soliloquy meant that even this seeming "naturalism" in stage behavior was actually a quite formal presentational style and not "natural acting" as we would use the term. One of the most famous of all director's statements is the one Hamlet gives to the players in Act III, Scene 2; it still sounds like excellent advice even for modern actors. So closely did the Shakespearian company work together that what emerged as a play was the result of their cooperative acting efforts rather than a design imposed by a director in the modern sense. Stage decorum—the

Figure 10–4

A small travelling company in the early Renaissance sets up a platform stage to perform for a standing audience.

proper lines said at the right time, entrances and exits, and the movement of props—was seen to by a company member called the book-holder, a position probably analogous on the one hand to the medieval regisseur with his baton and book, and on the other to our modern stage manager.

Just as the cooperative skill of a resident company produced Shakespeare's plays in England, it was the cooperative skill of travelling companies of actors that produced what we have come to call *commedia dell'arte* in Italy. This theatre form is exactly contemporary with Elizabethan-Jacobean drama. We have already spoken of it to some extent, but need to include it here in our progression. It had no resident playwrights and no standing theatres. Its company members were generally of one family, by birth or marriage, and both men and women performed. Usually one of the actors, by reason of his family position or his particular skills, was the company manager; he prepared the programs of the company, looked after their business affairs, and arranged the tours. In the most famous of these companies, *I Gelosi*, Francesco

Figure 10–5

Old sketches of commedia *actors performing.*

Andreini (1548–1624) performed these functions while acting Il Capitano for his entire career. His wife was the celebrated leading lady or *inamorata* of the company (Isabella, by name) whose beauty, grace, and skill are hymned in many a contemporary comment. The *commedia dell'arte* manager (like Francesco Andreini) drew up a kind of performance scenario which was a discursive story, broken up into scenes, indicating entrances, actions, and exits. It was posted "in the wings" and performers referred to it before going on stage. (The same device is used today by such improvisational troupes as the Second City.)

Each performer had his individual character in traditional costume and mask—Arlecchino, Brighella, Pantalone, Il Dottore, etc. —along with a store of previously memorized set speeches and previously practiced bits of business which were consonant with his character type. He would use these wherever the action of the given piece allowed for them. Otherwise, his speech and action were improvised, or created, directly on the stage in company with his fellow actors and in accordance with his character. (This theatre style is hence sometimes called *commedia dell'improviso*.)

The demands of this theatre form were very great. Performers had not only to be quick-witted and clear-spoken, they had also to be acrobats, dancers, and musicians. The story is told of Visentini, who could turn a somersault with a wine glass and not spill a drop; of Fiorilli who, at the age of eighty-three, could still box his ear with his toe; and of the great Isabella who could speak four languages fluently. The Italian *commedia* was actor's theatre at its acme, a highly professional institution.

Parallel with the heyday of the *commedia dell'arte* troupes in Italy was the formal theatre of the courts and the academies, playing the pastorals, comedies, and tragedies which were primarily written by the Renaissance scholars. Here the actors were amateurs, like Césare Borgia and his friends, and they participated in these special performances at festivals, weddings, and other courtly affairs. Naturally they needed more specific instruction and direction than the professionals, and they got it. One of the interesting documents of the Italian Renaissance is that called "The Dialogues of Leone di Somi," written about 1565, which gives most specific instructions concerning the casting, directing, and producing of these special events. In its preface di Somi says that his aim in writing is "to record, rather for myself than for others, in due order those most important rules and more necessary precepts of which I have often had to avail myself when obeying the commands of authorities"; i.e., to put on such a special performance. One of his cautions is that the producer should be careful to so dress his amateur actors that they will not be immediately recognized by their friends in the audience, for such immediate recognition is likely to spoil the illusion of the performance. Here is perhaps the first mention of the problem of representational *vs.* presentational style in acting. Di Somi's document, along with those of Serlio, Sabbattini, and Furttenbach (whom we will discuss further in the chapter on design) form what is in essence our first library of stage production. Di Somi's role is obvious: he is a director in the modern sense of the word, overseeing production in all its aspects, including casting, directing, designing, and lighting. We will not meet his like again for almost three centuries. With him, performers are to be used like any other element of production—as a part of the total stage picture.

Spanish Renaissance theatre companies were something of a

Figure 10–6

*Old lithograph of an
English pantomime
performance at Rich's
Old Covent Garden
with* commedia
characters circa 1740.

cross between the Elizabethan and the Italian *commedia,* though of entirely native growth. Women played the women's parts, except in very small traveling companies where boys were cast in the women's roles. Some companies played together for long periods of time as did the Elizabethans, although Spanish actors generally worked on a yearly contract. Some companies were shareholding, as were the Elizabethan companies, some paid set salaries to particular performers, the control being in the hands of the company manager, or *autor.* Parts were assigned by company consent, and rehearsals, while called and disciplined by the *autor,* were actually in the hands of the performers. Many and stringent rules governed the behavior of actors and actresses both on and off the stage, and the life of these traveling players (no company ever owned its own theatre as Shakespeare's company did) was incredibly hard. Augustin de Rojas amusingly described the life of such strolling players (of which he was one) in his "Entertaining Journey" (circa 1603). Spanish actors usually had to supply their own costumes (a very costly expense), whereas in England costumes were generally a company expense. For this and other reasons, many Spanish actors were declared bankrupt; while many English actors at the same time became wealthy (including Shakespeare). Like their fellows in the English theatre and the *commedia*, these Spanish performers were professionals, skilled in speaking, singing, dancing, and playing musical instruments. Their playwrights, like Lope de Vega and Calderon, were not usually attached in any way to the companies but supplied plays for agreed upon sums. In addition to playing the secular drama, they also played the *autos sacramentales* (the religious plays), usually for fixed sums of money, being hired for these by individuals or municipalities.

In the theatre of Molière's time, there was a dichotomy in acting style between the performance of tragedy and that of comedy, between the companies of the Bourgogne and the Marais and Molière's company. We have seen that French neoclassic tragedy was an adaptation of Greek and Roman models, and the style of play demanded a rhetorical, oratorical style in performance. In the Roman plays, particularly, actors announce themselves upon entrance, and speak in discursive style to the audience whenever they have something to "explain." The neoclassic tragedies contain much of this presentational aspect, having many long speeches which the actors delivered directly to the audience, in presentational style. These were known as *tirades*, and actors were judged on their ability to handle them, much as opera singers are rated even today for their rendition of the arias in opera. Movements were at a minimum and formalized, and Quintillian's rules for orators were adapted to stage deportment: gestures of hands never go above the shoulders or below the hips; facial expression is of paramount importance; in standing, the right foot must be advanced; etc.

Obviously, this declamatory style was unsuited to the comedy which Molière was developing, and he frequently lashed out against it. In *Les précieuses ridicules* he early impales the actors of the rival Bourgogne company by having one of his characters describe them thus: "They alone are capable of doing justice to plays; the rest are ignorant persons who recite their parts just as they talk, and do not know how to make the verses tell, or to pause at a fine passage; how can people know the fine passages if the actor does not emphasize them and thereby indicate that a burst of applause is expected?" Molière, all his life an actor who became increasingly popular with the public, and one who was intimately acquainted with *commedia* techniques, spent many years developing what he called a natural style of acting, along with a system of notation to help his actors acquire a more natural delivery. Something of what he meant by natural acting is detailed in both his *Critique de l'Ecole des femmes* and *L'Impromptu du Versailles*, where he appears in conversation with his company on matters of acting style. Its essence is a lack of inflated delivery, and actors playing to each other more than declaiming to the audience. Molière was *orator*, or manager, to his company, some of whom stayed with him for a lifetime of playing; it was a true ensemble, versatile and talented. As we know, it became the nucleus for the establishment of the Théâtre Française in 1680.

But though the style developed by Molière for his comedies was less formalized than that of the actors in the contemporary neoclassic tragedy, it is by no means "natural"; i.e., representational. His stage was simply a space where actors walked and talked and hardly ever even sat down. A part of his audience sat on the stage, so there was no front curtain; often the plays began with two characters talking as they enter, and ended with processions or dances. The most that we can say is that Molière's "reforms" made acting somewhat less formalized, a little more natural than that of most of his contemporaries.

The theatre of the Restoration exhibited the same pattern as that of the French: a highly formal, declamatory style in the heroic tragedies, and a somewhat less formal, somewhat more natural style in the comedies. But again, even in the comedies, the actors almost never sat down, and most of the action transpired on the deep and wide platform of the apron, rather than within the set. Restoration theatre also adopted the French practice of actresses playing the women's roles, and for the first time women appeared on the public stage in England. One significant result was the immediate expansion of women's roles in playwriting. The Restoration companies now had, in the persons of William Davenant and Thomas Killigrew, recognized *managers* (somewhat equivalent to the modern producer) who were neither actors nor playwrights, but who hired and paid the performers, chose the plays to be performed, and arranged production details of setting, costume, etc. Davenant and Killigrew had been named to their positions by the King and Killigrew, at least, had had little prior theatrical experience. This period marked the beginning of what would later prove a growing trend in theatre: the domination of production by initially nontheatrical people. But the performers, once hired, were fairly autonomous in their actual job of acting. Each player was hired to a line of parts; i.e., each had certain traditional roles which belonged to him, whose words he knew by heart and whose business he had "inherited" by tradition from the original creator of the part. New roles were assigned in accordance with an actor's line, and then became his property. As women began to take over the roles hitherto played by boys, they too developed lines just as the men had. By the middle of the eighteenth century, this pattern had solidified; rehearsals for "revivals" were laughably nominal (didn't everybody know his lines and business anyway?), and new plays were allotted no more than two weeks' rehearsal, the time chiefly being consumed in memorizing the lines. So David Garrick became the great hero and innovator when, from 1747 to 1776, as artistic director of Drury Lane, he introduced many reforms into the system.

Restoration times constitute the last historical moment when theatre played to a homogeneous and self-contained society, and even it was considerably reduced in size from what had obtained at earlier periods in history. The spacious times of great Elizabeth, the religiously oriented medieval society, the *polis* of ancient Greece had each had a built-in unifying principle of which theatre had been the reflection and a vital part of the entire whole. Even the theatre of Renaissance Italy had a centrality in the love of learning and curious art which was typical of that time. The theatre of Molière, Corneille, and Racine, while not so all-embracing in its audience, was unified in the rationalism of the intellectuals and frankly directed to a select audience capable of understanding its rationale. Restoration theatre was unified only in its selected audience of the court circles and its anti-Puritanism; the eighteenth century would change all that. The future would contain a search for particular audiences, and the unifying principles of production—heretofore inherent in the society itself—would gradually become the responsibility of particular theatres, and more especially of directors within those theatres. Garrick, then Kemble in England, Schroeder, then Goethe in Germany, Voltaire and Diderot in France, and Goldoni in Italy became, in effect, just such directors and theorists, although they were never so named and each considered something else his major commitment.

In the eighteenth century, too, the tide of printed matter which had had a slow beginning with the invention of the printing press toward the end of the fifteenth century, reached flood proportions, and the number of documents about theatrical matters increased enormously. Add to that the impetus toward analysis and codification which was characteristic of the eighteenth-century intellect, and the result is a whole series of papers investigating the properties of acting and laying down rules for its successful prosecution. Each of the above-named "directors," along with many others—actors and nonactors alike—considered, argued, declared, and/or issued fiats in this regard. When we read in these numerous commentaries that actors should have a "regard for nature," and that those who do are commended, we must remember that for the greater part of the century the Nature that was admired was not "natural nature" but "nature methodized."

Thomas Betterton began it all, or rather one Charles Gilden in the name of Betterton, by issuing in 1710 a presumed biography of the great Restoration actor, the largest part of which was devoted to a consideration of the duties and qualifications of "players" as Betterton might enunciate them. It is the first "book of acting" in English, and, of course, it makes the "appeal to Nature." But the "system of acting" which it espouses, while founded on the observation of nature, carefully catalogs "the passions and habits of the mind [which] discover themselves in our looks, actions and gestures," so that Nature is transmuted into Art; the "Beauties of Utterance" and the "Art of Gesture" never "transport the Speaker out of himself," even though a "strong Imagination" is necessary to bring the player's "Emotions to a Perfection." In 1741, the Italian, Luigi Riccoboni, was insisting that "If a Man enters strongly into a proper Enthusiasm and speaks in the Accents of the Soul, his Features will naturally form themselves

A Beggarly Account of Empty Boxes. PROTEUS *losing by his Benefit.*
No joke in THEATRICALS!

Figure 10–7

Richard Leacroft
Collection

*Performance in an
English provincial
theatre in the latter
part of the 18th century.*

into an Agreement with his Subject by the Alteration both of his Colour and Muscles." There the argument is joined and it continues to this day: Does one start with the *inner* feeling and let the rest follow, or does one start with the outer technique and build inward? Many of the arguments about the process of acting are summed up in this paradox.

David Garrick, called the greatest of English actors in his own day and ever since, wrote very little about his methods of work, but his career is so thoroughly documented that we are not much in doubt about them. He decried the stiffness of declamatory, oratorical delivery and spent much time in perfecting a style which placed emphasis upon movement and gesture suited to the words spoken, albeit this was done through careful practice and calculated skill, emotional identification with the character he was impersonating being anathema to him. He enforced strict discipline and rehearsal practices in his company and developed an ensemble spirit and skill which was the wonder of his contemporaries. Still, he was called an actor-manager and not a director—the term having not been invented in the modern sense. Diderot admired Garrick, and when he wrote his famous *Paradox* of *Acting* (1773) he insisted upon the cool head with the warm heart as the epitome of acting, substituting *judgment* for the *sensibility* which, along with *understanding* and *fire*, were usually held up as the most needed attributes of the actor. Goethe, from his autocratic position as director of the Court Theatre at Weimar, issued a document containing ninety rules for acting, which again, though appealing to nature, actually stressed an abstracted art, a technique-oriented performance. His compatriot, the actor Friedrich Schroeder, who in his long career played more than seven hundred different parts, said that every character must be so *individualized* that no repetitions from part to part are apparent in an actor's work; the actor must "fill out and be the character."

So it went. Actor-managers (Garrick, Schroeder, Kemble), playwright-managers (Goldoni, Voltaire, Goethe), actor-critics (Riccoboni) debated the nature of acting and espoused with their companies those techniques which *worked for them*. By the end of the century England was devoted to the decorous classicism of John Philip Kemble and Sarah Siddons; France to the similar quality of Talma and Clairon (for all the former's revolutionary ardor in his personal life); and Germany to the chameleon quality of Schroeder which was, nevertheless, always under perfect and reasonable control. "Ideal beauty" was the aim and the accomplishment—the epitome of the "reasonable" eighteenth "Century of Great Acting."

The Romantic Revolution of the early nineteenth century swept away the rules, classifications, and abstractions from nature which had prevailed in the eighteenth, and "inspiration" was glorified as the be-all and end-all of acting. The typical stars of this persuasion were Pavel Mochalov in Russia, Ludwig Devrient in Germany, Frédérick Lemaître in France, Tomasso Salvini in Italy, Edmund Kean in England, and Edwin Forrest in America. "Spiritual profundity and a flaming imagination are the two qualities which form the main components of talent," said Mochalov. Of Devrient it was said that "the strange and living figures created by him seemed to spring direct from his own imagination, conforming to no existing school, and owing nothing to any previous stage-creation." Hugo said of Lemaître that he "had movements, words, cries which shook audiences to their very depths." Salvini wrote in his autobiography that "I sought to live with my personage, and then to represent him as my imagination pictured him." Coleridge's remark about Kean is famous: "To see Kean was to read Shakespeare by flashes of lightning." And William Winter once characterized Forrest as "a vast animal, bewildered by a grain of genius." Though the dependence on inspiration and imagination, the throwing overboard of rules and discipline which characterized these players often resulted in very uneven performances and eventually led some of them (and many of their fellows) to a flamboyant theatricalism which initiated its own reaction, there was in them the grain of truth to an inner energy that would eventuate in the much heralded "realistic school" of acting at the end of the century.

Even while these stars flamed brilliantly in the theatrical skies, actors like Macready in England and Edwin Booth in America were developing more consistency in performance along with the requisite imagination and inspiration. By 1850, Ludwig Devrient's nephew, Eduard, was deploring the "pretentiousness" of romantic theatricalism and calling for "true naturalness." By 1852, Edmund Kean's son, Charles, was being complimented in the public press for his acting which had "a gentlemanly demeanor. . . . which intensifies the passion." The consuming flame of the previous generation's acting style had predictably burned itself out, and other emphases would take its place, although "personality actors" would sporadically command attention on the stage (like Sarah Bernhardt) and would later find their convenient home in the movies. The excesses of the romantic style subsided to the workmanlike performances of the actor-managers Henry Irving, Squire Bancroft, and Charles Matthews. In the last two decades of the century the French actor, Constant Coquelin, eloquently wrote of *The Art of the Actor* in fuller terms than any actor had done hitherto. He said that the "characteristic gift of the actor is . . . dualism; one part of him is the performer, the instrumentalist; another the instrument to be played on." The first must be the master of the second at all times. This analysis set the English critic William Archer into an investigation of the question about whether actors do and must *feel* the emotions they portray. The results of his investigations appeared as a monograph, *Masks or Faces?* (1888). The two documents (Coquelin's and Archer's) form an interesting compendium of age-old controversies concerning the nature of acting and the actor.

At the same time that the age of science was entering the theatre in the form of realism in playwriting, acting, and designing, the age of the director was also beginning. In its varying applications and emphases, science has been (as we have seen) the prime cause of the fragmenentation which so many critics and philosophers have observed in the modern world. The scientific age has destroyed the homogeneous social wholes which existed in past great ages, and a new unifying device became necessary in the art of theatre. What had earlier appeared as Greek theatre, Elizabethan theatre, neoclassic theatre, and Restoration theatre—reflections of the society which produced them—would now increasingly become Antoine's theatre, Meiningen's theatre, Stanislavsky's theatre, Max Reinhardt's theatre, the theatre of Jacques Copeau, Mayakovsky, Belasco, Brecht, Guthrie, Barrault, etc., etc., each with its own emphasis and direction. Its central core would not be determined by the creative energy and cooperation of the acting ensemble but by these directors who controlled, guided, and sometimes imposed a particular unification and style in the light of their individual visions. In considerably less than a hundred years, we have come to accept the role of the director as central and indispensable to theatrical production. The word director is the term we apply to this indispensable man in the United States. In England he is called the "producer," in France the *metteur en scène,* and in Germany and Russia the *régisseur,* but his function is the same in every place: to create the unifying concept of a given production and to control its elements.

The first director in the modern sense of the term was the early nineteenth-century French entrepreneur of melodrama, René Pixérécourt who, as we have seen, took upon himself exactly this unifying task and this general oversight; he even wrote many of the melodramas he produced. But the person generally acknowledged as the first modern director is George II, Duke of Saxe-Meiningen, probably because he worked with more serious (or at least more highly regarded) dramatic materials, his career is more thoroughly documented, and his company travelled to various metropolitan centers of the continent to perform. In any event, from 1874 to 1890 he made theatrical history in a new and spectacular way. For a number of years before the initial appearance of his troupe in Berlin (May 1, 1874), the Duke and his colleague, Ludwig Chronegk, had worked to train an originally

Figure 10–8

Museum of Modern Art
*The Duke of Saxe-
Meiningen drew
sketches to visualize for
himself and for his
company particular
moments in the stage
action. This is one from
a series for* Maid of
Orleans.

rather nondescript group of actors into a marvelously flexible acting ensemble which performed in meticulously designed and
historically accurate costumes in equally well-researched settings,
using very plastic movements and groupings which were minutely
worked out for maximum effectiveness. The Duke often made
moment-by-moment sketches (much like the "story board" of
modern-day cartoon movies) so that he and his company would
be constantly aware of the changing stage pattern. His productions were planned far in advance even of their first rehearsals,
and the actors wore facsimiles of their final costumes from the
first day of rehearsal on. There were no "star" performers; every
member of the ensemble was expected to work at his maximum
skill whether in a leading role or as a "walk-on" in a crowd scene.
No detail was too small, no amount of trouble too great to receive
loving attention and the lavish expenditure of time and energy
by George II. The results were revelations to successive audiences
in Berlin, London, Brussels, Moscow, Amsterdam, Stockholm,
Odessa, and many other cities. George II became familiarly
known as "the theatre Duke," and the artistic father of a whole
line of more or less autocratic directors from that day to this.

Reaching its apogee concurrently with that of classic realism itself, the Meiningen troupe was the very acme of external realism; actors were treated very much as stage properties, parts of the whole. Exactly analagous to the theatre Duke's methods and productions were those of America's first director autocrat, David Belasco. André Antoine, the first great modern French director, primarily founded his Théâtre Libre (1887) to give voice to new playwrights who had no hearing in the commercial theatre of the day. Circumstances forced him to work primarily with amateurs, so, as an actor himself, he became a teacher-director. He was no less autocratic (in his own way), with his fireman's whistle, than that natural-born autocrat, the theatre Duke. Believing as he did that the actions and feelings of the characters in the plays he produced were inevitably conditioned by the environment in which they lived, he insisted from the beginning of rehearsals on a complete facsimile setting. Within this environment he developed with his acting company, by trial and error, the "most truthful" presentation possible. This truth was not only to external reality but to the inner reality of characterization as well. So effectively did he train his performers that he consistently lost them to more remunerative theatre positions.

As director, Stanislavsky began as the autocrat devoted to the highly admired external realism of the Meiningens, working out very detailed production notes, which functioned as a kind of score to which every element—performers included—must conform. It was thus that he staged the first plays of Chekhov. That playwright's dissatisfaction with the results (even though the plays were critical successes), led Stanislavsky (an actor himself) into further researches and the development of his renowned psychological realism emphasizing both *inner* and *outer* truth. The general ferment of the turn of the century and the years following which questioned the value of facsimile staging, and which had its most eloquent spokesmen in Wagner, Appia, and Craig, led Stanislavsky further to crystallize his thinking and his search for "the primal source of theatre art." This primal source is, of course, the actor and his truth.

The avowed intent of each of the outstanding directors of the twentieth century has been to discover for himself this primal source of theatre art, and each has worked in his own way toward his own vision, has stamped his productions with a unique style. Copeau discovered his theatrical center in the *poet*, the first

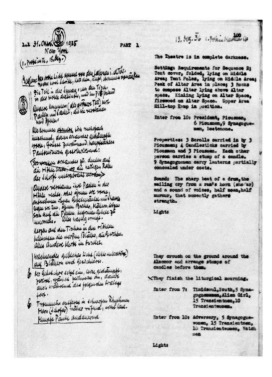

Figure 10–9

The Max Reinhardt Archive, SUNY, Binghamton

As directors, both Stanislavsky and Max Reinhardt prepared fully annotated scripts, containing every detail of performance, as in this regiebuch *for* The Eternal Road.

"creator" in theatre, who is to be served by the director as a kind of translator of his intentions, and by a dedicated body of actors who perfect themselves to give "scenic life" to this original vision. Copeau influenced the work of succeeding generations of French directors: Charles Dullin, Louis Jouvet, Jean Vilar, Michel Saint-Denis, Georges Pitoëff, Jean-Louis Barrault, and Roger Planchon. To some extent, each, according to his tastes and insights, agreed with Vilar's codification that "performance equals text plus interpreters."

The text was never so "equal" in Meyerhold's constructivist theatre or in the experiments of other Russian directors: Tairov, Vakhtangov, Okhlopkov, or in the theatre of Max Reinhardt and his followers. Reinhardt conceived that theatre was "a thing unto itself, following its own laws, its own path." He tried a wide variety of combinations of the theatrical elements, from the wordless *Sumurun* to the vastnesses of the Theatre of the Five Thousand and the elegance of the Redoutensaal, but always he stressed the *theatricality* of theatre. Leopold Jessner and Erwin Piscator, the first with his expressionistic productions, the second with his "agit-prop" techniques, shared Reinhardt's views. Influenced by

Piscator's work, Bertolt Brecht developed his theory of Epic Theatre, whose objective is to "astonish" the audience so that social changes can be brought about.

It is perhaps only in England that the director, per se, has not had overriding importance in the theatre. For there the outstanding modern directors have usually been the outstanding actors as well: John Gielgud, Laurence Olivier, and Michael Redgrave. These and others of note, like Tyrone Guthrie, Michael Langham, George Devine, Peter Brook, and Peter Hall, have each had varying degrees of experience as actors. Perhaps more than any other modern theatre, the English theatre has remained actor-centered. Some modern American directors began as actors—Harold Clurman, Elia Kazan, Orson Welles, and Ellis Raab—and in America the great reputation in theatre is generally that of the director: Joseph Anthony (once an actor), Alan Schneider, William Ball (also once an actor), Stuart Vaughan, Gerald Freedman, Tom O'Horgan, etc. While the newest trends in theatre, such as we have discussed in Part III, Chapter 9, which stress the "group image" may eventually lead to a deemphasis upon the role of the director, so far it has not done so; these groups are the reflections of the images of their founders and leaders. But their performances, at least, are more the result of cooperative group efforts than the traditional theatrical performance.

It must be evident from the foregoing that the nature of acting and the actor's place in the whole art of theatre is in a constant process of rediscovery. Nothing that is said or thought about acting today has not been thought or said or practiced at some point in the past. The seemingly newest of techniques or discoveries is, upon investigation, perceived to have had a prior existence. But the ephemerality of acting in its very nature has made these rediscoveries mandatory. Indeed, they *are* new to the people who discover them. Acting as a skill and as a profession is constantly being reborn. But, even with the differences of opinion which have always existed (sometimes sequentially and sometimes concurrently) about what constitutes acting and what the personal and professional qualities of the actor are, it is possible to discuss these matters both generally and specifically. This we now propose to do.

What we have been saying since the opening pages of this book —that theatre is *lived experience*, virtual life—is particularly epitomized in the actor. We have been making the point that theatre is *organic*, it is a living thing. The essence of life is in the *act*, the *doing*, the *actor* is the *doer*. But is it not then true that everyone who lives, acts? True. How then does that special person we call an actor differ from the general run of doers? In exactly the same way that the world of theatre differs from the world of reality—by extraction, by arrangement, by compression, by distortion, by emphasis, by selection—by all the processes that make theatre an art, or by which any art is made from "select and perspicuous material" which is not "embedded in a confusing and overwhelming matrix of other relations and events, as the realities of nature and of life are obscured in the moving universe of all reality." (See Chapter 2) Is acting then an art? Yes. Can it be learned? Yes, but just as in all the other arts that one can name, the *acquired skills* must meet the *commitment to excellence* and the *predisposition* to this particular artistic language (which we commonly call talent) in order to produce a highly valued end product. About great actors there is, and always has been, an extra, added dimension that we are fond of calling *star quality*—inspiration—which makes them the objects of adoration and emulation. I have always suspected that the essence of this quality is an unremitting dedication to absolute perfection such as most human beings (compromisers, all) can neither understand nor practice. Fortunately for the art of acting (as indeed for the arts in general), it is well that not all artists have this quality. Otherwise, how could plays be performed year after year and century after century? How could we ever have a symphony orchestra if everybody in it *must* sit in the first seat? A *predisposition* to the language of the given art must be present in the person who chooses to practice it, but he becomes proficient in the art by learning its techniques and materials and by perfecting himself in their use. Only after he thoroughly understands these techniques and materials is he in a position to be innovative and original.

The difficulty with acting as compared with the other arts, even the other arts of theatre, is that the actor is at one and the same time both the artist and the *tool* of the art. His *means of expression* is himself. This essential duality has been, in times past and in the present day, the source of much confusion and misunderstanding. All those questions about whether or not the actor *lives* his part, whether or not he *is* the character he portrays, whether

Figure 10–10

Royal Shakespeare
Company
*The actors in Marat-
Sade are not truly mad,
or they could not play
madmen. They are
impersonating inmates
of a madhouse. See
also 9–17.*
(Tom Hollyman)

or not he actually *feels* the emotions he projects, are connected
to the two-in-one state which is his being as an actor. The ease
and eagerness with which the public accepts the identification of
Lorne Greene with Ben Cartwright, of Don Adams with Agent
86, of James Arness with Marshal Dillon, refusing to believe that
the actors playing those roles may, in real life, have many characteristics different from those they exhibit as *characters*, is a
widespread example of these confusions. It is also, admittedly, a
compliment to the skill of the actors in creating believable characters.

As we have said before, the essential task of the actor is *impersonation*, the creation of a given character acting believably in
the given circumstances of the construct called a play (or movie,
or a television series). No actor, however he may deny the fact,
ever absolutely *becomes* the character he plays, or he could never
play another. Indeed, there are several characters one could think
of where he would not *live* to play another. Play is the key word;
the actor *seems* to become the character he is impersonating; the
audience accepts him as such; it believes him. But he accomplishes
this end through art. He intuits much, he investigates much, he
selects, arranges, experiments, discards, adds, and synthesizes—

Figure 10–11

Hanover College
*New theatre techniques
require an acrobat's
control of the actor's
physical being, as is
evident in this scene
from a "new" production
of Peer Gynt. Directed
and designed by Tom G.
Evans.*

he *works* to create the illusion of authentic being, the *virtual* life which is the theatre.

Now obviously, like any other artist, in order to achieve the end or purpose of his art, the actor must know the capabilities and possibilities of the tools and materials of his chosen art form. The actor's tool is himself, his living entity, and his material is the world of the play. Intuitively and consciously he discovers the nature of his medium and his tools and learns to use them.

As the person who is the tool of his art he has a physical being, an intellectual being, and an emotional or spiritual being. The physical being, since it is the most palpable, is the simplest subject for exploration and training. It is also the concrete and visible embodiment of the other two beings which constitute his whole. It is from this point of analysis that Delsarte, in the middle of the nineteenth century, constructed a whole system of acting by equating various physical configurations with specified feelings: "Rejection" required a slight turn to the right of the torso, a slight elevation of the left shoulder, an inclination of the head to the right, the right arm raised and bent at the elbow with the back of the hand against the forehead, eyes closed, and the left arm extended slightly at the level of the hip, hand turned back at the wrist—all worked out from the significance of various parts of the body in "signing" inner states. Delsarte was attempting a "scientific" analysis, but many of its details have long since been discredited. What we mean today when we talk about knowing and training the "physical being" of the actor is just that—the *physical* being. What is the nature of the skeleton, the musculature, the viscera, the organs? How are they organized into the torso, the limbs, the head? What are the possibilities of movement, of doing, in these organized entities—separately and in conjunction? If these questions would seem to imply that the actor, in his training, should become acrobat, contortionist, athelete, fencer, and dancer, that is exactly their intent. A body superbly trained, in excellent physical condition, capable of responding with assurance and control from the minutest movement of a small facial muscle to a great leap through space is the desired end. The accomplishment of most actors in this respect is approximate, but the stress in the techniques of the "new" avant-garde theatre, like that of Grotowski at the Polish Lab Theatre, is that, for one thing, make-up is unnecessary because actors' bodies must be trained so completely that they can change the actual appearance of their faces by specific muscle control.

A second part of this physical being, this palpable image, is the voice. We have mentioned before that when the great Sarah Bernhardt was once asked by a neophyte what were the three most important things for an actress to possess, she is said to have answered, "Voice, voice, and again voice." That is a particularly French emphasis; voice culture has long been a more serious pursuit among French actors than among almost any other national group; and there have been periods when "declamation" was indeed the actor's primary, if not sole, function. But such a situation ceased to exist long ago; as a matter of fact, the pendulum swung in the opposite direction for many of the actors of the "realistic school," who thought voice culture completely unimportant. But the necessity for voice culture for the actor becomes easily apparent through the simple experiment of putting a few ordinary human beings on the stage of, say, a 600-seat theatre and letting them talk in ordinary conversational tones. Aside from the fact that no one would hear them beyond the fifth row, no audience would be satisfied with the lack of selection, emphasis, and control—the complete lack of *art*—evidenced.

Figure 10–12

Minnesota
Theatre Company
*Such a scene as
illustrated here from
Henry V makes great
demands on the actor's
vocal as well as his
physical skill. See also
13–11. Directed by Sir
Tyrone Guthrie,
designed by Lewis
Brown.*

The actor must know the principles of voice production, the whole study of what we today call oral interpretation. His voice, like his body, must be a trained and flexible instrument, capable of meeting the demands of verse and prose on all levels and in all possible combinations, including singing.

At the same time that his physical being is developing in its possibilities and disciplines, his *inner being* must be undergoing the same process. Visible actions of individuals, such as sitting, standing, walking, running, shouting, whispering, intoning, laughing, and crying—all the *signs* possible of expression through the physical being—are selected and controlled by the inner being, the emotions and the intellect. It is with this inner being that Stanislavsky's famous "method" is primarily concerned. It is an "internal technique" designed to induce a "creative state" which enables the actor to bring "the life of the human spirit" to the stage. Through many starts and stops, mind changings and experimentations, chronicled in a list of books, Stanislavsky advocated an exploration and training of the inner being of the actor

Figure 10–13

Purdue
Professional Theatre
*Anne Revere as Mother
Courage shows the
synthesis of inner and
outer being which
creates a great
impersonation. See also
8–18. Directed by
Joseph G. Stockdale,
Jr., designed by Sam
Marks.*

which (although it was developed primarily in conjunction with realistic stage materials) has applicability for the art of the actor in no matter what circumstances he finds himself. It was as a method of training that its author conceived it. Relaxation, observation, concentration, sense memory, emotional recall, substitution, and improvisation—these are all *exercises* which sharpen the actor's *psychic* tools in *preparation* for his ultimate task, which is the impersonation of a given character, a method intended to sensitize the actor to main lines of action, to help him reason and intuit the type of character suitable to these actions, and to give him an approach to drawing out of himself what is necessary to make the character specific and suitable. The exercises hone his perceptions of the springs of emotion, fire his imagination, put psychological action under his control, and enable him to utilize the "magic if" which is at the core of acting. The psychoanalogical qualities of some of these exercises, and the self-expression implicit in many of them, led to abuses by some of Stanislavsky's self-styled disciples in the indulgence of their own dearly held personalities on the stage (the making over into themselves of whatever character they were presumably impersonating). But the total body of Stanislavsky's work indicates that these matters are simply training techniques for the inner being of the actor. He must then learn to use both inner and outer beings in the service of the play and the theatre. He must apply his tools to his materials.

Stanislavsky's "magic if" is the application of the tools to the materials: *If* I were a greengrocer, how would I greet the prime minister? *If* I were Estragon, what would I do when my shoes pinched? *If* I were Juliet, what would I do when it came time to drink the drug Friar Laurence gave me? The problem is twofold: (1) to know the given character intimately in its psychological and physical entities; and (2) to do what the assumed character would do in the given circumstances. Notice that there is no question about how the character *feels;* the emotional content is implicit in the being and the doing, in their exact and detailed imagining, or image-ing. This is "truth" in acting; this is the avoidance of cliché reactions, and the signing of amorphous emotional states. Faced with a character who is the construct of a playwright, how does the actor accomplish this truth? That eloquent actor, Coquelin, put it all very simply:

> When I have to create a role, I begin by reading the play with the greatest attention five or six times. First, I consider what position my character should occupy, on what plane in the picture I must put him. Then I study his psychology, knowing what he thinks, what he is morally. I deduce what he ought to be physically—his carriage, his manner of speaking, his gesture—I learn the part without thinking about it further; then, when I know it, I take up my man again, and closing my eyes I say to him, "Recite this for me."
>
> [*The Dual Personality of the Actor, 1887*]

It sounds easy; remember that Coquelin was a genius. More practically, the actor first *studies* his role, then he *creates* it. Or more practically still, he begins by studying, and continues the study while he begins and develops the creation. The beginning study is, indeed, a thorough acquaintance with the play as a whole; in Stanislavsky's terms, the actor (aided here by the perceptions of the director) determines the *superobjective* of the play; i.e., its idea, its Thought. Then he considers the objective of the character he is playing, from the point of view of what it is he *wants to do,* both in the play as a whole and in individual scenes or the even smaller units called "beats." He discovers this by: (1) What the character himself *says;* (2) What other characters say about him; (3) What the character himself *does;* and

(4) What other characters do because of him. Those are all the sources available in the script. He then goes on to place this character in his given environment: Gorki's cellar, Hamlet's castle, Lady Wishfort's boudoir, the Prozorov parlor—the details of time and place which give authentic life to the characterization. He is aided in this by his own study of the milieu, by the director's concept and aim, and by the working through with his fellow actors in rehearsal the moment-to-moment life of the play. He comes to each rehearsal with evidence of further study and imaginative creativity; the more he brings the more possibilities of selection there will be for him and for the director, who is the final controlling agent of the performance.

At some point in the rehearsal scheme the selection of details is accomplished, the overarching "spine" of the performance is determined, the transitions from beat to beat and scene to scene decided upon, and the rhythm of the piece established. Somewhere along the line the actor has learned the words the playwright has written—*just* as they were written, to every article and pause. If the playwright is skillful, and if the actor is creating his character truly and honestly, the words will be right; they *cannot be changed* because they belong to the character. Also somewhere along the line the actor has assimilated the properties of the costume he is to wear and the setting in which he is to perform. If he is somewhat literal-minded, he will try to use and wear approximations of his props and costumes during the rehearsal period, so that he gets the feel of them. The perceptive director will quickly see which actors in his company cannot create without these helps, or do so more easily, and will see that they are supplied. But it is perfectly possible for a highly imaginative and superbly prepared actor to create practically from thin air whatever he needs for his characterization. That is the real art of mime (witness Marcel Marceau) and the reason for those exercises in sense memory. I once directed a creative actor in a short play about Rembrandt (playing time about forty minutes), and I was amazed and gratified to discover that not only had he read everything about Rembrandt that he could lay his hands on and looked at every picture of Rembrandt's that he could discover in museums or art books, but he had also gotten the man into his very bones and sinews so that, on a bare stage, in his own rehearsal clothes, he *was* Rembrandt. When the "decorations" were added, his performance was overwhelming in its truth. It was one of the finest examples I have ever known of that "love of the art of theatre" for which nothing is too much trouble or pain.

For the dedicated actor, his work is a lifetime of study, of practice, of learning, and of doing. His observation of people and the world around him never stops. I know one actor who keeps an elaborate card file of his observations: an old man on a subway, the hands of the shoemaker, the way the bus driver sits, the back of the symphony conductor, etc., etc. to remind him of visual images which may be useful in characterization. Not only observation of the actual, present world constitutes the actor's laboratory, but everything he reads, all the possible knowledge of any kind that he can acquire become raw materials which are put through the crucible of his imagination in accomplishing his task of impersonation. Bernhardt said that the actor must be "familiar with the entire past of humanity."

Acting is the art of saying a thing on the stage as if you believed every word you utter to be as true as the eternal verities of life; it is the art of doing a thing on the stage as if the logic of the event demanded that precise act and no other; and of doing and saying the thing as spontaneously as if you were confronted with the situation in which you were acting, for the first time.

[John Barrymore, quoted in Cole and Chinoy, Actors on Acting, p. 515]

Perhaps one of the most difficult of stances for the actor to maintain is this very "illusion of the first time" of which Barrymore speaks. After all, the actor is speaking words he did not create, he has spoken them innumerable times in rehearsal, and he goes on speaking them night after night. How does he maintain this sense of discovery, this freshness, so that the lived life of the play remains always in the Now? The skilled actor has learned to live in the Now of the play; he has learned to see it fresh each time he approaches it. He uses his call time in the dressing room before performance to imagine himself once more into the world of the play; he prepares for some additional moments before he steps on stage, vividly re-creating for himself the circumstances of his character, so that he is in character when he appears before the audience. He has learned the concentration which shuts out personal concerns and extraneous circumstances, and his energies are totally directed to the creation which is his

Figure 10–14

Inner City Cultural
Center
*The actor creates anew
the reality of the play
each time it is
performed, as here, in
a scene from* A Raisin
in the Sun. *(AJDART
Archive)*

immediate reality. The more difficult and emotional the part, the
more demands there are for preparation and readiness. Michael
Redgrave talks about the hours he spends preparing for each
performance of a major role in tragedy; parts which are closer
to the actor's own reality take less preparation. But whether the
part be large or small, comedy or tragedy, the conscientious
actor assumes his character as he assumes his mask (make-up and
costume) and lives in the world of the play. And he sees to it that
nothing distracts him from this concentration. It is a demanding
and exacting pursuit, whose search is never ended, whose discipline is rigorous. It is no wonder then, that actors have been
considered a special breed of men—sometimes villified, but more
often revered and adored. The appreciative audience applauds the
skill and dedication of the performer who lives completely in the
world of the play for the duration of its performance, doing
nothing that will distract his audience's concentration from the
play's action or intervene in their understanding of the actor's
role. Along with the audience, actors are the only permanent part
of theatre from first to last; without them theatre would not exist.

Jean-Louis Barrault, one of the most versatile and interesting of modern actor-directors, says (*The Theatre of Jean-Louis Barrault*, New York: Hill and Wang, 1961) that there are three "styles" in which an actor can "face up" to a performance: (1) *à la broche*, (2) *à la souffle*, (3) *à la canne*. They form a kind of summary of acting techniques. The first, from *brochure* or text, is that wherein the actor has learned his part by heart and can recite it. The implication is that this method is undesirable and ineffective. The second, from *souffler* or prompter, is that which relies upon the prompter for words and movement; it is, of course, impossible. The third, from canvas or the floor of a boxing ring or public stage, is that in which the actor relies solely upon himself and is in full control of the performance, the "Complete Actor." It is the sum total of all the preparation, insight, discipline, and expression about which we have here talked concerning the work of the actor as an artist. It is the only tolerable stance for the actor in that very public place which is the stage of a theatre.

We have already mentioned in passing the role of the director. His person, his training, and his task as they exist in the modern theatre are easier to encompass than those of the actor, since he is a much more recent entity in the art of theatre. We have already dealt with the exigencies which led to his emergence; we now consider in some detail his task and how he accomplishes it.

In the simplest terms possible, the director is that member of the theatrical complex who has his eye on every detail that will finally result in the play performed for an audience. His task does not ordinarily entail anything concerned with getting the audience there, like publicity, box office management, and so forth. It quite naturally divides itself into two areas of activity, each equally important: (1) that which he does in conjunction with the acting company itself, and (2) that which he does apart from the acting company, by himself or with other members of the "theatrical team." We will start with the second area.

The initial task of the director is a solitary one: he chooses the play he will direct. If he is working with an ongoing and organized theatre group, such as a repertory house or a community or college theatre, he is likely to have a fairly free choice in this matter. In order to choose wisely, he must have a wide and deep acquaintance with theatre literature and theatre forms from the earliest times to the latest. He must have a quick and sensitive

Figure 10–15

Marymount College
*The director's concept
of the play derives from
a study of its content
and meaning; the image
of the* House of
Bernarda Alba *is that of
a compressed space
building to an explosion.*
(Daniel Berry)

appreciation of the possibilities of various theatrical *métier*. His choice will be guided not only by the intrinsic interest of the work itself, but also by his thorough knowledge of the capabilities of his working theatre group and the kind of audience for which the performance will be played. It is inexcusable that a responsible director choose a play solely on the basis of its challenge to his own abilities; to do so is insufferably selfish. The play cannot be realized in performance except through the devotion and hard work of a great many people besides himself; their interests and potentialities must be taken into account. And it is the height of foolishness to deliberately antagonize an ongoing audience by a particular choice of play, since any standing theatre company will shortly cease to exist if it does so.

This statement constitutes no apology for a consistent diet of "light" entertainment or "warmed-over Broadway," or even persistence in the presentation of "tried and true" scripts. It is perfectly possible (as I know from my own experience in several ongoing theatre companies) to do new scripts and untraditional plays even for tradition-oriented audiences, *if* the untraditional scripts do not absolutely outrage the sensibilities of the audience, and if the program for the season is balanced between the new and the familiar. Audiences are not to be treated with contempt; they are the final judge and jury of any theatrical event, and without them there is no theatre. The first obligation of a director in choosing a play for performance is to *know*, as intimately and as exactly as he can, the audience for whom it is intended.

Even the free-lance director, who exists and works outside the "standing" theatre, must *choose* the play he is to direct, though in this case his choice is an easier one. He is not confronted with the necessity of taking its audience into account in the choice (though he will be concerned with its hypothetical audience in its preparation); the producer or contractor for his services has that concern. The sole determining factor for the free-lance director in agreeing to prepare a script for production is that he is burning to do it; his interest in the script must be unequivocal, his artistic commitment to it absolute. No director will ever do a satisfactory and satisfying job of directing a play which he does not like, or which does not spark his interest and command his attention. He does himself, and those with whom he works, nothing but harm if the case is otherwise.

Next, having made the choice of the play, and still solitary, he embarks on the most delicate, most difficult, and the most necessary of his tasks—that from which all subsequent decisions will derive: the formulation of his *concept* of the play. This concept is by no means a mere statement in words of the so-called "theme" of the playwright's script. It is that totality of the theatrical construct which is its poetic, its metaphorical meaning. It involves not just the *words*, but the *image* of the production. It begins with the director's complete and understanding perception of the main intention of the playwright. It is arrived at by the application of a sensitive and creative imagination, fortified with extensive knowledge and experience, to the stuff of the play. Every director must have the visual acumen of the artist, the ear of the musician, and the space consciousness of the dancer. For plays speak in all these terms, and not just in words. As he reads and rereads his script, the image of the play formulates itself in his mind. He catches this image in notes, in sketches, by any means by which he can hold on to it. And the "truth" that he discovers is what animates the play, what makes it live. The key scenes help, and some directors start with these: the closet scene in *Hamlet*, the death of Atahualpa in *Royal Hunt of the Sun*, the proposal scene in *The Way of the World*.

The playwright's own scenic and character comments are aids,

Figure 10–16
Festival Theatre,
Stratford, Ontario

although they need not be prescriptions. When playwrights like Shaw and Williams and J. M. Barrie provide lyrical descriptions of characters and/or scenes these are not to be ignored, but used —not necessarily literally, even *preferably* not literally, but imaginatively. The director makes *associations* which help to define the play's image: Garcia Lorca's *The House of Bernarda Alba* has as its main intention to show that the suppression of natural instincts in oneself and others leads to disaster, hence the play's image is that of a box into which explosives are relentlessly packed until it bursts. Such an image governs the visual aspect of the play as well as its rhythm and pace. The setting must be that one "very white room" that the script mentions; even that last act, which the playwright mentions as being set "in the patio" is better played within this room to underline the feeling of confinement, of restriction. The messages from "the outside" will be heightened in tension as they are received within these confines. The ceiling must be low and threatening, the windows shuttered and barred. So the director builds his image. However he decides to interpret a play which is a "revival" (i.e., which has been previously performed elsewhere), he must honestly and diligently

THE ARTISTS

OF THE THEATRE

Figure 10–17

American Shakespeare
Festival Theatre

*Two concepts of the
same play, Shakespeare's
Love's Labour's Lost,
the first performed in
period costume at the
Festival Theatre in
Stratford, Ontario, the
second with no relation
to a particular
historical period at the
American Shakespeare
Festival Theatre.*

seek to encompass this central and all-important image. He will
not be an antiquarian, attempting to reproduce with fidelity and
in detail the original production of the play. That action was
performed for a different audience, under different circumstances.
But if the play has any validity at all for his present audience
(and otherwise it is not worth doing), it has this validity in its
central image. What inventiveness he then applies to make a contemporary comment will be truthfully and honestly arrived at and
not a gimmick to display his directorial virtuosity. To play *Hamlet*
as the case study of a neurotic young man is a serious abdication
of directorial responsibility; if this is your interest, do *Huui,
Huui* instead.

Having arrived intuitively and imaginatively at a central image,
the director then tests its validity by a close study of the text. If
he has to delete or transpose many speeches or scenes, or change
a number of character relationships, he is on the wrong track; he
had better try again. For the action the playwright intended is
written into the script; it is the director's job to find it. If he is
dealing with a new script, and has the playwright at hand to consult and work with, such consultations and work will result in

319

ACTOR AND DIRECTOR

meaningful clarifications and revisions only when director and playwright agree on the image of the play. In his continuing study of the text, the director exercises the peculiar skill (without which he is handicapped indeed) of seeing the performance in his head. He peoples his mental stage with his ideal vision of possible performers, sees them move in the pattern of the play and speak in the accents of the speeches; he "dresses" the stage with sets and lights. This mental activity, about which he may make notes and sketches as well, is a *preliminary* vision, which may go through many changes during the actualities of production. But it is a necessary *preconception.* He may fortify and clarify it by wide reading and study of other plays by his playwright, by commentaries and critiques of the play and/or playwright by others, by parallel reading in philosophy, social history, politics, or whatever other field has some bearing upon the work in hand. Out of all of this reading and study and imagining comes the *directorial concept:* the way of doing the play on the stage. When this mainspring of the production is arrived at, then the director can proceed with his other tasks. With some directors, like Max Reinhardt and the early Stanislavsky, this preliminary study produced a *Regiebuch* of minutely detailed prescriptions for every visual and auditory moment on the stage from beginning to end. The task of every other person then concerned became that of realizing this preconception as minutely and accurately as possible.

More typically, however, the director will follow his solitary musings with consultations. He will have decided the large outline of the movement in the play with its necessary exits, entrances, and sitting-downs, as well as playing areas, elevation, stairways, and so on, and he will probably have a rough ground plan either in mind or on paper. He talks this over with the designer, who has also familiarized himself with the script but not necessarily in as much detail. Director and designer agree on the necessary ground plans, on the style of the setting, its shapes and colors, the general role of the lighting, and the costuming. Each contributes of his talent and experience and knowledge to this interview (or series of interviews), but the director's primary aim is to maintain his vision of the play and see that the design which emerges serves his acting company to the ultimate extent, while the designer's primary aim is to see that the setting is visually

Figure 10–18
Booth Theatre
As rehearsals start, the director's ground-plan is transferred to the rehearsal space, with all areas marked out, and substitute furnishings in place, as in this rehearsal for The Flip Side, 1968.
(The New York Times)

pleasing and interesting, as well as serviceable to the actors and to the concept. Refining of details may be worked on during the rehearsal period, but before rehearsals begin the director must have in hand an accurate ground plan of the playing area, with all set pieces indicated in size and placement. If the set designer for the production is not also the costume and lighting designer, a similar process of consultation and agreement must be held by the director with these additional people, preferably as a group.

The director's next task is casting the parts; perhaps his most difficult task of all. Fortunate indeed—and very rare—is the director who sees his mentally conceived "ideal" cast appear before him in auditions. If he is working with an ongoing company, he will have chosen his play with an eye to specific actors for particular roles, and it only remains to verify by a combination of arranged readings whether or not his predetermination is likely to be right. But where he has to gather a cast from the profession at large, the community, or the school population, his task is arduous. His stage manager (having been chosen at some point prior to this moment) will arrange a series of auditions, supply scripts to prospective performers, and set up a place where the director can hear them and assess their potential for the play in hand. These auditions are best conducted privately, with no more personnel in the auditioning place than is absolutely necessary, because the director is asking the performer to expose himself in quite intimate ways of emotional being, wherein he ought not to feel constrained by extraneous audiences. The atmosphere of the audition should be friendly and gracious; the director should use all the techniques at his command to make the actor feel that he has done his very best in the audition. If possible, he should allow the actor to indicate what character or characters in the play he is interested in reading for. Then he should himself suggest others, if he feels the actor's possibilities would allow these. He should perhaps even ask the actor to present something outside the play in hand, if he thinks he can gain something from this. Preferably, the person with whom the auditionee reads should be another actor, so that he does not feel "hung-up" by his stage partner; but the director's attention is on the person auditioning. He should have a system of noting his visual, auditory, and psychological reactions to the person auditioning, so that at the end of auditions he can vividly remember and consider all his possi-

Figure 10–19

Peter Brook, as director, coaches Robert Merrill in fencing for a performance of Faust. *(The New York Times)*

bilities. He will no doubt want to eliminate some applicants immediately as not being suited for any part in the play at hand; he will probably want to have call-backs for a number of others. That is, with a smaller group of applicants, he will probably want to hear them again and try various combinations of possibilities. The end result of the casting procedure is the designation of a person to play each of the roles. During the casting procedure the perceptive director will note a number of things that actors bring (a particular cast of features, a vocal quality, or an evident psychological trait) which will enhance the play. His "ideal" preconception of the cast of characters may undergo varieties of changes. But he should end the auditions when he feels that, all things considered, he has approximated his ideal casting, or changed it for something better or more interesting. The purpose to be served is the play not that of the individual actor nor of the director.

So the cast is chosen. It is then assembled *in toto*, along with any other personnel the director desires present. Usually the director and the stage manager are the only noncast members present at this first meeting, because the director is here charged with the responsibility of creating a community of harmonious members

Figure 10–20

National Theatre
of the Deaf
*Technical effects are
worked out with the
actors in technical
rehearsals, as here for
The Critic. See also 7–9.*

who agree to the goals of the production and commit themselves
to it. This is best done in privacy, and in as gracious and friendly
surroundings as circumstances permit. The director is now assuming the second part of his task—his work with the acting company.
Tyrone Guthrie says in his book *A Life in the Theatre* (New
York: McGraw-Hill, 1959) that the director now wears two hats:
one as chairman of the meeting or factory foreman, the other as
a kind of entrepreneur who is to *evoke* the best possible performances from his cast.

Usually at this first meeting there is a "read through" of the
play, with the company seated around a table, along with a brief
discussion of the director's aims and concepts. David Belasco said
that he "preached his sermon" to his company at this time; Arthur
Hopkins said that his aim was to get from his actors what he
knew he wanted without their being aware of how it was done.
Jacques Copeau felt that these early meetings were vital to "nip
in the bud any incipient misunderstandings" and to clarify the
basic principles of the play's interpretation while the actors were
still at ease in their minds, not yet "having entered into their
parts." Each director will proceed in his own way, according to
his own personality and method, so long as the end result of this
first meeting is a prevailing feeling of cohesiveness, interest, and
enthusiasm.

At this time, some directors supply the cast with a complete
rehearsal schedule of times and places and actors necessary for

Figure 10–21

Wayne State University
*The disposition in
meaningful relationships
of many characters
on the stage is one of
the director's
responsibilities, as here
in a scene from a
Wayne State
University Production
of* Royal Hunt of the
Sun. *See also 6–13.
Directed by Don
Blakely, sets by Russell
Smith.*

each rehearsal; some make up rehearsal schedules a week or so in advance, and call actors as needed; some ask that all actors be present at all rehearsal calls whether or not they are involved in the scenes to be rehearsed. This last practice is a great time-waster and likely to provoke unnecessary resentments in the company. The experienced director, familiar with his material and quickly becoming acquainted with his cast, should be able to estimate how much work he can get done in a given amount of time and call only those cast members who will actually be rehearsing in a specific rehearsal period.

Depending on the type of play in hand and on the experience of his cast, the director may spend additional meetings in discussion of the play, before he "gets them on their feet," or begins blocking (arranging the stage movement). American directors usually "discuss" in this fashion; English directors usually scorn it. Laurence Olivier has been quoted as saying that "I'd rather have run the scene eight times than have wasted that time in chattering about abstractions." For all plays it is profitable that the actors understand at the outset how the director proposes to reduce the idea of the play to action in order that they may cooperate with the director. But the length and kind of discussions will vary. Small cast plays with deep symbolical or psychological overtones may need repeated and probing discussions at the outset. In large cast shows where the intricacies of characterization are likely to be centered on a small number of parts, it is

325

ACTOR AND DIRECTOR

Figure 10–22

Lincoln Center
Repertory Company
(*Peter Daness*)

usually better practice for the director to engage in probing discussions of characterization with one or more actors outside rehearsal hours, or limit the personnel of some rehearsals to only those cast members who are or should be involved in such discussions. Rehearsals, like performances, are for *doing* the play. In the doing, characterization grows and develops through the guidance of the director and by the inventiveness, imagination, and talent of the actors. During the rehearsal process the director is traffic manager, psychologist, nurse, sergeant-at-arms, teacher, "foreman of a factory, abbot of a monastery, and the superintendent of an analytic laboratory," as Tyrone Guthrie says. Most important is his relationship with the players: he must respect the personal dignity, integrity, and ability of each player, while at the same time persuading or cajoling or leading him into the performance the play needs. He must *evoke* this performance, not command it, for actors are sensitive human beings (or they would not be actors) whose performances can be destroyed by unthinking or unfeeling directors. Slipshod and inept work, of course, is not to be tolerated; it is a crime against the community. But beyond that, the director is at one and the same time the final arbiter of the shape and form of the play and an appreciative *audience of one*. In this atmosphere players will not fail to excel themselves.

THE ARTISTS

OF THE THEATRE

Figure 10–23

The Lincoln Center Repertory production of Danton's Death *and the Broadway musical, 1776, show different possibilities of handling large numbers of performers on stage. (Martha Swope)*

During rehearsals, the director encourages his players to be inventive and original, to "bring everything they can think of" to their parts. The rehearsals then become a process of refinement, selection, substitution, or even of new invention. The focus of each player is on his own part and its interaction with those of other players whose parts affect his; the focus of the director is on the relationship of all the parts to the whole. He is the only member present who constantly keeps the whole in his mind's eye, and shapes the progress of the rehearsals with that in view. His work with the production team continues *outside* of rehearsal time; the entire group convenes at technical and dress rehearsals.

Some directors, either before or during rehearsals, chart or block every movement of every actor and leave the actor to find the reasons for these movements as he progresses with his characterization. This stance is particularly applicable to large cast shows where many people are on stage at one and the same time. But even in such a show it is desirable to allow players some latitude of movement in a particular area, or when only one or two of them are on the stage, not only because it gives them confidence in themselves, but also because they just might come up with a better idea than that conceived by the director. But the practice of some directors in giving no consideration to stage movement before meeting the actors in rehearsal, and working it out completely (and over and over again) with the players is a terrible time-waster and consumes more energy than it is worth. In most theatre situations, the number of hours available for rehearsal precludes such wholesale experimention.

No matter how "free" a performance seems, every movement is one agreed upon beforehand; no matter how "natural" the outcome, the performance is, as it were, "nature methodized." Both actor and director will discover movements implicit in the lines of the text: there are "sitting down" lines, "standing up" lines, lines demanding overt movements, and others. These are much more frequent in playscripts than the stage directions written in by the playwrights; they may be said to be implicit stage directions, while those of the playwright are explicit. But the director has the additional responsibility of coordinating both implicit and explicit stage directions for the entire cast. His work evolves in space and time. He is concerned with the physical relationships of players to each other and to the setting. He *composes* a line of flowing movement occasionally coming to rest, which expresses the subtext of the play. What the players do—individually and in concert—must be guided by the director to achieve an overall unity, balance, variety, proportion, and rhythm.

Directors often schedule a "costume call" or "dress parade" some few days before dress rehearsal, when every player appears on stage in his costume, and the director and designers, from the house, observe him move in it and make notes about its suitability. Comments and preferences of the actors are taken into account, but only in so far as they conform to the necessities of the play. Technical rehearsals are held to iron out any difficulties of lighting, set changes, costume changes, properties, cues, curtains, and so forth—all the items that contribute to a smooth performance. Then come dress rehearsals, when that perceptive audience of one—the director—makes notes of adjustments necessary. By this time, of course, the cast has arrived at complete characterizations and a sense of ensemble; these notes make no major changes in those but are concerned with minor items (although they may be legion) that will produce the most perfect performance possible. At the last or next-to-last dress rehearsal, the director sets the curtain call, and with the last dress rehearsal his major creative work is finished, and the performance out of

Figure 10–24

Lincoln Center
Repertory Company
*The consummation of
the work and the vision
is the production which
the audience sees, as
here, John Hirsch's
production of* The Miser
*at the Vivian Beaumont
Theatre.*
(*Martha Swope*)

his hands. There is no more lonely person in the world than a
director during opening performance. The materials he has
worked with are largely intangible and mutable, script and performers are not so stable as paint and canvas. He has tried to
make his dream come true. In the minority of marvelous circumstances what he gets on opening night is even better than his
dream; in the majority of cases it is an approximation. But that
final arbiter—the audience—soon lets him know if his vision
and its realization comprise a satisfactory theatre experience. And
that is his joy and his peril. If the play he has directed has many
performances, a long run, he will come back to conduct brush-up
rehearsals, in order to take out the "improvements" which have
crept into the performance, and to see that his vision of the play
is maintained.

Louis Jouvet has said that the director is "the kind of lover who
draws his talent, invention and joy in his work from the talent,
invention and joy which he borrows from or inspires in others,"
and that the directing of a play is "a function of such sensitive-
ness that everything human can enter into it." In our fragmented
and disparate society, the director becomes the unifying force in
a given theatrical experience. He has sometimes been an autocrat

and dictator, he has sometimes been more acting coach than *metteur en scène*, and sometimes teacher more than anything else. But, ideally, he is something of all of these, in cooperation and balance, so that the process of giving life to the play he is directing has been a satisfying creative experience for all those connected with it, on both sides of the footlights. His final satisfaction is in the insights he has gained and expressed through intimate and creative contact with the imitation of life (in the Aristotelian sense) which is the art of theatre.

11

Designer and Architect

Now that we have concerned ourselves in some detail with the actor, who is the central fact of performance, and with that "specialized actor" who has in modern times become known as the director, we are prepared to move to the environment in which the living element of the theatre exists—to the *place of performance*. We shall consider its "necessities," its evolution, and the specialized theatre workers who are primarily concerned with it—the architect and the designer.

From the earliest of times, theatre space has been bifurcated: there has always been a place for the players and a place for the audience. In primitive societies, the former has often been no more than a cleared space, conveniently located, around which the audience, usually standing, could cluster. The original *orchestra*, or dancing place, of ancient Greek times appears to have been no more than this. But the topography of Greece, with its paucity of level space and its predominance of hills, presented a unique advantage in the arrangement of audience space vis-à-vis acting space. If the orchestra circle were located at the bottom of a hill, the members of the audience could dispose themselves on the incline of the hill itself, and so be in a most advantageous position for more people to see and hear more clearly. The most influential of ancient Greek theatre arrangements, that which came to be called the Theatre of Dionysus at Athens, had its orchestra at the foot of one of the slopes of the Acropolis, and originally, the audience seems to have sat on the ground itself. It was a very large orchestra circle, about eighty-five feet in diameter. It had to be level throughout, so the tangent farthest removed from the hillside itself was reinforced by a retaining wall perhaps five or six feet high. In the days when performers were solely members

Greek

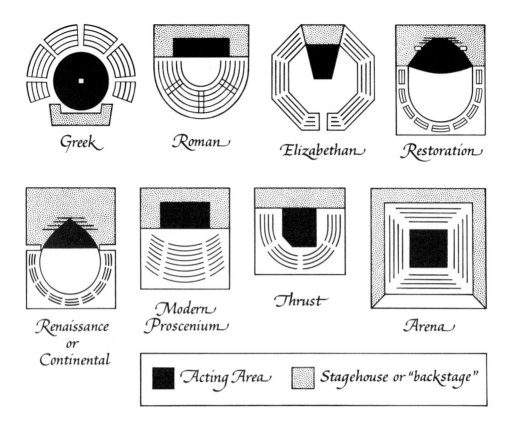

Greek   Roman   Elizabethan   Restoration

Renaissance   Modern   Thrust   Arena
or   Proscenium
Continental

| ■ Acting Area | ▨ Stagehouse or "backstage" |

Figure 11–1

Drawings showing the relationship of acting area, audience area, and "backstage" area.

of the large dithyrambic choruses, nothing further was needed for performance. The mass movements of the dancers created their own large effects.

But from the moment when the individual actor appeared on the scene, and plays were added to the festivals of dithyrambic competitions, additions had to be made to the playing space, and evolution of the playhouse was underway. The changes were first dictated by the necessities of the actor, and in turn they caused some changes in the audience space. At a minimum, all actors everywhere need four things: a place of entrance, a highly visible acting space, a place of exit, and a place to don or to change costumes. The visibility of the actor may be achieved by placing the audience on a level above him or by raising him above the level of the audience. In either case, the focus of the audience is more intently on the actor (he is more exclusively visible) if he also has a background which prevents the eyes of the audience from seeing over and around him to vistas not connected with his performance. And in order for the communication (which is the heart of theatre) to take place between actor and audience, the playing space must seem to have a direct and unencumbered line to every seating space.

For the play which is usually conceded to be the earliest extant of those of Aeschylus, *The Suppliants* (492 B.C.), nothing is needed in the action except the altar which was "standard" in the center of the orchestra; nobody changes costumes, and the three individually named "speaking" characters each has a retinue, so that entrances and exits are massed and processional through the same entrances which the audience had previously used. The unadorned orchestra would do very well for the performance, although there must have been some place for that huge crowd of performers to don their costumes and masks. By 472 B.C., when *The Persians* was presented, the action of the play demanded something more. There is the marvelous Ghost of Darius who presumably rises from his tomb (a spectacular entrance in any theatrical language), a Messenger who comes on unaccompanied, Queen Atossa who changes her costume during the action of the play, the Chorus of Persian Elders, and Xerxes, who comes on near the end of the play and must have been performed by one of the actors playing one of the other three individual parts (since no more than three major actors ever appeared in Greek tragedies), and hence he had to have a place to change his costume and mask.

There seems to be some archeological evidence for the fact that sometime before the date of this play a massive, T-shaped foundation was erected on the surface of the orchestra above the retaining wall, and the theory is that temporary structures needed for specific plays were erected in conjunction with this foundation. In *The Persians* a tomb at least would be needed, and perhaps a simulated palace for the Queen. And the tomb would have to be such as to allow for that startling appearance of the Ghost. It is interesting to speculate how these "set pieces" were accomplished, and how they worked, but more authentic information brings us to the year 465 B.C. or thereabouts, when a portion of the center of the hillside was somewhat hollowed out, the orchestra circle made a little smaller and moved closer to the hillside, and a wooden building erected in the thus vacated space above the retaining wall. The dirt from the hollowing-out process was de-

Figure 11–2

Metropolitan
Museum of Art
*This model of the
Theatre at Delphi about
160 A.D. shows the
structure of the
Hellenistic period, with
elevated acting platform.
See also the Theatre of
Dionysus, Athens in 4–1.
(The Dodge Fund, 1930)*

posited at the extremes of the elevation, and wooden benches were constructed for the audience, so that the rows of seats now encircled about three-quarters of the orchestra. So the actor acquired a background (the scene house) as well as a specialized place of entrance and exit and a "dressing room"—all in the one building, which was used in nonperformance times to store the wooden benches. The functional Greek theatre was complete.

In succeeding generations, the wooden scene house was replaced by a stone one, and in the next century the great architect Lycurgus refurbished the whole structure and laid out the audience area with concentric rows of stone benches. But these changes were in materials only, and in decoration, not in the fundamental relationships of the use of space. Some people think that a low platform for the actors was erected between the two projecting arms at the ends of the scene building, and that the total number of doors was increased to five, three being in the main face of the building and one in each projecting wing or *paraskena*. The platform is likely, because even in some of the very early plays the action calls for some sort of "reveal," for things presumably happening within the house, like the death of Agamemnon. This reveal is supposedly the *eccyclema*, a kind of wheeled platform that could be pushed out through the center doors. Also the descent of gods from above early demanded the

Figure 11–3

invention and use of the *mechane*, which was evidently a kind of cranelike construction built over and above the scene house. Aristotle says that Sophocles invented *Skenography*, which statement makes him the first named scene designer in history. Aristotle is not explicit about the meaning of the term or what it implied or contained, but it is supposed that what Sophocles did was to supply some painted additions to the permanent architectural facade of the orchestra backing in the form of painted, temporary screens set into or against the scene house.

By the latter half of the fourth century B.C., the predominant form of new plays was the Menander comedy, with no Chorus. The theatre architects did not dispense with the orchestra circle, because revivals of the old plays were still being given, but the theatres built at Priene, Assos, Ephesus and Delos had a two-story scene house, which encroached somewhat on the orchestra circles and had ramps leading up to the extended platform (about ten feet high) which formed the roof of the first story. Evidently the action of New Comedy took place there, in the more concentrated and circumscribed space which was better suited to the smaller casts and more intimate action. Probably those other set pieces which Vitruvius mentions in his manuscript of the first century of the Christian era were phenomena of this later Greek period. In any event, it seems to be true that both architecture and "scene

Figure 11–4

The auditorium of Theatre Atlanta uses a seating arrangement similar to that of classic theatres. (Larry Krantz. AJDARJ Archive)

design" in Greek times were formal and stylized; form followed function, and changes were made as the drama itself changed and developed.

The Roman theatre building with which we are familiar—those grandiose structures whose ruins dot Europe from England to Lebanon—have some similarities to the classic Greek theatre, particularly in the seating arrangements for the audience, but their origins are quite different. Even in classic Greek times (if the evidence of vase paintings fails us not) a kind of performance was given on raised platforms backed by curtains. These were evidently rustic farces; they were popular throughout Magna Graecia at fairs and in marketplaces and were performed by traveling troupes of actors. In order to be seen in these circumstances, and to call attention to themselves, the actors would need to perform on a surface elevated to at least shoulder-height, and they would need to have a place from which to enter and wherein to stay between entrances. The curtain-backed platform, or booth stage, was the natural solution. The Romans early adopted the booth stage from the Sicilian mimes and the mimes of Campania with which they came in contact, perhaps in the fourth century B.C. Republican Rome, austere and warlike, insisted on the stoic virtues and even passed an ordinance in 185 B.C. forbidding audiences to *sit* at theatrical performances. The tem-

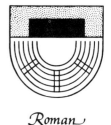

Roman

Figure 11–5

*Vase painting of an
ancient Greek* phylakes
*performance shows the
raised platform, backed
by curtains, which was
used for performance.*

porary, raised booth stage, with its back curtain through which
the actors emerged, was the only "theatre" permitted. As time
went on, the rules relaxed somewhat, temporary wooden seats
were sometimes built for the audience, and the backing for the
stage was of wood rather than simply being a curtain. But the
construction of a permanent theatre in Rome did not take place
until 55 B.C., when Pompey built it to honor Venus Victrix. With
the advent of the Empire, however, theatre building spurted, and
during the time of the Empire the Romans built more than one
hundred twenty-five theatres all over Europe and Asia Minor.

In Roman theatres, from first to last, the space for the actors was
a raised platform backed by the facade of the scene house. In the
permanent buildings, the scene house enclosed the stage on three
sides and a highly decorated wooden roof covered the stage. It
was an elaborated *rostrum*, or speaking place. In front of the stage
was an open space, five or six feet lower than the stage level,
which was a perfect semicircle paved with stone. The seats rose
on an incline, in sections, from the perimeter of this semicircle.
They were also of stone, and the whole structure, like half a cylin-
der, was almost invariably freestanding and made of brick faced
with marble. The scene house served for the entrance of all performers, for dressing rooms and offstage space, and it was as
high as the highest point of the inclined seats; the structure was

337

DESIGNER AND

ARCHITECT

Figure 11–6

*The Roman theatre of
Herodus Atticus in
Athens with its raised
platform and high scene
house.
(J. Christopher Roberts)*

a unit, a completely enclosed theatre building. The only portion
not permanently enclosed was above the audience, but even this
was often covered with a *vellum* or linen roof like a great horizontal sail. And on the small theatre in Pompeii they even built
a wooden roof over the entire theatre.

The very tall and imposing front of the scene building which
formed the background for the actors was an intricate design of
columns, architraves, pedestals, and statuary, and it had five doors
—three on the main wall and one each on the sides. For the
pantomimes, those elaborately danced extravaganzas, the stage
often contained most intricately designed set pieces, and, until the
performance began, the stage was covered from view of the audience by a curtain which dropped into a trough at the edge of the
stage. It is not hard to accept the fugitive contemporary descriptions of these elaborations, because we know of the Roman's skill
in engineering and structural design. Roman theatre architects and
designers worked on the grand scale, and it is easy to see how
(along with other sociological and political compulsions) the
theatre building itself forced Roman actors to ever more extravagant displays in order to register at all with their audiences.

The first theatres of the Middle Ages were the cathedrals them-

Figure 11–7

Richard Leacroft
Collection

*Performance in a
medieval great hall with
audience surrounding
the performance.*

selves, although the enclosing structure had little to do with the
form of the playing space once the Biblical episodes had multiplied
beyond a few. Then platforms were erected down the nave of the
church, one for each episode, so that the standing audience would
have a clear view of the action. (Cathedrals did not have seats or
pews; the congregation stood throughout services.) They *looked
up* at the performance and probably stood all around it. Each platform constituted a specific mounted scene, as factual (though not
realistic by any means) as the resources of the producers would
permit. This essential idea of a single, mounted scene for a particular episode remained constant for the production of the cycle
plays, even though the subsequent arrangements of presentation
varied once the productions moved out of the churches. As we
have seen, in England and in Spain these platform stages were put
on wheels to become *pageants* in the former country and *carros*
in the latter. In some parts of England, the platforms were arranged in "rounds" with cleared playing spaces in specified areas
between them. In Luzerne and a few other places on the Continent, they were arranged in town squares. At Valenciennes and
Mons they were arranged in a horizontal line backing a long
platform which became the chief playing area, and the single

DESIGNER AND

ARCHITECT

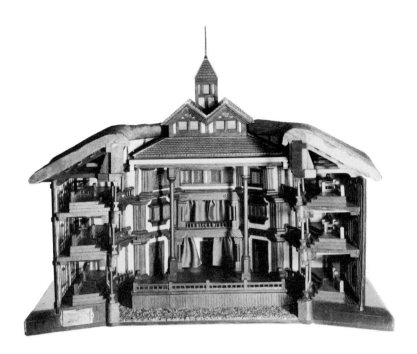

Figure 11–8

The Cleveland
Museum of Art
*Cut-away model of an
Elizabethan theatre,
showing its
characteristic acting
platform and
architectural
background.*
(Collection of the
Educational Department)

mounted scene was then called a *mansion*. This last arrangement constitutes a step toward a generalized stage with a fixed relationship to its audience—an arrangement which will develop into a theatre for the playing of various kinds of plays. Even in medieval times there was a rudimentary theatre form already existent, in widespread use, for the playing of a varied repertoire. This was the great hall of the typical medieval castle, with its dais before the fireplace and its screen wall opposite, pierced by two doors and having a gallery above it. Before this screen, and probably on a low platform, the actors used the doors for entrance and exit and played interludes and a variety of entertainment during and after great feasts. This arrangement, too, will have an influence on the use of space in future theatres.

Probably the closest we can come to a designer in the Middle Ages is the *maître des feyntes*, the master of tricks, or effects. He it was who invented the means for simulating the burning bush in the episode of Moses in the wilderness, the rain for the Flood, the miracle of the loaves and the fishes and that of the withering and flowering fig tree, the episode of the souls of Herod and Judas being carried through the air by devils, and the Hellmouth spouting flames and issuing thunder. Descriptions of these effects are

contained in some of the manuscripts preserved from the Middle Ages, such as those of productions from Mons, Bourges, and Valenciennes. We have already mentioned the sketches for the Luzerne plays, and the *Mystère d'Adam* includes extensive instructions about how it should be staged. Usually the workings of these "tricks" were jealously guarded secrets, and frequently several masters of effects were needed for elaborate and lengthy productions. The more intricate and spectacular these effects, of course, the more likely they were to appear in those productions given in stationary settings, although there is record of some surprising "trickwork" accomplished on the movable wagons as well. In Italy, where the production of religious plays stayed largely within the churches, such an artist-architect as Brunelleschi designed many involved productions of this kind.

By the early years of the sixteenth century, Italian noblemen were staging elaborate productions in the great halls of their castles. These were secular in nature, the Renaissance being in full swing in Italy by this time. By 1545, the designer Serlio (he called himself an architect, as did others similarly occupied) was writing a lengthy treatise on how such a large hall could be transformed into a theatre, saying that "I have always made a small

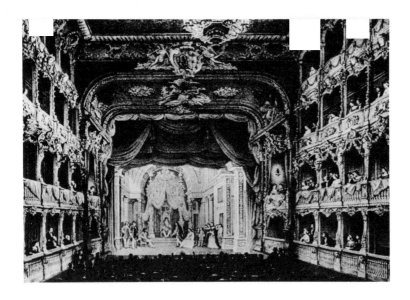

Figure 11–10

*A 19th century picture
of the Residenz Theatre,
Munich, the stage set
being the flat wing and
back shutter system in
use since the Italian
Renaissance, and the
curtain falling at the
edge of the stage, as
was customary in
Continental theatres.*

model of cardboard and wood carefully executed to scale." The
plans include the whole theatre space, not just the acting space,
and are interpretations of the rather obscure and sometimes fragmentary comments of first-century Vitruvius, whose long-lost
architectural treatise was discovered by Italian scholars in 1486.
Serlio's structure is built of wood, with curving rows of inclined
seats for the audience, a level, unencumbered space, then a flat
platform stage across one end of the room, raised, and behind it
an enclosed space exhibiting a perspective vista, with the floor
slanting slightly upward, or raked. Renaissance artists were universally enthralled with the rendering of perspective; Serlio's
scene translated this preoccupation to the stage, in three-dimensional terms. Since his "scenes" could be built to specification
for particular performances in these temporary theatres, there
was no need to provide for scene changing. So the perspctive was
quite solidly built, either as a tragic scene, a comic scene, or a
"satyric" (bucolic) scene, according as he read Vitruvius' recom-
mendations. The actor performed *in front of, not within* this
setting. It is merely an elaboration of the old booth stage, the
shelf for acting with an unchanging background. The permanent
structure of the Teatro Olimpico, opened with great fanfare at
Vicenza in 1585, is the solidified embodiment of the idea. It was
designed by the great Renaissance architect, Andrea Palladio, and
finished by Vincenzo Scamozzi. It can still be seen.

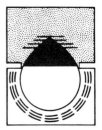

*Renaissance
or
Continental*

The Elizabethan theatre is another embodiment of the shelf-for-acting stage. We have described it in some detail elsewhere, and here need only point out that its raised platform stage had one great difference from the Italian adaptation of the booth stage: the Elizabethan shelf was attached to its background only along one edge, so that audiences could surround the action on three sides at least, and since the theatre structure was open to the skies, the stage itself was covered by a roof. This roof functioned not only as protection for the actors, but also as a "Heaven" from which chariots, etc. could be lowered for mystifying appearances, and the stage floor had one or more covered-over openings, or traps, for "risings." The background of this shelf was in no sense pictorial, but architectural and unchanging. Set pieces and other scenic suggestions were placed on the stage as they were needed but in any event were rudimentary. The actor made his entrances and exits by means of two doors in the background wall, where he also found provision for an "above," an acting position heretofore achieved on the booth stage by the simple expedient of a ladder set behind the back curtain. The actor James Burbage seems to have invented this theatre, and his company began playing in it in 1576. There is no direct influence from Italian to English ideas, although both can be said to have developed from the earlier and universal concept of the booth stage and/or the medieval pageant wagon.

From this point on, the scene *à la Italienne* and the English platform stage pursue separate courses for about a century. It is the *background* element which the Italians develop; the shelf-for-acting the English. It is the same shelf-for-acting that characterizes the Spanish public theatres of the time as well, and the building itself is equally open to the sky. The simple booth stage, of course, continued to be used by the traveling companies of *commedia* players for another century and a half at least, and the basic form of the booth stage is still in use in widely divergent theatrical presentations. Both the English and the Italian systems were influenced by the "effects" tradition of medieval playing as well. The English platform stage concentrated these effects largely in the stage action itself, whereas the Italian system largely came to concentrate effects in scenery.

The Teatro Olimpico and the various great halls and ballrooms which preceded it as "theatres" were roofed-over spaces, and

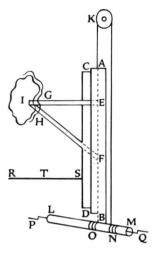

Figure 11–11

Sabbattini's sketch of a complicated stage machine.

DESIGNER AND

ARCHITECT

Figure 11–12

Richard Leacroft
Collection

*A 19th century print
of the Covent Garden
theatre in England,
showing the
characteristic stage
apron which had been
a feature of English
theatres since the
Restoration.*

subsequent Continental developments stayed within this structure. As French theatre developed it would also move its booths
indoors. The English theatre would achieve a roofed-over public
theatre at the Restoration in 1660, but its interior would have
significant differences from its Continental contemporaries.

Serlio's static back-scene was a single perspective vista; Scamozzi's back-scene in the Olimpico had seven perspective vistas
visible behind five openings (like the doors of the classic stage
house), three behind the great center opening, and one each
behind the other four. All the perspectives were static and un-
changeable. In 1588 Scamozzi built a small-scale theatre at
Sabionetta, under commission from the Duke of Mantua. Probably because of its small size, it had only one permanent vista seen
through a large, arched and decorated portal—the prototype of
the proscenium arch through subsequent centuries. But the static
scene, as illustration for the action transpiring before it, was useful
for only a limited type of theatrical production. And Italian ap-
petites already conditioned by the transformations of scenic representations in the religious plays were whetted by the burgeoning
fashion of lavish *intermezzi*, with rapidly changing scenes. The
"new thing" became the designs of such architects as Bernardo
Buontalenti and Giambattista Aleotti, who (in the latter half of

THE ARTISTS
OF THE THEATRE

Figure 11–13

An Inigo Jones design (1635) for a painted backdrop showing the designer's lines by which the scene painters can enlarge the drawing—a technique still in use.

the sixteenth and the early part of the seventeenth centuries) developed a system of flat wings (wooden frames covered with canvas, running in tracks, or grooves, on the floor), so that changes could take place and the scenes be "transformed" in full view of the audience. The canvas frames could be painted in various ways; they could be shaped as trees, clouds, houses, or whatever was called for; they could be arranged in groups, so that drawing off the first would reveal the second, and so on; the groups could be set at intervals from front to back of the stage, in diminishing perspective; the back could be finished off with a pair of these (now called shutters because they are bigger than the wings and come together), or by a backdrop (a large curtain of painted cloth either rolled, dropped, or raised to change it). Such a setting was capable of almost infinite variety, elaboration, and flexibility. Traps and overhead machines could be added to increase the intricacy of the scenes. This stage practice endured as a predominant style until well toward the end of the nineteenth century.

It was not only Serlio who wrote treatises on the problems of stage design, but notably also Nicola Sabbattini (c. 1574–1654), and Joseph Furttenbach (1591–1667), a German architect who had spent several years in Italy. Their detailed instructions for the design, building, and operation of intricate settings, machines, and

345

DESIGNER AND

ARCHITECT

Figure 11–14

Museum of Modern Art

*A Juvarra sketch of
Piazza prepared for
Nocturnal Illumination
showing the position of
one set of side wings
and a backdrop.*

lighting instruments are marvelously interesting theatre documents. They were practicing "theatre architects" who, like Di Somi and Serlio, set down expositions of their theories and practices. But many other designers were at work as well. Artists whose lasting fame placed them outside of theatre—like Mantegna, Da Vinci, Peruzzi, Andrea Del Sarto, and Gherardi—spent large portions of their time creating the milieu for a wide variety of theatrical performances. And there were some, like San Gallo, Torelli, Vigarani, and Servandoni—in addition to those we have named as "writers" about scenery—who devoted their full attention to theatrical matters, and whose fame lives by their accomplishments in theatre.

Inigo Jones brought the Italian scenic practices to England when he became designer-architect for court productions in the reign of James I. Somewhat less elaborate "maskings" had occasionally taken place at court since the institution of the Office of the Revels by Henry VIII in 1544. The essence of the new "Italian" style was that the actors performed *within* the set, and become a part of the changing visual image. As the complexity of such a practice increases, the actor tends to be no more than an additional stage decoration, an artifact for the visual delight of the audience; literature and the unadorned power of the spoken word tend to

Figure 11–15

Museum of the City of
New York

*Charles Witham's
design for the throne
room scene of Booth's
King Lear, showing the
use of borders to dress
the top of the stage.
See also 3–4 and 4–8.*

be lost. The audience arrangement, therefore, is necessarily one
which stresses the visual. The whole of the audience must be seated
in front of the picture, with the most important (because the only
completely undistorted) viewing position squarely on a perpendicular to the center of the stage—the royal seat of the masking
house at Whitehall or the royal box in many Continental theatres
and opera houses. Other members of the audience surrounded the
royal seat on various arrangements of chairs, or looked down
upon it and the stage from boxes arranged in tiers on the three
sides of the audience space. Such stage settings and appurtenances were exceedingly expensive to construct and operate and
were for some time confined to the largesse of noblemen and
royalty. Public theatres pursued a different course, although as
soon as they could manage it (historically speaking) they incorporated as much of this splendor as they could afford.

The English Restoration theatre was a curious combination of
the public and "private" practices that had preceded it. One of
the royal patentees, William Davenant, had been a colleague to
Inigo Jones in the production of court masques before the Civil
War and the Commonwealth, so he was very much aware of the
effectiveness of changeable scenery. The theatre he installed in a

347

DESIGNER AND

ARCHITECT

Figure 11–16

State Theatre, Bremen
*Painted backdrops are
still in use in modern
times as this
contemporary scene
from a German
production attests.
Directed by Fritz André
Kracht.*

converted tennis court in 1661 opened with provision for change-able scenery, and the subsequent theatre buildings erected by Killigrew and Davenant all incorporated this feature. But the English viewing and acting traditions of the platform stage (as well as the English theatre's emphasis upon the spoken word) put these changeable scenes upstage, behind the architectural pro-scenium arch. This "frame" was itself behind the main acting area—a wide and deep "proscenium," or apron, to which en-trances were made through two permanently installed doors on either side, still a feature of London's Old Vic. Restoration actors continued to use scenery as background, and at least a part of the audience partially surrounded the actors (as in Shakespeare's theatre) in the boxes and galleries that overlooked the apron. The rest of the audience was seated on benches on an inclined floor or in the remaining boxes or galleries surrounding that floor, or pit. Little or no attempt was made to include the actor in the setting; the production was in no sense *illusionistic.*

By the beginning of the nineteenth century in England, the pres-sures of growing audiences had reduced the size of the apron to make way for more seats; some entrances now *had* to be made through the side wings of the scene itself. Then came the romantic plays with their emphasis upon illusion. Shortly, these combined pressures forced even the English actor behind the proscenium arch and within the scenery, where his Continental colleagues had been for many preceding years. The triumph of the picture-frame (illusionistic) stage was complete. The nineteenth century was the great age of "scene painting" and "trickwork," and all plays, of whatever genre, were treated in the illusionistic style, intricate and changing scenes being invented for all of them. It was a part of the show that the changes were visible to the de-lighted audience.

Then toward the end of the century, as we have seen, came the incursions of realism, affecting stage production practices even before the plays themselves: real furniture, practical doors and windows, the box set—and hence the necessity of lowering the front curtain between scenes if there was to be a change of scene. Also during the nineteenth century the old methods of theatre lighting were displaced first by gas and then by electricity, the better (or at least more brilliant) lighting requiring more refined scene-painting techniques and bringing in the possibility of dim-ming and then completely extinguishing the house lights for the performance. By the last quarter of the nineteenth century the "peepshow" theatre was complete: a brightly lighted box, with a facsimile set, revealed to a blacked-out house by the rise of the front curtain. The stage action was completely contained within a "picture frame" and the actors played to each other, essentially, rather than to the audience; they did not "break the frame."

This theatre style became so entrenched that the announced "reforms" of Richard Wagner in the building of his great Bayreuth Festspielhaus (which opened in 1876) affected only the audience arrangements; the stage was perfectly "picture frame" and intri-cately equipped. But the audience sat in fan-shaped rows of seats with no intervening aisles, on an inclined floor that gave every seat a good view; the plan was the beginning of the end for the old "hen-coop" Italian opera house theatre with its rows of boxes overlooking a pit (now called the orchestra).

Then came the antifacsimile movement in theatre design fathered by Adolphe Appia and Gordon Craig. At first there was no at-tempt to break the stage out of the box behind the picture frame but simply to reform the contents of the box. The emphasis was

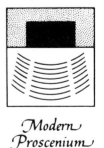

Modern Proscenium

349
DESIGNER AND
ARCHITECT

Figure 11–17

Appia and Craig both worked to simplify stage design, as this sketch by Craig for a scene in Macbeth *indicates.*

to be taken off the scenery, and put upon the actor, who, as the *living thing* in the production was obviously most important to the living theatre. The stage space, said Appia, is to be conceived of as *living space;* "stage decoration is regulated by the presence of the living body" of the actor. This is the truth of theatre (a truth *re*discovered and not invented for the first time, as we can see) : that the actor, the *doer* is the soul of theatre. Whatever is on the stage with him must take its life from him, must serve him, must be meaningless without him. We cannot duplicate nature on the stage, anyway, so let us find this deeper truth. Abstract forms, bathed in "living color" (thanks to the developing use of electric lights) would enable the appropriately costumed actor to create the illusion of whatever time or place or action was proper for the play. All of this would be guided by the unifying genius of the director-designer, who would have absolute control over all the elements of production. These theories inspired the work of numerous designers in the twentieth century; to even name them all would be impossible, and they extended to the second and third generations of disciples. Jessner, Piscator, and Reinhardt in Germany; Meyerhold, Tairov, and Gamrekelli in Russia; Copeau, Pitoëff, and Fuerst in France; Norman Wilkinson, Claude Bragdon, and Roger Furse in England; Robert Edmond Jones, Donald Oenslager, and Jo Mielziner in the United States form a typical,

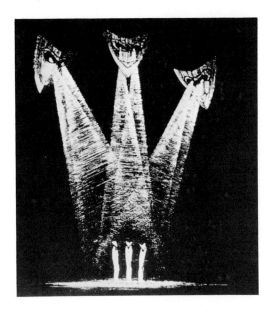

Figure 11–18

*Robert Edmond Jones'
sketch for the witches'
scene in* Macbeth
*follows Craig's
principles, and puts its
chief emphasis on
lighting.*

but by no means exhaustive listing. Modern scene design—its principles and its practices—could properly be said to have its almost sole inspiration with Appia and Craig.

Changes in the actor-audience relationship by the actor's breaking out of the picture frame are further extensions of the anti-illusion, or antifacsimile stage. This movement began with Max Reinhardt in 1919, when he installed in the Grosse Schauspielhaus in Berlin a wide and deep extension of the proscenium-arched stage. The extension thrust itself out and the audience was "wrapped around" three sides of it. The whole edifice, seating about 3500 people, was too big for any but the largest effects and soon fell into disuse. But the "new" idea of thrusting the stage out beyond the proscenium arch in order to put the actor into more intimate and direct touch with his audience is one which has spread as a design concept in many new and reconstructed theatre buildings in both Europe and America. The Vivian Beaumont Theatre at Lincoln Center incorporates precisely this idea: the thrust stage (which can be lowered out of sight) backed by a deep proscenium stage (which is rarely used). Buildings incorporating a permanent thrust stage with wraparound seats are now usually called "open stage" theatres, because the background for the thrust is not a proscenium stage with its appurtenances, but a more or less permanent architectural backing. The stage is "open"

Thrust

DESIGNER AND

ARCHITECT

Figure 11–19

A development of the new movement in scene design was the use of the sky-dome, here indicated by a Schinkel design for The Magic Flute.

Figure 11–20

Lincoln Center Repertory Theatre

The thrust stage (a modern application of old principles) of the ANTA-Washington Square Theatre set with platforms for the production of Arthur Miller's After the Fall. *(Inge Morath, Magnum Photos)*

Figure 11–21

Trinity Square Repertory Theatre

The arena stage of the Trinity Square Repertory Company with a performance of The Old Glory *in progress. (AIDART Archive)*

because there is no proscenium arch anywhere. The Festival Theatre at Stratford, Ontario, and the Guthrie Theatre in Minneapolis are both of this type. The third antiillusionistic development is the "arena stage," where the playing area is surrounded on all sides by the audience. With this type of acting space, lighting and the elevation of the seats must define the actors and focus the attention of the audience on them; the floor area of the arena then becomes the "background."

In recent years there have been many experiments in varying the relationships of players to audiences. Some theatre interiors are flexible so that both acting space and audience space can be changed in size and location from production to production. It has also become fashionable to extend performances beyond the fixed prosceniums of houses so constructed by platforms, steps, the use of the aisles by performers, and so on. But in all of these, in any given performance, there is a clear definition between what is acting space and what is audience space. The new, so-called environmental theatre (as we have mentioned previously) attempts to destroy this definition, and one of the "givens" in any specific performance is that actors will displace segments of the audience and usurp their space for use as a playing area. Whether such an infraction of an incredibly ancient convention in the theatre can become established (or even for very long be *tolerated*) has yet to be proved. Even in the medieval "rounds" and other seeming historical precedents of actors mixing with audiences, there were always theatre functionaries whose duty it was to see that neither actor nor audience actually displaced one another from their predetermined allocations of space. And it is difficult to see how an actor, who is "a thing apart" by the very nature of his calling and its practice in the theatre, would want to give up his special stance for very long and merge himself with the audience. Such tactics seem to me not only misguided, but ultimately self-defeating and a denial of the basic core of theatre: that special audience-actor relationship which facilitates and makes pleasurable and meaningful their essential communication.

For some years now the actual building of theatres has been entrusted to the professional person we call today the architect— not in the old sense of theatre architect who was the designer of the interiors (and sometimes of the exteriors) of theatres, but a man who builds all kinds of buildings, not just theatres. The

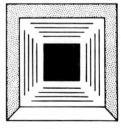

Arena

Figure 11–22

University of Iowa
*The nature of the action
in* Death of a Salesman
*demands a multiple
stage setting of various
interiors and an
exterior, all present on
stage at the same time.
See also 6–15. Directed
by Gregory Foley,
designed by A. S.
Gillette.*

wisest of these now "consult" with theatre specialists in the planning stages, so that a satisfactory end product is more likely to occur. But the deficiencies of many standing theatres in sight-lines, acoustics, backstage space, dressing rooms, work space and *usability* bear mute evidence to the fact that there are (and have not been for a long time) very few real theatre architects. With the many more new theatres that are beginning to be built these days, perhaps we can look hopefully forward to the viability of such a specialization.

Within the last decade there has been an unprecedented boom in the building and planning of arts centers and theatres. In the United States alone the number of such facilities is well over three hundred, with increasing emphases and resultant additional plans growing out of the burgeoning of state arts councils. The majority of these facilities incorporate theatre space. The building of cultural centers has become a matter of civic pride, and one prediction has it that within the next ten years no city of more than 100,000 population will be without such a center, either actual or planned. Now, all of this sounds very much like that cultural explosion which people in the arts have been desiring for the last half century. But the construction of buildings is no

Figure 11–23

Another solution for multiple setting is the unlocalized platform construction evident in this scene from the Broadway production of Dylan, *and that in 11–20.*

(Friedman-Abeles)

guarantee that culture, or more particularly, *theatre* will fill them. Indeed, to erect a building and then try to find something to fill it is proceeding in exactly the reverse direction. What you are then building is a monument, like the J. F. Kennedy Center for the Performing Arts in Washington. Such a procedure is particularly fatal for theatre, because the essence of theatre is the performance of live actors for a live and present audience.

It is the witness of history that theatre forms are intimately related to actual performance, that the structure grows *with* the performance and *because* of it. At least a sizeable portion of all the hundreds of thousands of dollars currently being raised to produce monumental theatre buildings might better be spent to develop performing groups who would then help to create the *living space* for the performance and the audience. No community will ever have anything more than a monument unless it first recognizes the organic nature of theatre, its *livingness,* and gives first consideration to the development of *real* theatre (the playing of plays) and only after that to the means of housing them. Theatre artists must determine the development and the form of theatre buildings, not chambers of commerce. Only then will we be able to rejoice in the burgeoning of theatre as an art form. The plan-

Figure 11–24

The Max Reinhardt
Archive, SUNY,
Binghamton

ning of theatre buildings must be the *result* of the existence of a living and growing theatre art. Theatre architects must be theatre artists and responsive to the needs of performance; the technology of construction must be designed to fit the art of theatre. Fortunately, there are hopeful signs that this very thing is taking place, particularly in the design and construction of such theatres as the Tyrone Guthrie in Minneapolis, the Ruth Taylor at Trinity University in Texas, and the San Diego Community Theatre in California, and it is, of course, the manner in which Lincoln Center in New York was developed and constructed.

Scene designers, unlike modern architects, have for a long time been specialized, skilled, and highly regarded members of the theatrical community. As we have at least intimated in the preceding chapter and immediately above, no respectable designer these days would undertake to supply the milieu for a play without studying the play itself carefully and consulting with the director. All designers accept without question the statement of Robert Edmond Jones in his immensely influential treatise, *The Dramatic Imagination* (1941), that it is the obligation of the scenic artist to "see the high original intention of the dramatist" and to work to "affirm and ennoble the art of the actor."

Ideally, the modern stage designer plans every aspect of the visual embodiment of the given production: setting, costumes, and

Figure 11–25

Two modes of dealing with design for The Merchant of Venice *are illustrated in the realistic setting for a Reinhardt production and in the constructivist Exeter setting. See also 5–4.*

lighting. This total creative act was the kind performed by Robert Edmond Jones. Gordon Craig, of course, called for this function to be that of the director as well—the *total* theatre artist. On some levels and in some places (where time, talents, and energy are available and commensurate to the task) no doubt there are such theatre artists. But a division of labor early occurred between the director with his primary responsibility to the actors, and the designer with his toward the visual elements. There are still a few successful designers, like Cecil Beaton, who do sets, lighting, and costumes for given productions. But there has been a further division of labor, at least in the commercial theatre generally, so that not only the design function but each of its principle elements is accomplished by an individual specialist. In some college and university theatres and sometimes in community and repertory theatres, the design function is still performed by a single person. More frequently in these kinds of theatres, the costume designer will be a separate functionary, and the setting and lighting will be planned by a single specialist, although the chief designer retains final control of the total production. We will talk here about the design function as a unit, keeping in mind that when the areas are separated, each specialist must work in complete cooperation and consultation with the other, just as the designer per se must work with the director. The end to be desired is a unified effect, all ele-

ments working together to enhance the total production. There is some value in the saving of time and energies to having a single designer perform all three functions; on the other hand, the specialized insights of differentiated experts can often spark creative efforts on the part of the total group that might not otherwise come to the surface. In any event, the resources of the particular producing group and the amount of time available for production will, in the final analysis, determine how the design personnel are deployed.

In addition to the creative imagination which is the absolute prerequisite for any theatre artist, the designer must have an unerring command of composition in line and color. Like the director, he must have the ability to work in concentrated and fruitful fashion not only by himself but also with other people. He must also have a good working knowledge of the other theatre arts: enough acting so that he recognizes and appreciates the problems of actors, and enough directing so that he can (above all) communicate creatively with his director-colleague. Finally, he must have an intimate working knowledge of the theatre crafts: set construction, costume construction, and the setting of lights.

The designer's work will be conditioned by the theatre space for which the production is intended, and by the directorial concept of the work in hand. He will need to take into account the size of the theatre, the proximity of the audience to the playing

Figure 11–26

Designer's sketches of settings may be rather impressionistic as this one by Fritz Erler for a Reinhardt production of Macbeth. *See also 5–4, and 11–22 and 11–23.*

Figure 11–27

The Max Reinhardt Archive, SUNY, Binghamton

Or they may be bold and definite like this design by Oskar Strnad for a Reinhardt production of Danton's Death. *See also 10–22.*

358

THE ARTISTS

OF THE THEATRE

Figure 11–28
ANTA
*Sometimes the designer
makes a model of the
set, like this one for
Incident at Vichy. See
another model 6–2; see
also 12–3.
(Inge Morath, Magnum
Photos)*

space, and the size and shape of the playing space. He will also need to be conversant enough with a variety of theatrical styles so that he can draw upon this knowledge to deepen and enrich the concept of the director for the given play. It is the designer who ultimately provides "a local habitation" for the play.

No less than the director, he is concerned with the play's central image; before he can begin to think in concrete terms of set and costume he must make his own series of associations, his own gathering of notes and sketches, his own specification of the central idea of the play. In Wilder's *The Skin of Our Teeth* the central image is the persistence of Man, his indomitable courage, his inventiveness, his *being*. So the actual *house* of the Antrobus family could be sketchy and impermanent, but the clothes must be actual and detailed. Maybe the walls of the room should be simply two-dimensional, painted flats with gaps between them so that the world shows through. Shall we use a cyclorama backing? How should the house on the stage look? American Gothic? That would fit with the colloquial American speech of the play. So the designer goes on with his questions and answers, his preliminary decisions and sketches. Will these decisions amplify and extend the play's metaphor in the consciousness of this audience for whom the play will be performed, or will their realization simply call attention to themselves, be mere gimmicks? These matters are all, of course, ironed out with the director.

359

DESIGNER AND

ARCHITECT

Figure 11–29

Sometimes the designer plans for projected scenery, as in this production at the Baylor University Theatre.
(Windy Drum Studio)

Once the form and shape of the play is determined, the designer concerns himself with the clarification and formalizing of the ground plan so that the director will have his space relationships worked out as he proceeds to rehearsals with his company. The ground plan itself is a kind of sculpture base for the completed setting, agreed upon by designer and director, and their mutual concept will depend to no small degree upon the director's knowledge of stagecraft and scene design. Taking into account the needs of the play for doors, windows, stairways, furniture, or whatever "working elements" are called for, the designer then proceeds to "detail" the setting, to make "renderings," colored sketches of the settings, or "models," three-dimensional, scaled replicas of the settings. Unless the designer has a staff which works under him, he continues the detailing of the setting by making working drawings for the stage carpenter and crew who will build the set. These must be accurate in every measurement and feature of construction. In large theatrical establishments there are paint crews as well as shop crews, but even in cases where a paint crew does the large areas of "laying in" the color, the designer himself frequently does the detail work and mixes the colors. In any event, he supervises the setting up of the scenes on

Figure 11–30
APA-Phoenix Company

Figure 11–31

American Conservatory Theatre

The designer follows the director's concept in supplying costumes as well as settings for a particular production. The end product may vary as widely as these two designs for the same play—Molière's The Misanthrope—one in period costume and setting, the other in modern dress. See also 4–14.

Figure 11–32

American Shakespeare
Festival Theatre

*Costumes are carefully
fitted and adjusted in
the costume shop.*
(Jim McDonald)

the stage itself and works with the lighting designer to light it properly. If he does the total design job, he of course has the lighting set-up and use in mind throughout his entire design process.

It is only in the present day that so many possible "styles" are available to directors and designers. In past theatrical times the homogeneous nature of given theatres raised no such questions about "style." Shakespeare wrote for the Globe stage, Sophocles for the Theatre of Dionysus at Athens, Congreve for the particular apron-stage of the Restoration. And not only for those stages did they write, but for those particular audiences. The designer today must know the theatrical conditions for which particular plays were written, no less than the director must possess this knowledge. But it is hardly likely (except in the rarest of circumstances) that he will try to reproduce those theatrical conditions in his design. He is working for a NOW audience, and with actors whose very physical size and shape differ from those of the players who first performed the play. So he makes adjustments. The masks of the Greek theatre were conventions which were not only right but necessary in the Theatre of Dionysus; are they either right or necessary in a modern proscenium (or even open

Figure 11–33

New York Shakespeare
Festival Public Theatre
*The costume shop also
often turns out armor
for productions
requiring it, as seen here
in making costumes
for Henry IV.*
(George E. Joseph)

stage) theatre today? Do they add a dimension of grandeur and legend to the present performance, or do they merely inhibit the expression of the actors and confuse the audience? Can we achieve the abstract, heroic quality of *Oedipus Rex* by means other than masks? And again we are back to the original question: how does this play *speak* and *mean* to *this* audience at *this* time, and how can the visual elements of the production speak and mean in that way? Revivals must be *translated* for modern audiences without violating the original intent, just as plays written in foreign languages must be translated without violating the originals.

The designer must also be concerned with the *flow* of the play. If there is more than one set scene, how will the changes be effected? Then, what problems are presented by the projected settings and costumes for the actors—both onstage and off? Costumes are, on the one hand, a part of the décor, the visual aspect of the performance, and hence must harmonize in color and style with the stage settings. On the other hand, they are essential elements of characterization for the actors, and hence must reflect the stage character and aid the actor in his characterization. Costumes are designed for plays, but also for *people*; any designer who forgets this fact is in for a lot of grief. Within reason, actors can become accustomed to tight-fitting garments, trains, hats, capes, etc. (actors are very adaptable people in this regard; besides, they *love* costume shows), but the designer must always bear in mind that any given costume should aid the actor not hinder him in his essential task of characterization. The successful designer of costumes has as unerring eye for line and shape as well as for color. It is obvious that the athletic build of modern women, for instance, is a far cry from the smaller, more delicate physical structure of the usual Restoration belle, yet the designer of a costume for Millamant must, by his judicious arrangement of line, color, and decoration, make his modern Amazon believable in her Restoration finery. Costuming requires special care and consideration for the theatre style; obvious zippers on a costume that is pre-twentieth century, for instance, can destroy the illusion which is being created by other elements of the play's milieu, particularly in open-stage and arena productions. Costumes which, by their nature, cover up a player pretty completely are difficult enough, but when the kind of costume demanded is scant or revealing, the designer's problems increase, for now the physical being of the actor becomes an even greater element to be reckoned with in preserving the aesthetic integrity of the total design. (Maybe Gordon Craig was right in suggesting that actors be replaced by "super-marionettes.") The factors and details which the designer must take into account are many, but his success in doing so—his insistence upon perfection in all details—will figure large in the total success of the production. Needless to say, both settings and costumes must be ready far enough in advance of opening night to give the acting company time to become acclimated to them, to *live* in them.

Setting and costume (and lighting as well) must be expressive of the mood and spirit of the play, of its historical and geographical locale, and of the particular segment of society which it presents. They must also conform to the artistic principles of arrangement and adjustment for line, form, and mass so that the visual impact of the play has harmony and balance. Finally, these visual elements must be serviceable in meeting the needs of the stage action, both from the point of view of actors and director and for the demands of production in the shifting and storing of scenes, the wearing and changing of costumes. The best stage decor is not simply *illustrative* of the play, but an *organic* part of the theatrical construct.

To put the matter another way, let us say that the designer does not just decide to do a "constructivist" *Tartuffe*, or an "expressionist" *Richard III*, or an "environmental" *Antigone*, or a "realist" *Merchant of Venice*, although any of these might make for some theatrical fireworks. Along with the director, he determines the concept of the present production within the limits of the given metaphor of the play itself, the expressed intention of the playwright, and the "style" grows from that. The famous Mielziner setting for *Death of a Salesman* is an organic part of the play because its impressionistic techniques are implicit in the form of the play. Lee Simonson's spectacular unit setting for *Hamlet* adds visual impact to the play's centrality, and facilitates the swift-moving scenes which are so integral to its effect. Fortunately for theatre, the vogue for minutely realized facsimile stages has long since passed, and no designer is these days expected to transfer the interior of a Child's Restaurant to the stage, nor the very wallpaper from a down-at-the-heels boardinghouse room. But every play has its "givens." Even on an open stage the setting for Chekhov's *The Three Sisters* must convey the decorative clutter of that nineteenth-century provincial Russian household, and even on a traditional proscenium-arch stage the setting must allow for the uncluttered flow of Shakespearian scenes. Arena stages present special problems in design because the action must be visible from all sides; but if the designer regards these special problems as challenges capable of solution the results can be exciting. The only insoluable problem in designing for arena staging is the play whose *primary* effect is a scenic one. The illusion of a prison can be achieved for Edwin Justus Mayer's *Children of Darkness* by making the chief scenic element a diagonally free-hanging "barred" window in forced perspective so lighted that the bars fall in shadows across the gray-carpeted floor of the stage; the garden scene in *The Importance of Being Earnest* puts delicate, white wrought iron furniture on a light green floor with painted flower borders; the ever smiling picture of Father in *The Glass Menagerie* is an actor holding an empty frame before his face who appears whenever the picture is referred to. In arena staging, the design unit is a cube of space, all six sides of which must be taken into account, as well as the volume.

Figure 11–34

National Theatre
of the Deaf

*Some productions
require special designs
for make-up, as in this
Theatre of the Deaf
presentation of* Gianni
Schicchi.

With the open-stage arrangement, the designer has at least one
wall which he can utilize. It then becomes, for instance, the location of that all-important window through which Bluntschli enters
in the first act of *Arms and the Man;* having decided to use it for
that inescapable purpose, the designer then is posed other problems as to its disposition in the parlor and garden scenes. But
hardly any audience today expects facsimile settings no matter
what the form of the stage. The tendency, on the contrary, seems
to be that of finding ways to "bring the show closer to the audience" by extending the action beyond the proscenium arch in
houses where that architectural feature remains. Selective realism
is the style most designers follow these days in plays which have
a natural, or real, milieu. That is to say, the desired end for the
stage picture is not that of a seeming photograph, but of a selection of details which will give the impression of place and time,
the illusion of reality. It is no longer necessary on the stage to
"roof in" a room, or even to have its walls solidly built of tightly
lashed flats of equal height, so long as the lack of these does not
in any way lessen the mood the play establishes. O'Neill's *Ah,
Wilderness!* can be played successfully on an almost bare stage,
since its central meaning is primarily in the character relationships
which are independent of surroundings.

Figure 11–35
Everyman Player
Productions
*Or as in the production
of* The Book of Job.
*Directed by O. R.
Corey, designed by
Irene Corey.*

What the set designer must keep in mind always is that the setting is a kind of symbol for the meaning of the play, that it must reflect and enhance the total statement. Having discovered all of the possible stage items which might be pertinent to the play and its present production concept, he eliminates all those which are not necessary either to the action or the mood, then arranges the most significant in a way most artistically in harmony and most useful to the acting company and the director.

Perhaps the most spectacular of tools available to the director and designer in the modern theatre is lighting. Adolphe Appia would be pleased at the creative uses to which it has been put in modern productions, and no director in his right mind would today neglect or negate the depths and dimensions which lighting can give. One is almost inclined to say that if a budgetary choice must be made between scenery and lighting, the choice should fall on lighting because it is almost infinitely variable and flexible. Its inherent qualities of direction, definition, intensity, and color make it a powerful evoker of mood and focus. The kind, location, and use of lighting instruments must be of vital concern to designer and director alike, regardless of the style or period of the play and without respect to the form of the theatre. Indeed, lighting becomes especially important in arena and open stage theatres,

Figure 11–36
Carnegie-Mellon
University

which by their nature cannot accommodate elaborate stage set-tings. In representational performances the light sources are hidden and the changes made subtly; in presentational perform-ances the light sources are often frankly a part of the stage décor, and the lighting shifts become an integral part of the stage action. The recent Nicol Williamson *Hamlet* (1969) is an example of the latter lighting technique. The increasing intricacy of lighting in-struments and electrical requirements have tended to make the lighting of a performance the responsibility of a specialized theatre artist called the "lighting designer." But both director and scene designer need to be sensitively aware of the possibilities of lighting with respect to all of its qualities. Colored light not only changes the color values of pigment and cloth, but it also has a definite emotional effect on both performers and audiences.

The lighting designer (whether he be a specialized individual or the general designer) works within the limits of some general rules: bright and sharp general lighting for farces and comedies, with everything distinct and clear; directional and chiaroscuro lighting for mood and serious plays. But within these extreme limits are a multitude of choices. The proficient lighting designer knows not only the various types of instruments for lighting and control but also the technical problems involved in their use. In

Figure 11–37

University of Arkansas
*Lighting is an important
element of design in
both the setting for*
Summertree, *directed
by Henry Boettcher
(11–36), and in the one
for* The Scarecrow,
*directed by Cleveland
Harrison (11–37).*

addition, he is no less aware than other artists in the theatre of the needs of the production, and he works closely with the director and other designers to bring this to full realization. If he is a truly sensitive artist he is likely to prefer a control system for the lighting which will allow its operator to respond to the rhythm and movement of each performance of a particular play, rather than one which is preset and unvarying in its operation. For one of the excitements of the art of theatre is the responsiveness of a performance to its ambience of place and audience. Though the casual observer may feel that successive performances of the same play by the same cast are identical performances, any interested person who takes the trouble to observe can discover that such successive performances are by no means identical. The theatrical performance is a lived experience, and no truly lived experience is ever identical to any other, however similar they may seem. Of course it has been the effort of the entire production company to bring about a set of agreements concerning how this play shall be lived through for the audience. Not only the large outlines, but contingencies and details have received attention; presumably the play is "set" when it is ready for its audience. But that audience itself makes changes in the performance; that is the secret of the living theatre. "They're very quick

Figure 11–38

Bavarian State Theatre

All elements work together to make a memorable theatre experience—The Sleeping Princess at the Bavarian State Theatre *Directed by Fritz André Kracht.*

Figure 11–39

The setting often carries the burden of establishing the mood of the play, as does this Otto Rheigbert design for Drums in the Night.

tonight." "What a house!" "Haven't gotten to them yet." "A little sluggish in the reaction department." These are all remarks which one might hear backstage at almost any time. For not only the theatre as a whole, but every individual performance in it is conditioned by its audience. All the artists of the theatre are aware of this fact; they live their lives and practice their professions in its light. It is the immediate interaction of audience and performance which makes theatre the most exciting of all the arts.

12
Playwright and Critic

The last of the theatre artists to come under our consideration are the two whose province is words. Actually, in a time sequence of production, the playwright is the first of all of those we have talked about; the critic is last. But the nature of the medium in which they primarily deal, and various other affinities in their separate crafts, make this coupling a convenient one. We have already, in Part III, said much about the interactions and mutual influences of playwrights and critics in their historic and aesthetic relationship. It is impossible to discuss the theatre of past times without such a focus, because the written word has been, until very recent years, almost our sole record of those past times, and certainly of anything so ephemeral, so bound to time passing, as a theatrical performance. It is largely by means of the written word that we have learned, not only the materials which formed the bases for thousands upon thousands of theatrical perform-ances, but also a great deal about how these performances were presented, how effective they were, and what sorts of people were involved with them on both sides of the figurative footlights. We have seen that the written play has for centuries—with few exceptions—been the heart of theatre, the point of departure, the chief shaping instrument of the total construct which is theatre. And we have also seen that the theoretical critic has sometimes had a very great influence upon the writing of plays. Our purpose in this discussion, then, will be to speak primarily of the *process* of playwriting, the status of the playwright in the theatre, and the ideal functions of the critic. In discussing the function of the critic we hope to make clear that, to some extent at least, every playgoer is a critic, exercising his understanding and knowledge to influence in significant ways the shape and form of theatre.

The fortunes of playwrights have varied widely from age to age. The poet-dramatists of ancient Greece were evidently highly respected and prosperous members of their society, and, as we have seen, their functions in theatre went far beyond the writing of the plays. They were types of universal theatrical geniuses who have had sporadic reincarnations from time to time, even down to the present. Shakespeare and Molière were of the same universal type, their involvement in the theatrical enterprise being much more than the supplying of words for actors to speak. Shaw frequently directed his own plays, and the contemporary Peter Ustinov is not only playwright, but actor and director as well. There have been myriad lesser examples of multiple-functioning individuals, and it is interesting and significant to note that those dramatists whom succeeding generations have called "great" have been—almost without exception—individuals who not only wrote scripts but also acted in them, directed them, and were involved in the total stage production. They were masters of the art of theatre and did not confine their energies solely to the writing of plays.

Playwriting is not primarily a literary art. If it were, the store of great plays would be considerably larger than it is. But who today, except interested scholars, is aware that Byron, Shelley, Browning, and Tennyson, as well as Charles Lamb, Dickens, and Henry James all wrote plays, none of which live in theatrical memory but exist only as curiosities? For the truth of the matter is that none of these men—great literary geniuses all—were men of the theatre. They did not know it intimately by working in it from day to day in its complex of diversified activities. Scratch almost any successful playwright and you will reveal underneath an individual who has involved himself with the theatrical art *as a whole*. Playwriting is not a "closet" activity. No doubt one of the reasons we currently bemoan our present lack of "great plays," is that the present century has too often excluded playwrights from the theatre, and sent them off to "write" somewhere else, accepting their solitary accomplishments when they had theatrical possibilities but delegating their production to other theatre artists. Great plays are very unlikely to be produced with this kind of arrangement. Various hopeful reactions are visible on the current theatrical scene: The Open Theatre and its stress on "cooperative playmaking," the New Dramatists Committee, the

American Place Theatre, and the Eugene O'Neill Memorial Foundation which nurture the theatrical education of promising writers, many attempts in colleges and universities (as well as in nonschool organizations) to set the playwright in the midst of the theatrical complex so that the necessary cross-fertilization can take place. But it has been so long a time—by now—that the playwright has been, perforce, a solitary literary writer, that it will take a good deal more concentration on such reinvolvement, by a great many more theatrical establishments, before much progress will be realized.

The playwright must *think in dramatic terms*. He must do so from the beginning and throughout. His descriptive title— whether it be "playwright" or "dramatist"—states the nature of his work. Play*wright* is not one who sets down the words of a play (to *write*), but one who *makes*, or *fashions* a play, as a wheel*wright* makes wheels. The dramatist is he who *does* (drama-*to do*), not he who writes. The soul of the play is the conceived and presented *action*, not the words with which it is expressed. Any writer of plays who begins with the words has made a bad beginning. It is even possible for a playwright to rise to great heights without that marvelous facility with words which is the mark of the literary genius. More than a little of Eugene O'Neill's *writing* is embarrassingly inept, while that of Tennessee Williams is almost without exception felicitous and admirable; yet few there be who would not, without hesitation, name O'Neill the greater playwright. It is the conceived action of O'Neill's works which puts him in the forefront of modern playwriting, not his skill as a manipulator of words.

The question in the theatre is always "What happens? What do these people do?" And a satisfactory answer is seldom "They think, they feel." For in the theatre especially (even more so than in life itself), we intuit the thinking and the feeling from what we observe in the doing. That is where the playwright must start: with *the thing done*. That is why he needs to be in the theatre, where the action is, observing and absorbing and being a part of that particular art form whose very language is action, instead of in the contemplative solitude of his study. He must get this language of action into his very marrow and sinew; the words come later. Then, in addition and quite practically speaking, his actual theatre experience will hone, refine, and discipline his

Figure 12–1

Théâtre de la Cité

Language in the theatre is always the language of action. The Three Musketeers, Roger Planchon production. (René Basset)

imagination to the possibilities of expression in the theatre and will further inspire him to explore these possibilities to their fullest extent.

In other words, the playwright cannot be a solitary, introverted genius, like the lyric poet or the spinner of tales. He must be a complete theatre man, because his precious words (and I do not denigrate them; I am myself in love with words) are merely one part of the theatrical construct. Even the words the playwright uses must be of action all compact, must be the sign and signal of the action; the words themselves must *act*. This is what he must learn, first and foremost, forever and ever. Words in the theatre are not descriptive, as they most often are in narrative fiction and other forms of literary art; in the theatre they are a part of the action being lived through on the stage. As with any work of art, there is something mysterious and undefinable in the creation of a play. Michelangelo used to say that his great skill as a sculptor lay in recognizing and releasing the forms that were *implicit* in the stone with which he worked. In some similar way the playwright recognizes and releases the forms implicit in the matrix of theatre, which is itself a microcosm of life. No great plays or even very good ones have ever been written by prescription, by fleshing out an assigned or chosen form; this is hack work. The action implicit in the core is the life of the play; the rest of the structure supports that life, as the flesh and bones of the body support its mysterious life, which is something apart from, in addition to, their corporeal reality. Theatre is an *organic* structure.

It is perfectly possible, of course, to practice structure, to exercise its parts, as one exercises the arms and the legs. No serious playwright neglects such practice. But likewise, no artist considers his practice pieces, his exercises, the finished work. In a work of art in any media, the structure, the skillful manipulation of parts which is the end result of long practice, is subordinated to and the servant of the animating *life* of the work. The playwright can (and should) practice plotting with its constituent elements of exposition, rising action, climax and dénouement. He can (and should) practice characterization, with due care to its revelation in speech and action. He can practice the building in of suspense, surprise, and foreshadowing. He needs to be in command of his tools. But the completed play is more than these; as in theatre everywhere and at all times, the whole is greater than the sum of all its parts. This necessity for practice in order to perfect his skills is one of the important reasons why developing playwrights need to be connected with producing theatre units, so that they can see their practice exercises in the medium for which they are intended —theatrical production. Obviously such practice situations should be sheltered as much as possible; no artist does his practice exercises in public. But since the audience is so integral a part of the theatre matrix, the playwright is in something of a dilemma. For his first efforts he is probably wise to make this necessary audience as private as possible, and as perceptive; such audiences can help him to develop his skills. Nothing is more disastrous to the long and steady growth of artists than our modern (particularly American) penchant for instant perfection and instant success, as if an art were analogous to brewing "instant" coffee. This syndrome attaches not only to the playwright (although more particularly in his case), but to actors and directors as well. Much of the playwriting and many of the productions in various school situations and in the many apotheoses of the off-Broadway theatre (wherever the particular Broadway may be) are in the nature of such practice exercises, as they should be. But there is a real need for all the artists of the theatre, and the public as well, to make a distinction between *practice* and artistic accomplishment and not take one to be the other. Almost nothing is sadder or more dispiriting than to witness *any* theatre worker who has had insufficient practice in his craft presented as an artist. Such presentation does neither him nor theatre any good. If the presentation is acclaimed (and this sometimes happens; chance is an inescapable component of theatre), he is misled as to his true level of skill; if it is derided (and this more frequently happens), he is discouraged and downcast. Both situations usually make him incapable of further progress and development. The formulation and dissemination of sensible standards in the art of theatre is the responsibility of all who love the art, but more especially of the critics, whose particular responsibility we will consider in some detail a little further on.

The "how-to-write-a-play" books are legion, and too many people, for whom these are their sole contacts with theatre, think that such prescriptions will show them how to turn out a masterpiece, real or approximate. I would guess that the number of "plays written" in the United States alone in any given year number into the thousands. Over the years I have heard too many neophyte playwrights complain that they are indeed writing —where can they find a theatre group to produce their plays, or an agent to sell them? Most of them are prescription playwrights or—worse yet—completely intuitive without the least vestige of craft or skill. It is just as foolish to say categorically that "playwrights are born, not made," as to aver that playmaking is a skill which can be learned. The truth lies somewhere between the two. Or perhaps we should say the truth is made in both statements taken together; "Playwrights are born, then made." For as with any art, there must be native disposition to the medium concerned (in this case to the dramatic), but there are also many points of skill that can be acquired. W. T. Price, one of the first to write a how-to book (1892), who started a school for dramatists in New York in 1901, said, "What can be learned can be taught." While it is true that the writing of a successful play depends a great deal upon the possession of a particular talent which cannot be imparted, certain technical aspects of playwriting (as in others of the fine arts) can be taught directly and efficiently. What cannot be taught is the dramatic sense which perceives materials in terms of plot and character and their interaction. The writing of dialogue is also a particular gift. In these areas the teacher can function only as a perceptive critic, pointing out flaws and inconsist-

Figure 12–2

Festival Theatre,
Stratford, Ontario

*Characterization and its
revelation in action is
the fundamental
concern of the
playwright.* The
Government Inspector.
(*Peter Smith*)

encies. But the playwright can learn (and hence can be taught) how to make the most of his gifts in the theatre through developing skill in exposition, using complications to build suspense, arranging minor crises toward the climax, introducing needed attitudes and facts at their optimum point, and eliminating anything that detracts from the emotional unity of the play. Some of this can be done in a writing situation, but the laboratory of the theatre—a "practice theatre"—is the most effective working ground for the playwright learning his skills. Jesse Lynch Williams had the right idea when he said that an audience is necessary to "play on" just as strings are necessary in the piano for it to be "played on." "The drama's laws the drama's patrons give,/And we that live to please must please to live," was the way Samuel Johnson put it.

There is probably no more vivid illustration of the process of playmaking, or at least of its genesis, than Pirandello's play, *Six Characters in Search of an Author*. These hapless creatures, with their reiterated story, are clamoring to be put into a play. It is just so that characters and plot drop themselves from somewhere into the playwright's imagination, and when he can no longer stand the pressure of their pleading, he makes a play for them. It is the immensely talented Edward Albee who says that he writes a play when he can no longer bear *not* writing it. The playwright feeds his imagination from his reading, from his experience, from his observation of and participation in life. He rarely conceives a play for the purpose of demonstrating a social or political idea. Samuel Raphaelson, playwright and teacher, cautions that "the method which starts with a theme and then rummages around for characters and a plot to fit it" is a dangerous method. The emotion, the thought, must grow from the plot and characters, not the other way around. The plot, the characters and their dialogue form the conceived action; their arrangement and refinement make the play. The conception is the "inspiration"; the arrangements and refinement are techniques. The former cannot be successfully taught or learned, although it is possible to create atmospheres which are conducive to visits of the Muse. The latter is the business of all how-to books and of courses in playwriting.

Thornton Wilder once said that it is the task of the playwright to so "coordinate his play, through the selection of episodes and speeches, that, though he is himself not visible, his point of view and his governing intention [i.e., concept] will impose themselves on the spectator's attention, not as dogmatic assertion or motto, but as self-evident truth and inevitable deduction." Since the very form that he has chosen as his means of expression means that there will be several intermediaries between his statement and its eventual audience, he must make that statement in such a way that its strength is chiefly in the unfolding of the idea through a succession of events which is the action of the play. This *unfolding* may take the form of a closely knit plot, a narration, or it may be a series of scenes unrelated by cause and effect, as in many modern plays. But in either event the *extrinsic* meaning (the overt communication signed in the visual and auditory symbols presented) must illuminate and reveal the *intrinsic* meaning (the myth, the ambiguity, the irony, the unifying concept, the theme or idea, the basic expression which is the impulse of the playwright to make the play). Whatever the strategy the playwright chooses for his statement, his tactics must embody a *forward movement* because he is presenting his play to the group mind which is an audience who are involved in the lived experience of the play by reason of this movement with its suspense, its pushing toward a future, as life itself inevitably does.

Since the province of the play is that of a virtual present moving toward a virtual future, the agents of that action are primarily

Figure 12–3

Brighton Theatre Royal
*The plot, the characters,
and the dialogue form
the conceived action of
a play.* Incident at
Vichy, *with Alec
Guinness and Anthony
Quayle. See also 11–28.
(Magnum Photos)*

characters. The playwright's concern with characterization defines itself in two ways. The compression of stage life insists that characters be given highly characteristic utterances which will be the auditory signs of their nature and intent, and that they be placed in concrete situations which define them by action, which is the visual sign. The playwright's control of the eventual presentation depends upon the inevitableness of his choice of these auditory and visual signs. These "signs of characterization" will be animated by the skill of the player, it is true, but the eventual effectiveness of that animation should be in the written signs, so that the character the playwright conceives is not unduly distorted by the personality of the actor who plays it. Many of the great roles in the plays of past times were especially written to fit the abilities of particular players, but they remain great roles because each has its own vitality outside the personality of its first embodiment. There are perhaps an equal number of roles especially written for particular actors (like L'Aiglon for Sarah Bernhardt, Metamora for Edwin Forrest, and Rip Van Winkle for Joseph Jefferson) which died with their performers because their vitality was chiefly in the particularized performance of those individual actors and not in the characterization conceived by the playwright. An inferior play may be temporarily enhanced by the imaginations and interpretive skills of the theatre artists who intervene between the play and its audiences, but it will not live beyond that particular embodiment. The late great Tallulah Bankhead is said to have remarked to Alexander Woollcott when both were members of the audience at just such a presentation: "You know, Alec, there is less in this than meets the eye."

Jacques Copeau saw the playwright as "the true origin and life of all drama," whom every other theatre worker must serve in "sincerity and modesty, maturity, reflection." That concept is under some challenge in the present day by various "actor's theatres" and the type of virtuoso director who considers scripts merely as materials available for shaping into forms that please his fancy. But the *permanent* theatre—that which lasts beyond the ephemerality of immediate performance—is likely to continue depending upon the original insights and visions of playwrights. For it is, even today, the playwright who conceives the action which is the heart of theatre, structures it as the skeleton structures the human body, and clothes it in the flesh and blood of dialogue and mood, thus making possible the work of directors, actors, and designers in producing a living reality in the theatre for their mutual audience, which always is at least half of any theatrical performance.

The other theatre artist whose chief function is as a "dealer in words" is the critic. In the popular mind—and in the minds of more than a few theatre people—the critic has no standing as a theatre artist. Often, indeed, he is considered *the enemy*, standing outside the passionate commitment of performers and production staff, and invidiously or facetiously pointing out flaws in the theatrical realization. In fairness, let it be said that the conduct of some individuals in their exercise of criticism does deserve this scornful evaluation. But we have been talking "ideals" here— fundamentals, first principles—the understanding and appreciation of which are the foundation stones with which to build varying structures, the concepts by which to measure a variety of specific realizations.

It was almost a century ago that Matthew Arnold defined criticism as "a disinterested endeavor to learn and propagate the best that is known and thought in the world, and thus to establish a current of fresh and true ideas." In every phrase and nuance, this statement can be applied specifically to the person and the work of the theatre critic. The critic is impartial, he is knowledgeable, he is open to new ideas, he is in love with theatre.

At the outset, then, we can ignore the reporter of theatrical events, the writer of theatrical commentaries, the purveyors of theatrical gossip, the usual run of reviewers; they will be worthy of attention only when their true knowledge of the art of theatre and their experience of it turn them into critics.

We have previously observed the seminal character of Aristotle as a critic in the largest and best sense of the term, and the preceding pages hold the names of many others: Horace, the Renaissance critics, Dryden, Voltaire and Diderot, Lessing and Goethe, Zola, and Shaw (who moved from criticism to the writing of plays). Charles Lamb and William Hazlitt graced the early nineteenth century with their theatrical criticisms, William Archer, William Winter, Brander Mathews, and Henry James the latter part of the century. The early twentieth century produced George Jean Nathan, Stark Young, Clayton Hamilton, John Mason Brown, and Joseph Wood Krutch, to whose ranks were subsequently added the late great John Gassner, as well as Eric Bentley, Brooks Atkinson, Harold Clurman, James Agee, Robert Brustein, John Simon, Kenneth Tynan, and Walter Kerr. Perhaps the most universal of all recent critics—and certainly the most prolific writer—is John Gassner, whose intimate knowledge of the total spectrum of theatre from earliest to latest times only served to enhance his enthusiasm and interest in current trends and developments; he most truly embodies the Arnoldian principle. But all of these mentioned here have, to a very large extent, achieved the status of true critic, whose insights and judgments have lasting value.

Genuine dramatic criticism is rarely achieved by either first or second night critics, who dash from performance to typewriter so that the notice can appear in the next day's newspaper. Such reviews can often do no more than describe or narrate the evening's happenings, or display the clever turns of phrase in which these writers become adept. One of the classics of such witticisms is John Mason Brown's comment upon the opening of Tallulah Bankhead in *Antony and Cleopatra*: "Tallulah Bankhead barged down the Nile as Cleopatra last night—and sank." Another example is the recent comment of a prominent critic on a certain fashionable "artistic director," that the term is "a double misnomer if there ever was one." Such "clever remarks," apt as they may be, do not constitute genuine dramatic criticism; they are mere "wisecracking." One is more likely to find the reasoned judgment which is the soul of true criticism in periodicals and books, where the writer's "recollection in tranquillity" can bring his critical faculties more pertinently into play. George Jean Nathan insisted that it is "infinitely a more difficult thing to write good dramatic criticism than to write good drama." While one may smile a bit at the heat and exaggeration of the statement, there is more than a grain of truth in it. The playwright is partisan and need only be true to his single vision; the critic must be non-partisan and true to the "best that has been known and thought" in theatre. He must be widely conversant and thoroughly sympathetic with a broad variety of plays and theatre styles as well as playwriting and stagecraft; he must, as a member of the audience, be able to give himself over wholly to the production he is instantly viewing; he must be judicious and illuminating in his comments.

Perhaps more necessary to the critic than to any other of the artists of the theatre (excepting the director) is a thorough grasp of all the literatures and the traditions of all the stages of the world; he must have a sound and usable knowledge of theatre history. He must also be thoroughly grounded in dramatic theory and criticism, not only in the principles of its application, but in its historical development. Cases have been made for impressionist critics like Anatole France, who said "the good critic relates the adventures of his soul among works of art." But the validity of all impressionist criticism lies solely with the writer of it. We would be inclined, for instance, to accept the impressions of such a one as Anatole France, for we know him to be a person with catholicity of taste and rich resources of personality and experience. But when the impressionist technique is applied by less competent witnesses, it becomes an excuse for laziness and results in a series of willful reactions which are a far cry from authoritative criticism.

No sounder criteria for the judgment of a given work of art has ever been stated than that of Goethe in the form of his three questions: What is the artist trying to do? How well has he done it? Is it worth the doing? Here is the sum and substance of criticism, involving understanding and judgment—*first* the understanding, and *then* the judgment.

The critic is a constant learner. In order to be able to answer

Figure 12–4

The extrinsic *meaning of the play must illuminate and reveal the* intrinsic *meaning.* The Blacks. *See also 9–12. (Martha Swope)*

Goethe's first question, he needs both a broad and general culture and a particular equipment for the work in hand. His knowledge must be not of the theatre only but of the other arts, of history and of psychology—of all the humanistic studies which give him a deeper understanding of man and his world—for man and his world are the ultimate subjects of any play ever played. The ideal critic is the ideal Renaissance man who takes all knowledge as his province and is continually seeking to enlarge his personal horizons. But, ideally also, he should have had, somewhere in his background of experience, actual and meaningful work in as many kinds of theatrical artistry as possible. Harold Clurman is a practicing director as well as a critic; Walter Kerr has been both director and teacher; John Gassner's involvement in theatre matters has been so broad as to frustrate cataloguing. But having had actual theatre experience, the critic must develop an objectivity about it, must learn to use it as a tool for the understanding of the totality of theatre and not as a "point of view" which dictates judgments. Eric Bentley's almost exclusive involvement with literature, for instance, makes him an injudicious and somewhat scornful critic of any theatre experience which does not include a "great script."

What the true critic does is to bring all of his knowledge and all of his experience to the formulation of certain principles of theatrical art to which he is committed; a body of *beliefs* which he expounds, and with which he illustrates his criticisms. Mr. Clurman, for instance, asks always of a performance "is it humanly relevant?" In such a book as *Lies Like Truth*, which is a compilation of reviews written between 1947 and 1957, it becomes apparent that his process of consideration for a new work involves not only his answer to the question of whether and why he likes it, but also where it stands in relation to other work of the same dramatist, where that dramatist stands in relation to the theatre he writes for, and where his theatre stands in relation to society in general. Thus he encompasses the whole of Goethe's principles, ending with a value judgment founded upon wide and deep knowledge and experience.

It is not the critic's business to announce how plays *should be* made (the history of criticism offers too many sad examples of the futility of that approach), but rather to explain how they *are* made, how a given play at a given time and place *has been* made. Each play that is produced may demand of the critic that he shall broaden or alter what he knows already: Croce was right when he said that every play is a unique experience. The critic must forever keep a freshness of approach, a willingness to be convinced, a complete "illusion of the first time." It is reflection and consideration which relates each new experience to the body of one's knowledge and beliefs, which connects *this* play to all those that have come before it and sees its possibilities in relation to all those that may follow.

Some critics feel that they are better able to judge a given performance if indeed it is absolutely fresh and new to them both as to script and as to production. Some feel themselves better equipped if, even for a new script, they have previously read the play and formed an idea of the play's essential meaning. Obviously, for the many productions a critic sees of plays which are not new scripts, he will, perforce, have formed some prior judgment of its meaning. But in either case he will need to ask himself if the "image" or concept of the production is indeed that of the dramatist. To neglect this question, even in the case of a new script, is to stint in his task. As we have seen, the latitude of "interpretation" varies from play to play, and the critic must assess whether or not this particular interpretation falls outside these latitudes for the given play. A recent production of Ibsen's

Peer Gynt, for instance, was criticized because the director had "transmogrified it into a soul-less sequence of slapdash scenes, now bursting into musical-comedy song, now into plebian farce." Such distortion of a classic is obviously the imposition of the particular director and is no organic part of the play. Undue artiness and self-conscious preciosity can be the unfortunate result of an attempt to "update" or to translate for present audiences one of the plays of the standard repertory. To play *Hamlet* "hippie-style" (as was done recently in New York), with beads and jeans and casual jauntiness is an unwarranted distortion and denigration of the play's central image, especially since the attempt to retain the poetic speech of the original set so incongruously with the "translation."

The critic will further ask himself how the playwright's intent is communicated to the audience in this production. The answer will involve a consideration of the chosen action, of the sequence of events, of the characters, their dialogue, the established mood, and the scenic investiture—all those components which make the play as form. Productions of new scripts he will measure in terms of the unity of action, the balance and proportion of the scenes, the emphasis and rhythm with which they are presented, the harmony of all the elements. The same criteria he applies to "revivals," but here his consideration is tempered by his intimate knowledge of the original intent as compared with the present incarnation. When he sees (as recently happened in New York) a production of Alberto Casella's *Death Takes a Holiday* incorporating an *illustration* of the news of the Algerian war by bringing onstage a whole group of French and Arab fighters to pantomime the news report, he can dismiss it out of hand as a bad production. For such a needless scene not only interrupts the flow of the playwright's action, but becomes a ridiculous insult to the intelligence of the audience, which was quite right in laughing at it.

Obviously bad productions of obviously inferior plays the critic does well to dimiss in some such peremptory fashion as Clayton Hamilton suggests: "Last evening a play called *Crime*, by John Smith, was produced at Brown's theatre, with Mary Jones in the leading role. The audience seemed to like it (or seemed not to). There is nothing in it that requires critical consideration." But his obligation is greater to productions of plays which have had a long and honorable history in the theatre. Even if the production is bad—probably *especially* if the production is bad—he must point out where and how and why it failed to meet its obligation to the playwright's concept.

While it is true that "every play should be criticized after its kind," the genuine dramatic critic is, to some significant extent, a teacher. His ultimate responsibility is not to the theatre in and of itself alone, but to the public—to the audiences real or potential without whom there is no theatre. To some extent, he acts as a mediator between the theatre artist and the public, explaining the former to the latter, and encouraging understanding and appreciation through his own insights and observations which he cogently communicates. But more directly he is that "appreciative audience of one" who rightly assesses theatrical productions and *teaches* audiences, out of the fullness of his understanding and experience, what is good or not good, and why and how this is so. In other words, we might express the nature of criticism in the following way: (1) The critic has in mind the image of the play; (2) he also has in mind a standard suitable for the play; (3) he compares what he sees with that image and that standard; (4) he decides how far short the particular production falls in script and in interpretation; and (5) he expresses that judgment for *his* audience: the public. Just as Jefferson insisted that democracy needs an educated electorate, the critic insists that theatre needs an educated audience, and he bends his efforts to achieve this.

It is fashionable nowadays to aver that audiences are stupid, that they will accept anything in the way of entertainment that is glossily packaged and/or cleverly ballyhooed, or (especially now) that has some prurient or salacious air about it. But the theatre that has contempt for its audience will surely die. If audiences are to be led to a more meaningful theatre, to a juster appreciation of the life-enhancing properties of theatre, to its centrality in illuminating the human condition, it is the critics who (by inclination, training and ability) must lead the way. There will probably always be a segment of the theatre-going public which looks to the theatre for nothing except an escape mechanism; the "tired-businessman's syndrome" I call it. And there will also probably always be a tiny segment of intellectual snobs who look to theatre for a special and esoteric experience. But *real theatre,* the broad and deep stream which has nourished mankind since the dawn of history, will wither and dry up unless theatre artists in general—and theatre critics in particular—develop ever widening audiences who know with deepening knowledge and love with deepening devotion the particular image of man that is recurrently lived in the theatres of the world.

The critic of theatrical presentations which call themselves "professional" has an absolute obligation to bring to his criticism all the knowledge and taste which it is possible to exercise, without consideration for the feelings of producers, designers, or players; he must put his attention to the focus and the truth of the total production. He also is under the necessity of stating his assessment of the *worth* of the production in terms of its value for audiences. It is not enough that he admire the polish and expertise of the acting, directing, and setting of an ultimately insignificant frippery of a play. He must make a *value* judgment of the total meaning with respect to the weight or worth of the basic materials as well as its stage realization. This is not to say that he should dismiss out-of-hand the "minor" play, but that he should point out that it is, indeed, minor—and why. His abilities and sensibilities must alert audiences to significances and insignificances, or he shirks his role. There is a place for *The Odd Couples* of the theatre, but let us not confuse them with the *Marat-Sades* and the *Lion*(s) *in Winter.* The critic who is truly interested in preparing (as Clayton Hamilton says) "the way for new creative effort by establishing a current of fresh and true ideas," will state and explain why a possibly inferior production of a vital new play is more important and more worthy of support than the glossiest of tired old clichés. He will always be on the lookout for fresh and interesting talent in the writing, directing, designing, and acting of plays; he will always look hopefully to the future but will also always insist on the highest standards in every area.

The critic of other-than-professional productions has a difficult role to play. Unquestionably, he must maintain his standards of excellence while at the same time he exercises an understanding and appreciation of the circumstances of performance. I sometimes think that there should be no critics in the usual sense for this type of performance. At any rate, such a critic will profitably concentrate on the play's central image and concept and comment on the extent to which these have been realized. He does well to

Figure 12–5

The audience is always at least half of any theatrical event. . .
(*George E. Joseph*)

Figure 12–6
No matter how small it may be.
(*George E. Joseph*)

avoid reference to individual performances unless they are out-standing. And he does very ill indeed for both players and audiences if he finds merit where there is none. Few things are so ultimately destructive of excellence in the theatre as "puff reviews." Perhaps a good rule of thumb is one (formulated in somewhat flowery language but sound in principle) contained in Price's *The Technique of the Drama* (1892):

The critical temperament is kindly and forgiving; it exalts the true, kindles the fire of timid hearts in capable breasts, and is only fierce in words of dispraise where presumptuous imbecility uses a false authority to mislead.

We have said earlier that every member of every audience is, to some extent, a critic. His immediate and spontaneous reaction is most likely to be a simple "I like it," or an equally simple, "I don't like it." Each reaction, conditioned as it is by the sum total of the individual's knowledge, experience, prejudices, and life style, is perfectly legitimate if he recognizes it for what it is: an expression of the fact that the witnessed performance *agrees* or *disagrees* with his personal predilections and constitutes no judgment on the artistic worth of the presentation. If such an audience member wishes to proceed in making a value judgment on the artistic merit of a given performance, he must equip himself for the task; i.e., he must, to some extent, go through the process we have outlined here for valid criticism. First of all, he must acquire some understanding of and some feeling for the nature of the theatre experience. He must develop some standards concerning the contribution of each theatre artist and for what may reasonably be expected of a production. In addition, he must apprehend the currents of thought in the world of which he is a part, so that he can relate his theatre experience to that world. If he knows, for instance, something of the wide reaches of theatre history and criticism, he can fit the present production into the general scheme of various periods, forms, and modes. If he is acquainted with the various elements of the theatrical construct and how they function in the whole, he can compare the present production with standards thus developed. If he is baffled by what he sees, he can always learn more, investigate further. He can analyze the writings of critics and playwrights of past and present times to spark his own thinking, and with each exposure to a theatre experience (he should try many, of many kinds) his judgment will be more sure and he will have a better understanding of what he likes or does not like. He will then be an *informed critic* and not merely a consumer. An audience member thus educated and sensitized is invaluable to the well-being and the development of the art of theatre itself, and he certainly, at the same time, enlarges his own enjoyment and understanding of this most fascinating of art forms.

Much of our consideration of the critic has concerned itself with the application of his abilities to individual performances. This method is not only the most convenient but, of necessity, the only sound approach. For the very nature of criticism is inductive, or descriptive, built upon the observation of a multitude of particular instances. The act of creation precedes the act of criticism; Aristotle's great critical work was descriptive of plays written many decades before. We have seen how that inductively arrived at manuscript was distorted into a set of rules which became prescriptive, and the difficulties which ensued in the attempts of many playwrights to fit their creations to those rules. But we have also seen that the true value of the *Poetics* is its perceptive analysis of the nature of the theatrical act itself, in its fundamental aspect of art, of feeling and form.

The great theoretical critics of any age, who write not of one particular performance alone, or of a series of such performances, but of the total art of theatre, are no less wedded to an aggregate of individual creative acts (or plays) than was Aristotle. Hazlitt, Lamb, Schlegel, Schopenhauer, Meredith, Santayana, Knights, Frye, Kitto, Olson, Esslin and Styan—and all the "creative critics" who have enlarged our understanding and our sympathies by their writings about theatre—have arrived at that pinnacle through their patient consideration of the individual creative works of the plays themselves. It is the breadth of their knowledge and the force of their insights which has raised criticism itself to an art, a necessary and component art of theatre. "A work of art is above all an adventure of the mind"; says Ionesco, "it is the creation of an autonomous world introduced into our world from fundamental truths." Although he did not mean his statement to apply especially or exclusively to the art of criticism, it does have here a special applicability. It is the particular responsibility of the critic to make known those "fundamental truths" through his "endeavor to learn and propagate the best that is known and thought in the world," so that (again in Arnold's words) he can help to "establish a current of fresh and true ideas."

V
The Allied Arts: Movies and Television

13

Cinema

In the not quite two generations during which moving pictures have been a reality, they have been called by different names: the flicks, the movies, the cinema, the film. The arrangement of that progression is a microcosm for the development of, and the respect for, the medium. In its earliest appearance and uses it was a toy and a curiosity, then a great popular entertainment medium, then a cult, and finally it bids fair to become an art. The last three incarnations are still simultaneously existing: entertainment, cult, and art. But its entertainment priority has, in the last fifteen years or so, been largely usurped by television. Therefore, "cultists" have appeared on the scene bemoaning the lost glories of "pure cinema" and praising the appearance of "art films" and "underground movies." But within the last six or seven years there has also been a genuine attempt to develop an "aesthetic" of cinema, and film courses and film activities have multiplied in the colleges and universities of the United States—a sure sign that the flicks have been intellectualized and "artified."

If, indeed, cinema is now an art form, it is the only art which has been developed almost completely within the twentieth century, and for that reason alone it might be said to reflect most exactly the world which created it. Superficially, it is a compendium and combination of twentieth-century concerns: scientific investigation, mechanization, automatic duplication, a stress on objects and environments, complicated distribution methods, big business and "quick money," and the "success syndrome." Various facets of its brief and brilliant career can be used as cogent illustrations of each of these concerns. But right now, at the moment when cinema might be said to have reached its maturity, a more pertinent inquiry is that which is directed towards understanding it as an autonomous phenomenon, an expression of modern man in relation to his world—a modern art. Materials for an aesthetic of film are still being gathered, and there are sometimes wide divergences of opinion from one critic to another (sometimes even a bald statement that the very concept of film criticism is impossible). Any statements which we make here, any conclusions at which we may arrive, must of course be tentative and subject to revision; it is difficult to "recollect in tranquillity" that which is so pervasively and newly present. But it is not impossible, and the constant linking of theatre, film, and television in the public mind requires that distinctions be made. There are some similarities, but there are also wide and significant differences. None of the three is served by a system of thinking which lumps them indiscriminately together as "entertainment." We shall, therefore, in this chapter make what discriminations we can with respect to cinema and treat television separately in the next chapter.

The first and most obvious distinction one can make is that the world of film is a very wide one, embracing a whole series of applications which not even the most devoted film enthusiast would call entertainment. The peculiar and eminently useful qualities of the whole film complex have been profitably applied to scientific studies involving the techniques of time lapse, slow motion, high speed, X-ray, and microscopic filming and projection. Occasionally the beauty and perfection of some of these "studies" will raise them to the realm of art or entertainment, but they are not generally and originally so intended. We will exclude them from our consideration here. Another category is the application of film to the solution of teaching problems in various traditional subject matters like mathematics, economics, physics, chemistry, astronomy, and others—those visual aids which have proved so useful in so many classrooms. They, too, have no artistic pretensions but are frankly pragmatic and didactic. The third category is that of news films, whose popularity and usefulness have now largely been transferred to television, although news films are still being made and distributed. Then follows a group of film types a little harder to classify: sports films, travelogues, and documentaries. Each functions to some extent as entertainment, but our exclusion of them from the present consideration is based on their primarily informational purpose. Again, in individual instances, they may rise to the realm of art by their perfection and beauty, as does the famous documentary of Pare Lorentz's called *The River* (1937), or *Night Mail*, which Basil Wright and Harry Watt produced in 1936. Finally, we exclude here, though somewhat regretfully, the whole body of cartoon films, as being tangential to our study, and worthy of a separate and extensive treatment of their own. We will, however, have some occasion to refer to them in our brief consideration of the history of the motion picture.

We are left, then, with the so-called "fictional films" which deal primarily with human beings, and whose chief *raison d'être* is to entertain, delight, amuse, or otherwise present themselves to an audience which gathers particularly to see them. Even this division of the total film complex is a rather wide one, embracing comedy shorts, serials, program pictures, spectacles, "feature" films, and "art" films. But the line of their development is fairly clear, and it is these for which distinctions need to be made with respect to their relationship to theatre. These are the films which primarily aspire to the appellation of "art," and the ones about which critical comment chiefly concerns itself. In the beginning, few such distinctions as those above could have been made, but by now these various types are fairly well established and autonomous, with the nonfiction or nonart films continuing a viable and vital existence of their own and needing no assessment or consideration as art. Before we consider in some detail the means, methods, and effects of "the film as art," it might be useful to sketch briefly the development of "film as film."

This history of the motion picture can conveniently be divided into the following periods:

Before 1895—discovery and development of basic equipment
  1896–1905—basic applications or "types" established
  1906–1916—development of the "feature film"
  1917–1927—prime of the "silent film"
  1928–1939—perfecting of the "talking film"
  1940–1950—new exploration in the "language of film"
  1951–1960—"independents," color, and "wide screen"
  1961–   —predominance of the "art" film

Obviously, such a "division into periods" is a somewhat arbitrary affair, as any historically-minded person can attest. Any historical development is a continuously unfolding progression or process, and both date limitations and "legends" in the above tabulation are open to question and revision. But the listing is, at any rate, a convenient way of keeping the progression in mind.

The production of moving pictures, at its lowest common denominator, required the development of certain devices: primarily the projector and the film camera; secondarily, screens, projection booths, and studios. Each of these devices had separate beginnings and developed at different rates of speed; all, plus moving picture theatres, are necessary to the realization of the activity we call "going to the movies." They constitute a whole series of "interventions" between the "pure act" of performers and the eventual audience. Movies could "happen" only in the twentieth century, but some of the constituent elements have a long history.

The basic principle of the camera goes all the way back to Aristotle, who noticed that an image of the sun could pass through a small hole and be seen on a surface behind the hole. By the early Renaissance the intrepid Leonardo da Vinci had sketched into his notebooks a device later called the *camera obscura* by which an artist could sketch on a piece of white paper the image projected by the light of the sun through a small hole into a darkened room or box. Others, too, were working on the Aristotelian principle; over the next two centuries, mirrors, lenses, and shutters were added to the "box" in order to capture a better image more quickly. A concomitant problem was that of "fixing" or retaining the image. Various scientists and inventors struggled with this problem throughout almost the whole of the nineteenth century: Niépce and Daguerre in France, Fox Talbot and F. S. Archer in England, the group of experimenters associated with the Eastman Company in Rochester, New York, as well as several others. Experiments with various combinations of chemicals on bases of paper, tin, glass, and celluloid, finally produced in 1887 that phenomenon called *film*.

Meanwhile, the mysteries of projectors had been under investigation and development. About three hundred years ago the magic lantern appeared, and various forms of this device led a separate existence for some two hundred years, enlarging and casting upon walls or other surfaces by means of various combinations of lenses and light sources images drawn and painted on glass slides or disks. It is just such a device that the indefatigable Samuel Pepys mentions in his *Diary* for August 19, 1666: "Mr. Reeves

. . . did also bring a lanthorne with pictures in glasse, to make strange things appear on a wall, very pretty." Refinements of this device are still with us, of course, in various forms of slide projectors. Its application to the eventual picture-in-motion will wait until the middle of the nineteenth century.

The third contributing factor to the development of motion pictures is the scientific observation of the optical phenomenon known as "persistence of vision." From very early times man has been aware of the tendency of his eyes to an after-image when, for instance, he continues momentarily to see a glowing spot after turning his eyes away from a bright light. Observations and optical experiments in the early nineteenth century produced a series of gadgets which depended upon the persistence of vision for their effect: the thaumatrope (a disk with, for instance, a bird on one side and a cage on the other which, when spun, seemed to show the bird *in* the cage); various other spinning tops which made colors flow together; Plateau's anorthoscope, which enabled one to look at a distorted image through a revolving slotted disk and see an undistorted image; and the zoëtrope, which mounted a series of slightly different drawings inside a slotted drum— when the drum was revolved, the images seen through the slots seemed to move. The principle is the same as that of the "riffle books" which sometime later (and for a very long time after) simulated motion through a series of slightly differing drawings on separate pages which are "thumbed" rapidly. All cartoon films are refinements of the "riffle book" and zoëtrope principles. Pictures "move" because the image of the first one seen persists in the human eye long enough for the second to take its place. The actually existing realities of film are a strip or series of slightly differing pictures shown sequentially at an appropriate rate of speed.

Between 1845 and 1853, an Austrian army officer by the name of Franz von Uchatius combined the zoëtrope principle with that of the projector to show "moving pictures" as an aid to teaching recruits. The pictures were, of course, drawings, but here is perhaps the first instance of moving pictures used for instructional purposes. As photography concurrently developed, carefully posed photographs were substituted for the drawings of the earlier experiments. The next great leap forward seems to have been that of Edward Muybridge who devised a means of lining up first twelve and then twenty-four cameras whose shutters were tripped in succession to "freeze" the continuing movement of a horse. This he accomplished on Leland Stanford's estate in Palo Alto, California, in 1878. He seems to have thrown these "moving" images on a screen by means of a projector he called a zoögyroscope, at a meeting of the San Francisco Art Association some two years later. Other comparable experiments were being done in both France (chiefly by Jules Étienne Marey) and in England (by Louis Le Prince and William Friese-Greene).

By the early years of the 1890s, many men were building devices that incorporated the newly perfected film in both cameras and projectors, including not only the above, but also Emile Reynaud and the Lumière brothers in France, the Skladanowsky brothers in Germany, and William Dickson, Woodville Latham, and Thomas Alva Edison in the United States. Reynaud seems to have been the first to think of perforating the film to control its movement through the projecting lens, Edison the first to conceive that motion and sound should be recorded and reproduced simultaneously (although this feat was not really accomplished until years later), and the Lumières the first to produce a projector with an adequate light source. Edison, concentrating chiefly on the *recording* of sound and sight images, at first was opposed to any device for showing the new "moving picture" films to large audiences by projection, on the ground that this would destroy their novelty. He developed the Kinetographe, a viewing cabinet with fifty feet of film inside moving around spools with a single "peep-hole," and a useful camera, the Kinetoscope. The Edison filming was done in what is probably the first studio, his "black Maria"—a tar-paper shack at his New Jersey laboratories. A part of its roof opened to the sunlight which was necessary to make the photographs. It was the use of Edison films in projectors developed by William Jenkins and Thomas Armat that led to the first public showing of motion pictures to a large audience in New York at Koster and Bial's Music Hall on April 23, 1896, as part of the vaudeville bill at that house. Edison's earlier peep-show idea continued a separate life, and such machines are still to be found in penny arcades. In Europe, Reynaud had devoted himself to the production of animated drawings, and as early as 1892 was showing them to the public for an admission price. The Lumières in Paris opened their "Cinématographe" show to the public in December, 1895, and the Englishman R. W. Paul showed his "Theatrograph" in March of 1896 in London. That widespread experimentation was going on throughout the nineteenth century is summarized in the figure of nearly 600 patents issued by 1900 in Western Europe and the United States for devices connected with the development of motion pictures.

All of this experimentation and development was by scientists and engineers interested in optical problems, the study of motion, and still photography. Only the early Daguerre whose "tinplates" were a way of "fixing" a photographic image, was in any way connected with theatre; he had been a scene designer. But the immediate popularity of the public showings of this "scientific" equipment led to the involvement of theatre people. Kenneth Macgowan, in his rambling history of the motion picture *Behind the Screen*, tells us that one of the 50-foot strips of film (one minute of "showing time") used in the Koster and Bial house in 1896 was a scene from Charles Hale Hoyt's play, *A Milk White Flag*, obviously especially photographed in the "black Maria." Other short subjects (each about one minute in length) were advertised by the Music Hall: Sea Waves, Umbrella Dance, The Barber Shop, Burlesque Boxing, Butterfly Dance, The Bar Room, Venice with Gondolas, Kaiser Wilhelm reviewing his troops, etc.

Lumière supposedly created the first fiction film in a short sequence called *L'Arroseur arrosé*, in which a puzzled gardener looks into the nozzle of his hose and is sprayed with water when a mischievous boy removes his foot from the hose behind the gardener. He showed it in Paris in 1895. Because he had developed a more portable camera than the American machine, he sent men all over Europe to film scenes (including the coronation of Nicholas II of Russia in 1896) and to show the films in hundreds of cities and towns. This "location shooting" and "distribution system," Macgowan feels, is the origin of a fad for faked newsreels (staged away from the actual scenes) of such events as the Dreyfus affair, the Spanish-American War, the Boxer Rebellion, and the eruption of Mt. Pelée. In America, the literal size and weight of the cameras also forced "stagings" of events on roof tops, in studios, and out-of-doors. With the continuing improvement of equipment and techniques, films proliferated in number and variety and grew in length. The showing of 16 frames per second became standard, and the length of a "reel" was set

Figure 13–1

Museum of Modern Art
Scene from The Great
Train Robbery, *first
American film of note
and probably the first
"Western." It was filmed
in New Jersey in 1903.*

at 1000 feet, or about 16 minutes of showing time. News events, short travelogues, and comic episodes were the favored subject matters. Camera men gradually learned how to move from a single episode in a single setting to a second episode in a different setting, "editing" their film before showing it and "intercutting" from scene to scene. McKinley's campaign and inauguration were recorded on film, as were episodes in the Russo-Japanese War, the Boer War, and trips to various exotic parts of the world. The wonders of the microscope were filmed as early as 1903. By trial and error in the manipulation of lenses and cameras, the techniques of panning (moving the camera to follow action), fades, and dissolves (means of transitions between scenes) were perfected.

Georges Méliès, a conjuror and proprietor of the variety house known as the Théâtre Robert-Houdin in Paris, became particularly inventive of special effects and, in 1897, built a glassed-in studio (sunlight is mandatory for filming). Between that date and 1904 he produced there faked newsreels, a fantasy called *Cinderella*, another called *A Trip to the Moon* (in 30 scenes), and *An Impossible Voyage* (in 43 scenes). Although he generally used a stationary camera in a studio throughout the whole period of his work, he is responsible for inventing and developing a great many of the optical tricks still employed in movies today. In addition,

402

THE ALLIED ARTS:

MOVIES AND

TELEVISION

he early turned the attention of an eager audience to imaginative storytelling, designing scenery and costumes as well as camera tricks and special effects, and preparing ahead of time a carefully worked out plan for shooting the scenes. By the time he retired in 1913, he had made over 500 films.

In England and America, film makers concentrated more exclusively on "natural surroundings" for all their various kinds of films, and it is particularly fitting that the first American film of note was a one-reel "western" (made in New Jersey) called *The Great Train Robbery* (1903). Conceived and produced by Edwin S. Porter, it included both indoor and outdoor scenes, a conflict between "the good guys" and "the bad guys," shootings and a chase: the traditional ingredients of the preeminently American form of movies from that day to this—the "western." Among other films, he also produced a 14-scene *Uncle Tom's Cabin* which (at least in the advertising catalogue which contained a description of it) is credited with being the first film to introduce subtitles, or "announcements with brief descriptions" between the scenes. By 1905, the basic techniques of filming, editing, and projecting had been established. The many short films made were shown at fairs, as part of the bill in vaudeville houses, and in "store theatres." There was also an occasional building converted or erected for the sole purpose of showing films, but the most famous and highly touted of all these was that which opened in McKeesport, Pa., near Pittsburgh—the Nickelodeon of John P. Harris in 1905. He showed a 15-minute program for a nickel admission, and within two years there were 3,000 nickelodeons spread throughout the United States, 10,000 by 1910. Motion pictures had become a big business. This sudden spread of low-cost entertainment was not without its critics and detractors. Typical of antimovie statements was that made by the *Chicago Tribune* that "there is no voice to defend the five cent theatre . . . its influence is wholly vicious." But there were other voices raised, including that of Jane Addams of Hull House, to the effect that this "poor man's show" might well become his university. A generation later the same defenses and attacks would be applied to television.

Defense and attack notwithstanding, nickelodeons (with prices raised to a dime) continued to flourish, with a seemingly insatiable public, and the "industry" began to burgeon. As Macgowan points out (*Behind the Screen*, p. 137), the period between 1906 and 1916 saw "The dawn of the feature film, the film star, the first distinguished director, the first picture palaces, and the place called Hollywood." Dozens of companies and scores of people (most of them not hitherto involved in theatrical affairs) turned their attention to the production of films, and the great names began to appear: Adolph Zukor, Jesse B. Lasky, C. B. De Mille, Samuel Goldwyn, Mack Sennett, and David Wark Griffith, to name only a few. The movement began which persists to some extent even today: that of stage performers and directors to the screen. In the United States, the making of feature films (a film so called had to meet a minimum standard of at least five reels), was first undertaken in and around New York, the center of both the technology and the performers. By 1910, Griffith was taking his Biograph players to the West Coast for filming in the winter months, and by 1915 more filming was being done there than on the East Coast—Hollywood had been born. By this time there were more than ten million "movie fans" in the United States, and the movie houses were becoming cleaner and more comfortable. They were also raising their prices to 15 and 20 cents. In 1914 Mitchell Mark opened the Strand in New York, a "movie palace" with 3,300 seats and a 30-piece orchestra to play the musical accompaniments. Smaller houses used organs and pianos.

At the same time, the viability of longer films was being explored and proven. A 9-reel Italian spectacular, *Quo Vadis*, and a 4-reel *Queen Elizabeth* starring Sarah Bernhardt had been successfully presented (with increased admission prices) in New York. The first full-length motion picture having its exterior scenes shot in California had been *The Count of Monte Cristo* in 1908. (Its interior scenes were shot in Chicago.) But the culmination of this early period of feature film making was D. W. Griffith's still famous *The Birth of a Nation* in 1915. It was a 12-reel epic about the Civil War, for which many theatres charged as much as $2 admission. It is said to have earned more than $18 million over a period of some twelve years.

Griffith was a New York stage actor in 1908, when he reluctantly agreed to direct a film for the Biograph Company, with whom he had previously been supplementing his income as an actor in one-reel productions. He had also tried his hand at playwriting and poetry and had even written a movie scenario based on *La Tosca*.

Figure 13–2

Museum of Modern Art
*Scene from D. W.
Griffith's* The Birth of a
Nation, *filmed in 1915.
Griffith was the first
motion-picture man to
use the camera as an
instrument in shaping a
new experience of
seeing.*

Figure 13–3

*Joseph Ruttenberg, 1916.
Early cameras were
hand-cranked.
See 13–12.
(Photo courtesy
American Society of
Cinematographers)*

His first film as director was entitled *The Adventures of Dolly.*
No one today, American or foreign, writes about the development, the techniques, or the "art" of cinema without referring to,
giving credit to, and admiring the early skills and artistry which
Griffith achieved. In many ways he may be said to be the true
"father of the motion picture," although he himself said that he
owed much to the pioneer work of Méliès. Although trained for
the stage, he seems to have been the first "motion picture man"
to understand that the camera is not the correlative of a theatre
audience, a recording machine for a series of shots, but an actual
instrument in the shaping of a new experience of seeing. What
these achievements were we shall consider a little further on when
we talk about the aesthetics of film. By the time the end of his
career came in 1931, he had directed and/or produced literally
hundreds of full-length films and was a byword throughout the
world. With the overwhelming success of *The Birth of a Nation,*
movies became respectable as a form of entertainment for all
social classes.

  For the ten years following 1915, the Hollywood product domi-
nated the screens of the world; almost 850 feature films were produced there in 1918 alone. Many New York stage players were
lured to the films by the promise of instant and worldwide fame

and by the actuality of astronomical salaries. These included John Barrymore, Douglas Fairbanks, William S. Hart, Florence Reed, Mary Boland, and many others. But the cinema also developed its own "stars," like Mary Pickford, Wallace Reid, "Fatty" Arbuckle, the Gish sisters, the Talmadge sisters, Tom Mix, Chester Conklin, Mabel Normand, and Charlie Chaplin. Screen salaries rose to the thousands of dollars weekly and the hundreds of thousands annually. The theatrical "agent" appeared and the seven-year contract. Movie "palaces" seating up to 6000 people were lavishly strewn across the breadth of the country, largely under control of the film-making syndicates. Their somewhat fluctuating but ordinarily lavish income covered not only the ever increasing costs of production, but also provided unheard of sums in profits for the moguls, like Louis B. Mayer, Irving Thalberg, De Mille, Lasky, and Goldwyn. Though the budgets for the pictures were big, the profits were bigger: *The Covered Wagon* (1923) cost about $750,000 to produce and its *profit* brought Paramount about $1.5 million. The ratio for many other pictures of the period stood at about the same level. This was very big business indeed. Many fortunes were made by producers, directors, and players (none by *writers*, that I know of), and the extravagant style of living that the next decades would ascribe to Hollywood grew then into a way of life. Payments for "screen rights" to their work would bring some dramatists and fiction writers income from the new field, but since the screen was devoid of spoken words, the works would be considerably transformed in the making.

It was the great public demand for movies, of course, which made possible the incredible lavishness of the film scene. The moviegoing public, in the years of World War I and after, consisted primarily of the younger generation, chiefly of the middle and well-to-do segments of society. They not only dictated profound changes in the conduct of motion-picture houses but also in the content of the films themselves. The post-World War I period of the flapper and the hip flask was one of revolution against the "stuffy" mores of the prewar generation, and the movies reflected this revolution in film content stressing boudoirs, vamps like Theda Bara and Clara Bow (the "It" girl), and riotous living in lavish surroundings. Rudolph Valentino became the idol of millions of romance-seeking movie patrons. The luxuriousness

of movie decor was reflected in the pretentiousness of the "cathedrals of the cinema" which were erected in large numbers of
cities. Their opulence had no counterpart in the ordinary lives of
their patrons, but they were beloved as were the movies they
showed. Most typical and lavish of these was the Roxy in New
York, which opened in 1927 with 6250 seats, a Chinese room, an
Empire room, lush carpeting and baroque decoration to the tune
of $8 million in construction costs. But in only one of its early
weeks the box office grossed nearly $150,000. It, like many of its
counterparts elsewhere, offered a program which included not
only a feature film, but newsreels, short subjects, and a live
vaudeville show.

On the Continent, the advances made by Max Reinhardt and
Ernst Lubitsch in Germany, Ambrosio and Pasquali in Italy,
Méliès and the *film d'art* (photographed stage plays) in France,
Victor Seastrom and Mauritz Stiller in Sweden were effectively
interrupted by World War I. After the war, Lubitsch, Seastrom,
and Stiller went to work in Hollywood, and the most significant
developments in European film came from the activities of Eisenstein and Pudovkin in Russia, Carl Mayer, F. W. Murnau, and
Fritz Lang in Germany, and Carl Dreyer in Denmark. One of the
most famous, memorable and influential of films was that of Carl
Mayer: the expressionistic and innovative *The Cabinet of Doctor
Caligari* (1919). Almost equally influential have been Murnau's
Nosferatu (1922) and Carl Dreyer's *The Passion of Joan of Arc*
(1928) which is filmed almost completely in close-ups. Fritz Lang
was to win his greatest success with his first "talkie": *M* (1931),
although he had been making films throughout the 1920s. Pudovkin and Eisenstein, working in the revolutionary fervor of the
New Russia, produced in the twenties and thirties films which
became the admiration of many diverse film makers because of
their filming and editing techniques.

Then, in 1928, came the advent of sound. The "silents," of
course, had almost invariably been accompanied in their distribution by specially composed or arranged scores to be played by the
resident musicians in the various theatres during the showings of
the films. The emotional underscoring and emphasis thus supplied
had been a long-recognized supplement to the pictures themselves.
It was the great success of the Warner Company's film starring
Al Jolson which sounded the death knell of silent films. In *The*

Figure 13–4

Museum of Modern Art
Carl Mayer's The
Cabinet of Dr. Caligari
*(1919) probably stands
at the beginning of the
controversy between
those who regard film
as a personal
arrangement of aesthetic
surfaces and those who
conceive of it as reality
in depth.*

Jazz Singer, released in October, 1927, Jolson not only sang several songs which were recorded on the film itself but also spoke several lines of dialogue, the most prophetic of which was "You ain't heard nothin' yet." Scientists had been struggling with the problem of "talking pictures" since the days in the 1880s when Edison had first attempted to record both sound and sight. The experiments had gone through many metamorphoses, including the use of phonograph cylinders and disks, but it was primarily the work of the radio manufacturers in their development of the photoelectric cell, the vacuum tube, the microphone, and the loudspeaker who eventually made sound on film possible. Basically, the system involves the translation of sound waves into light waves, their recording on film, and the retranslation into sound waves through the electric eye, amplifiers, and speakers.

Some producers, many performers, and large segments of the public audience did not welcome the addition of spoken dialogue to what they conceived to be a "perfect" artistic creation—the "silent" film. But a larger proportion either saw its possibilities for extending the "reality" of the cinema, or simply and frankly enjoyed hearing their movie idols talk. So within a matter of months, the studios were converted to the production of "speak-

Figure 13–5

Museum of Modern Art
*Charlie Chaplin, as
actor and director, was
perfectly in command of
the language of film;*
City Lights *is one of his
famous silent films.*

ing films," and hundreds upon hundreds of moving picture houses in the next several months were "wired for sound." Many films being edited for distribution were also provided with "sound track" before they were issued. All of these changes were immensely expensive but by fortuitous circumstances most of the work had been accomplished before the stock market crash of October, 1929. The new public interest in "dialogued films" cushioned the blow of the Great Depression for the movie producers; in fact, it would appear that the depression did not even touch this "luxury" industry. Between 1929 and 1931, the number of sound-equipped theatres and the size of the total audience in the United States almost doubled. Sociologists and psychologists might point to this phenomenon as proof that the chief function of the movies is as "an escape from reality." It was in December of 1932 that the cavernous reaches of Radio City Music Hall were opened, and it is still today a "first-run" house with all the appurtenances of the "good old days"—various short subjects and a "stage show" on the program and lavish lobbies and audience space. The old and ornate Roxy, however, was finally demolished in the late 1960s, marking a kind of end to the most flamboyant period of movie-making.

In any event, sound created problems for directors and actors.

Figure 13–6

Museum of Modern Art
*The filming of a
motion picture, with
star, director, cameraman
and crews, is illustrated
in this "backstage"
shot from* Sunset
Boulevard.

Many of the latter, having had their sole career and training in the silent films, saw an abrupt end to their careers because their voices were untrained or unsuitable. A great many "voice coaches" were imported to Hollywood in these years to meet the crisis. Silent screen stars (like Ronald Colman, Claudette Colbert, Marie Dressler, and William Powell) who had had previous stage experience, had no difficulty in making the transition. But in the 1930s the ranks of "talking stars" were swelled in Hollywood by the importation of a great influx of stage stars including Fredric March, George Arliss, Helen Hayes, Alfred Lunt, Lynn Fontanne, Leslie Howard, Cary Grant, Fred Astaire, Paul Muni, Spencer Tracy, and many others. Some of these stayed in cinema from that time forward; others divided their careers between stage and screen. The same phenomenon would occur after World War II when television developed; both stage and screen stars would "defect" to the new medium. The new necessities for spoken dialogue also brought numbers of playwrights and directors from the theatre to the cinema, among them John Howard Lawson, Clifford Odets, George Cukor, King Vidor, Rouben Mamoulian, Lewis Milestone, Josef von Sternberg, John Ford, and Frank Capra. The new element of recorded dialogue, at the beginning, caused some retrogression in camera techniques until it was well integrated and ways were discovered to deal with it. By 1940,

410

THE ALLIED ARTS:
MOVIES AND
TELEVISION

Figure 13–7

*Strips of film are "read"
after shooting.*

however, as André Bazin, the French critic, points out, American and French production of sound film "had reached a well-balanced stage of maturity." (*What Is Cinema?* p. 29.) In addition to the "western," a continuing favorite, the other major kinds of film production were devoted to comedy and burlesque (*Mr. Smith Goes to Washington* and the Marx Brothers), dance and vaudeville (Fred Astaire and Ginger Rogers), horror and fantasy (*Frankenstein, The Invisible Man*), as well as many crime and gangster films like *Scarface* (1932), and some psychological and social dramas, like Renoir's *The Grand Illusion* (1937) and Fritz Lang's *Black Fury* (1935).

In the decade of the 1940s new areas of realism were explored in subject matter by such directors and producers as Rossellini (*Paisan,* 1945) and De Sica (*The Bicycle Thief,* 1948) in Italy, Darryl Zanuck (*The Snake Pit,* 1948) and Doré Schary (*Battleground,* 1949) in the United States, and various others in France, Scandinavia, and Russia. But it was really the challenge of television from 1947 on that caused major changes in the film industry. Though the growth of film making in various parts of Europe had caused a slow decline in the total number of feature films made in Hollywood from its high point in the middle twenties, American film making continued to prosper. The advent of television, with its free and convenient entertainment, caused a near disaster. It is estimated that the number of moving-picture houses in the United States dropped from more than 20,000 to about 14,000 in the years from 1945 to 1955, and the total audience was cut to about half. Receipts fell accordingly. At first Hollywood answered in typical fashion with "bigger and better" pictures: De Mille's mammoth *Ten Commandments* (1956) and William Wyler's *Ben Hur* (1957). Methods of filming and projecting were revised in order to produce a picture not showable on the home screen: Cinerama, Cinemascope, VistaVision, 3-D, Todd-AO. Massive and lavish color productions were also made. But by the end of the fifties everyone knew that television was here to stay, and movies everywhere turned to their own unique tasks, developing subject matters and treatments not suitable for the home screens on the one hand; on the other, they found uses for empty studios by making films especially for showing on television. An increasing trend in production through the latter years of the fifties and into the sixties has also been that of the "independents," stars and directors who finance and produce individual films which are then distributed through the major companies. There has also been a greater tendency to "run-away" productions—i.e., those not primarily filmed in studios and back lots, but "on location" in many parts of the world. Location shooting is presumably more "real" and hence more desirable than that on simulated sets in southern California. Also, it sometimes happens that shooting a film (or a major portion of it) abroad saves production costs because wages are lower overseas. Hundreds of smaller picture houses were also built in the 1950s, chiefly in metropolitan areas and college communities. These showed primarily foreign language pictures and unusual English and American pictures to the smaller audiences who were looking for more adult fare than was available in the larger, more commercial houses. These so-called art houses had a definite effect on public taste and on the more creative artists in the movie industry.

By the latter years of the sixties a kind of equilibrium had been established, with new and exciting film releases from Italy, France, the Scandinavian countries, Russia, and Japan, as well as the United States. It seemed to be fairly well established that the cinema would not be "done to death" by the home screen. Its short but stormy history might well pause for a calm assessment. In the last few years such written assessments have become numerous and, as we stated earlier, film seems to be metamorphosing quite generally into an art rather than a business. Already there are those who see it as a "minority art" like theatre, but perhaps it is only that there is a more diversified choice available now than was the case twenty years ago. Colossal sums of money are still invested in the making of movies.

If cinema has indeed become an art, then it is surely like none that the world has known before. Never before in the history of civilization has there been an art so totally dependent for its very existence upon a complicated array of technological devices. And not since the building of the great cathedrals in the Middle Ages has there been an art in which it is so difficult to distinguish absolutely the contributions of particular individuals to the final art product. We have been in the habit of identifying films by the names of producers or directors, and the public eye ordinarily distinguishes them by the appearance in them of certain beloved stars. But, for better or for worse, the majority of feature films are the results of highly complicated processes involving numerous intricate decisions on the part of many people, all of whom have "a finger in the pie."

In the theatre, even in the new and "experimental" forms, it is comparatively easy for a member of an audience to fix the responsibility for the production he is experiencing. He sees *in toto* the scenic investiture and its relationship to the auditorium and the play; he is there in fact with the players and can engage in the theatrical transaction with them; if he has an eye for concept and interpretation, he can assess the work of the director; if he knows the play, he can judge the rightness of the interpretation. But the spectator at a feature film is allowed no such immediacies; he is several times removed from the original making of the presentation. Even the most expert of observers would have a very hard time distinguishing the work of the director from that of the cameraman or the editor, since the final film product is so largely dependent upon the mutual work of all three. One of our cultural clichés is that theatre is the actor's medium and film is the director's medium; the statement is true only if we subsume under the word *director* the work of cameraman and editor, or cutter. It would often be more true to say that film is the *producer's* medium, for the producer is the czar of the motion picture world. Theatrical producers are a different breed entirely, generally rely-

Figure 13–8

Museum of Modern Art
*The Odessa steps
sequence represented by
this single shot from
Eisenstein's* Potemkin
*was made by the use of
the camera technique
called "trucking," and
is a classic in film
history.
(From the Film Library
of Rosa Madell, Artkino
Pictures, Inc.)*

ing for artistic decisions upon the artists of theatre we have previously discussed, and confining their activities to organization of
the theatrical venture and the securing of production costs.

It is the movie producer, in the ordinary course of events, who
decides to make a particular film. He has become intrigued with
a certain play or novel, and he acquires it as a "property." Or
he is intrigued with a particular theme, as Goldwyn was about the
problems of returning servicemen in 1946, when he produced *The
Best Years of Our Lives.* Or he is looking for film possibilities for
certain players. Or he is simply anxious to "cash in" on a certain
trend in public interest, say, like dope addiction, or campus dis-
orders, or the black protest, or juvenile delinquents, or sexual
deviation. In any event, what he has is an *idea*, either one that
he has thought up himself or one that has been suggested to him.
Generally he will immediately call in a director (if he is not one
himself), and a writer or writers whom he feels might be particularly helpful in "developing" this idea. He explains his idea
in as much detail as he is capable of or (in the case of an already
written story or play which he has acquired) solicits the opinion
of the director on its viability as a film. The writer (usually a
salaried employee of the studio) is sent off to prepare a *synop-*

Figure 13–9

Culver Pictures, Inc.
Footlight Parade, *an
early Busby Berkeley
musical spectacular,
produced by Warner,
used, among many
techniques, this one of
the high-angle shot.*

sis, which is a brief, expository statement of the presumed aim and subject of the picture, written with an eye to its dramatic and visual possibilities. If this synopsis is acceptable to producer and director (i.e., if they agree that the property has filmic possibilities), the writer is directed to prepare a *treatment*. This is a detailed outline of structure, characters, scenes, and transitions, with possibly a sample or two of dialogue included for a few of the scenes. This treatment may be revised several times on the basis of suggestions by producer, director, cameraman, star or principal players, even by designers and by lawyers. Writers may be changed or additional writers assigned to the project at this point.

If the treatment is finally accepted, the writer or writers begin to prepare the actual *screenplay* or *shooting script*. While this process is going on, costume designer and set designer will be proceeding, with the help of the research department, to prepare the milieu of the play. The producer and director are casting the show, and the former is also figuring costs and setting budgets. The cameraman and the cutter may already be involved in the project, the former planning angles, set-ups, and lighting, the latter making sure that there will be sufficient *coverage* of all

Figure 13–10

Museum of Modern Art
*This shot of Fred
Astaire and Ginger
Rogers in* Top Hat *is
made from a medium-
low angle to call
attention to the
footwork of the pair.
(Copyright RKO
Radio Pictures, a
division of RKO
General, Inc.)*

scenes, actions, etc. so that the most effective selections can be made for the *final cut*. Sometimes the art director cntributes a series of *continuity sketches* to the development of the screenplay, which may again be revised several times before any actual filming begins. Inevitably, the screenplay will be revised *during* shooting. If all of this sounds as if the screenwriter has very little chance for originality and none at all for autonomy, that is precisely the case. Yet, perversely, there are frequent enough successes of "original" screenplays like *Woman of the Year, Sunset Boulevard, On the Waterfront,* and *The Defiant Ones* to keep alive the idea among neophyte writers (and some not so neophyte) that there is a real market for originals. Successive perusal of a large number of "screen credit" listings will effectively correct that idea.

The director and cameraman then proceed to the filming, or *shooting*, of the script. Nominally, the director is responsible for every moment-to-moment segment of this process. Actually, he is in constant consultation with his cameraman and even his cutter to determine the immensely complicated matter of the order in which the scenes and sequences will be shot, the angles and set-ups which will be required to cover "adequately" all possibilities of character, scene, etc., and how the scenes and sequences will be lighted. He and the cameraman decide the movements of

Figure 13–11

Museum of Modern Art
*This still from Olivier's
Henry V is from a pan
shot of an approaching
army, one of the
thrilling creations by
which Olivier translated
Shakespeare's play into
satisfying cinematic
terms. See also 10–12.
(Photo Arrow)*

the camera, and the latter plots with his assistants how these moves will be carried out and the lighting arranged. In the ordinary course of events, all action transpiring in a given setting or locale is filmed sequentially, whether or not there are intervening locales or settings in the script, in order to save both time and money. Such an arrangement means that the director must be supremely familiar with the continuity, so that no matter how small a segment of it he is "shooting" at a given time, he can help the performers be "ready" for the segment being filmed. A given segment may require several set-ups or arrangements of cameras and lights to complete it. It is also the director who decides whether or not any given *take* or filming of a series of frames for a given sequence is to be the "final" one. Each take is carefully numbered by the cameraman, and small segments of the action may be filmed over and over again until the director achieves one which he thinks is the ultimate possibility. The amount of film used in shooting an entire script is many times the number of feet which will finally comprise the finished film; all exigencies must be foreseen insofar as possible; there must be sufficient possibilities for the cutter to make the optimum choice, and enough *cover shots* to take care of emergencies. It is a tedious and time-consuming process, this filming.

Producer, director, cameraman, cutter, and writer usually view *rushes,* or the processed raw film, as soon as possible after the filming itself, in order to determine if there need to be changes or *retakes.* When a sufficient number of rushes are on hand, or the filming has been completed, the cutter begins to view and select frame by frame (i.e., each individual picture) those sequences which will be included in the mile to two miles of film which will comprise the final film. Usually, these days, the director sits with the cutter for this job, but at several periods in the past, editing was solely the cutter's responsibility; directors have now gained more "artistic control." The optical printer aids them in their task, which includes not only the selection of particular frames, but their sequential arrangement and the insertion of transitional devices where needed: cuts, wipes, fades, and dissolves. This assembling of the *rough cut* proceeds concurrently with the editing of the sound track—the deletion or addition of noises and sound effects as well as the correction of dialogue if necessary and the synchronizing of it to the visual film. (Dialogue is usually recorded at the same time the scenes are shot but on a separate *track* or film. In musicals, songs are generally prerecorded, then played during the takes, with the singers mouthing the words.) The final cut is then *scored,* or supplied with the musical background, a new print processed, and the film is ready for preview, or its first exposure to an audience. It has taken just about as long to get to this point since the completion of filming as it did to do the filming itself, from start to finish. Revisions are possible all along the way and are still in order after the preview and before the film is released. Everybody—even an audience—finally has a say in the finished product, for once a film is finished, there it remains, immutable and unchanging (unless it falls into the hands of some television station's "late show" and is butchered to the requirements of time slots and commercials).

It will be noted here (and rightly) that the actor has very little autonomy or latitude in the film-making process. One advantage he does have over the stage actor: he can be sure that any given moment of his performance, as selected by director and cutter for inclusion in the final film, will be his optimum for that moment. (He may have done it over in the filming more than a dozen times.) If he is playing a minor character in the film he may never have seen the complete script, or indeed any script at all, and have very little idea of how he "fits in" until he sees the preview.

He may not even have been "on the set," for more than a few days or a few hours. He is totally dependent on the director for his characterization in all its aspects. Even major actors and stars are similarly dependent upon the director, the cameraman, and the cutter, for no matter how talented or capable an actor may be, the very process of film making has reduced him to an "object," an image in sound and sight which must take its place along with all the other images which make up the final print. Many a beloved scene has ended up on the cutting-room floor—one of the calculated hazards of the profession, and one of the reasons why so many latter-day film actors have become their own producers and sometimes their own directors. It is true that there are occasional directors, like John Huston, and perhaps Ingmar Bergman, who depend on the skill of their performers for much of their cinematic effectiveness. It has even become possible for screen actors to have some rehearsals before shooting, and sometimes they will use stand-ins to see how they will look in the scene, thus cutting down their dependence upon the director. But, by and large, the value of a screen player lies in his face and his malleability to the director's vision of the sequence being filmed. Robert Bresson, the French director, goes so far as to say that "acting" on the part of film performers "only gets in the way" of the film image.

The total process of film making is exceedingly wasteful and expensive by its very nature, even though *process shots, special effects,* and working in constructed sets within studios rather than travelling to *locations* can help to reduce expenses. Few full-length movies today, however unpretentious, can escape production costs of under $500,000–$750,000; the more usual budget is $1.5–$2 million, with many "big" films multiplying that sum several times over. The *Cleopatra* (1963) which starred Elizabeth Taylor cost over $40 million. If one is given to deploring the cost of putting man on the moon, one would do well to consider the sums expended on producing recent "blockbusters," to say nothing of the additional sums expended in advertising and distributing them to audiences who have paid exhorbitant admission prices to see that which they would have been just as well off not seeing at all. It's a crazy world!

Fortunately for the sanity of the movie-consumer, he need not be concerned with costs except as they affect his own pocket-

Figure 13–12

Cameraman using a boom to film a scene on location in Puerto Rico in the successful cinematic translation of the novel, Lord of the Flies. *(Jean Hollyman)*

book through the price of tickets at the box office. He can enjoy his "aesthetic distance" and ruminate about the "artistry" with which he is presented. He can ask himself "What is cinema?" as André Bazin has done in his book to which we previously referred. Our answer here will not be the same in all respects as that of M. Bazin, but since he has been called "the Aristotle of the cinema" by competent commentators, we must give his point of view due respect, even while we disagree or delete or add to his vision.

As early as 1915, the American poet, Vachel Lindsay, published *The Art of the Motion Picture* (New York: Macmillan Co.), in which he insisted on a separate aesthetic for the new medium based on the fact that its essential being lies not in its capacity for reproducing life, but in the movement of the camera itself. Apollinaire, Gilbert Seldes, and Hugo Münsterberg voiced similar opinions at about the same time. From that time to this, however, there have been very few writers about film who have grappled with the aesthetic problem of film; I have listed the most cogent

of these in the bibliography at the end of this book. Some of the confusion is due to a dichotomy which has existed since full-length films were first made. At about the same time that Vachel Lindsay was writing his book, a group of French intellectuals and artists, led by the painter Léopold Sauvage, insisted that the motion picture was a branch of the graphic arts, not a "theatre art" or a "photographic art." Lindsay had chiefly been impressed with its picturing of masses of human beings in motion. The Surrealists supported the Sauvage position; the popular production of films stressed its dramatic and narrative values. There has always been a minority group of film makers whose point of view has been opposed to the popular one; the post-television "new wave" in cinema seems the popularization of many of these earlier minority views. The argument again seems new which opposes the idea of film as the expression of reality in depth and supports that of film as a personal arrangement of aesthetic surfaces. It is at this point that Bazin's statement about the *myth of*

Figure 13–13

Museum of Modern Art
This is a long-shot of Moses in de Mille's 1923 version of The Ten Commandments, *illustrating the kind of thing movies can do best—great crowd scenes realistically depicted.*
(Copyright © 1956 by Paramount Pictures Corporation)

421

CINEMA

cinema is particularly helpful. Cinema, he says, is simply the latest manifestation of the incredibly ancient human urge toward the "preservation of life by a representation of life," the magic which defies mutability and conquers death. So the ancient Egyptians made mummies, the Romans portrait busts, and later ages paintings. Until the Renaissance, these representations were largely content to stress the "spiritual reality" of their subjects, and the symbol thus expressed frequently "transcended its model." But the scientific and secular emphases which have been ascendent in the world since the Renaissance have caused a conflict in the graphic arts by adding the objective aim of "duplication of the world outside." So baroque painting and sculpture tried to capture movement itself in swirling lines and contorted figures. The aim was constantly toward greater realism until, as André Malraux has pointed out, the moving picture released the plastic arts from their obsession. A careful study and understanding of the drives and experiments which led to the development of the camera and projection machine reveals that their aim also was always to capture reality. (Remember that Edison tried mightily to record and reproduce sound *along with* sight in the very early days.) Perhaps some of the enchantment of the early, chiefly working class audiences for the movies lay in film's satisfaction of a deep, unrecognized proclivity of mankind to the magic inherent in the "preservation of life by the representation of life." Inadequacies of technology prevented for more than a decade the full realization of the realistic representation in both sight *and* sound, but the drive was always in that direction, and the coming of "sound movies" inevitable.

In some ways it was fortunate that the possibilities of the "silents" had a chance to be explored fully before the dimension of spoken dialogue had to be dealt with, but those critics who nominate the silents as "pure cinema" and deplore spoken dialogue are in error. For the capturing of the reality of human life inevitably involves the spoken word as well as the visual image. True cinema deals with images of sight *and* sound. Even the "silents," as we have seen, were concerned with the importance of sound (though not the sound of speech) through the accompaniment of music.

With photography, there entered, for the first time in man's long history, an inanimate object between the subject of the

Figure 13–14

Museum of Modern Art

This is a medium shot from the film made of Pasternak's novel, Dr. Zhivago, a long and scenically beautiful film. (© *Metro-Goldwyn-Mayer, Jnc. 1965*)

representation and the person making it: the camera. As Bazin says, "This production by automatic means has radically affected our psychology of the image." Although an excellent drawing may communicate more about its subject than a photograph (in that it conveys a spiritual reality along with its duplication of the model), the photograph has an "irrational power" to impress us, by its faithful reproduction, as the thing itself, embalmed in time, rescued from corruption, "change mummified as it were." And when the illusion of motion is added to the photograph by the rapid showing of a consecutive series of them (which is the principle of the motion picture), we have succeeded in embalming time itself, its very duration. At last man seems to have conquered the chief of his old, recalcitrant enemies. His logic tells him that his victory is an illusion, but his psychology accepts the illusion and glories in it.

The camera sees more, and differently, than the human eye; the microphone hears more, and differently, than the human ear. Eye and ear make unconscious selections, blockages, focuses; camera and microphone are unselective, all-embracing, *objective.* So long as their automatic capacities record this uncomplicated, objective

Figure 13–15

Museum of Modern Art
Zefferelli uses the
"two-shot" to bring
intimacy and poignancy
to this scene from
Romeo and Juliet. See
also 5–5 and 6–5.
(Copyright © 1968 by
Paramount Pictures
Corporation)

world, they are operating in the realm of science, and we tend to accept their objectivity as "truth." Microphotography, documentaries, some of the very early 50-foot films of trains, horses, and other natural phenomena were as close to this ideal as one could get. But as soon as a human agent intervenes to *select* and *arrange* the objective images of sight and sound, *art* begins to supplant science.

Since, as John Howard Lawson says, "A film statement is *organized* [italics mine] in images and sounds" (*Film: The Creative Process*, p. 175), it is possible to discuss and analyze those principles of organization. The cinema has a *language*, a *syntax*. Even in the most primitive of filming situations—the simple opening of the eye of the camera to the world around it—some selection is apparent. The human agent who operates the mechanical contrivance selects a segment of the world toward which to direct that eye. The strength and beauty of Robert Flaherty's *Nanook of the North* (1922) lay largely in its paradoxical character of seeming entirely open and factual with respect to the documenting of Eskimo life, while Flaherty's skill in the selection and arrangement of scenes and camera positions (to say nothing of many retakes) is apparent and real to the artist in film. The operator of the camera does, from the outset, make decisions about what shall be included in the picture, what excluded. He decides how close the camera will be to its subject, how far away. In other words, he *composes* a picture. His composition is selected consciously to direct the attention of his potential audience to those aspects of the chosen reality which he feels will be most powerful in eliciting the effects he is seeking. The individually registered moment of a particular scene is called a *frame* of the continuous film, but in the psychology of the cinema this appellation is a misnomer. For a cinematic frame is something quite different from a picture frame. The latter is set about a picture to mark it off from its surroundings, to focus attention, to function *centrifically*; it has substance and actuality. The cinematic frame however refers not to the solid and sometimes ornate object which exerts a centrifugal force on the picture it surrounds, but to the *contents* of the frame, or the picture itself. The cinematic frame operates in a directly opposite way to the picture frame. Its force is *centripetal*; its viewer is conscious always of additional surroundings to its contents, the reality of a world which opens out from this single frozen moment. The images of people and objects in a cinematic frame leave it and return to it; their world does not cease to exist nor is it marked off from its presumed surroundings. The cinematic frame *opens out* on all sides.

Camera movement reinforces this centripetal feeling. The *close-up* of an actor's face does not detach it from his body; in a moment we will see his whole person. The close-up of a doorknob turning in a thriller does not detach it from the whole door; we are conscious as we look at it, not only of the entire door, but of the spaces into which it leads on both sides of it. When the camera *pans* a shot of mountain tops, for instance, it moves from left to right, blocking out a portion of the view on the left as it reveals more of it on the right, and the movement has the ability to *include* much more than is seen at a given moment. The effectiveness of both close-up and pan shot were a part of film "vocabulary" as early as Edwin S. Porter's *The Great Train Robbery* in 1903. He also used a kind of primitive *trucking shot* by mounting his camera, at one point, on top of the train, although it was primarily used in that position to film the bandits fighting for control of the engine. The trucking shot is an extension of panning; in the latter, the camera remains in one spot but moves on its axis to follow a scene; in the former, the camera is mounted on a moving vehicle and travels with the action. Eisenstein's famous scene of the steps in *Potemkin* (1925) was accomplished by trucking.

Figure 13–16

The popular shot-in-depth makes an effective filming of one of the scenes visualized for the translation to film of Tennessee Williams' play, Suddenly Last Summer.

The camera eye can also be moved perpendicularly as well as horizontally. A person or an object photographed from a *low angle* (looking up at it) is endowed with impressiveness, size, or menace; if the shooting (taking the picture) is done from a *high angle*, a somewhat opposite effect is achieved. Flexible camera mountings, booms, cranes, even helicopters and airplanes have provided possibilities for a great variety of angle shots. Close-ups and pans can be combined with angles to give even more possibilities. The French director, Alexandre Astruc, uses the phrase *caméra stylé* (writing camera) to express, in part, this sense of movement and flexibility. The illusion of distance from camera eye to object or person can be achieved by moving the camera towards or away from it. In this respect, the language of cinema speaks not only of the close-up, but also of the *medium shot* and the *long shot*—degrees of distance which include more or less of the primary subject and the surroundings. The long shot, say, of two figures is an "establishing shot" which includes not only the full figures themselves, but also a fairly wide view of their surroundings, hence it is taken from a distance. The medium shot moves closer and excludes all the surroundings except that which is in immediate proximity to the two figures which are shown in their entirety but now "filling the screen." Before arriving at a close-up, an intermediate position is that of the *two-shot*, which shows the two figures closer to the camera's eye, so that (for instance) they are seen only from the waist up, and most of the background is eliminated. In the true close-up only the face and head of *one* figure is seen, with practically no background at all. A variation of this is the *over-the-shoulder shot* which views a single face literally over the shoulder of the other figure. Sometimes this shot shows the face of the person speaking, sometimes that of the person being spoken to, thus registering *a reaction*. The *shot in depth*, for which Bazin praises Orson Welles and William Wyler, is simply a type of long shot which had a particular aesthetic effect in emphasizing the continuity of dramatic space and forcing the viewer to make his own selections of focus instead of having the camera command that focus by close-up techniques. It is also possible to achieve varying distances between camera and figure being photographed by having the figure move toward or away from the camera within the scene itself.

Obviously, the widely variable movement of the camera and the

Figure 13–17

Museum of Modern Art
*The shot-in-depth is
used also in Becket,
another play
successfully translated
to the screen.
(Copyright © 1964 by
Paramount Film Service,
Ltd.)*

more limited movement of figures within the scenes photographed allow for an incredibly varied series of *stills* or individual frames. The quality of those stills can be further "directed" by the use of various kinds of filters, lenses, and mattes on the camera itself, as well as by variation in the focus of the lenses. Filters (colored plates placed over the lenses) affect the quality of light entering the camera. A yellow filter will, for instance, make white areas gray, a red filter (such as Eisenstein used in his Mexican film) will make an almost colorless sky look threateningly dark. As any theatre person knows (and any photographer), the qualities of light have telling psychological effects in the perception of images, to say nothing of the direction or angle from which the light comes. Various kinds of lenses also influence the quality of the photographs taken. A wide-angle lens tends to force the perspective and exaggerate the speed of movement. A long-focus lens (the ultimate of which is the telescopic lens) tends to eliminate distance. Lenses can also be used in *soft* or *sharp* focus—the former tending to blur or "romanticize" images, the latter showing them in stark relief. Mattes can change the shape of the image on the screen by applying a kind of stencil cutout to the lens (such as a circular or oval hole) which blocks

428

THE ALLIED ARTS:

MOVIES AND

TELEVISION

out portions of the scene. Méliès was particularly fond of this camera trick, and various applications of it have, for instance, provided for those hilarious comments of Robert Benchley vignetted into the action of some of the old "Road" pictures of Bing Crosby and Bob Hope, as well as the "double-screen" effect frequently seen in comedies and on television, and "composites" of various kinds.

All these various possibilities, then, for the production of a wide variety of approaches in the use of the camera comprise the *vocabulary* of the cinema; the individual frames are, as it were, the words which function in relation to each other. They are arranged into sentences or scenes; these are in turn arranged into paragraphs or sequences; and a succession of these sequences or paragraphs are arranged to form the finished work. This is the syntax of film, as Terry Ramsaye named it long ago in the days of the silents. Lawson and Bazin both point out that the *sound images* become another working element in this syntax but, to date, outside of such films as Eisenstein's *Alexander Nevsky* (1938) which was "orchestrated" to a score by Prokofieff, and a few others, film makers have not generally been as skillful in handling sound images as they have been with visual images. This is true partly because sound has no equivalent to the "still," no static element which can be isolated and manipulated; as Lawson says, "The world of sound remains largely unexplored." (p. 180)

In its elemental word, or still, cinema has a relationship to painting, as photography does, in composition: the relationship of masses, planes, and lines, the values of light and shadow. But in the moving picture these "photographs" are changing at the rate of 24 per second (the speed of sound films as compared to the 16 of the early silents). The central fact of cinema is this *progression*, the shifting compositions which give it a dynamic quality and which develop its centripetal force. The juxtaposed images of sight and the accompanying or counterpointing images of sound give the motion picture its peculiar and inimitable "art." This progression is the quality of the *cinematic*.

Organizing the filmic statement is done both in the shooting and the editing of the film; ideally the director controls both processes. The term *montage* is usually applied to this process of organization. As soon as a "still" composition begins to move, it suggests

Figure 13–18

Museum of Modern Art

Ingmar Bergman probably used a red lens filter to enhance the ominous appearance of the sky in this famous scene from The Seventh Seal. *(Courtesy Janus Films, Inc.)*

sequence and interaction (contrast, conflict, reinforcement, balance, and rhythm). *Internal montage* (a term not popular with American writers about film) is that which occurs during the shooting of the film as director and cameraman arrange and shoot the various takes and scenes. It involves all of the possibilities for the juxtaposition of images inherent in the camera itself and in its movement. There is no comparable term (unless we suggest external montage) except *editing* or *cutting,* for montage not included in the filming process itself. These two terms (editing and cutting) are those which American film makers usually apply to the organizing of the film after shooting; the French call editing *montage* or *putting together;* the Russians adopted the French usage, and the term acquired special meanings through the practices and statements of Eisenstein. In any event, Eisenstein's explanation of montage is a very useful one: ". . . the juxtaposition of two separate shots by splicing them together resembles not so much a simple sum of one shot plus another shot—as it does a *creation*" (*The Film Sense,* p. 8). The whole is more than the sum of its parts; the impact of two elements juxtaposed is *greater* and *other* than that of the two elements viewed separately. Bazin lists three kinds of montage other than that which he calls the "invisible," and which we have called "internal" above; namely, parallel montage, accelerated montage, and montage by attraction. (*What is Cinema?,* p. 25) Actually, what he calls accelerated montage is now largely accomplished by camera techniques; the illusion, for instance, of the steadily increasing speed of a locomotive. What he calls parallel montage is the creation of early American film directors—notably D. W. Griffith —in conveying the sense of two actions taking place simultaneously in two different geographic locations by means of alternating sequences from each. It is the old "meanwhile-back-at-the-ranch" technique, an absolutely fundamental part of the film language. According to Kenneth Macgowan, not only American but also English film makers had developed this technique before 1905. It is sometimes known as *intercutting;* i.e., two segments of action filmed separately are cut in pieces and spliced together alternately to give the impression of simultaneity. This manipulation of time and space is one of the unique qualities of the filmic art and has remained so until the present day. It is the technique above all others for which Griffith is admired around the world. The skill of such editing lies in determining the optimum moment for the switch from one sequence to the other, and the proper running time for each sequence. The effectiveness of every chase scene that ever was, from the Keystone Cops to *North by Northwest* lies here. Suspense and tension are the emotional states generated by it.

Montage by attraction is that which is particularly designed to influence several kinds of emotional reaction, and it was brought to perfection by the Russian film makers, particularly Eisenstein. Bazin has a good definition: "the reënforcing of the meaning of one image by association with another image not necessarily part of the same episode." (p. 25) It operates by an association of ideas, by means of a metaphor. The intercuts between a sequence of a butcher slaughtering a bull and one in which a group of soldiers massacre a huge crowd of fleeing civilians, as planned by Eisenstein for his film *Strike,* is a classic example of such montage. Another classic example is that in Pudovkin's *Mother* (1926), in which the sequence of a man in prison reading a note from his mother is intercut with a variety of short sequences signalling a counterpoint of happiness and freedom: flowers in spring, a baby being picked up into the air, etc., etc. Such montage is a means of "emotional scoring" and has some of the elements of expressionism in it. Not quite so abstract or "pure" is the intercut which juxtaposes with mass scenes sequences of single faces or figures, or cuts to symbolic inanimate objects in the sequence of a dramatic scene. What the director-editor does in his montage is to influence the field of consciousness of the viewer and thus direct

Figure 13–19

A wide-angle lens emphasizes perspective in this photograph of the filming of a sequence for another play translated to film, Arthur Miller's A View from the Bridge. *See also 3–3.*

his emotional response to the film by a careful selection of possible images and their juxtaposition. At its worst, montage is simply cinematographic fireworks calling attention to the ingenuity of the director-editor and confusing the audience with the abrupt, ill-related changes. At its best, it is a powerful means of generating and sustaining emotional response to the film.

In addition to the syntax implicit in filming and explicit in editing, the grammar of film has what Kenneth Macgowan calls punctuation marks (*Behind the Screen*, p. 413). These are the *lap dissolve* and the *fade* and variations thereof. The fade is the period, or full stop. It is effected by the gradual darkening of the screen image to blackness and then a gradual lightening to disclose a new scene or setting. It has been likened to the curtain or the blackout in the theatre. Since the advent of the "talkies," techniques of the *wipe* have sometimes been substituted for the fade. The wipe involves the "pushing off" of a scene by a new scene which appears at one edge of the screen and moves across it, replacing the former scene. A variant is the *diagonal wipe.* Another is the *soft wipe*, with diffused edges, which is a little easier on the eyes. A final variant is the *spiralling out* which is visually self-explanatory. The exclamation mark of film grammar is the *swish-pan* (particularly beloved of television these days)

Figure 13–20

Museum of Modern Art
*Sharp focus is the
appropriate camera
technique for* High Noon
(1952), *which is a
landmark film in the
de-romanticizing of the
Westerns.*

in which a blur of highlights and what seem like racing shadows pass before our eyes as the camera pans swiftly from one scene to the next. The final technique of cinematic grammar is likened to a semicolon, and is the *lap dissolve*, in which two images are superimposed, the first fading out while the next fades in. It is generally used to indicate a short gap of time or a change of place within a sequence when the sharper effect of cutting would be inappropriate. All of these editing effects are now achieved through the machine called the optical printer and are decided upon in the editing process.

The film language analyzed here is applicable in the expression of all kinds of filmic statements, from animated cartoons to historic epics. It has been used with a great deal more freedom and virtuosity in short subjects, cartoons, and "art" films than in the films with extended narrative and dramatic content which we usually associate with the term *cinema*. The final combination of the fragmented bits of photographed film in the process of editing constitutes, in whole or in part (depending upon how much is inherent in the actual filming) the bringing together of those elements which give the finished film pace, variety, flow, economy of expression, and timing. The perfection of artistry in the films of Charlie Chaplin lies not solely in his personal abilities as a per-

Figure 13–21

Museum of Modern Art

The effectiveness and importance of lighting is evident in this shot from the post-World War II Italian neo-realist film, The Bicycle Thief.

former, but in the uniqueness with which the very language of film suits his particular abilities. As John Howard Lawson points out, Chaplin films are particularly fruitful for a study of cinematic structure (*Film: The Creative Process*, pp. 323 ff.). This structure is not the same as that for a stage play, as anyone can prove to himself by noting the ineffectualness of any stage play literally transferred to the screen. Conversely, the film scenario has its life almost totally in the finished film (while, as we have seen, playscripts have frequently become literature) and published scenarios are rare. The film structure has only three parts: premise, progression, and climax. The *premise* is the opening sequence or sequences which set the mood and establish the theme. The rapid succession of sequences at the opening of Tony Richardson's *Tom Jones* (1963), in the style of the silent film with subtitles, not only swiftly accomplishes necessary exposition, but introduces the major characters and sets the playful comic tone. The swiftly changing images at the opening of Fellini's 8½, in which the predominant one is that of the movie producer trapped in a car in a traffic jam, set the image of entrapment and alienation for the film. The swift succession of Chaplin's opening scenes in *The Gold Rush*, each with its threat of violence only just averted, and the news of Citizen Kane's death exploding in a flood of newsreel shots in Welles's film both function as proper premises in their respective films.

The *progression* which is the middle part of the cinematic structure may be said to consist of a series of "movements" which may take the form of conventional plot (as in the majority of narrative films), or a series of variations on a theme (as in many of the films of Resnais, Antonioni, Fellini, and Roman Polanski's 1962 film, *Knife in the Water*). The "new wave" films tend to have the slimmest of "story lines," using cliché situations in order to build variations on themes of alienation and violence, or bourgeois decadence. But even in more conventionally plotted progressions, the chief reliance is on a sucession of images in sight and sound which build suspense and tension; on the stage, suspense and tension are usually inherent in the dialogue and the actions of the players. The skill with which John Huston builds his images in the admirable *Treasure of the Sierra Madre* (1948), or Ingmar Bergman in *The Seventh Seal* (1957) are cases in point. Here all the resources of the cinematic language are brought to bear. Pace and flow and timing are of the utmost importance; there must also be variety in the tension which is built and momentarily released to build again; there must be a strict economy of expression. Words must never simply explain a visual image; visual images must never simply illustrate words. In the movies, the visual images are almost always more important than dialogue. Although, as Bazin notes in writing about Robert Bresson's *The Diary of a Country Priest*, Bresson declared that he had made an absolutely faithful transcript of Bernanos' book, what he actually did was to transform the narrative "into visuals" and images of sound that are truthful to the total concept of the original rather than a literal transcript of it. It is a *translation* of the book into cinematic language, just as Olivier's glorious *Henry V* is a translation of Shakespeare's play to film.

The *climax* is not simply the ending of the film, the conclusion of the particular series of events detailed in the progression, but should also include a judgment on "*why* it happens, *what* it means and *how* it affects our lives and conduct," as Lawson says. It is partly Lawson's ideological commitment which makes this statement so positive, but insofar as it implies a climax growing out of the preceding statements of the film and a content and resolution which makes the film memorable to us, he is right. He

is inclined always to insist on "social significance" in film but (this bias having been recognized) he has many perceptive comments to make about film form, some of which we have used in this exposition. Endings of movies tend to "open out" the scene, like the pan shots at the end of Truffault's *Fahrenheit 451* (1966) or John Ford's *Young Cassidy* (1964), or the pulling away of the camera from a final close-up to a long shot. Such endings tend to impress the final image of film in its centripetal reality, uniting the filmed events with the contiguous surrounding world.

It is in this respect that film differs radically from theatre, which is entirely centrifugal and anthropocentric. Because film audiences pay admissions to a building which resembles a theatre in its arrangements and watch imaged characters move through the events of a story, film has often been equated with theatre. The impression has also gained currency from the fact that there has been, historically, a considerable transfer of personnel between the two media. But the basic premise of cinema, its methods of work, its means, and its effects are fundamentally different from those of theatre. It cannot be judged by the same standards, nor should its experience be equated with the theatrical experience; it is too different.

Figure 13–22

Museum of Modern Art
The central image of entrapment is constantly reinforced in varying visual images in Fellini's 8½. (Copyright © 1963 by Avco Embassy Pictures Corp.)

436

Figure 13–23

Museum of Modern Art
Robert Bresson's Diary
of a Country Priest *is
one of the most
successful of translations
from novel to film.*

Theatre is centrifugal. It draws audience and players into a vortex of mutually lived experience. There is no theatre without an audience. Film is otherwise; the fact of film exists exclusive of audience. The central thesis of theatre is a transaction which takes place between players and audience. In film, the performance is autonomous, self-sustaining; nothing an audience can do will change the film in any detail; it is a finished and completed work. We do not mean to imply that the spectators at a movie are always and completely objective, never drawn into the "spell" of the cinema statement. Quite the contrary. Effective movies cast a peculiarly compelling spell; they are meticulously structured to do just that. But it is an isolated spell, working its magic impersonally to the same calculated extent each time it is shown. Its effect is hypnotic rather than communicative. The actor in the theatre makes a personal relationship with the members of his audience; the cinematic relationship is *intimate* but not *personal*. The cinema audience can often see every pore in the skin of its favorite movie star's face, yet he is less *real* than the actor on the stage. (Note the verification of this statement in the excitement engendered when a movie star appears in person anywhere, anytime: mobs fight to see him "in the flesh," to touch him.) Several modern movies, like those of Bergman, Antonioni, and Pasolini for example, have been increasingly concerned with states of feeling and psychological nuances. But cinematic technique in expressing these human factors necessarily differs from that of theatre. Emotion in cinema is evoked not by psychological penetration (as it is in the great monologues of theatre, for instance, or the multiplication of signs in speech and action), but by the juxtaposition and flow of images. Even the immensely talented Laurence Olivier was unable to translate Hamlet's great soliloquy into cinematic terms, and simply let us watch him "think" it, moving his lips on certain passages to establish that the words were indeed his. Perhaps those words, of themselves a living and action-packed entity, are untranslatable into cinematic images, being solely and completely conceived in theatre terms.

The experience of cinema has more consonances with the reading of novels than it does with the experience of theatre. The mass audience in cinema is indeed a crowd, but a fragmented crowd, a mass of individuals, each of whom enters into communion with the images on the screen in personal terms, as in a dream. Each commits himself to the dream as to a personal time-machine which plunges him backward or foward and immerses him in the minutiae of an embalmed time and/or place. His point of view is not fixed, but ever changing, as the camera moves him through space and time. In the theatre, the member of the audience views the performance from a fixed perspective; in the cinema (by its very nature) the perspective is always in flux. The camera, like the teller of the tale in the novel form, moves the audience to whatever position for viewing it chooses, and focuses the attention on whatever details of person or place it selects for attention, as the novel does in its descriptive passages. The minutiae of reality in discursive form which is inherent in film has often made the translation of novels to the film form more successful than that of plays (cf. *Great Expectations* and *Dr. Zhivago*). The theatre is much more recalcitrant, not only because the action of theatre is so frequently inherent in the words of the play (and the cinematic language is not words but images), but also because theatre seems to be, as Bazin says, "at the end of an irreversible process of aesthetic refinement." (p. 83)

The theatre is anthropocentric: man stands at its center. It is inconceivable that theatre should exist without the actor. Cinema can and does exist without him. A banging door, a leaf in the wind, a line of swallows across the sky, an arrangement of pots and pans on a kitchen stove or before a hearth, the open leaves of a book, a pair of shoes under a chair, waves beating on a shore, rocks tumbling down a hill—all of these are dramatic entities in cinema and impossible of the same effect in theatre. In theatre the action proceeds from the players and flows to the decor; in cinema the movement is often the other way. It was Jean Cocteau who once said that viewing cinema was like looking though a keyhole; it is truly in cinema that the "décor acts." As we have seen, the camera puts at the disposal of the director, and hence the spectator, all the resources of the microscope and the telescope; the *mise en scène* assumes the position of ultimate importance. "Things are in the saddle and ride mankind." Is this one factor which makes cinema the child of the twentieth century?

In the cinema everything that is shown must have an inalienable reality; even dream sequences and fantasy are expressed in realistic terms of things and people. Occasional departures from this rule, like *The Cabinet of Dr. Caligari* with its expressionistic décor, and Cocteau's *Beauty and the Beast* with its adventure into surrealism, stand only as exceptions which prove the rule. This inevitable tie to the reality of things is one with the myth of cinema, a part of its fascination and its charm, as well as one of its limitations. It is the factualness of the cinematic representation of other times and places which ineluctably draws the spectator into the moving images and makes him a part of the action, and with it of the total universe which stretches out on all sides of the movie screen. Skies and trees and streets and houses and doors and windows and roads in film all lead out centripetally to the surrounding world, as they must. The theatre, on the other hand, creates its own microcosm, and, being man-centered rather than thing-centered, does not need the specificity of detail without which cinema can hardly exist. Appia was right; the "cinema-theatre" of Antoine and the realists was a contradiction in terms, just as the "theatre-cinema" of the literal transcription of stage plays to the screen has always proved a failure. For each medium speaks in its own language; one must understand the language before one can "get the message," even if one tends to accept McLuhan's pronouncement that "the medium is the message."

It is no mere happenstance that the film with the longest record of popularity and the most consistent record of success is the epic, or "spectacular," in which a minutely itemized world of other times is brought dazzlingly to life on the screen. Griffith's voice was prophetic in 1915; historical epics have been a constant on our screens, and some of the best of film productions: Eisenstein's *Potemkin* (1925), David O. Selznick's *Gone with the Wind* (1939), and Stanley Kubrick's *Spartacus* (1960) to name only a few of the most outstanding ones. From first to last there has also been a constant making and remaking of Bible epics: De Mille alone has made two different *The Ten Commandments* (1923, 1956), and *King of Kings* (1927). Even in 1965, George Stevens directed *The Greatest Story Ever Told*. The peculiar qualities of the film medium rise to their greatest intensity in treatments of this kind. A host of Italian film makers have discovered the lure of the past and continue to make "costume spectaculars" year after year. The same illusion of past times being present that the historical epics present is also to be found in another rich vein of filmic materials: biographies. Paul Muni alone was, during the 1930s, Louis Pasteur, Emile Zola, and Juarez—and very convincing in each. Charlton Heston has played a number of famous men from The Cid to Michelangelo and "Chinese" Gordon, and the bright young English star Peter O'Toole had his first great success in *Lawrence of Arabia* (1963).

The same qualities of richness and spaciousness that the film technique can bring to these historical epics and biographies, it can also attach to novels, always a rich source of materials. Several of Dickens' works have been done on film, and film makers found him as interesting and rewarding as the melodrama houses in London had previously. He is still being dramatized, the latest effort being a 1968 *Oliver*. We have discussed previously how and why novels make such good filmic materials. Dozens of great and not so great novelists have supplied the basic materials for "film treatment," the latest in a long line being Lawrence Durrell, whose *Alexandria Quartet* has been made into the 1969 *Justine*. Steinbeck's *The Grapes of Wrath* and *East of Eden* have both seen excellent screen treatments, as has Hemingway's *For Whom the Bell Tolls* and *A Farewell to Arms* (twice). Even Pasternak's difficult and lengthy *Dr. Zhivago* was rather successfully translated into a spectacular and visually beautiful film in 1965. The list could go on indefinitely. So long as the emphasis in the novels

Figure 13–24

Museum of Modern Art

The African Queen is one of cinema's great screenplays; the boat itself is as important an "actor" as either Katharine Hepburn or Humphrey Bogart.

Figure 13–25

Museum of Modern Art

The film treatment of Margaret Mitchell's long Civil War novel, Gone with the Wind, is properly epic and panoramic. Here, one of the quieter scenes. (© Metro-Goldwyn-Mayer, Inc. 1939)

translated to the screen is primarily narrative and descriptive, the screen treatments are likely to be eminently satisfactory. But when the novel is primarily philosophical, like James Hilton's *Lost Horizon* or Melville's *Moby Dick*, filming tends to reduce it to a visually beautiful but thematically empty presentation, satisfying if one does not know the book but inadequate otherwise. The scope and sweep possible in the film medium has also made it particularly suitable for musicals, that particularly American invention, and any casual movie-goer can name dozens of such successful ventures.

Another kind of material which cinema has made uniquely its own is, of course, the western. Like the epic, this has been a constant and popular type. From *The Great Train Robbery* (1903) to *True Grit* (1969), cowboys, horses, and the wide open spaces have enthralled legions. Again, the nature of the film medium is particularly suited to this material. Until very recent years this form of melodrama (for so it is) was pure and unadulterated, no one questioning the simplified characters and the naive narratives. But reality began to creep into the form with *High Noon* in 1952, *The Misfits* (1960, with screenplay by Arthur Miller), and *How the West Was Won* (1962). By 1965, the cherished western melodrama was the subject of burlesque in *Cat Ballou*. Are we becoming too sophisticated now for the black and white ethics of the "true" western?

The nineteenth-century melodrama was exactly the right fare for films, with its constant theme of "Man Alive in a World of Danger," for the camera could make the dangers and the risks more fearful and more convincing, hence the inevitable happy ending more pleasurable and satisfying. Not only the spectacular melodramas like *Ben Hur* and *Uncle Tom's Cabin* moved to the new medium, but the host of mystery, war and patriotism, spy and crime melodrama as well. The very technique of movie making, with its special facilities for incremental suspense and surprise through the use of montage and trick effects made movies particularly congenial to these materials, to say nothing of their superior control of "trickwork" and make-up. So there have been a whole line of war films up to and including *The Bridge at Remagen* and *Castle Keep* in 1969. So Alfred Hitchcock as a director has made a brilliant career, since his 1935 *The 39 Steps*, of "thrillers" on both screen and television. So James Bond has

Figure 13-26

Museum of Modern Art
*Film is particularly
congenial to farce, and
the Marx Brothers (here
in* A Night at the
Opera) *carried farce
technique to its
ultimate. (© Metro-
Goldwyn-Mayer, Inc.
1935)*

become a modern byword of the melodramatic hero, in that particular "spy" category of which nineteenth-century theatregoers were so fond. And a long line of crime pictures, chiefly starring Edward G. Robinson, George Raft, and Humphrey Bogart, have been constantly issued.

The nature of the film medium early proved a most congenial home for farce. As a matter of fact, much of the best farce that has ever been seen was on the screen in early movies: Charlie Chaplin, Harold Lloyd, Buster Keaton, Charles Conklin, the Keystone Cops, Laurel and Hardy, and the Marx Brothers. Pure farce, as we have seen, is not so much dependent upon words but upon physical action for its effects. Hence the silent screen not only gave it a home but increased its effectiveness in bringing closer to the eye of each spectator the minutiae of the farceur's battle with *things* as obstacles which stood in his way; it made them seem more real, while at the same time allowing for more overt beatings and other physical violence because, after all, these were not real people to whom these things were happening but images on a screen. The blows were softened in black and white moving pictures; it was easy to become, as John Simon recently phrased it, "voyeurs of violence." So the Marx Brothers and The Three Stooges became the modern *zanies* of a modern *commedia dell'arte* and Chaplin, King of Clowns. Chaplin even achieved

Aristophanic caricature in *The Great Dictator* (1940) and a telling measure of satire in *Modern Times* (1936). The genre has persisted in movies; the Beatles made *Help!* in 1965, and Stanley Kubrick used the old traditions to a good cinematic effect in *Dr. Strangelove; or, How I Learned To Stop Worrying and Love the Bomb* in 1963. English film makers have proved especially adroit in farce-comedy, in such films as *Kind Hearts and Coronets* (1948), *The Lavender Hill Mob* (1951), *The Ladykillers* (1955), and the series of "How, Now" films which have been issued from time to time. Cinema can be said to have invented the historical epic, and to have so adroitly taken over various genres of melodrama, farce, and farce-comedy as to have made them its own.

Romantic comedy and sentimental comedy have likewise fared well in the movies, but genres having more serious content (unless they were historical or biographical) have not been so ubiquitous nor so competently handled. The drama of ideas—that dramatic vehicle in which is contained what John Howard Lawson calls "social significance"—has never been plentiful on movie screens. D. W. Griffith came a costly cropper with his 1916 *Intolerance*, in spite of its cinematic qualities, and until television drained off a large portion of the less thoughtful movie audience, examples of films with social significance are the exception rather than the rule. Occasionally there was a picture like *The Big House* (1930) which exposed prison abuses, or like *I Am a Fugitive from a Chain Gang* (1932) which is said to have effected some reform in Southern penal practices, or William Wellman's *The Ox-Bow Incident* (1943) which made a pungent social comment, or Kazan's *Gentleman's Agreement* (1947). But the larger number of such films did not appear until the fifties and sixties, when relaxations of censorship combined with a more receptive audience to make them possible. Otto Preminger's picture about drug addiction, *The Man with the Golden Arm* (1955) caused a flurry of concern, but *Synanon*, on the same subject, appeared without a ripple in 1964.

The neorealists (as they called themselves) of the post-World War II period, of whom the Italian film makers were the most prolific, did much to change the content and point of view of cinema, with Rossellini's *Paisan* (1946), De Sica's *The Bicycle Thief* (1946), and Visconti's *The Earth Will Tremble* (1948). But the newest cinematic genre today is that of the tragicomedy,

Figure 13–27

A modern film farce,
M.A.S.H., *shows the
influences of the
absurdists and the black
humorists.* (20th
Century-Fox)

dealing primarily with the theme of alienation. The Italians Antonioni and Fellini, the Frenchmen Bresson, Resnais, Truffault, and Godard, Karel Reisz in England with such a film as *Morgan!* (1966), and Ingmar Bergman have produced films which are not only characteristic of modern cinematic techniques but also thoughtful and meaningful considerations of man's relation to his world. It is Bergman who has become the most admired of modern film makers, both for his dedication and his achievement. Curiously enough, he has said that he finds "the Wild West more stimulating than Antonioni and Bergman." But he finds it necessary, for his own integrity, to grapple with moral problems, and to proceed from an "artistically ethical standpoint." He has made himself "three commandments": (1) "Thou shalt be entertaining at all times, (2) Thou shalt obey thy artistic conscience at all times, and (3) Thou shalt make each film as if it were thy last." He is the definitive artist of the cinematic world against whom others measure themselves. His understanding of the nature of film is deep, his commitment to it absolute. Locations, characterizations, and atmosphere are easy enough to achieve on film, he says, but then you come to that "vital third dimension" without which any film is merely dead: "montage, rhythm and the relation of one picture to another." That is not so easy, and that is the secret at the center of the cinematic art.

As we have seen, there have been many attempts to transfer stage plays to film. It was early discovered, through the *film d'art*, that simply opening the eye of the camera to the stage production resulted in a completely ineffectual film. Even "translating" a stage play into cinematic terms does not invariably assure its success in that medium, as the 1962 failure of the film *Five Finger Exercise* will prove. But, conversely, the success of *Twelve Angry Men* (1957), *Inherit the Wind* (1960), *Becket* (1964), *The Lion in Winter* (1969), and the Olivier Shakespeare films (*Hamlet* possibly excepted) have proved that the endeavor is perfectly possible if the translation into cinematic terms is imaginatively and sensitively done. It is through such translations that the cinematic world has seen almost its sole examples of that revered theatrical genre of tragedy. It would be difficult to think of even a few "original tragedies" in the history of film. Perhaps the genre is too "aesthetically refined" (to use Bazin's phrase) to translate effectively.

Thus we see that film is most successful when it is most itself; when its materials match its means to produce its characteristic effects. The whole minority movement of experimental film making has continued to explore these materials, means, and effects. Avant-garde and "underground" film makers are continuing to test the principles by which the majority art has lived, and we may increasingly find that they have more and more to give to the realization of the peculiar genius of the art of cinema. For only as it is true to itself will it be an art, a twentieth-century art, a *public art*. For, as Bergman has said, "I do not intend my work to be solely for my own edification or for the few but for the public in general; the demands of the public are imperative." It is only as ever widening segments of the public are educated in the artistic discipline of cinema that the spurious and cheap will be eliminated and the production of true cinema enlarged. There is a real and urgent need for effective and knowledgeable film critics to engage in the "disinterested endeavor to learn and propagate the best that is known and thought in the [film] world, and thus to establish a current of fresh and true ideas."

"There is not any such thing as film criticism," says David Slavitt ("Critics and Criticism," in *Man and the Movies*, Penguin

Books, 1967, p. 336), after having spent a good portion of his life reviewing films for periodicals. The trouble is that such reviews, appearing in proliferation, are all too often written by people "promoted from covering weddings or shipping news or fires in Brooklyn to the dubious eminence." (Ibid, p. 344) They have absolutely no conception of the art of film, so they concentrate on *content* rather than on form or style, and approve or disapprove if the subject matter pleases or displeases them. And for years on end, it made no difference *what* they said—the mass audience just went to the movies anyway. Circumstances changed somewhat (as we have seen) with the advent of television, but it is still possible to count on the fingers of one hand the names of first-rate film critics in America: the late Robert Warshaw, Judith Crist, Pauline Kael, Brendan Gill, and Dwight Macdonald. The creative critics of film (in the sense that we have dealt with such critics for theatre) are almost nonexistent. So it is incumbent upon film-goers and students to develop criteria of aesthetic judgment for film. Perhaps from such an informed and committed public will eventually come a number of capable critics and a large body of significant criticism. It is a consummation devoutly to be wished.

14

Television

In many ways, television's "finest hour" may be said to have taken place on July 20, 1969, when literally billions of people, all over the globe called Earth, watched the civilian astronaut Neil Armstrong take man's first step on the Moon. That occasion was the epitome of television, its consummation and the core of its meaning. And, outside of the event having its own inherent drama, it had nothing at all to do with theatre or film. It was a tremendously costly, tremendously *immediate* and wholly thrilling happening. That grainy, wavering picture, that muffled, almost indistinguishable voice coming from so great a distance summed up the wonder that must have overtaken the first viewers of electronically transmitted images about forty years ago. The hours of reporting surrounding the central event illustrated the capacities of the electronic medium developed since those first days: news of the progress of the flight, interviews, demonstrations, remote "pick-ups" from various places in the world and in outer space—all in beautifully registered color, around the clock, for days on end. Though there were hours when the transmission was continuous, there were also many hours (at least in the United States) when the transmission was interrupted for commercials and "station identifications," and the whole episode came to a crashing anticlimax on August 13, when "Man on the Moon: An Epic Journey in Space" ran its last "trailer" as an introduction to a boring telecast of the "state dinner" held for the astronauts in San Francisco. Even the skill of Walter Cronkite, who had been so magnificent and vital during the hours when Apollo 11 was on its mission, could not overcome the tedium of the affair and the conviction that it should never have been televised at all. Something which began with a bang was ending in a

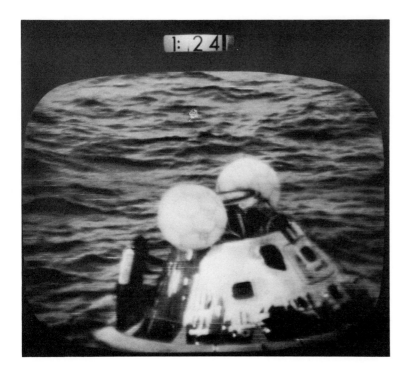

Figure 14–1

Television's "finest hour": splashdown after man's first walk on the moon, as it appeared on the home screen. (Photograph courtesy Columbia Broadcasting System, Inc.)

whimper; the whole "package," from first to last, contained all that was best and much that was worst in television—a true paradigm.

Theatre is anthropocentric; cinema is filmic, television is electronic. The communication of theatre is effected through the human body; that of the cinema through strips of film; that of television through thin air, the impalpable waves broadcast by a transmitter and picked up by a receiver. Television is in its infancy, its potential largely unrealized. The visionaries of its future range all the way from the Orwellian nightmare of "Big Brother is watching you," to the Utopian concept of universal peace, brotherhood, education, and prosperity. Some of its uses can be called in as examples for either vision; the truth lies somewhere between the two. We seem to have a tiger by the tail, and whether he will turn and devour us, or become a domesticated and powerful servant, is the subject of many an argument and disquisition. The fact of the matter is that television—in and of itself—is neutral. It is an invention, a discovery, a mechanism, a technology that man *uses*. It can be used wisely or unwisely, well or badly. If our choices are good ones, if the future of television is to be better than its present for the benefit of mankind, then it behooves us to understand it, to be aware of its potentialities, of its accomplishments and failures. Television, like cinema, is only tangentially and partially related to theatre, but theatre people can have a great stake in its future, just as they quickly became involved in its short past and participate in its present. More than any other means, it is a *universal medium* of communication; before we conclude our consideration of theatre (one of man's oldest means of communication), let us see what we can understand about this newest one.

November 2, 1936, is usually the date set as "the beginning of television," because it was on that date that the British Broadcasting Corporation initiated the first public system of television transmission from its studios in Alexandra Palace on the northern edge of London. For three months they alternated in the use of two technical systems which had been developed. Among performers who appeared in that period were George Bernard Shaw and a new actress named Greer Garson. In February, 1937, it was decided that in the future, transmission would be by the electronics system as built by Isaac Shoenberg and Charles S. Franklyn; the discarded system was that of John Baird.

But, as in the case of the development of movies, many experiments had preceded this decision and this public event. As early as 1878, Sir William Crookes invented a cathode-ray tube which, with some changes, became an integral part of television. In 1884, the German Paul Nipkow invented a mechanical scanning disc to "take pictures" and transmit them by light rays, and by 1888 another German physicist, Heinrich Hertz, had demonstrated the relationship between light waves and electrical waves. By 1895, Marconi had developed the first *wireless* telegraph, and by 1900 an American physicist, Reginald A. Fessenden, applied these techniques to *voice* transmission. In 1904, John Fleming, an English electrical engineer, invented the vacuum tube, and three years later Lee De Forest, an American, produced a much superior model. By 1925, Baird and Charles Jenkins, an American, had assembled from all of these discoveries in radio, optics, and photography a method for transmitting pictures through the air. The system which finally prevailed in the British Broadcasting Corporation experiment mentioned above, however, was based on the development of more efficient scanning and transmitting systems first conceived by Vladimir Zworkyn and Philo T. Farnsworth (working separately) just two years before. By the late twenties, the iconoscope camera and the kinescope picture tube had both been developed. By 1930 and 1931, the National Broadcasting Company (NBC) and the Columbia Broadcasting System (CBS), both giants of radio broadcasting, had begun experimental television transmission in New York. Then came the broadcasts from Alexandra Palace. Then, just in time for the 1939 World's Fair, NBC began regular public broadcasting.

In both Britain and the United States, television broadcasting was suspended during World War II, but during that time the Radio Corporation of America developed the image orthicon tube, and other technical advances were made. In 1940, the Federal Communications Commission (FCC) approved a plan for commercial television broadcasting, and NBC and CBS were licensed. On September 17, 1946, the first postwar television sets went on sale. During the next year, 178,000 sets were manufactured; and by the end of 1952 over 20 million sets were in use. By the end of 1953, the first program in color had been broadcast, and in April of 1956, a Chicago station became the first to broadcast all its live programs in color. By 1960, all European countries except Andorra, Liechtenstein, San Marino, and Vatican City had regular television services, as did Nigeria, Japan, and the Philippines. By 1965, television stations in more than ninety countries were serving an audience of over 750 million persons, and it is estimated that by the early seventies this audience will have doubled in size. In November, 1963, 300 million persons on four continents watched the televised funeral of John F. Kennedy; in July, 1969, for the moon launch, another continent had been added and the audience figure approached four *billion*. The breathtaking advance of television over the entire globe in less than twenty-five years is not only a tribute to modern technology but reason enough to pause and consider what manner of thing this is, and how it affects man's mode of life on the earth.

Conversely to the known facts in the development of motion pictures, television was early conceived of as a luxury which would appeal primarily to the well-to-do. But events proved otherwise, and it was not long before television aerials were remarked in the ghettos of all large cities, over the huts of the *barrios* of Rio de Janeiro, the tents of nomads, and the roofs of villagers. The poor man had made the medium his own, and the intellectual tended to scoff and call it "the boob tube." It is, however, a dwindling minority of persons who refuse to give house room to a television set, and the Union of South Africa is the only sizeable country which has not licensed television transmission. The social significance of television broadcasting is universally recognized, and all countries impose certain minimum program requirements and otherwise regulate its operation. In countries like the United States, where the largest number of television stations are in the hands of private, commercial operators, the regulatory agency takes the form of our FCC, issuing periodic licenses after an operational review. Besides the United States, Japan is the only other major power to commit television to private enterprise in this fashion. In Italy, Sweden, and Switzerland the government is a partner with private corporations "set up in the public interest." A third category is the public corporation or authority, like those in the United Kingdom, France, West Germany, and Belgium, which has considerable independence although the state retains final control. The fourth category is that wherein the state itself runs the service as a department or a unit of the government, such as happens in the Soviet Union and most other East European countries. Almost universally (except in the United States), television services are supported by license fees collected from set owners, plus government subventions. Many systems in various parts of the world supplement these funds with fees collected from commercial advertising. But outside the United States, commercial advertisers are not the chief source of support for the operating funds television needs. Consequently there is generally more freedom in program planning, and fewer commercials interrupt the broadcasts than is the case in the United States. The more prosperous countries have more than one program system— one for minority tastes, the others for varying degrees of popular tastes and for "educational" uses. Commercials are often relegated, as in Italy and West Germany, to a certain segment of evening broadcasting, when all commercials are given at once, without respect to particular programs which are "sponsored." We are given to understand that this "carnival of sales" is a popular feature in the countries which have it.

Professor Burton Paulu lists seven factors which influence the development of broadcasting in all the countries which have thus far begun it (*Radio and Television Broadcasting on the European Continent*, 1967). These are: (1) geography, (2) history and politics, (3) religious traditions, (4) educational and cultural status, (5) language, (6) national economic standards, and (7) relations between neighboring countries. Size, shape, and terrain of the national territory dictate the number of transmitters necessary and the kind of coverage pattern used. Countries with a tradition of freedom of the press (like the United Kingdom and the United States), develop free systems of broadcasting, while highly centralized governments (like France under De Gaulle and the Soviet Union) develop unified broadcasting systems. Countries with a strong dominant religion (Portugal, Spain, Greece, and Turkey) often forbid or curtail broadcasts by minority faiths; the Eastern countries of Europe tend to prohibit *any* religious broadcasts. Literacy levels affect program needs and sometimes result in highly effective educational programs, like Italy's very popular "It's Never Too Late." Varieties of languages within national boundaries make for complications in programming and tend to stress television broadcasting of materials in which language is not a crucial factor, like sports. Highly industrialized countries and those with a large supply of consumer goods tend to devote larger segments of time to commercial advertising; they also have more money to spend on programming. Most European countries not only produce programming for their own nationals but also do some broadcasting intended for extranationals.

Various associations, like Eurovision, arrange simultaneous coverage of major European events and provide for exchange of appropriate programs. The Scandinavian countries are linked by Nordvision, and the Communist countries by Intervision. Japan is currently taking the lead in developing Asiavision, and a Central American Television Network (CATVN) has been in existence since 1964. The International Telecommunication Union of the United Nations, with headquarters in Geneva, facilitates cooperation between countries and among various regional groupings. The Telstar and Early Bird satellites have provided for instantaneous transmissions between Europe and America, but experience has demonstrated that their usefulness is limited because of the time gaps involved. Except in extraordinary cases, more effective programming can be realized through the exchange

of filmed and taped programs. The day is almost upon us, however, when a worldwide television system will be formed by the
combination of satellites and the regional networks.

Universally, the programs broadcast can be divided into two
basic kinds: informational and entertainment. The former includes
news and public events, and political, religious, and educational
(for adults as well as for children) programs. The latter includes
sports, music, documentaries (which may also be informational),
light entertainment, and theatre. More than half of all broadcast
time is devoted to entertainment, and in this category, by far the
most in demand are sports and light entertainment. Various surveys and studies universally confirm this fact. "When the history
of the medium is written, it may be said that Big Brother met his
match in Lucille Ball, and lost," says Wilson P. Dizard (*Television: A World View*, p. 132). The spectacular effectiveness of
television in the coverage of public events and the dissemination
of news has been demonstrated over and over again. The exploits
of both American and Soviet astronauts, the Coronation of Queen
Elizabeth II, the investiture of Charles as Prince of Wales, the
journeys and appearances of popes, the Ecumenical Council,
royal weddings, parliamentary openings, international conclaves,
political campaigns and elections—these and many more public
events have provided the television audience with a thrilling sense
of immediate presence at these events of interest, much as Walter
Cronkite's famous old historical series, "You Are There," did for
the many past events which it reconstructed. Elaborate cooperative arrangements are often made to make possible the airing of
these events. Here television is often at its best.

The availability of television to politics and public figures bids
fair to revolutionize political campaigning not only in the United
States but in other parts of the world as well. Both De Gaulle
and Fidel Castro have used the medium as a personal political
arm, and Nasser tended to do the same. The late Everett Dirksen
in the United States became a "TV personality," and (for good
or bad) many public figures now tend to be judged on their
effectiveness in television appearances. Church services and school
programs of many kinds now reach a much larger segment of the
public than formerly could attend those institutions in person.
The United States has had its "Church of the Air" and its
"Sunrise Semester" even in its commercially oriented medium. In

Figure 14–2

Television and politics: the Nixon-Kennedy debates, as seen in the studio, with lights, microphones, and cameras in operation for this live broadcast. (Photograph courtesy Columbia Broadcasting System, Inc.)

Europe, generally, the organization of the broadcasting system allots more time to educational programs than does that of the United States, where educational television is still struggling with the problem of adequate means to accomplish its ends. In the United States, television is an industry, and is usually so spoken of by both the public and the medium; in Europe it is generally regarded as a public service, not subject to the competitive pressures of industry either for types of programs presented or for the checking of "popularity" by rating polls. There is more room for variety and diversity in programming under such a system.

But everywhere (as we mentioned immediately above), the largest audiences are for televised sports events and programs of light entertainment. Quiz shows and game shows draw large audiences not only in the United States but also in many other parts of the world. The millions of Americans glued to the television screen for the Saturday afternoon football games or the nightly major league baseball games have their counterparts in Japan's broadcasts of *beisbol*, and in all other parts of the world

reached by television by those who watch wrestling, boxing, skiing, basketball, skating, track events, soccer, and a wide variety of peculiarly national sporting events. Sports broadcasts most easily cross language barriers on television, for the visual portion is self-sustaining, while any necessary audio portion can be added by a commentator in any given native language. Documentaries, too, which are usually prepared with a commentary in "voice over" style, are easily transported over language barriers, although their number and variety are far less than those of sporting events. Music, too, is a universal language; it can be effectively broadcast without any dependence on visuals. In the United States the broadcasting of serious music has largely disappeared from television, and has its only continuing life on radio, chiefly the FM stations. In Europe, too, more music is broadcast over radio than over television. But there, where both radio and television are likely to be under the same supervisory control, several national networks maintain their own orchestras for live broadcasts (as NBC used to do), and televised programs of serious music are much more frequent than in the United States.

Curiously enough, however, the televising of opera performances forms a very small percentage of broadcast time, even in opera-loving Italy. Much more time is devoted to the production of plays, both originals and adaptations. In 1965, for instance, the

Figure 14–3

Typical of popular light entertainment on television are the talk shows, like that of David Frost, here with guest Groucho Marx.

Figure 14–4

Captain Kangaroo *is a recent example of imaginative programming for children. (Photograph courtesy Columbia Broadcasting System, Inc.)*

456

THE ALLIED ARTS:

MOVIES AND

TELEVISION

Figure 14–5

Occasional specials, like the CBS Children's Film Festival (here a scene from Testadirapa*) enliven the television scene. (Photograph courtesy Columbia Broadcasting System, Inc.)*

Italian television network devoted 5.6 per cent of its total time to the presentation of dramatic works, as compared to 1.2 per cent for opera and ballet. In Europe generally, television drama is a strong part of the total programming, never having been replaced by light entertainment as it has largely been in the United States. A part of this condition can, of course, be ascribed to the fact that (in contradistinction to the prevailing practice in the United States), most European networks have "supplementary programming" so that, while drama may be airing on one system, the more popular sports and/or light entertainment is simultaneously airing on another. Since neither is directly sponsored, there is no question of comparative "ratings" for popularity; the theatre pieces are generally acknowledged as appealing to smaller audiences but being equally as desirable and necessary as the more popular materials. In the United States we speak nostalgically of "the golden age of television drama" as being the years of the fifties, when Playhouse 90, the Philco-Goodyear Playhouse, Studio One, the Kraft TV Theatre and others developed the talents of Paddy Chayevsky, Rod Serling, Horton Foote, Tad Mosel, and others and presented adaptations of stage plays, novels, and short stories. Today the drama on American television is reduced to the occasional "special" like the Hallmark Hall of Fame.

The decline in the production of these "playhouse" dramas has

457

Figure 14–6

Among the most popular fare on television are the situation comedy series, domestic variety, such as The-Mothers-in-Law. *This studio shot shows not only a scene in an episode, but also the elaborate lighting equipment used in studio filming. (Photograph courtesy Columbia Broadcasting System, Inc.)*

been marked by a corresponding increase in "dramatic series," like "The Defenders," "I Spy," "Bewitched," "Mission: Impossible," "Bonanza," "The Outcasts," etc., in which continuing characters appear week after week in a series of slightly different circumstances with different minor characters or guest stars. The declining revenues of film studios in the early fifties, which led them to accommodate themselves to the new medium, spurred the production of such series in otherwise vacant studios. Each show is *filmed* and *edited* in six to eight days, and generally in the Hollywood studios and back lots (although a few, like "The Defenders" and "East Side, West Side" have been filmed in New York). These "telefilms," then, are shown on the national networks in a regularly scheduled "time slot," the season schedule running from early September to late May. In order to be aired they are presold to commercial sponsors through advertising agencies who "buy" them on the strength of a pilot (one weekly segment), and the presumed effectiveness of the story situation planned for the series and the drawing power of the "regulars" in the series. Many more pilots are made each spring and summer than ever become series, and every season some of the series are withdrawn from the air before they are completed, either because

Figure 14–7

The Beverly Hillbillies
*is one of the American
comedy series exported
throughout the world.
Here the manipulation
of microphones is
apparent as the bear-
trainer stands by during
shooting. (Photograph
courtesy Columbia
Broadcasting System,
Inc.)*

the sponsor becomes disenchanted with them, or their ratings do not come up to expectations.

The successful ones—those which get good ratings and which please their sponsors, then "go into syndication," for outright sale or for rental to other United States networks or stations and to the foreign market. The sales are usually made in groups of thirteen segments (considered a cycle), and they can be shown for a number of years. Yearly sales of American telefilms abroad are now about $1 hundred million, and the most popular "exports" are "I Love Lucy," "Bonanza," and "Perry Mason," each having been sold in more than sixty markets and having been dubbed into German, Spanish, Japanese, Italian, French, and Portuguese, and running with subtitles in a dozen other languages. "Peyton Place," "The Beverly Hillbillies," "The Virginian," "The Man from UNCLE," "Gomer Pyle," "Lassie," "Rin Tin Tin," "Gunsmoke," "Daniel Boone," and "The Untouchables" are only slightly less popular in world markets. Needless to say, the television screens have offered actors a wider audience than even cinema, and some continuing income from the constant reruns long after the first filmings (and first payments) were originally made. There is some reciprocity for British television in the show-

Figure 14-8

Some series are made on location, as the perennially popular and widely distributed Lassie. Here the same techniques are used as in the movies.

ing on American screens of such series as "The Avengers," "The Saint," "The Prisoner," "The Adventures of Robin Hood," etc., but by far the greatest traffic in telefilms moves *out* of the United States and not into it.

United States producers also sell a number of "variety shows," which have been filmed or recorded on tape, to foreign markets. The names of Ed Sullivan, Perry Como, Fred Astaire, Gary Moore, and Jackie Gleason are known around the world. This type of program (classified as light entertainment) is most profitably and skillfully produced in the United States; smaller countries have fewer outstanding "personalities" upon which to draw in producing such programs. American-made moving pictures too, originally filmed for showing in movie houses, are likewise sold to foreign markets, just as they have been sold to American networks for television transmission. The very quantity of such American "products," and the vigor with which their sales are pursued in world markets has aroused some bitterness in foreign television circles and has led at least one American foreign service officer to conclude the following.

We need to be represented on overseas television by something more than the standard formula of cowboy serials, detective films, pratfall comedies, and an occasional news documentary. An overseas viewer would be hard put to believe, from what he sees on his screen, that contemporary America is a leader in the lively arts such as drama, architecture, painting, and sculpture, or to understand the workings of our economic system or our current struggle to build a truly democratic multiracial society.

[*Dizard, pp. 284 f.*]

Pressures of sponsor preferences and the impossibility of maintaining on American air (with its almost completely commercial orientation) programs which would appeal primarily to minority tastes, have largely reduced American television fare to the blandness of sentimental "situation comedy," romantic western tales, and various kinds of detective and crime melodrama. The recent conflict over the "Smothers Brothers Show" serves to remind us that there is little place on American television for satire. In Europe, on the contrary (except of course in Communist countries) the satirical review holds an honored place. In spite of some adverse governmental reactions to such programs as the Dutch

Figure 14–9

Location shooting of the adventure series, Daniel Boone, often entails the use of a boom camera, and each episode is a small film. (20th Century-Fox Television production, NBC photo)

"That's How It Happens To Be," and the German "Hello Neigh-bor," "Panorama," and "Report," such broadcasts continue to be much more frequent in the countries of Europe than they are in the United States.

Television as a whole is much more subject to regulation and censorship than any other informational or entertainment medium, and not only in nations (like those having Communist govern-ments) where it is regarded chiefly as a propaganda instrument. In the first place, the nature of the medium requires regulation in the mere assigning of channels and frequencies. In addition, it is the only medium received directly and instantaneously into the home without previewing, and its domestic output can often be heard abroad. For these reasons (and no doubt others) workers in television are often hedged about with restrictions in subject matter, points of view, and language that are not to be found in other media, or at least to no such extent. The problem of censor-ship is a thorny one and offers no easy solutions. In the United States we are inclined to rely upon the industry's self-censorship, as we largely have in the matter of moving pictures. We have warned television producers that, after all, they are "guests in the living-rooms" of American families, and should "govern them-selves accordingly." But the obviously great variation which exists in the interpretation of what constitutes an "acceptable guest" has led to very different judgments on the "worth" or "value" of television. A few years back, Newton K. Minow, then director of the FCC, characterized television as "a vast wasteland," and there have been recurring strictures about the psychological and social consequences of televised violence. The problem in our own time is especially acute because of the simultaneous expansion of movies and television and the collapse of a universally recognized regulating ethic.

Perhaps Ken Taylor, a prominent British writer for television, is worth listening to for a moment here. Writing for the Summer, 1964, *Journal* of the British Society of Film and Television Arts, he notes that we exist in a society which is "freed from the ethical restraints which define conventions" and that "when nothing is unspeakable, the unthinkable cannot be defined," and "the great truths in consequence are either debased or denied." Therefore, "sex is for giggles," and "death is for giggles." He feels strongly that artists (and particularly writers for television) have an ob-

Figure 14–10

This scene from Checkmate represents the popularity of medical stories as television fare. (Photograph courtesy Columbia Broadcasting System, Jnc.)

ligation "to recreate a sense of moral purpose in our society." He goes on to say that they have "a duty to emphasize that men and women possess brains as well as sexual organs . . . that gentleness and wisdom have more human value than a pair of tits," and he concludes that "if these things are no longer true for us and have no meaning, I hold that the sooner we are obliterated by our own stupidity the better it will be." That is creative criticism, and a challenge which needs to be accepted and acted upon.

The writer of television drama, particularly in the United States, works within restrictions much more stringent than those in other forms. He is inexorably bound by the clock and the time schedule within which television operates. The 15-minute segment of time is the operating unit. There are "commerical breaks" at the quarter hours and commericals, as well as "station breaks," at the half hour and the hour. Therefore, the writer's action must be planned to fit these requirements. The dialogue and action immediately preceding one of these breaks must be such that its impact will carry through the break itself, so that the audience will not lose interest and "switch to another channel." Because, for the first time in entertainment history, an audience can instantaneously reject a performance, the first few moments of the presentation must likewise quickly engage the interest of the viewer. One of the "tricks" developed by television writers is that of presenting an intriguing segment of action at the outset, then superimposing

upon a quieter segment the "credits" which usually come at the beginning of a movie film—a technique which films (quite unnecessarily) have recently adopted. The movie audience, after all, has paid an admission price and is highly unlikely to walk out on the opening scenes of the film; whereas the television presentation is "free," and the audience is subject to the inherent distractions of the home environment. So the successful television writer quickly learns to "start with a bang," often by showing an enigmatic high point of the total action, then using flashback to complete his exposition. The total length of a given television drama may be as short as a half hour (less time for commericals and station breaks), or as long as 90 minutes, but the usual time is an hour (again less the usual deductions). With such a strict and unalterable time pattern, the writer must choose a fairly uncomplicated and forceful action, keep exposition to a minimum, select dialogue with ruthless attention to the significance of every word, and see that the essential scheme for each character is quickly apparent and interesting. It is obvious that such characters can

464

THE ALLIED ARTS:

MOVIES AND

TELEVISION

have little roundness or depth; there is no time to develop them. It is possible, however, for some character development to take place in the television series, where the chief character or characters appear over a period of weeks. Such development (or perhaps "extended revelation" would be a better term) has occurred in such series as "Dr. Kildare," "Mr. Novak," and "The Fugitive." But generally, even in a series, the central characters are likely to have definitely set and unchanging characteristics (like Matt Dillon in "Gunsmoke") which are reemphasized week after week in new combinations of surrounding circumstances. The technique of placing a well-known character or characters in new situations which time after time bring out his essential characteristics is the "stock-in-trade" of the successful series. Each of the well-known figures is a type character: the father figure, the wanderer, the clever detective, the reporter, the idealistic doctor, the impetuous young man, etc., etc. (Menander and Plautus are far from dead.)

Because there can be so little in the way of character development, the chief element of interest in television drama (both series and single presentation) is that of situation, of circumstance, of setting. So series "regulars" are set down in various parts of the world (as are Bill Cosby and Robert Culp in "I Spy"), are confronted with a series of crimes to solve (as is Raymond Burr in "Ironside"), or faced with a series of domestic problems (like Fred MacMurray in "My Three Sons"). The "domestic problem" series has had a long and continuing interest for television viewers. It has varied all the way from the outlandish exaggeration of the typical daytime "soap opera," which has all the characteristics of the "true confession" pulp magazines or newspaper "sob" stories, to the more balanced and truthful presentations of such series as "Father Know Best." Like the cinema, the effectiveness of telefilm depends on the factualness of setting, and the succession of images presented. The same techniques of shots, angles, montage, and cutting are applicable. Within the literalness of the given scene, these filmic procedures progress by association in the creation and release of tensions, the building of suspense. The tensions and suspense inherent in espionage tales, trials, detective work, and operating room procedures have made television shows built around these materials "naturals" in the medium. With milieus less naturally suspenseful, like the social

Figure 14–12

The visually beautiful Cinderella was an imaginatively conceived and executed special. Here a cameraman and crew stand by, and a monitor screen is in evidence. (Photograph courtesy Columbia Broadcasting System, Inc.)

work scene in "East Side, West Side," or the state legislative assembly scene in "Slattery's People," the writer must more directly depend on personal confrontations and interactions among his characters for his effects. That both these excellently written and acted series quickly disappeared from the air is an indication that the nature of television (as it is presently organized and administered, at least), precludes subtlety, and emphasizes the broad stroke, the "crash effect." It is true, too, of course, that the mass audience, in no age noted for its acuity, dictates an emphasis upon the broad effect, the clear-cut distinction (for instance) between "good guys" and "bad guys" in the typical and mythlike western. But the urgency of "grabbing" the audience at the outset of a television show and holding them through the commericals emphasizes the exaggeration of effects and the use of "gimmicks." More honest and meaningful writing is possible where the pressure of the commercial system is not so great, as in some of the presentations on the educational channels in the United States and in most of the European networks.

The very stringencies and compression demanded by the television format can *sometimes* produce a more effective and truthful drama than more leisurely forms. For instance, the original tele-

466

THE ALLIED ARTS:

MOVIES AND

TELEVISION

vision presentations of Rod Serling's *Requiem for a Heavyweight* and Paddy Chayevsky's *Marty* were much more effective and artistic than the full-length movies made from each. In both cases, the authors had conceived the action *in terms of a one-hour television show*, and the compression thus imposed gave a unity and power that were dissipated by the additions made in the longer film form. Here, perhaps, is the truth of the successful television drama: that it be *conceived in terms of television*. We have seen that successful moving pictures adapted from stage plays or novels are, in essence, *translations* into filmic language; the same holds true for television adaptations. Much more attention needs to be given to the form, the means, and the effects of television as a medium for drama. Then perhaps we can eventually develop an aesthetic of television, as we have recently succeeded in doing for film. It is useless to talk of "the art of television," when these necessary explorations are in so primitive a state. In the United States, television is largely a branch of the Madison Avenue advertising establishment; in the rest of the world it is more generally a *public service*. Only in rare and isolated incidents have the peculiar advantages of the television medium been used to produce a true work of art, as in the case of the two plays mentioned above, to which could be added the production of Megan Terry's futuristic play, *Home*, and the imaginative Repertoire Workshop presentation of *Circle of the Mind*, a Michael Godreau "electronic dance fantasy," presented in July, 1969. In the latter, both the visual and sound images effectively exploited the full possibilities of the electronic medium in changing patterns of movement and sound. But such creativity is all too rare in a medium which seems to have committed itself almost completely to an "ersatz" realism which had hitherto been the sole province of the cinema. The pervasive immediacy of news, public events, and sports (which television handles with admirable skill, and which constitute its most impressive use), have by association influenced dramatic writing for television by stressing *actuality* in presentation. But the television picture is differently constituted from the succession of photographs which make up a film; there are electronic possibilities for original uses of television which are, to date, largely unexplored. Television still needs to "find itself" before it can make any sizeable contribution to the creative arts. Telefilms and kinescope and tape recordings are not the

Figure 14–13

The "golden age of television drama" produced such effective programs as Requiem for a Heavyweight, *which was more effective on the television screen than in the later movie version. (Photograph courtesy Columbia Broadcasting System, Inc.)*

answer, since they are largely tied to the photographic process; it is the nonphotographic qualities of television which offer the best possibilities for new and creative presentations. What these may be is still very much an open question.

The making of telefilms, whether dramatic or documentary, follows in its essential details exactly the process by which moving picture films are made. It is in the broadcasting of "live" shows that television is unique and most itself. The heart of the television studio is the *control room*, where the exact image to be transmitted over the air is chosen. Its essence is a bank of television screens, each one connected by cable to one television camera in the studio. During the "airing," or transmission of a given program, the *director* sits in the control room, along with a timekeeper and several technicians, and observes the images on the *monitor screens*. He has two essential functions during this time. The first is to decide which of the possible images shall be broadcast at a given moment, either as a clear image, a dissolve to the next image, or a superimposition of one image on another. The second is to "direct" what is happening on the "floor" of the studio through a headset and phone connection to each of his *assistants* in the studio. These directions chiefly concern camera movement and use, because the movement of actors has been prerehearsed before airing. Possible camera angles and

Figure 14–14

Amahl and the Night Visitors *is re-broadcast at intervals and represents a high level of television programming.* (*George E. Joseph*)

movements have also been previously decided upon, and there may have been a studio rehearsal similar to a full dress rehearsal in the theatre, but the ultimate images on the home screens are decided by the director in the control booth at the time of the broadcast. He is in active control of the performance as it proceeds, and is responsible for keeping it within the time limits as well.

In this respect (his work in the control booth) the television director differs from his counterpart in both theatre and cinema. It is an exacting and difficult job. His other directorial duties are analogous to those in the other media: with the producer, he casts the show; with the scenic, costume, and lighting designers he decides on the visual elements of the production. He then rehearses with the cast, usually in out-of-studio space and for a short period of time, usually a week. During the rehearsal period he not only guides the performers in their movements and characterization, but he also makes decisions about the eventual camera shots. A few hours are generally set aside just before the broadcast for the director to rehearse with the camera crew, and perhaps then for a "run through" with cast and crews. The director's task is not finished until the given program has completed its broadcast.

The use of multiple cameras simultaneously is another unique feature of the television medium. Each camera is equipped with a "turret" of differing lenses which can be quickly changed for different kinds of shots. Cameras can also be tilted, panned, or moved by "dollies," or cranes or booms, just as moving picture cameras can be moved. But the television camera is not a self-contained recording device like the moving picture camera. It is (as we mentioned above) connected by cable to the monitor screen in the control booth. The camera men follow the instructions of the director implicitly, whether given beforehand or improvisationally created during the broadcast. They do not know if the image they are "shooting" is the one that is being broadcast at a given moment, since that broadcast decision is made in the control room by the director. But the use of multiple cameras allows for interesting changes in perspective or in size, a playing around with space relationships which is unique to television. A long shot on one camera, superimposed or "split screen" with a close-up on another, for instance, can create a "dream sequence" or the image of a man dancing on the edge of a tea cup, or various other tricks. Multiple cameras can also be used to fill the screen with duplications of the same performer or action, in the manner of Andy Warhol's "portrait" of Marilyn Monroe. Even negative images and reverse images can be broadcast. The almost universal preoccupation of television with realism makes little or no use of the possibilities inherent in the presence of multiple cameras in the studio: concentration is generally on conventional filmic techniques. In the United States, at least, it seems as if innovative television techniques are more often used in commercials than in the programs themselves.

The director is also aided in the live broadcast by three or more *production assistants,* who receive his instructions on the floor during the broadcast. One usually relays instructions to the actors, one to the camera men, and one to the lighting and set crews. Certain programs may use more than three production assistants, depending on the complications involved. There is also often a *floor manager,* who coordinates all the activities transpiring on the floor of the studio during the broadcast. The *technical director* has aided the director in working out technical problems during the preparation period, and he sits with the director in the control booth during the broadcast to assist. The *audio engineer* is in charge of sound, including the placement of

Figure 14–15

*Successful stage plays,
like* The Crucible, *are
sometimes adapted and
shown on television.
See also 3–7.
(Photograph courtesy
Columbia Broadcasting
System, Jnc.)*

microphones and the pick-up and broadcast of all sound. Microphones are usually manipulated on booms, just out of camera
range, to pick up the voices of performers, although it has become
something of a convention for the "talk" shows, like that of
Johnny Carson, to use a visible microphone. In any event, the
audio engineer must coordinate the sound images with the visual
images throughout and provide for their effective transmission.

The television actor finds himself with some advantages over
his colleagues in other media, but also with some distinct disadvantages. The actor in the live television show can build and
play his performance from start to finish, like the actor in theatre.
He does not have to play it by bits and pieces, or out of sequential
order, as the film actor usually does. He also has some sense of
playing to an actual audience, though his immediate audience
consists primarily of cameras. Even in those television shows
which permit studio audiences, the whole technical arrangement
is for the benefit of the home audience, and cameras, microphones, and other equipment may effectively screen the studio
audience from the performers. The size of the home audience

may add a bit to the tension of the actors, in that any error of whatever size wil be seen by millions of people. (The move to telefilmed rather than live performances was to some extent motivated by the desire to eliminate such possible errors.) But most observers and critics agree that there is a spontaneity and vitality in live performances that is often missing in telefilmed shows. Some actors have found that the absence of a literal, in-person audience in television studios deprives them of the feeling of communication with a live audience which is so much a part of the theatre experience. Others have found that the very absence of a live audience, which must be reckoned with in any theatrical performance, has enabled them to concentrate more fully and completely on the role being played. In television, it is the director's job, anyway, to choose the elements of performance which will be broadcast; the actor need simply concentrate on his role.

Because the final broadcast is so much the director's choice, and because the rehearsal period for television shows is generally so short, the television actor, like his counterpart in cinema, is much more dependent upon his director than is the stage actor. He also works, most generally, in much more confined quarters than either stage or film actor, so that his movements are smaller and his gestures more constrained. Both he and the director are constantly aware that the performance will be seen on a screen no larger than 23 inches in diagonal measurement, and the performance must be scaled to the appropriate dimension. In addition to considering the size of the screen, they are also aware that the audience will be much closer to the performance, in the living rooms of homes, than are audiences of either stage or moving picture. Like the film actor, the television actor need pay no attention to the matter of voice projection, for the microphones are always present to pick up his slightest whisper. Also like the film actor, he can rely to a large extent upon facial expressions rather than larger bodily movement or dialogue to convey emotional states; the cameras can close in and catch these nuances. Close-ups are often more effective on television than in the movies, because the size of the head cannot be so distorted on the small home screen as it often seems on the motion-picture screen.

Leading actors in television series have some of the disadvantages of stage actors in a long-run play, in that they are playing the same character for month after month, and the performance is likely to "go stale." The stage actor in the long-run show has the continuing excitement of new audiences to help keep his performance "fresh"; the television series star has new situations confronting him in each episode. But the characterization which he presents is usually done in such elemental terms that the series star is more likely to tire more quickly of his role than is the stage star who is probably dealing with more challenging materials. The television star finds his compensation in the infinitely greater sums of money he makes in television, and many actors have found it possible to augment their incomes very appreciably by working in television.

Most actors would agree that their basic task of *impersonation* remains their chief responsibility whether they are performing in the theatre, for film, or on television. But they are also likely to agree that the *means* by which they accomplish this task, the techniques which they employ in its realization, vary from medium to medium. Performers who have had a long career on the stage are likely to miss the stimulation of a live audience in film and television; film stars are likely to be wary of live television shows because they do not offer the same chances for minute-by-minute perfection of detail that is possible in film. But the developing actor today works in all three media and finds that each has its demands—and its satisfactions. The British actor, Dilys Hamlett, sums up the latter this way: in the theatre the reward is "performance in the presence of an audience; this is a wonderful thing, uniquely exciting"; in television, the reward comes "from reaching out to a vast audience through the television camera and one's instinctive response to the technical needs and the particular excitement of the television studio"; and in film the actor finds his reward in "its wonderful chance of completing the performance stage by stage, detail by detail." The wise performer shapes and scales his performance to the nature and the needs of the medium in which he is working; only thus can he be successful in all three of those open to him.

Television is the newest way of bringing the performing arts to the widest possible audience. But this function is by no means its sole—or perhaps even its most important—one. It is true enough to say that the potentialities of television for disseminating and

Figure 14–16

Stage performers often reach very wide audiences through television. Tallulah Bankhead and Luther Adler in Hedda Gabler. *(George E. Joseph)*

strengthening man's age-old involvement with art (which helps him to understand himself and his world) are very great, and have hardly begun to be realized. While it is true that the statistics-gatherers at the moment have "proved" that far and away the most popular (by the numbers) transmissions of television are sports and light entertainment, there is equal "proof" that more serious and meaningful presentations also have very large audiences which are growing in size. Though the ten million or so people who watched "East Side, West Side" was not an impressive enough percentage of the total possible audience to insure the continuance of that excellent series in the commerical grab-bag that is American television, ten million people is unquestionably a *big* number of people. Their preferences need more attention than they are likely to get within the competitive structure of American television. A few farsighted sponsors like Hallmark, Esso, Firestone, Xerox, and United States Steel have been willing to sponsor programs directed to "minority" tastes, but they are the exception rather than the rule. "Educational" television,

474

THE ALLIED ARTS:

MOVIES AND

TELEVISION

through the National Educational Television network, has tried to supply quality programming for minority tastes, and recently the Ford Foundation has underwritten the efforts of the Public Broadcast Laboratory to do the same. But these noncommercial endeavors have suffered from a chronic lack of funds; they are the indigent stepchildren of the broadcast family. If one is searching for a scapegoat for the imbalance which exists in American television programming, one would probably have to go back to the 1940 decision of the FCC which allocated all the then available channels to commerical operators, with only minor provisions for educational and other public-service uses. It was at that point that television in the United States began to be an industry rather than a public service (to say nothing of an "art").

Other countries, entering the television field at somewhat later dates, or (like the United Kingdom) having a different orientation toward the uses of a public medium, arranged systems of surveillance and development which better insured protection of and service to minority audiences. It is true that, despite the fact that Europe has fewer television stations than the United States, European broadcasting does achieve wider diversity than that in the United States. European audiences often have many more real choices among programs at a given time than those in the United States, because there it is practically universal practice to maintain "second" or "third" program networks to offer the opera, ballet, theatre, and other kinds of programs not offered on the more popularly oriented "first" program.

Everyone agrees that American television must offer more diversity in programming, that what appears on the home screens (and consequently around the world) should be a more accurate reflection of the American culture in all its multifariousness. But there is little agreement as to how this can best be done. The hopes of the advocates of "subscription" or "pay-TV" have been somewhat dashed by recent inconclusive experiments in this direction. And there seems little reason to suppose that the majority of commercial advertisers who pay for television production in order to sell their products will be inclined to follow the lead of the big and wealthy corporations whom we have mentioned above as having sponsored minority programming.

Extensive government control of programming (such as exists in some other countries) is so incompatible to the American temper as to be inconceivable. We might more profitably consider the immediate and total divorce between advertisers and program content and control. Some such system as prevails in Italy and West Germany is not unthinkable. There all advertising is relegated to a set time period each day, and advertisers do not directly "sponsor" any specific program. Advertising revenues might thus be reduced to some degree, but there seems to be little reason why American owners of television sets should not also pay a license fee, as owners in other parts of the world do. The funds thus acquired would increase income sources for production costs, and the payment of the license fee might give set owners some feeling of a personal stake in television operation instead of the present feeling that they are merely targets for a huge sales-pitch. Creative writers, producers, and directors might then have more incentive to reflect the multiplicity of points of view and tastes which are present in the potential American television audience, and truly artistic and significant programming might become more available. Thus the tastes of television's great mass audience might be educated to higher levels of culture, not by saying "Watch this; it's better than what you're looking at," but by providing wider possibilities of choice for the viewing public. No doubt there will always be those who will tune in only to the inconsequential and insignificant. But, if the limited experience of other television systems is any criteria, better and "more serious" programming will have a surprisingly large and enlarging appeal.

The time is NOW for a good, hard look at this ubiquitous and highly influential media, and for reforms which would lead the way to the realization of a true "art of television" commensurate with its potential and equal to the effectiveness which the "informational" aspect of the medium has already achieved. It is an immensely hard and complicated question but not impossible of solution; the only way to accomplish a journey is to take the first step. An aroused and informed public opinion is, in a democracy, that first step; others will and must follow. Let the lovers of art and of mankind constitute themselves creative critics of television, and we are on the way toward making this incredible technology which is television the servant of mankind in its entirety rather than the intrusive huckster it all too frequently is. Someone has wisely said that everything that appears on television, no matter how trivial, says something about the attitudes and points of view of the society of which it is a part. There have been frequent enough heartening signs of some maturity in this newest of the mass media, like some of those we have mentioned here. But, particularly in the United States, there must be a significant change in the organization and structure of television if a more widespread and more lasting maturity is not to be too soon cut off or die aborning. It is an articulate body of consumer-critics which television needs most badly: a body of people who know the possibilities of the medium and who insist with the "industry" that its artistic values be augmented. The consumer, for instance, who is aware of the age-long values of good theatre will, with his knowledge of the television medium, make his voice effectively heard in support of more and better "TV theatre" for this large and enlarging audience.

Theatre is an art of long standing, with an intricate and varied history, and a structure of materials, forms, means, and effects that has been the subject of much study and creative criticism. It has long been one of the most effective of the arts in aiding man to understand himself and his world, in reflecting, refining, and ordering that world. Cinema, a reality for less than a century, has made rapid strides in selecting and arranging its own materials, forms, means, and effects, and many critics would call it an art. But television, so newly arrived in the world, has yet to find itself in its special nature and being, so far as its potential as art is concerned. It is true that dramatic materials can be contained in each of these three media, and that the special techniques of all are borrowed and loaned from each to each. But since each is differently constituted and uses different means to effect its ends, it must handle its dramatic materials (drawn from the surrounding world) in the manner best suited to it. As television develops the ability to do this, it will join theatre and cinema as a true art.

Postscript: Vocations and Avocations

This book was neither conceived nor written as a professional guide to theatre careers. But it may not be amiss here to mention something of those possibilities, since they have immeasurably improved in the United States over the past ten or fifteen years, and since there are likely to be more such opportunities in the future, though the exact shape of some of them may not yet be clear.

The public image of a vocation in the theatre has for too long been that of the conspicuous performer in New York or Hollywood, with the recent addition of the national television networks. It is as if all lawyers must be Supreme Court justices, all doctors Surgeons General, and all teachers occupants of endowed chairs in major universities. The concept is patently ridiculous. Rewarding and self-fulfilling careers are to be found within the framework of the theatre arts for many kinds of talents and in many areas of work. The sole indispensable and basic requirement for anyone contemplating any facet of theatre as a lifework is that, as Stanislavsky said, he must *love the art*, not himself in the art. The very nature of the art also requires that its practitioners love mankind, in all its bewildering diversity, with all its hopes and fears and desires and aspirations, and that they see theatre (of whatever kind or variety) as potentially the most human and humanizing of the arts, a powerful tool in the struggle of mankind against despair and darkness. Then it only remains for the interested individual to make a fair and objective estimate of his own special talents, abilities, and interests, augment and develop them by suitable training and experience, then find a way *or make one* to his objective.

The professional in theatre is defined in precisely the same way as the professional in any other field: he is the person who, by reason of his native talent, his training, and his *choice*, makes theatre his lifework, the source of his income, and his major satisfaction. In the United States, as the structure of the professions is presently arranged, the theatre professional is likely to be either a theatre teacher or attached to a nonschool producing organization. In addition, there is probably more room in the theatre profession for the "free-lance" artist than in most other professions, although that status is usually reserved for the unusually qualified, the adventurous, or the self-confident.

Because theatre lives in the *doing*, let us speak first about opportunities for doing theatre outside the educational structure, which (by its nature) is primarily concerned with humanistic education and preprofessional training. As we have stated and implied in all the foregoing discussion throughout this book, the person who elects theatre as his profession, in any one of its various specializations, must be thoroughly familiar with the whole structure, and must constantly keep up with new developments. (The same could be said for any lawyer, doctor, or teacher.) For the qualified candidate today more than seventy regional theatres scattered throughout the United States offer professional opportunities for working. Most of these are nonprofit organizations, autonomous in their operation but exchanging ideas and information chiefly through the Theatre Communications Group of the Ford Foundation. They are supported primarily by community involvement in fund-raising and subscription campaigns, although state arts councils, some federal funding by grants-in-aid, and various foundations have recently augmented their incomes. Each was started by a visionary group or individual who knew the community well and planned and worked hard and carefully to make the vision a reality. There is no reason why their same pattern cannot be repeated in hundreds of other locations by devoted and hard-working people who are willing to endure an inevitable amount of frustration and difficulty to realize their goals finally. Meanwhile, the present regional theatres stand as monuments of achievement and potential sources of employment for new theatre workers. When you cannot find a theatre, make one—if you have the nerve for it.

It is not at all necessary these days (and certainly not desirable) for the dedicated theatre worker to head for New York upon the completion of his training. Theatre is more frequently, and often more significantly, being made *outside* New York now. Regional theatres are even supplying plays and performances, first developed in the "provinces," to the New York theatre scene. The vitality and growth of the theatre outside New York is one of the most heartening aspects of American cultural development. But New York remains the "Mecca" of theatre in the United States, as Paris does in France for its regional theatres, and London does for the theatres of the English provinces. The immensely expensive "commercial" theatre there still sets standards of production, and often of taste, for the whole country. It is regrettable that theatres in other parts of the country too often (probably at the demand of their audiences) offer a too constant diet of "Broadway hits." For the strength of regional theatre inevitably lies in developing an individual style and repertory, as Roger Planchon has done with his company in Lyons, as the American Conservatory Theatre has done in San Francisco, and the Association of Producing Artists (APA) has done notably in New York, and elsewhere.

The glamorous "top dog" of Broadway production is hedged about with so many economic difficulties that it offers little scope for the exercise of many theatrical talents; it has no room at all for beginners, and very little for anyone else. The small proportion of theatre professionals employed on Broadway in any given season has by this time become legendary. Even the off-Broadway theatre, notable for experimentation and low production costs in the fifties, has developed into an "establishment," with production costs hovering around $50,000 per show, and income severely limited by the small size of the houses. But the number of off-Broadway productions, in recent seasons, has equalled or exceeded the number produced *on* Broadway, and the off-Broadway establishment still offers a sizeable number of opportunities for theatre personnel of all kinds. As in the professional regional theatres and on the Broadway stage, actors must be members of Actors' Equity to work off Broadway. Within the last half-dozen years, however, a thriving circuit of "found" theatres, most often producing in spaces not originally intended for theatre, have been designated "off-off-Broadway." These are constantly in flux, often ephemeral in their existence, but exhilarating and experimental in their productions. They are performing now as the off-Broadway houses did about a dozen years ago, and offer the best entry for new talent into the New York theatre scene.

There are any number of specialized companies as well, both standing and touring: the "national" companies which tour Broadway shows, various ethnic theatres, adult companies playing for children's audiences, street theatre groups, and others. In some of these, the living to be made is likely to be precarious and the work intermittent; but few professional theatre workers have ever been assured of continuing job security—*in*security is one of the hazards of the profession.

More job security is available for the professional who becomes a theatre teacher, but for him the required qualifications are in many ways greater, and the artistic rewards less immediate. The theatre teacher must be, as it were, a "double" professional: in theatre *and* in teaching. That is, he must be thoroughly prepared in all areas of theatre, with a specialization in one, and he must be an *educator*, with background and skills in teaching. What he does as a theatre teacher is for the benefit of his students, and he must often accept an artistic product which is less than perfectly realized, if the process of achieving it has entailed a significant learning experience for the students involved. No educational theatre is ever well served by the apologist who excuses an inept production on the basis that "after all, they are just students." The theatre teacher must insist, always, on a rigorous professionalism and the attainment of the highest possible degree of perfection, or he does his students a disservice. But the very fact that he is dealing with young, comparatively inexperienced personnel will sometimes make his production dream impossible of realization in its fullest, most artistic sense. No one should ever become a teacher of anything if he is not daily excited by the process of discovery and development in his students, which he is there to aid and guide. No one should be a theatre teacher who in not convinced that theatre is one of the best avenues through which such development and discovery can take place.

Because literally thousands of colleges and universities in the United States devote a portion of their resources to theatre production, there is a good supply of job opportunities in this area. They are fewer for actor-teachers than for director-teachers or designer- and technician-teachers. But in every instance, only a portion of the individual's time and energy is spent in actual production; the rest is in the classroom. Even the process of actual production is often necessarily a teaching process, as it should be in educational theatre. But there are many excellently equipped theatre plants in American colleges and universities, and often the college or university theatre supplies theatre fare to a whole community, with well-chosen and beautifully staged performances. The college-level theatre career is in many ways a most rewarding one, but it must be one which is *chosen* and not settled for, or the frustrations can become overwhelming; one is very likely to be an inadequate and unhappy teacher if he arrives in a teaching position because he could not "make it" in the non-school professional theatre. Almost all colleges now require at least a master's degree for permanent appointments to their faculties, and those which offer graduate work in theatre (except in unusual circumstances) require of their prospective faculty the doctoral degree. These are matters which the new careerist must take into account.

Secondary schools also offer expanding opportunities for the prospective theatre teacher who is particularly interested in the teenage student. More and more secondary schools are each year adding work in theatre; the field is definitely expanding. But the theatre person who wishes to teach on the secondary level would do well to be prepared in one of the "standard" fields, like English, or art, or music, or general speech, because it is unlikely that he will find a position where his total time is given to theatre subjects. Teaching theatre at the high school level has its own great and particular rewards, as the many professionals now at work in this field can attest. Of the tens of thousands of secondary schools in the United States, the majority give at least a senior class play every year. Many of them do much more. Teachers knowledgeable in theatre are in desperately short supply at the secondary level. Skills are needed not only in the actual teaching and production but in curriculum planning and research. The student for whom secondary level teaching is the desired goal will find many challenges. He will usually need a bachelor's degree and a teaching license prior to his appointment to a teaching post.

There is also room at the elementary school level for the theatre teacher, though the candidate here would be wise to be prepared in creative dramatics as well as the more usual theatre skills. In the elementary schools, generally, theatre takes the form of activities supplementing classroom instruction, rather than that of production. But many interesting examples could be cited of children's productions which have genuine educational value, and working in theatre with children is a very rewarding and stimulating experience. The unself-consciousness and devotion with which children approach an activity they love makes working with them in theatre very often a pure joy. Again, the student who chooses this level at which to teach will very likely have to be prepared as well in one of the disciplines of the traditional curriculum, and will generally be expected to have completed the bachelor's degree and to have qualified for a teaching license.

The potential theatre professional must choose his career with a full knowledge of both the advantages and disadvantages of the particular position to which he aspires; he must also assess his personal attributes and talents as fairly as possible, so that he is more likely than not to succeed in the task he sets out to accomplish, and more likely than not to find satisfaction and fulfillment in it.

Another area of theatre work where the professional may find a post is in one of the thousands of community theatres that dot the land. The professional in such an organization may well be the only paid worker, and he is likely to be manager, director, or designer—or a combination of the three. Performers and all other staff will be people for whom theatre is an avocation—they will be amateurs—people who love the theatre but who do not make their living in it. The amateur theatre movement had its start in the United States in the early years of the present century, and it has continued to thrive. Many of these community-based operations now employ one or more full-time professionals to aid and guide them, and many play to enthusiastic and devoted audiences. The community theatre scene can be immensely rewarding for the professional who enjoys working with volunteers, and who does not mind the irregular working schedule which such a situation mandates. In addition to the personal rewards he finds, he can also advance the cause of theatre by developing more sensitive appreciations concerning theatre in both his volunteer company and his audience. It is an area of work worthy of consideration.

Finally, for the majority of students who take theatre courses in college, theatre will be chiefly an avocation in their adult lives.

Some will, indeed, be active in some producing theatre organization, such as a community theatre or a children's theatre. Some may volunteer their time to settlement houses or other service organizations to work in theatre with adults or children. Some may do no more than attend plays, or go to the movies, or watch television in their spare time. But, if theatre is truly an avocation, if they are truly *amateurs* of theatre, their lives will be enriched by their contacts with the art (since there is no art so apt to foster an understanding of man and his world) and the art itself will profit from their perceptive participation.

Cinema and television, in their technological aspects, add to the roster of possibilities for theatre careers. In addition to the writers, directors, actors, designers, technicians, administrators, and teachers who are as necessary to cinema and television as they are to theatre itself, these newer media add the posts of cameramen, sound engineers, editors, and various other technical specialties. Since the end products of cinema and television are so varied and so various, and applications of their techniques are still developing, it is impossible here to list all the possibilities they offer. Since both are, to some extent, mass media—a part of that burgeoning discipline called communication arts—the student who considers a career (in whole or in part) in one of these media should investigate their components most carefully and prepare himself with the appropriate knowledge and skills. Perhaps the only caution one needs to give to a person aspiring for a career in films or television is that the college graduate should be willing to begin "at the bottom" of the job structure in these industries, and thus be better able to move with new developments to positions of more distinction.

Although it is perfectly true that immense personal incomes are the reward of only a very small portion of the great numbers of people engaged in theatre and its allied arts, and although they sometimes prove to be a "chicken-today-feathers-tomorrow" kind of existence for many others, rewarding and productive jobs are to be found in all three areas, and certainly much to be done by devoted and creative people to make these arts more meaningful to all levels of the general public. They can be both the "hyacinths to feed thy soul" of the old Hindu proverb and a powerful instrument for social change. The imagination of man, which created theatre, cinema, and television, is boundless. These creations are in constant need of new infusions of imagination to keep them constantly alive and growing. Each generation must discover them anew and foster their growth with creative criticism and creative work, so that the best of them may continue to enrich the lives of all mankind.

Having chosen for myself the profession of theatre educator, let me close on a note of special pleading. It has always seemed to me that educational theatre provides a preeminent opportunity for putting both teachers and students in touch with some of the best minds that have contemplated and imitated life's struggles in the theatres of the world, that it challenges both to live up to its rigorous but rewarding discipline while at the same time it affords the opportunity of reflection on one's life in progress, deepens one's perceptions, and—perhaps—finally enables one to discover the reason why he lives. In other words (to bring the ending back to the beginning after the circular pattern we have established) it makes life *meaningful*.

Selected List of Books for Additional Reading

The following list of books suggests titles useful for further reading in the areas covered by the present volume. It is by no means exhaustive, and it does not include any plays or play anthologies. Plays are now so widely printed in such a variety of collections that the instructor and student will have no difficulty in locating them. The reading of plays is, of course, integral and basic to any consideration of the nature of theatre.

I. Historical Surveys and Collections

CLARK, BARRETT H. *European Theories of the Drama* (Rev. Ed.). New York, Crown Publishers, 1947.

DIZARD, WILSON P. *Television: A World View.* Syracuse, N.Y., Syracuse University Press, 1966.

GASSNER, JOHN. *Masters of the Drama.* New York, Crown Publishers, 1947.

GASSNER, JOHN, and RALPH E. ALLEN. *Theatre and Drama in the Making.* Boston, Houghton Mifflin, 1964.

KOHLER, CARL. *A History of Costume* (tr. by Alexander Dallas). New York, Dover Publications, 1963.

MACGOWAN, KENNETH. *Behind the Screen: The History and Techniques of the Motion Picture.* New York, Delacorte Press, 1965.

MACGOWAN, KENNETH, and WILLIAM MELNITZ. *The Living Stage.* Englewood Cliffs, N.J., Prentice-Hall, 1955.

NAGLER, ALOIS M. *Sources of Theatrical History.* New York, Theatre Annual, 1952.

NICOLL, ALLARDYCE. *The Development of the Theatre* (3rd ed., rev.). New York, Harcourt Brace Jovanovich, 1948.

ROBERTS, VERA MOWRY. *On Stage: A History of Theatre.* New York, Harper & Row, 1962.

SOUTHERN, RICHARD. *Seven Ages of the Theatre.* New York, Hill & Wang, 1957.

STUART, D. C. *The Development of Dramatic Art.* New York, Appleton-Century-Crofts, 1928.

II. General Works in Aesthetic and Dramatic Theory

ABEL, LIONEL. *Metatheatre: A New View of Dramatic Form.* New York, Hill & Wang, 1963.

ARTAUD, ANTONIN. *The Theatre and Its Double.* New York, Grove Press, 1958.

BENTLEY, ERIC. *What Is Theatre?* Boston, Beacon Press, 1956.

BUTCHER, S. H. *Aristotle's Theory of Poetry and Fine Art.* New York, Reynal and Co., 1953.

FRYE, NORTHROP. *Anatomy of Criticism.* Princeton, N.J., Princeton University Press, 1957.

LANGER, SUSANNE K. *Feeling and Form.* New York, Charles Scribner's Sons, 1953.

NICOLL, ALLARDYCE. *The Theory of Drama.* London, Harrap, 1931.

PRALL, D. W. *Aesthetic Judgment.* New York, Thomas Y. Crowell Co., 1929.

STYAN, J. L. *The Dramatic Experience.* Cambridge, Eng., Cambridge University Press, 1965.

THOMPSON, ALAN REYNOLDS. *The Anatomy of Drama.* Berkeley, University of California Press, 1942.

A. Tragedy

ANDERSON, MAXWELL. *The Essence of Tragedy and Other Footnotes and Papers.* Washington, D.C., Anderson House, 1937.

BENSON, CARL, and TAYLOR LITTLETON. *The Idea of Tragedy.* Glenview Ill., Scott, Foresman, 1966.

BROOKS, CLEANTH (ed.). *Tragic Themes in Western Literature.* New Haven, Yale University Press, 1955.

CORRIGAN, ROBERT W. *Tragedy: Vision and Form.* San Francisco, Chandler Publishing Co., 1965.

FRYE, PROSSER HALL. *Romance and Tragedy.* Lincoln, University of Nebraska Press, 1961.

HEILMAN, ROBERT B. *Tragedy and Melodrama: Versions of Experience.* Seattle, University of Washington Press, 1968.

KERR, WALTER. *Tragedy and Comedy.* New York, Simon & Schuster, Inc., 1967.

MANDEL, OSCAR. *A Definition of Tragedy.* New York, New York University Press, 1961.

MYERS, HENRY ALONZO. *Tragedy: A View of Life.* Ithaca, N.Y., Cornell University Press, 1956.

OLSON, ELDER. *Tragedy and the Theory of Drama.* Detroit, Wayne State University Press, 1961.

STEINER, GEORGE. *The Death of Tragedy.* New York, Knopf, 1961.

WILLIAMS, RAYMOND. *Modern Tragedy*. Stanford, Calif., Stanford University Press, 1966.

B. *Comedy*

BERGSON, HENRI. *Laughter* (tr. by Brereton and Rothwell). New York, Macmillan, 1917.

CORRIGAN, ROBERT W. *Comedy: Meaning and Form*. San Francisco, Chandler Publishing Co., 1965.

EASTMAN, MAX. *Enjoyment of Laughter*. New York, Simon & Schuster, Inc., 1942.

ENCK, JNO, J., ELIZABETH T. FORTER, ALVIN WHITLEY. *The Comic in Theory and Practice*. New York, Appleton-Century-Crofts, 1960.

FEIBLEMAN, JAMES. *In Praise of Comedy: A Study in Its Theory and Practice*. New York, Russell & Russell, 1939.

KRONENBERGER, LOUIS. *The Thread of Laughter*. New York, Knopf, 1952.

LEACOCK, STEPHEN. *Humor, Its Theory and Technique*. Toronto, Dodd, Mead & Co., 1935.

LAUTER, PAUL. *Theories of Comedy*. New York, Doubleday & Co., 1964.

MEREDITH, GEORGE. *Essay on the Idea of Comedy and the Uses of the Comic Spirit*. New York, Charles Scribner's Sons, 1918.

OLSON, ELDER. *The Theory of Comedy*. Bloomington, Indiana University Press, 1968.

REPPLIER, AGNES. *In Pursuit of Laughter*. Boston, Houghton Mifflin Co., 1936.

SYPHER, WYLIE. *Comedy*. New York, Garden City Publishing Co., 1956.

C. *Other forms*

BOOTH, MICHAEL R. *English Melodrama*. London, Herbert Jenkins, 1965.

BRUSTEIN, ROBERT. *The Theatre of Revolt*. Boston, Little, Brown and Co., 1962.

DISHER, M. WILLSON. *Melodrama*. New York, Macmillan, 1954.

ESSLIN, MARTIN. *The Theatre of the Absurd*. New York, Doubleday & Co., 1961.

GRIMSTEAD, DAVID. *Melodrama Unveiled: American Theatre and Culture, 1800–1850*. Chicago, University of Chicago Press, 1968.

GUTHKE, KARL S. *Modern Tragicomedy*. New York, Random House, 1966.

HERRICK, MARVIN T. *Tragicomedy*. Urbana, University of Illinois Press, 1955.

KIRBY, MICHAEL. *Happenings: An Illustrated Anthology*. New York, E. P. Dutton, 1966.

KRUTCH, JOSEPH WOOD. *"Modernism" in Modern Drama*. Ithaca, N.Y., Cornell University Press, 1953.

LUMLEY, FREDERICK. *New Trends in Twentieth Century Drama*. New York, Oxford University Press, 1967.

STYAN, J. D. *The Dark Comedy: The Development of Modern Comic Tragedy.* Cambridge, Eng., Cambridge University Press, 1962.

WELLWARTH, GEORGE. *The Theatre of Protest and Paradox: Developments in the Avant-Garde Drama.* New York, New York University Press, 1964.

III. The Theatre Arts

CANFIELD, CURTIS. *The Craft of Play Directing.* New York, Holt, Rinehart and Winston, 1963.

COLE, TOBY, and HELEN KRICH CHINOY (eds.) *Actors on Acting* (Rev. Ed). New York, Crown Publishers, 1970.

COLE, TOBY, and HELEN KRICH CHINOY. *Directors on Directing* (Rev. Ed.). New York, Bobbs-Merrill, 1963.

DEAN, ALEXANDER. *Fundamentals of Play Directing* (Revised by Lawrence Carra). New York, Holt, Rinehart and Winston, 1965.

GILLETTE, A. S. *An Introduction to Scenic Design.* New York, Harper & Row, 1967.

LAWSON, JOHN HOWARD. *Theory and Technique of Playwriting.* New York, Hill & Wang, 1960.

MCCANDLESS, STANLEY. *A Method of Lighting the Stage* (4th ed.). New York, Theatre Arts Books, 1958.

MCGAW, CHARLES. *Acting is Believing: A Basic Method* (2nd ed.). New York, Holt, Rinehart and Winston, 1966.

OENSLAGER, DONALD. *Scenery Then and Now.* New York, Norton, 1936.

ROCKWOOD, JEROME. *The Craftsmen of Dionysus: An Approach to Acting.* Glenview, Ill., Scott, Foresman, 1966.

SELDEN, SAMUEL, and HUNTON D. SELLMAN. *Stage Scenery and Lighting* (3rd ed.). New York, Appleton-Century-Crofts, 1959.

SPOLIN, VIOLA. *Improvisation in the Theatre.* Chicago, Northwestern University Press, 1963.

WAGER, WALTER (ed.). *The Playwrights Speak.* Intro. by Harold Clurman. New York, Delacorte Press, 1967.

IV. Cinema and Television

ARNHEIM, RUDOLPH. *Film as Art.* Berkeley, University of California Press, 1953.

BAZIN, ANDRÉ. *What Is Cinema?* (Essays selected and edited by Hugh Gray.) Berkeley, University of California Press, 1967.

BLUEM, A. WILLIAM, and ROGER MANVILLE (eds.), *Television: The Creative Experience: A Survey of Anglo-American Progress.* New York, Hastings House, 1967.

EISENSTEIN, SERGEI M. *The Film Sense* (tr. and edited by Jay Leyda). New York, Harcourt Brace Jovanovich, 1942.

HAZARD, PATRICK D. *TV as Art: Some Essays in Criticism.* Champaign, Ill., National Council of Teachers of English, 1966.

KNIGHT, ARTHUR. *The Liveliest Art.* New York, Macmillan, 1957.

KRACAUER, SIEGFRIED. *Theory of Film: The Redemption of Physical Reality.* New York, Oxford University Press, 1960.

LAWSON, JOHN HOWARD. *Film: The Creative Process* (2nd ed.). New York, Hill & Wang, 1967.

MCLUHAN, MARSHALL. *Understanding Media.* London, Routledge and Kegan Paul, Ltd., 1964.

PAULU, BURTON. *Radio and Television Broadcasting on the European Continent.* Minneapolis, University of Minnesota Press, 1967.

ROBINSON, W. R. (ed.). *Man and the Movies.* Baltimore, Md., Penguin Books, 1969.

SCHRAMM, WILBUR. *Mass Media and National Development.* Stanford, Calif., Stanford University Press, 1964.

VARDAC, NICHOLAS A. *Stage to Screen.* Cambridge, Mass., Harvard University Press, 1949.

V. Useful Periodicals

Cahiers du Cinema. (Published monthly in Paris.)

Educational Theatre Journal. (Published by the American Educational Theatre Association.)

Film Culture. (Published quarterly in New York.)

Film Quarterly. (Published by University of California Press at Berkeley.)

Journal of Broadcasting. (Published quarterly at University of Southern California.)

NAEB Journal. (Published by the National Association of Educational Broadcasters from Urbana, Illinois.)

Players Magazine. (Published by National Collegiate Players from Northern Illinois University.)

Quarterly Journal of Speech. (Published by The Speech Association of America.)

S.F.T.A. Journal. (Published by the Society of Film and Television Arts, London, England.)

Show Biz. (Weekly trade paper published in New York.)

Sight and Sound. (Published quarterly in London.)

Speech Monographs (Published by The Speech Association of America.)

Television Quarterly. (Published by the Newhouse Communications Center at Syracuse University, New York.)

The Drama Review. (TDR, formerly *Tulane Drama Review,* published by New York University.)

Theatre Survey: The American Journal of Theatre History. (Published by the University of Pittsburgh.)

Theatre Today. (Published by Advanced Institute for Development of American Repertory Theatre—AIDART, City University of New York.)

Variety. (Weekly trade paper published in New York.)

Washington International Arts Letter. (Monthly news sheet published from Washington, D.C.)

Index

Figures in italics refer to pages on which illustrations appear.

Acharnians, The, 83, 181, 192
Act IV Café Theatre, *17*, 17–18
Act Without Words, 257
Adamov, Arthur, 244, 250, 251
Adding Machine, The, 111, 164, 167, 255
Adler, Luther, *474*
Adventures of Dolly, The, 405
Aeschylus, 81, 82, 132, 143–144, 283, 333
African Queen, The, 441
After the Fall, 352
Agamemnon, 64, 84, 144
Ah, Wilderness!, 208, 366
Ajax, 144
Akropolis, 275, 276
Albee, Edward, 244, 254, 378
Alchemist, The, 91, *198*
Alleyn, Edward, 288
"Amahl and the Night Visitors," *469*
Amédée, 246, 257
America Hurrah!, 14, 15, 273
American Dream, The, 249, 254, 256
Anderson, Maxwell, 141, 164–165, 208
Andrews, Bert, *38*
Anouilh, 167, 238
Antigone, 52, 53, 64, 82, 133, 144, 162, 167, 271, 366
Antoine, André, 105, 106, 300, 302, 439
Antonioni, Michelangelo, 435, 437, 445
Antony and Cleopatra, 79, 382
Apollinaire, 248, 249, 420

Appia, Adolphe, 302, 349, *350, 350,* 439
Archer, William, 60–61, 299, 382
Arena Stage, Washington, D.C., *111, 268,* 353, 366–367
Aristophanes, 50, 81, 83, 84, 176, 181, 192–193, *195,* 199, 211
Aristotle, 48, 49–52, 54, 62, 65–71, 74–75, 82, 109, 141, 142–143, 147, 175, 192, 229, 243, 335, 382, 391, 398
    (*See also* Aristotelian principles)
Aristotelian principles, 91, 105, 147–149, 158–159, 168–172, 179–190, 192–195, 251, 254–257, 259, 261
Arms and the Man, 20, 21, 122, 188, 197, 366
Arnold, Matthew, 381, 391
Arsenic and Old Lace, 187–188
Artaud, Antonin, 115, 239, 244, 249–251, 256, 261, 269, 273
Astaire, Fred, 410, 411, *416,* 460
Atelje 212, *246*

Balcony, The, 54, 115, *252, 254, 256,* 257
Bald Soprano, The, 56, 68, *247,* 251, *256*
Bankhead, Tallulah, 381, 382, *474*
Barrault, Jean-Louis, 284, 300, 303, 315
Barrie, J. M., 208, 318
Barry, Philip, 203
Barrymore, John, 313, 406

Bazin, André, 411, 420, 421, 427, 429, 430, 431, 435, 438
Beauty and the Beast, 439
Beck, Julian, 269–270, *270–271, 273, 278*
Becket, 59, *428,* 446
Beckett, Samuel, 66, 68, 115, 239, 250, 251, 254, 255, 257
Beggar on Horseback, 211
Behan, Brendan, *235,* 244
Bel Geddes, Norman, *37, 42*
Belasco, David, 300, 302, 324
Ben Hur, 412, 442
Bentley, Eric, 219, 382, 384
Bergman, Ingmar, 419, 430, 435, 437, 445
Bernhardt, Sarah, 39, 299, 308, 313, 380, 404
"Beverly Hillbillies, The," 459, *459*
Bicycle Thief, The, 411, *434,* 444
Birds, The, 192–193
Birth of a Nation, The, 404, 405, *405*
Blacks, The, 54, 259, *384*
Blood Wedding, 164, 169
Bogart, Humphrey, *441,* 443
Bolt, Robert, 114, 170
"Bonanza," 458, 459
Book of Job, The, 365
Booth, Edwin, 218, 299
Booth, Michael, 218
Born Yesterday, 188, *212*
Boucicault, Dion, 102
Bourgeois Gentilhomme, Le, 60, 181, 200
Bread and Puppet Theatre, The, 277

493

Brecht, Bertolt, 113, 168, 237, 238, 270, 271, 300, 304
Brecht, Stefan, 271, 273
Bresson, Robert, 419, *437*, 445
Brook, Peter, 244, 250, *264*, 304, 323
Büchner, Georg, 164
Burbage, James, 154, 343
Burbage, Richard, 288
Burke, John Daly, 222
Burlesque, 196–198

Cabinet of Doctor Caligari, The, 407, *408*, 439
Café La Mama, 250, 269
Cage, John, 263
Cameraman, 416–418, 424–429
Camino Real, 232
Campbell, Douglas, 42, *125*, 202, 221
Camus, Albert, 243, 249
Cannibals, The, *264*
Capra, Frank, 410
Caretaker, The, 57, 64, 231, 234, 237, 239
Castelvetro, 148, 149
Castle Keep, 442
Cat Ballou, 442
Cato, 99
Caucasian Chalk Circle, The, 237, *240*
Celestina, 229
Ceremony of Innocence, 170
Chaikin, Joseph, 269, 270, 273, 274
Chairs, The, 254, 256
Chaplin, Charlie, 406, *409*, 433–434, 443–444
Characters, 51, 62–67, 100–102, 105, 110, 135–137, 150, 158–159, 163–164, 169–170, 183–186, 193, 194, 209–210, 215, 221–224, 238–239, 255–256, 464–465
Charley's Aunt, 125, *191*, 194
Chausée, La, 215
Chayevsky, Paddy, 457, 467
"Checkmate," *463*
Chekhov, Anton, 59, 108, 233–235, 302, 366
Cherry Lane Theatre, *248, 258*, 270, 271
Cherry Orchard, The, 64, 69
Chichester Festival, 122
Children of Darkness, 365
Child's Play, 227

Chronegk, Ludwig, 300–301
Chronicle plays, *90*, 90–91, 114
Cid, Le, 64, 150, 152, 440
Cinderella, 402, *466*
Cinema (*See* Motion pictures)
Circle of the Mind, 467
City Lights, *409*
City Scale, 266
Classic mode, 77–80, 142–147, 149–150, 153–154
Cleopatra, 419
Clurman, Harold, 304, 382, 384, 385
Cocteau, Jean, 251, 439
Cohan, George M., 197
Colbert, Claudette, 410
Collection, The, 277
Colman, Ronald, 410
Comedy of Errors, The, 205, 206
Commedia dell'arte, 93, *93*, 184, 199, 211, 289–291
Community theatres, 483–484
Como, Perry, 460
Composite arts, 37
Conklin, Charles, 443
Conklin Chester, 406
Conscious Lovers, The, 101, 215
Constant Prince, The, 275
"Constructivism," 111–112
Copeau, Jacques, 300, 302–303, 324, 350, 381
Coquelin, Constant, 299, 311
Corey, Irene, *365*
Corey, O. R., *365*
Coriolanus, 64
Corneille, Pierre, 150, 152, 153, 160, 295
Corrigan, Robert, 218
Cosby, Bill, 465
Costume designer, 363–365
Costumes, 71, 86, 102, *126*, 126–127, 145, 155, *155, 156*, 293, *361, 362, 363*, 363–365
Count of Monte Cristo, The, 404
Country Wife, The, 64, 100, 185, 202
Court Theatre at Weimar, 298
Covent Garden Theatre, London, 102, *344*
Covered Wagon, The, 406
Coward, Noel, 203
Craig, Gordon, 302, 349, *350*, 357, 364
Cratinus, 177
Creon, 59, 64, 65
Crist, Judith, 447

Critic, The, *195*, 197, 324
Critics, 381–391, 403, 446–447
Croce, Benedetto, 48, 51, 131, 385
Cromwell, 160
Cronkite, Walter, 448, 454
Crosby, Bing, 429
Crucible, The, 54, *64*, 164, 169, 170, *471*
Cukor, George, 410
Culp, Robert, 465
Cunningham, Merce, 263
Curley McDimple, 197
Curmudgeon, The, 194
Cycle plays, 86–88, 90–91, 199, 215, 229, 287
Cyrano de Bergerac, 57, 59, 64, 65, 102, 160–161
Cysat, Renwald, 287

Dames at Sea, 197
Dance, 37, 38, 262–263
"Daniel Boone," 459, *461*
Danton's Death, *358*
Darwin, 106, 163, 168, 169
Davenant, William, 295, 347–348
da Vinci, Leonardo, 346, 398
Day of Absence, 267
Death of a Salesman, 54, 164, *172, 354*, 365
Death Takes a Holiday, 386
Deceiver of Seville, 90–91
"Defenders, The," 458
Defiant Ones, The, 416
De Forest, Lee, 450
Deirdre, 164
Delacorte Theatre, 11–13
De Mille, C. B., 406, 409, 412, 440
Dénouement, 61–62, 181, 238, 254
De Sica, Vittorio, 411, 444
Designer, 283–284, 321–322, 340–342, 350–351, *352, 353*, 356–360, 362–369
Desire Under the Elms, 167, 172
Desperate Hours, The, 227
Dial "M" for Murder, 227
Dialogue, 68, 79, 151, 224–225, 239, 418
Diary of a Country Priest, 435, *437*
Diderot, 52, 100, 163, 215, 231, 296, 297–298, 382
Die Räuber, 215
Disher, M. Willson, 220

di Somi, Leone, 291, 345
Dizard, Wilson P., 454
Doctor's Dilemma, The, 107, 107, 205
Doll's House, A, 106
Downer, Alan, 155
Dr. Faustus, 94, 275
Dr. Strangelove, 444
Dr. Zhivago, 423, 438, 440
Dressler, Marie, 410
Dreyer, Carl, 407
Drums in the Night, 370
Drury Lane Theatre, 102, 217, 295
Duchess of Malfi, The, 94, 159
Dullin, Charles, 303
Dunlap, William, 225
Dunnock, Mildred, 95
Dylan, 355

Each in His Own Way, 238
Earth Will Tremble, The, 444
East of Eden, 440
East Lynne, 220, 220
"East Side, West Side," 458, 466, 474
Eat, 264, 266
Edison, Thomas Alva, 400, 408, 422
8½, 434, 436
18 Happenings in 6 Parts, 261, 272
Eisenstein, Sergei, 407, 414, 415, 429, 430, 431, 440
Electra, 114
Elizabethan theatre, 120, 124, 135, 153–155, 215, 340
Emperor Jones, The, 65, 69, 164, 172
"Emperor's New Clothes, The," 77–78
End of Summer, 203
Endgame, 126, 253, 255
Enemy of the People, An, 106
English theatre, 89–90, 99–100, 105, 153, 217–218, 347–348
Enrico IV, 240
Entertainer, The, 239
"Entertaining Journey," 293
"Environmental theatre," 114, 269–276, 353
Epic play, 112–114
Ernst, Max, 262
Esslin, Martin, 243, 256, 391
Eternal Road, The, 303
Euripides, 81, 132, 144, 211, 285

Every Man in His Humour, 91
Everyman, 88, 110
Exit the King, 254, 255
Exposition, 56–58, 182, 237–238
Expressionism, 110–111, 115, 167, 172

Fahrenheit 451, 436
Fairbanks, Douglas, 225, 406
Farce, 88, 191–195, 221, 443–444
Farewell to Arms, A, 440
Father of the Family, 52
Father Uxbridge Wants To Marry, 17–18, 17, 69
Faust, 65, 323
Faustus Lights the Lights, 270
Feibleman, James K., 207
Fellini, 434, 435, 436, 445
Female Patriotism, 222
Fergusson, Francis, 2, 39, 150, 158, 163, 169
Fessenden, Reginald A., 450
Films, *see* Motion pictures
Five Finger Exercise, 446
Flaherty, Robert, 424–425
Flazen, Ludwig, 274
Flea in Her Ear, A, 190
Fleming, John, 450
Flip Side, The, 320
Flynn, Errol, 225
Folk plays, 88
Fontanne, Lynn, 410
Foote, Horton, 457
Foote, W. S., 224
Footlight Parade, 415
Ford, John, 410, 436
Form, 75, 76, 79–89, 101, 104–116, 143–145, 148, 219, 244–245, 264–267,269
Forrest, Edwin, 298, 299, 380
Fourberies de Scapin, Les, 200
Frankenstein, 411
Freedman, Gerald, 12, 123, 215, 260, 304
French theatre, 96–97, 102–103, 105, 216–217, 293–294
Freud, Sigmund, 163, 165, 168–169, 178
Friar Bacon and Friar Bungay, 94
Friel, Brian, 57
Friese-Greene, William, 400
Frost, David, 456
Frost, Robert, 28
Fry, Christopher, 208, 209

Frye, Northrop, 182, 207, 208, 391
"Fugitive, The," 465
Furse, Roger, 350
Furttenbach, Joseph, 291, 345
Futz, 246

Gagliano, Frank, 17, 69
Gallows Humor, 238
Gammer Gurton's Needle, 194
Garcia Lorca, 164, 171, 174, 318
Garrick, David, 295, 296, 297–298
Garson, Barbara, 197
Garson, Greer, 450
Gary, Harold, 18
Gas I, 167
Gas II, 167
Gassner, John, 101, 113, 114, 382, 384
Gelber, Jack 244
Genet, Jean, 115, 250, 251, 254
Gentleman's Agreement, 444
George II, Duke of Saxe-Meiningen, 300–301
German theatre, 102, 160, 215
Ghelderode, 16–17, 235, 238, 244
Gherardi, 346
Ghost Sonata, The, 236, 237
Ghosts, 106, 107, 109, 164, 166
Gianni Schicchi, 364
Gielgud, John, 284, 304
Gilbert and Sullivan, 197, 198
Gill, Brendan, 447
Giraudoux, Jean, 114, 172–173, 174, 181, 251
Glass Menagerie, The, 69, 167, 237, 365
Gleason, Jackie, 460
Godard, Jean-Luc, 445
Godreau, Michael, 467
Goethe, Johann Wolfgang von, 5, 102, 138, 160, 214, 216, 296, 298, 382, 384, 385
Goetz von Berlichigen, 160, 215
Gold Rush, The 434
Golden Boy, 167
Goldoni, 296, 298
Goldsmith, Oliver, 181, 194, 208
Goldwyn, Samuel, 404, 406, 414
"Gomer Pyle," 459
Gone with the Wind, 440, 441
Good Woman of Setzuan, The, 64, 237
Gordon, "Chinese," 440
Government Inspector, The, 378

Graham, Martha, 263
Grand Illusion, The, 411
Grant, Cary, 410
Grapes of Wrath, The, 440
Great Dictator, The, 444
Great Expectations, 438
Great Train Robbery, The, 402, 425, 442
Great White Hope, The, 268
Greatest Story Ever Told, The, 440
Greek chorus, 82, 124, 143–146
Greek National Theatre, 145–146
Greek Theatre, 79–85, 91, 120, 124, *125,* 126, 135, 176, 284–286, 331–332
Greene, Robert, 208
Griffith, David Wark, 404, 405, *405,* 431, 440, 444
Grimsted, David, 224
Grotowski, Jerzy, 244, 269, 270, 274–276, *276,* 307
Guerrilla theatre, 277–278
Guinness, Alec, *119,* 380
Guitry, Sacha, 248
"Gunsmoke," 459, 465
Gutenberg technology, 25, 116, 267
Guthke, Karl S., 109, 232
Guthrie, Tyrone, *78, 124,* 125, *156,* 230, 300, 304, *309,* 324, 326

Hair!, 260
Hairy Ape, The, 164, 167, 172
Hall, Peter, 304
Halprin, Ann, 263, 269
Hamilton, Clayton, 49, 382, 386, 388
Hamlet, 25, *36,* 59, 60, 64, 91, 133, 136, 154, 155, 156–157, *158,* 161, 162, 275, 317, 318, 366, 368, 386
Hamlett, Dilys, 473
Happenings, 248–249, 261–267, 269
Happy Days, 248, 254
Harris, John P., 402
Hart, William S., 406
Hauptmann, Gerhart, 164, 167, 170
Havel, Vaclav, 256
Hayes, Helen, 410
Hazlitt, William, 382, 391

Hedda Gabler, 140, 164, 166, 474
Helena's Husband, 197
"Hello Neighbor," 462
Help!, 444
Henry IV, 11–13, *12,* 57, 90, *90, 363*
Henry V, 57, 309, 417, 435
Hepburn, Katharine, *441*
Hernani, 64, 102, 103, 160
Hertz, Heinrich, 450
Heston, Charlton, 440
Higginson, Thomas Wentworth, 27
High Noon, 433, 442
High Tor, 208
Hingle, Pat, 18, *19*
Hitchcock, Alfred, 442
Hochhuth, Rolf, 114
Holcroft, Thomas, 217
Holiday, 203
Holms, John Cecil, 181
Home, 467
Homecoming, The, 241
Homer, 62, 192
Hope, Bob, 429
Hopkins, Arthur, 324
Hostage, The, 235, 237
House of Atreus, The, 124, 125
House of Bernarda Alba, The, 316, 318
Howard, Leslie, 410
How I Learned to Stop Worrying and Love the Bomb, 444
How the West Was Won, 442
Hugo, Victor, 102, 103, 160, 298
Huui, Huui, 260, 319
Huston, John, 419, 435

I Am a Fugitive from a Chain Gang, 444
"I Spy," 458, 465
Ibsen, Henrik, 61, 106, 107–108, 109, 164, 165–166, 171–172, 205, 286–287
I Gelosi, 289–290
"I Love Lucy," 459
Imaginary Invalid, The, 199
Impersonation convention, 118–120, 284, 306–307, 311–313, 473–474
Importance of Being Earnest, The, 69, 187, 202, 203, 365
Impossible Voyage, An, 402
In the Matter of J. Robert Oppenheimer, 268

Inchcape Bell, The, 224
Incident at Vichy, 359, 380
Inherit the Wind, 446
Intolerance, 444
Intruder, The, 110
Invisible Man, The, 411
Ionesco, Eugene, 68, 115, 232, 239, 244, 246, 250, 251, 254, 255, 257, 258, 391
Iphigenia in Aulis, 40
"Ironside," 466
Irving, Henry, 218, 299
Italian Renaissance theatre, 91–92, 93, 289–291
Italian Straw Hat, An, 178, 194
"It's Never Too Late," 453

Jack, or the Submission, 255
James, Henry, 373, 382
Jarry, Alfred, 115, 246–248, 271
Jazz Singer, The, 407–408
Jefferson, Joseph, 380
Jenkins, Charles, 450
Jessner, Leopold, 303, 350
Jew of Malta, The, 64, 214
Johnson, James Weldon, 29
Johnson, Samuel, 67, 231
Jolson, Al, 407
Jones, Inigo, 345, 346, 347
Jones, Robert Edmond, 165, 350, *351,* 357
Jonson, Ben, 91, 152–153, 199–200, 230
Jouvet, Louis, 303, 329
Justine, 440

Kaiser, Georg, 167
Kaprow, Allan, 261, 262, 263, 264, 266, 269, 272
Kaufman, George S., 197
Kazan, Elia, 304, 444
Kean, Charles, 299
Kean, Edmund, 298, 299
Keaton, Buster, 443
Kemble, John Philip, 296, 298
Kennedy, Arthur, 18
Kernodle, George R., *211,* 244
Kerr, Walter, 131, 382, 384
Kesselring, Joseph, 187
Keyhole, The, 257
Keystone Cops, 431, 444
Killigrew, Thomas, 295
Kind Hearts and Coronets, 444
King of Kings, 440
King Lear, 58, 67, *92, 94,* 159, 162, *347*

Kirby, Michael, 261, 263–264, 265, 266, 267, 269
Knife in the Water, 435
Kopit, Arthur, 257
"Kraft TV Theatre," 457
Krapp's Last Tape, 258
Krutch, Joseph Wood, 167, 219, 382
Kubrick, Stanley, 440, 444
Kyd, Thomas, 91

Lady Killers, The, 444
Lady from the Sea, The, 109, 166
Lady's Not for Burning, The, 188, 208, 209
Lamb, Charles, 373, 382, 391
Lang, Fritz, 407, 411
Langer, Susanne K., 31, 32–33, 34, 37, 39, 42, 132
Langham, Michael, 182, 304
Language, 66–68, 101, 115, 137–138, 146, 159, 164, 170–171, 186–187, 193, 210, 224–225, 256– 257, 374–375, 375
Lanson, Gustave, 185
Lasky, Jesse B., 404, 406
"Lassie," 459, 460
Latham, Woodville, 400
Laurel and Hardy, 443
L'Avare, 200
Lavender Hill Mob, The, 444
Lawrence of Arabia, 440
Lawson, John Howard, 410, 424, 429, 434, 435
Lebel, Jean-Jacques, 261, 263, 269
Lemaître, Frédérick, 298
Lessing, Gotthold Ephraim, 5, 100, 141, 160, 163, 232, 382
Lesson, The, 254, 256
Lewis, Matthew Gregory, 216
Lighting, 70–71, 119, 367, 368–369, 434, 458
Lillo, George, 100, 138–139, 163–164, 215
Lincoln Center, 356
Lindsay, Vachel, 420, 421
Linoleum Happening, 272
Lion in Winter, The, 388, 446
Little Foxes, The, 227
Little Mary Sunshine, 197
Living Theatre, The, 236, 250, 269, 270–271, 273, 277, 278
Lloyd, Harold, 443
London Assurance, 102

London Merchant, The, 100, 163–164, 215
Long Day's Journey into Night, A, 59, 167
Look Back in Anger, 237
Lorca, *see* Garcia Lorca
Lord of the Flies, 420
Lorentz, Pare, 397
Lost Horizon, 442
"Love of Life," 464
Love for Love, 100
Lovers, 57
Lovers in the Metro, 256
Love's Labour's Lost, 205, 319
Lubitsch, Ernst, 407
Lumière brothers, 400, 401
Lunt, Alfred, 410
Luv, 183
Lyly, John, 208
Lysistrata, 189

M, 407
Macbeth, 57, 59, 69, 138, 140, 156–157, 351, 358
MacBird!, 197
Macdonald, Dwight, 447
Macgowan, Kenneth, 401, 403–404, 431, 432
McLuhan, Marshall, 25, 116, 257, 439
MacMurray, Fred, 465
Madwoman of Chaillot, The, 64, 181
Maeterlinck, Maurice, 108, 109–110
Maistre Pierre Pathelin, 88, 194, 199
Major Barbara, 106, 205
Make-up, 307–308, 364
Malina, Judith, 269–270
Man for All Seasons, A, 114, 170
"Man on the Moon: An Epic Journey in Space," 448, 449
Man and Superman, 68
Man Who Came to Dinner, The, 194
Mandel, Oscar, 135, 139, 142
Mandragola, 91, 92
Mannheim Court Theatre, 102
Man's a Man, A, 113, 238, 270
Marat-Sade, 264, 388
Mark, Mitchell, 404
Marlowe, Christopher, 95, 152, 154, 288

Martyrdom of Saint Apollonia, 287, 288
Marx Brothers, 411, 443, 456
Marx, Groucho, 194, 456
Marxism, 167–169
M.A.S.H., 445
Masks, 125, 126, 133, 145, 170, 177, 259, 362–363
Masse-Mensch, 110–11, 167, 237
Master Builder, The, 109, 133, 164, 166
Matthews, Charles, 299
Mayer, Carl, 407
Mayer, Edwin Justus, 365
Mayer, Louis B., 406
McLuhan, Marshall, 25, 116, 257, 439
Measures Taken, The, 113
Medea, 64
Méliès, Georges, 402, 405, 407, 429
Member of the Wedding, The, 233, 237
Memorandum, The, 253, 256
Menander, 84, 91, 176, 181, 194, 195, 335, 465
Merchant of Venice, The, 122, 357, 366
Mercier, Sebastièn, 215, 231
Meredith, George, 189, 207, 391
Merrill, Robert, 323
Merry Wives of Windsor, The, 182, 183, 205
Meyerhold, Vsevolod, 111–112, 303, 350
Middle Ages theatre, 85–89, 126, 199, 286–287, 338–341
Midsummer Night's Dream, A, 67, 92, 94, 117, 181, 182, 188, 196–197, 205
Mielziner, Jo, 42, 120, 172, 350, 365
Miles Gloriosus, 181, 194
Miller, Arthur, 18, 54, 78, 141, 164, 169, 170, 174, 237, 442
Minow, Newton K., 462
Miracle, The, 37, 42
Misalliance, 204
Misanthrope, The, 58, 65, 96, 97, 200, 201, 361
Miser, The, 181, 182, 329
Miss Sara Sampson, 100, 163
Modern Times, 444
Moeller, Philip, 197
Moiseiwitsch, Tanya, 230

Molière, 5, 57, 62, 76, 96, 98, 99, 178, 179, 181, 182, 183, 184, 185, 189, 198, 200, 201, 203, 293–294, 295, 373
Mood, 79, 101, 107–108, 138–139, 161, 171, 187–188, 235, 237
More, Thomas, 137, 152, 170
Mosel, Tad, 457
Motel, 255, 257
Mother, 431
Mother Courage, 237, 240, 310
"Mothers-in-Law, The," 458
Motion pictures, 395–447
Mourning Becomes Electra, 59–60, 164, *165*, 167, 170
Mr. Smith Goes to Washington, 411
Mrs. Warren's Profession, 106, 107, 205

Nanook of the North, 424
Nathan, George Jean, 382, 383
Naturalism, 105–106, 294, 298
Neoclassicism, 96–100, *96*, 102–103, 127, 147–152, 231
New Tenant, The, 257
New York Shakespeare Festival, 4, 11–14, *12*, 28, *123*, *214*, *253*, *260*, *363*
Nickelodeons, 403–404
Night Must Fall, 227
Night at the Opera, A, 433
No Exit, 238
Nipkow, Paul, 450

Oberammergau Passion Play, 87, *88*
O'Casey, Sean, 235, 237
Odd Couple, The, 184, 195, 388
Odets, Clifford, 114, 167, 410
Oedipus Rex, 58, 59, 60, 62, 78, 82, 83, 125, 161, 162, 221, 363
Of Mice and Men, 164
Of Thee I Sing, 188, 197
Oh, Dad, Poor Dad, etc., 257
Oh, What a Lovely War!, 260
Oliver, *417*, 440
Olivier, Laurence, 118, 122–123, 136, 239, 284, 304, 325, 435, 446
Olson, Elder, 131, *165*, 187, 245, 391
O'Neill, Eugene, 59, 65, 69, 79, 164, 166–167, 169–170, 172, 174, 208, 366, 374

Open Theatre, The, *14*, *15*, *250*, 269, 270, 273–274, 373
Osborne, John, 235, 237, 239, 244
Othello, *41*, 59, 61, 122–123, *157*
Our American Cousin, *103*
Our Town, 56–57, 209, *209*
"Outcasts, The," 458
Ox-Bow Incident, The, 444

Pageant Players, 272, 277
Paisan, 411, 444
Palladio, Andrea, 342
Pantagleize, 16–17, *16*
Papp, Joseph, 4, 253, *260*
Paradise Now, 271, 278
Peace, *186*, 192
Peer Gynt, 109, *307*, 386
Pepys, Samuel, 11, 398
Performance Group, The, *250*, 269
Persians, The, 82, 144, 333
Phèdre, 58, *95*, 98, 133, 140, 151
Philadelphia Story, The, 203
Piazza, *346*
Pinter, Harold, 57, 234, 235, 237, 239, 244
Pirandello, Luigi, 62, 238, 239, 242
Piscator, Erwin, 303, 304, 350
Pitoëff, Georges, 303, 350
Pixérécourt, René, 102–103, 217, 227, 300
Planchon, Roger, 13, *13*, 303, *375*, 480
Plato, 31, 50, 176
Plautus, 91, 176, 181, 184, 194, 214, 228–229, 286, 465
Play of Daniel, The, *127*
Play of Herod, The, *87*
Playboy of the Western World, 236
Plot, 51, 54–62, 81–82, 94–95, 101, 105–106, 135, 159, 169, 180–183, 193–194, 200, 208–209, 220–221, 237–238, 254–255, 266–267, 435
Pocket Theatre, 14–15
Poetry, 27–29, 37–38, 68, 137, 151–152, 164, 171
Polish Lab Theatre, *250*, 269, 274–276, *276*, 307
Porter, Edwin S., 403, 425
Potemkin, *414*, 425, 440
Prall, D. W., 32, 33, 43, 49

Price, The, 18–20, *19*, 54, 78
Price, W. T., 377, 389
Prometheus Bound, 134
Pudovkin, 407, 431
Pygmalion, 214

Quo Vadis, 404

Raab, Ellis, *16*, 304
Racine, Jean, 96, 135, 138, 139, 150, 151, 153, 160, 163, 164, 173, 295
Rain, 226, 227
Raisin in the Sun, *314*
Raphaelson, Samuel, 379
Realism, 101–102, 105–109, 411–412, 439
Red, White and Maddox, 268
Rehearsals, 324–325, 327–328
Reid, Kate, 18, *19*
Reinhardt, Max, *92*, 300, 350, *357*, *358*, 407
Renaissance theatre, 89–92, 147–148, 152–153, 229, 341–342
Requiem for a Heavyweight, 467, *468*
Resnais, Alain, 435, 445
Restoration theatre, 204, 294–296
Revere, Anne, *310*
Revivals, 47, 145–146, 161–162, 295, 318–319, 362–363
Rhinoceros, 254, 255
Riccoboni, Luigi, 296–297
Rice, Elmer, 111, 164, 167, 255
Richard III, *119*, 365
Rogers, Ginger, 411, *416*
Roman theatre, 84–85, 176, 286, 336–338
Romantic mode, 76–79, 88–90, *92*, 94, 103–105, 110, 152–161, 205–210
Romeo and Juliet, *123*, 135, 155, *155*, *424*
Rosencrantz and Guildenstern Are Dead, *241*
Rossellini, Roberto, 411, 444
Rostand, Edmond, 102, 160, 161
Rousseau, Jean-Jacques, 214–215
Royal Hunt of the Sun, The, 170, *170*, *317*, *325*

Sabbattini, Nicola, 291, *343*, 345
Saroyan, William, 7, 208, 209, 211
Satiric mode, 84, 93, 178, 198, 461–462

Satyr play, 76, 83, 196, 229
Saxe-Meiningen, *see* George II
Scaliger, 141, 148, 149
Scamozzi, Vincenzo, 342, 344
Scarecrow, The, 367
Scenery convention, 70–71, 103, *119, 123,* 124, 189, 347–348, *360*
Schiller, Friedrich, 31, 102, 214, 216
School for Scandal, The, 123, 204
Schroeder, Friedrich, 296, 298
Screens, The, 54
Sculpture, *33, 34–37*
Second City, 290
Second Shepherd's Play, The, 64, 86, 229
Selznick, David O., 440
Serling, Rod, 457, 467
Serlio, Sebastian, 291, 341–342
Servant of Two Masters, The, 94
Seven Against Thebes, 82
Seventh Seal, The, 430, 435
Seyler, Athene, 185
Shaffer, Peter, 170
Shakespeare, William, 5, 66, 67–68, 76–77, 79, 90, 94–95, 136, 138, 139, 153,156–157, 163, *163,* 173, 181, 197, 205, 207, 208, 231, 233, 287–289, 293, 362, 373, 446
Shaw, George Bernard, 5, 20, 68, 106, 107–108, 122, 168, 197, 205, 318, 382, 450
She Stoops to Conquer, 64, 181
Sheridan, Richard Brinsley, 197, 204
Shoemaker's Holiday, The, 94, 182
Show-Off, The, 210
Siddons, Sarah, 298
Sidney, Sir Philip, 153, 229, 230
Silvera, Frank, *92*
Simon, John, 382, 443
Simonson, Lee, *36,* 365
Six Characters in Search of an Author, 378
Skin of Our Teeth, The, 42, 57, 64, 113, 121, 209, 359
Slavitt, David, 446–447
Sleeping Princess, The, 370
Slonim, Marc, 111–112
"Smothers Brothers Show," 461
Society, 105

Song of the Lusitanian Bogey, 266
Sophocles, *52,* 53, 76, *78,* 81, 82, 132, 138, 143, 163, 283, 285, 335, 362
Spanish Renaissance theatre, 90–91, 291–293
Spanish Tragedy, The, 64, 91, 214
Spectacle, 79, 101, 105, 139–140, 159, 188–189, 193, 226–227, 256–257
Stage, 11, 13, 86, 102, 112, 155, 170
Stage gestures convention, *121,* 122–123
Stage movement, 327–328
Stage settings, *33, 36, 37,* 57, 81, 102, 105, *120,* 124–*125,* 154–155, 172, 204, 333–334, *354, 355,* 465–466
Stage speech convention, 121–122
Stage time convention, 78–79, 120–121, 254–255, 467
Stanislavsky, Constantin, 233–234, 300, 302, 309–312
State Department Interventionists, 278
"Static theatre," 110, 237
Steiner, George, 152
Sternberg, Josef von, 410
Stevens, George, 440
Stiller, Mauritz, 407
Stop the World, 265
Straight, Beatrice, *95*
Streetcar Named Desire, A, 167
Strindberg, August, 110, 164
Strnad, Oskar, *358,* 404
Stuart, D. C., 110
Styan, J. L., 205, 233, 391
Summer of the Seventeenth Doll, The, 178
Summer and Smoke, 237
Summertree, 367
"Sunrise Semester," 454
Sunset Boulevard, 410, 416
Suppliants, The, 82, 143–144, 333
Surrealism, 248, 262
Sweet Bird of Youth, 238
Symbolism, 109–110, 166, 180–181, 237
Synanon, 444

Synge, J. M., 164, 208, 235, 238

Taille, Jean de la, 148, 149
Tairov, 303, 350
Taming of the Shrew, The, 61, 64, 205
Tardieu, Jean, 251, 256, **257**
Tartuffe, 13–14, *14,* 57, 60, 62, 63, 200, 201, *201,* 203, 365
Taste of Honey, A, 237
Taylor, Ken, 462–463
Teatro Olimpico, 342, 343–344
Tempest, The, 123
Ten Commandments, The, 412, 421, 440
Terry, Megan, 273, 467
Thalberg, Irving, 406
Theatre of Dionysus, 81–84, 331–332, 362
Theatre of the Five Thousand, 303
Théâtre Libre, 302
Théâtre de l'Oeuvre, 246–248
Theatre of Reason, 150
Théâtre Robert-Houdin, Paris, 402
Theatre of the Soul, 110
Theme *see* Thought
Thieves' Carnival, 241
39 Steps, The, 442
Thomas, Dylan, 208
Thought, 51–54, *52,* 75–76, 107, 134–135, 158, 168–169, 179–180, 192, 205, 243–244, 251, 254, 359
Three Men on a Horse, 181, 195
Three Musketeers, The, 375
Three Sisters, The, 230, 365
Three Stooges, 443
Tiger at the Gates, 234
Titus Andronicus, 214, *215*
To Damascus, 110
Tobacco Road, 227
Toller, Ernst, 110–111, 167, 237
Touch of the Poet, A, 121
Transformations, 252
Trip to the Moon, A, 402
Truffault, François, 436, 445
Twelfth Night, 84, 178, *206*
Twelve Angry Men, 446
Tzetzes, John, 176–177

Ubu Roi, 246–248, *246,* 271
Uncle Tom's Cabin, 402, 442
Uncle Vanya, 108
"Untouchables, The," 459

Valentino, Rudolph, 406
Van Druten, John, 235
van Itallie, Claude, 14–15, 255, 273
Vaughn, Stuart, 304
Vega, Lope de, 5, 90, 209, 293
Vestris, Mme., 102
Victims of Duty, 257, 258
Vidor, King, 410
Viet Rock, 273
View from the Bridge, A, 237, 432
Vilar, Jean, 303
"Virginian, The," 459
Visit, The, 228, 233, 238
Vitrac, Roger, 249
Vitruvius, 342
Vivian Beaumont Theatre, 13–14, *329*, 351
Voice culture, 40–41, 68–69, 308, 309
Volpone, 91
Voltaire, 5, 296, 298, 387
von Laban, Rudolf, 262
von Uchatius, Franz, 399
Vorenberg, William, *168*

Wagner, Richard, 5, 302, 349
Waiting for Godot, 56, 66, 68, 122, 251, *252*, 254, 255, 256, 257, 259
Waiting for Lefty, 114
Walpole, Horace, 215–216
Waltz of the Toreadors, The, 238
Warhol, Andy, 106, 470
Way of the World, The, 100, 185, 202, 204, 317
Weavers, The, 162, 164, 167
Well of the Saints, The, 238
Welles, Orson, 304, 427, 435
Wellman, William, 444
Wellwarth, George, 243–244
West Indian, The, 101, 215
Westerns, 442
Who's Afraid of Virginia Woolf?, 229, 233
Wigman, Mary, 262
Wild Duck, The, 109
Wilde, Oscar, 203
Wilder, Thornton, 49, 56–57, 69, 113, 118, 208, 209, 211, 245, 259, 279

Wilkinson, Norman, 350
Williams, Jesse Lynch, 378
Williams, Raymond, 142
Williams, Tennessee, 68, 167, 235–236, 237, 238, 239, 318, 374, *426*
Williamson, Nicol, 118, 368
"Winners, The," 57
Winter, William, 299, 382
Winterset, 164, *168*
Woman of the Year, 416
Woollcott, Alexander, 381
Woyzeck, 164
Wyler, William, 412, 427

Yellow Jack, 120
Yerma, 164, *166*
"You Are There," 454
You Can't Take It with You, 184, *184*, 188
Young Cassidy, 436
Your Own Thing, 38

Zanuck, Darryl, 411
Zola, Emile, 105–106, 382, 440